Ireland in the Coming Times

IRELAND IN THE COMING TIMES:

Essays to Celebrate T. K. Whitaker's 80 Years

Edited by Fionán Ó Muircheartaigh

IPA

INSTITUTE OF PUBLIC
ADMINISTRATION

First published 1997
Institute of Public Administration
57–61 Lansdowne Road
Dublin 4
Ireland

ISBN   1 872002 93 5 hbk
            1 872002 44 7 pbk

British Library Cataloguing-in-Publication Data
A catalogue record for this book is available from the British Library.

Cover design by Creative Inputs, Dublin
Typeset in 10/12.5 Classical Garamond by Computertype Ltd., Dublin
Printed by Betaprint, Dublin

Contents

Contents

Buíochas

Ta an t-eagarthóir buíoch dos na h-áisínteachtaí seo ach go h-áirithe: an Roinn Airgeadais agus an Banc Ceannais a chuidigh leis an tógra, agus an Foras Riaracháin a thoiligh an leabhar a chur i gcló. Ta sé buíoch freisin don ESRI, a fháiltigh é le linn dó bheith mar T.K.Whitaker Research Fellow.

Thug na daoine seo a leanas cúnamh ar leith: Paddy Mullarkey, Maurice O'Connell agus John Gallagher. Ní bheadh leabhar ar bith ann murach tacaíocht ó fhoireannn an Fhoras Riaracháin, agus go h-áirithe ó Tony McNamara. Rinne Finbarr O'Shea an-obair ag cur slacht ar na téacsanna agus á gcur i láthair ar bhealach so-léite. Thug Mary Cleary agus Kathleen Harte cúnamh freisin ó am go h-am.

Léigh John O'Connell ón Roinn Airgeadais, Kieran Kennedy, Seán Cromien, Miriam Hederman O'Brien agus Alan Gray dréachtannna aiste an eagarthóra ar chúrsaí chaiteachais phuiblí agus rinne moltaí lena leasú. Tá sé an bhuíoch dóibh.

Acknowledgements

The editor would like to acknowledge the support of the following agencies and organisations: the Department of Finance, the Central Bank who assisted him with this project, and the Institute of Public Administration who agreed to publish the book. He would also like to thank the Director and staff of the Economic and Social Research Institute.

Certain people were of particular assistance: Paddy Mullarkey, Maurice O'Connell and John Gallagher. Without the support and assistance of the staff of the Institute of Public Administration, and particularly Tony McNamara this project would never have been brought to fruition. Finbarr O'Shea did trojan work in arranging the text in a clear and readable way. Mary Cleary and Kathleen Harte also helped from time to time.

The reading of earlier drafts of the editor's own essay on public expenditure by John O'Connell, Kieran Kennedy, Miriam Hederman O'Brien, Seán Cromien and Alan Gray is also much appreciated.

Notes on Authors

Peter Sutherland is chairman of Goldman Sachs International and of British Petroleum plc. From July 1993 to May 1995 he was director general of GATT and, upon its establishment in 1994, the World Trade Organisation. Between 1981 and 1984 he was Attorney General of Ireland, and from 1985 to 1989, was a commissioner of the European Communities.

Alan W. Gray is managing director of Indecon International Economic Consultants. He was chief economic consultant with the pan-European consultancy practice of Price Waterhouse. He also worked in the economic affairs department of the Central Bank of Ireland and as economic advisor in the Department of Industry and Energy. His books include *EU Structural Funds and Other Public Sector Investments* and *The Economic Consequences of Peace in Ireland*. He has directed major consultancy assignments in North America, Japan and Europe.

Dr Willem Frederik Duisenberg is president of the European Monetary Institute, Frankfurt. A graduate (cum laude) of the University of Groningen where he received his doctorate in 1965, he joined the IMF in Washington in that year. In 1969 he returned to the Netherlands to join De Nederlandsche Bank as advisor to the governing board. He was professor of macroeconomics at the University of Amsterdam, 1970–73, and was subsequently appointed Dutch Minister for Finance. He was a Member of Parliament (1977-1978). He was appointed president of the board of De Nederlandsche Bank in 1982, a post he held until 1997. Dr Duisenberg was a member of the council of the European Monetary Institute from January 1994 until June 1997. He has been president since July 1997.

Fionán Ó Muircheartaigh was appointed T.K. Whitaker Research Fellow at the Economic and Social Research Institute, Dublin in September 1994. He is a graduate of University College and Trinity College, Dublin and Oxford University. He was head of the policy and planning division of the Department of Industry and Energy (1981–84), assistant secretary at the Department of Tourism, Forestry and Fisheries (1986–87). He served as secretary, Department of the Marine, 1987–94, and chairman of the Salmon Research Agency in Newport, County Mayo, 1994–97. He was chairman of the Oslo Commission 1992–94. In 1996 he headed the Irish delegation to the UN/ILO International Labour Conference and chaired the Committee on the Convention on Wages, Hours of Work and Manning which secured tripartite agreement for the convention which was adopted by that conference. Previous articles include 'The Changing Burden of Income Taxation', 'Equalisation of Opportunity: Statistical Aspects' (with R.C. Geary), 'The Future for Oil Prices' (with D. McAleese), 'Economic Appraisal of Commercial Salmon Fisheries in Ireland and their Residual Value'.

Miriam Hederman O'Brien is a director of Allied Irish Banks plc, chairman of the Institute of Fiscal Studies, member of the Top-Level Appointments Committee (for senior civil servants in Ireland), and chairman of the international executive of the European Cultural Foundation. She has served as chairman of the Broadcasting Complaints Commission, the Commission on Taxation (1980–85), the Commission on Funding the Health Services (1987-89), and the Expert Group Enquiry into the National Blood Transfusion Service (1995).

Douglas Gageby is one of Ireland's leading journalists. After army service he joined the *Irish Press* in 1945, then worked on the *Sunday Press*, and was editor of the Irish News Agency in 1952–53. In 1954 he became first editor of the *Evening Press*. In 1959 he joined *The Irish Times* as joint managing director. He served two periods as editor of that paper, from 1963 to 1974, and from 1977 to 1987. Under his stewardship that paper increased substantially its circulation and its coverage of Northern Ireland affairs.

Finola Kennedy is chairman of the Housing Finance Agency plc. She is a lecturer of economics and an author. Her publications include *Public Social Expenditure* (1975), *Family, Economy and Government in Ireland* (1989) and the *Minority Report of the Second Commission on the Status of Women* (1993). She has served on a number of government commissions and review bodies, including the Constitution Review Group and the Child Benefit Group of which she was chairman.

Liam Ryan is professor of sociology in St Patrick's University College, Maynooth. He is a graduate of Maynooth College and St Louis University, USA. He lectured previously at University College, Cork. He has written and lectured widely on social and development issues, and has taken a particular interest in penal reform and prisons. He was a member of the Committee of Inquiry into the Penal System (1985) and more recently of the expert group to advise the Minister for Justice on the establishment of a Prisons Board. He continues to be active in promoting reform of penal establishments. He was a member of the Higher Education Authority (1975–85).

Áine Hyland is professor of education and head of department in University College, Cork. She is joint editor of a three-volume collection of extracts from documents relating to education in Ireland, north and south, from the earliest times to 1992. She also has published articles and papers on various aspects of educational history and policy from both an Irish and a comparative perspective. She has been a member of a number of government commissions and review bodies, including the group appointed to advise on the technological sector (1997), the Constitution Review Group (1995–96), and the Technical Working Group on the Future of Higher Education. She is currently a member of the Technical Working Group of the Commission on School Accommodation Needs and was recently appointed chair of the new Commission to Review the College Admissions System (points system).

John Coolahan is professor of education at St Patrick's University College, Maynooth. Among his recent public service roles were advisor to the Department of Education on the Green Paper on Education (1991), secretary general and chief rapporteur of the National Education Convention (1993), chairman of the Roundtable on Regionalisation in Education (1994), advisor to the Department of Education on a Policy for Lifelong Learning (1996). At international level he has been chairman of the Academic Committee of the Association for Teacher Education in Europe, was a contributor to the OECD comparative study on performance standards in education, leader and chief reporter of the OECD team on the country reviews of education in Poland and in the Russian Federation. He is currently vice president of the study group to advise the European Commission on education and training policy for the future.

Miriam M. Wiley is head of the Health Policy Research Centre and senior research officer at the Economic and Social Research Institute, Dublin. She is a graduate of Trinity College, Dublin, the London School of Economics and Brandeis University, Boston. She has been a member of the Health Research Board since 1987, and has published widely on health care financing, reform, management, organisation and delivery. She has also worked with the World Health Organisation, the OECD, the World Bank, the US Office of Technology Assessment and the European Commission.

Peter Bacon is a distinguished professional economist. He has worked in various positions in the private sector, including a period as managing director of Goodbody Stockbrokers. In the public sector he has worked both as an executive and as a ministerial advisor. He currently leads an international consultancy practice, Peter Bacon and Associates. His overseas experience includes work with developed countries, the OECD, the World Bank and the EU.

T.P. Hardiman graduated in engineering and science from University College, Dublin in the early 1950s. His early career was in broadcasting, and he served as director general of Radio Telefís Éireann for seven years. He holds directorships in industry, commerce and finance. He is chairman of IBM Ireland and a director of IBM, Europe. He was executive chairman of the National Board of Science and Technology, is chairman of the University Industry Programme at University College Dublin and is a trustee of Lynn University, Florida, and its subsidiary, the American College, Dublin. He is active in European industrial affairs and in international communications policy issues. He is a fellow of the Institution of Engineers of Ireland, the Irish Management Institute, and the Marketing Institute of Ireland. He was decorated with the order of the Rising Sun, Star, by the Emperor of Japan in April 1986.

Eoin P. O'Neill is director of the Innovation Centre in Trinity College, Dublin. He is active in the generation of new ventures arising from the products of university research, and in collaboration with industry in the study and development of the innovation process itself. He has worked, *inter alia*, with Westinghouse Corp. and the Institute for Industrial Research and Standards, and was chief technical advisor at the Department of Industry and Energy. He served as a member of several important government energy reviews, including the Review of the Town Gas Industry, and the Electricity Review (the Jacobsen Report). His work experience includes industrial and academic scientific research in Ireland, the UK and the United States, and the development of scientific programmes with Japan.

Seamus J. Sheehy is professor of agricultural economics in University College, Dublin. He is a leading Irish expert on agribusiness and is a specialist on the impact of EU membership on agriculture. He advocated quotas in the early 1980s as the least harmful means, for farmers and the Irish economy, of controlling surpluses. More recently he has been highlighting the shifting balance of advantage against quotas as the Uruguay Round trade agreement progresses and as EU enlargement approaches. He supported the MacSharry reforms as being the best means of responding to growing international pressure to liberalise agricultural trade. He is a board member of Allied Irish Banks plc and of Greencore plc.

James Deegan is lecturer in economics and director of the National Centre for Tourism Policy Studies at the University of Limerick. He has lectured widely on tourism issues in Ireland and overseas. He has also conducted research for the European Commission and governmental agencies.

Donal A. Dineen is professor of economics and head of department and is also associate dean of the College of Business at the University of

Limerick. In addition to tourism policy his other interests include the labour market and local economic development, about which he has written extensively. He is active in the international consultancy field.

Proinsias MacCana is senior professor emeritus at the School of Celtic Studies of the Dublin Institute for Advanced Studies. He was a professor at that Institute from 1961 to 1963, professor of Welsh at University College, Dublin from 1963 to 1971, professor of old (including medieval) Irish at University College Dublin from 1971 to 1985, senior professor at the Dublin Institute for Advanced Studies from 1985 to 1996, and annual visiting professor at Harvard University from 1987 to 1992. He is a former president of the Royal Irish Academy.

Gerard Hogan is lecturer in law at Trinity College, Dublin. He is a fellow of Trinity College and a senior counsel. He has published widely and is editor (with Gerry Whyte) of the third edition of J.M. Kelly, *The Irish Constitution* and author (with Professor Gwynn Morgan) of *Administrative Law in Ireland*. He is a member of the Committee on Court Practice and Procedure and was a member of the Constitution Review Group, 1995–96.

Bill Jackson is chief of external relations with the United Nations Volunteers Programme, based at its headquarters in Bonn. He was chief executive of the Agency for Personal Service Overseas (APSO) from 1974 to 1979 when Ken Whitaker was its first chairman. A classics and social studies graduate of Trinity College, Dublin, he worked previously with Oxfam and the University of Keele. He is a past president of the International Student Movement of the United Nations.

Ken Whelan is director of the Salmon Research Agency of Ireland. He worked previously for the Inland Fisheries Trust and the Central Fisheries Board of Ireland. He has served as secretary of the Institute of Fisheries Management (Irish Branch) and is a member of the council of management of the Atlantic Salmon Trust (UK). He has published widely on salmon and related topics.

Introduction

FIONÁN Ó MUIRCHEARTAIGH

KEN Whitaker was eighty in December 1996. He served his country with distinction in many roles, but particularly as secretary of the Department of Finance, governor of the Central Bank, chancellor of the National University of Ireland and, most recently, chairman of the Constitution Review Group. He has been active in Irish public service for over sixty years. It is now almost forty years since the government approved the preparation of the first cohesive economic strategy document, *Economic Development* (1958), of which he was the principal author and architect.

Our paths crossed fortuitously in the line of duty, first in the context of the Salmon Research Agency where, on his proposal, I succeeded him in the chair. He subsequently agreed to chair two important reviews – one on the Common Fisheries Policy and the other on the sea trout crisis – for the Department of the Marine when I was secretary there. My appointment by the government to the Economic and Social Research Institute as T.K. Whitaker Research Fellow facilitated increased contact.

That assignment inspired me with the idea, and furnished the opportunity, of marking Ken Whitaker's first eighty years with a celebratory volume. The authors were specifically enjoined to look to the future and to identify in their chosen areas the vectors for development in the twenty-first century. Given a free hand with their contributions, a generic topic was suggested reflecting their interests or experience. Certain desiderata were proposed. Ideally, developments in the chosen area would be reviewed, the issues of most concern for the future identified, and the author's considered or preferred emphasis for future policy direction outlined.

The title of the book, *Ireland in the Coming Times*, echoes that of a well-known poem of W.B. Yeats, of which more later. The title was chosen to be, at once, descriptive of the content and evocative of the changes wrought by time. The book has four parts. These reflect the range and scope of Ken Whitaker's interests and contributions. Following a biographical note, the first part surveys the broad economic context, nationally and internationally. The second part addresses social questions. The third section, dealing with domestic economic sectors, outlines the experience of and prospects for industry, services, agriculture and tourism, as well as the increasingly pivotal role of science and innovation. The final section contains essays on a variety of other policy areas in which Ken Whitaker has made a contribution: the Irish language, the constitution, volunteer service in the development aid context, and salmon and sea trout. I set out below some personal reflections arising from these essays.

Globalisation, markets, trade and competition

The globalisation of markets and the development of competition will be the dominant features of the economic scene in Europe and the world in the coming years. The march of free trade has become a stampede.

Sutherland, who has contributed directly to the strengthening of some key international institutions and agreements in the area of markets (the EU, GATT and the World Trade Organisation), shows how the modern economy is characterised by the re-emergence of the liberalisation of trade, but on a scale and at a pace that are unprecedented. The speed and efficiency of transfer of competitive goods are the dominant influence on the prosperity of nations as the new millennium approaches. Advances in telecommunications, technology, and transport have facilitated the transfer of services and information across boundaries with a speed and facility, and in volumes, that were never before contemplated. The reduction in the proportionate cost of transfer of goods and services has transformed the nature of economic activity, is progressively redefining the structure of production, and is transforming concepts of autonomy and independence into relationships of ever-closer association and interdependence.

Specifically European aspects are addressed by Duisenberg and Gray. In Europe, Economic and Monetary Union is an expression of the pursuit of more efficient and competitive markets; it is aimed at further reducing barriers to intra-European trade and at facilitating trade and investment with other economic blocks by reducing currency uncertainties and fluctuations. Potential implications for Ireland are addressed by Duisenberg. Gray sets out some of the issues which require particular attention in the European context, including the policy interface with the EU, maintaining the public finances at a level consistent with a competitive environment for foreign direct investment, competitive employment costs, flexibility in public sector costs, and maintenance of a competitive framework in Ireland, within the EU and in world trade. The role of the EU in company taxation and the planning of the response to enlargement are critical areas.

For the future, the general prescription for national development is to work through the EU and to exploit the opportunities for competitiveness which this situation affords. Major concerns will be the adaptation and likely reduction of the state sector, the encouragement of competition, and increased flexibility in labour markets. The critical role of foreign direct investment is highlighted, as is the importance of retaining a competitive edge in this regard. Investment in education, and its linkage to modern industry are cited, as are the need to establish performance-related rewards and the continual updating of skills.

This general framework of increasingly vigorous markets and competition is reflected in the essays of Bacon, Sheehy, Dineen and Deegan, which address the various economic sectors. Industry and services, agriculture and tourism are all at the mercy of the general forces of the market. It is the combination of the needs and aspirations of the consumers with the ability of industry and services to adapt to meet those needs in the market through the use and adaptation of knowledge, innovation and the application of technology which will be the determinant of success and prosperity for those industries in the future.

Bacon points not only to the process of changing markets, but to the changing nature of the products themselves and the inclusion of an increasing service element in the products sold. The retrospective sections in many of the sectoral essays illustrate how proactivity brought success while inactivity led to stagnation and decline. Sheehy stresses the need for agriculture to secure its future by rapid and timely adjustment to the needs of the market and by achievement of comparative advantage through appropriate improvements in efficiency, adjustment of scale, and development of products. International services have received new emphasis with the re-emergence of tourism as a growth area and the development of the financial services, computer software and medical services industries.

Adapt and prosper: procrastinate and decline.

Social provision and its future

Social issues are addressed in the second part of the book.

The responses of poverty, deprivation, unemployment and old age, and their evolution and prospect, are traced in Finola Kennedy's essay.

The progressive expansion of the range and scope of social supports and the extension of eligibility for benefits have been made possible by economic growth. In the absence of appropriate anticipation and funding of predicted liabilities, the sustainability of present benefits into the future is critically dependent on the continuation of that growth.

Welfare has increased enormously in complexity and cost, and there has been a decline in insured as against uninsured welfare payments; the proportion of social welfare benefits that are funded through contributions, even on a current basis, is therefore declining. The interaction of social welfare, income and tax has attracted increasing attention in recent years, and some important initiatives were taken by Michael Woods when Minister for Social Welfare, and Richard Bruton when Minister for Enterprise and Employment to mitigate negative impacts on incentives to work.

The growth of welfare recipient numbers in periods of prosperity points up a challenge for the future in the highly competitive global market economy. Economic reversal will create higher demand for cyclical social payments for which there is an entitlement, and at precisely the point when the resources available to the exchequer are being squeezed by economic contraction. It will be practically impossible to insulate the social sector from economic developments generally. For this reason, it is necessary to plan, in a systematic way, for future provision of social payments, if their value is to be protected in recessionary periods without prejudicing economic recovery. It is also clear that social supports will be defined not just in the context of norms in Ireland; they will also have to take account of European practice and the resources available to meet the other various commitments of government.

Related issues of social deprivation are dealt with in Ryan's essay on prisons and Jackson's essay on volunteer development aid, which address particular aspects of the challenges in our approach to the treatment of some of the least fortunate citizens of Ireland and the world. Ken Whitaker has, of course, been active in both areas in his career as, *inter alia*, chairman of the Committee of Inquiry into the Penal System and first chairman of the Agency for Personal Service Overseas.

Education and health are major elements of government's social programmes. The essays in this volume by Hyland, Coolahan and Wiley suggest that the need for change and the introduction of new forms and ideas is well understood in these sectors. The achievements in terms of improved access to education, the removal of some of the financial barriers to participation, and the work on reform of curricula and structures are noteworthy. Numbers in full-time education have increased greatly, particularly at second and third level. Participation at third level has risen from 4 per cent to over 50 per cent of school-leavers over the last thirty years. There is a systematic effort to have worthwhile consultative processes, and there is a new emphasis on tackling social exclusion from education; as well as consciousness of the need to review and update curriculum content and teacher skills.

Yet it is not clear that these massive sectors are currently constituted in a way that makes best use of the human and financial resources that are available The relative insulation from effective consumer/producer interaction, and in some cases from calibration and measurement of their output, and the relatively low level of investment in ongoing training are likely to lead to a suboptimal return to our investments in these areas. The magnitude of the challenge faced in education and health in the efficient provision of public services is daunting. There is a real need to develop mechanisms that encourage expansion of those suppliers who meet customer demands as efficiently as possible. How can the practice and performance of good schools and hospitals be spread to schools and hospitals that perform less well? Are the policies for further and continuing in-service education and training, and in particular the policies that address the mobility of skilled health and education personnel and the administration of health and education, sufficient for the scale of change which is necessary? Does the structure of rewards re-enforce better performing health and education professionals? Are the professional bodies sufficiently oriented towards promotion and improvement of weaker schools and hospitals? These areas will require institutional and organisational change on a significant scale if their full potential is to be realised in an era of change. More information for the public on the performance of schools and hospitals is needed if strategies to improve performance of weaker schools and hospitals is to be effectively monitored and pursued.

One particularly important current concern in health policy is how the economic burden of ill-health can be equitably distributed. The community rating principle as operated in the past by the Department of Health and the Voluntary Health Insurance Board i.e. charging the same rate for participation in a scheme regardless of age – provided a useful mechanism to achieve this end when there was a single insurance provider. With the advent of competition between insurers, regulation of schemes alone is unlikely to be sufficient to achieve a similar effect. While it is clearly in the interest of the individual consumer to encourage competition, some schemes will, inevitably attract disproportionate numbers of low-risk customers. Combining competition with regulation which secures an equitable basis for sharing the burden of ill-health in the community is a defining challenge for the future, for the regulators and for society.

The role of government

Aspects of the role of government are addressed in Hederman O'Brien's essay on taxation and my own on public expenditure. Concurrence of the citizenry with the taxation arrangements and the importance of getting the tax structure right are emphasised. The system was described in the reports of the Commission on Taxation as 'unfair, muddled and complicated'. These considerations, when combined with the competitive imperative and the financial opportunity conferred by recent growth, make attention to the desiderata set out by the Commission on Taxation of contemporary relevance. Hederman O'Brien points out that thorough-going tax reform needs to be undertaken early in the lifetime of a new government. A definitive break from the past with attention to the competitive and disincentive effects of income taxation is suggested as pivotal to future efficacy and acceptability of the tax system.

The review of historical experience suggests that the irresistible force of public expenditure will come up against an immovable object – the discipline of financial markets and international competition. These forces will be reinforced by Economic and Monetary Union. The autonomy of the government and the people in the area of economic management is progressively being constrained by the increasing interdependence of the world economy.

In the years since Whitaker's work on *Economic Development*, central government expenditures have grown sixfold, while income has grown approximately fourfold. The characteristic budgetary trend of the 1960s – the increase in capital expenditures, absolutely and proportionately – has been reversed. The decline in the capital programme has been very marked. Increased European funding has stimulated a recovery of capital spending in recent years, but public expenditure nonetheless has become considerably more current in character. Within the current budget there has been, over the period, a progressive switch from economic to social programmes. While this pattern may not give ground for alarm, neither should it be a matter of indifference. The prognosis suggests that some contraction of the government's share in the economy may be in prospect. Difficult choices for public expenditure will arise in any event.

The balance between current and capital expenditures is a key issue for sustainable development. The prosperity which we now enjoy has been supported to a significant extent by the investment in economic and productive public infrastructure. The ultimate test of the adequacy of the capital programme is availability – in a timely way and at a competitive price – of necessary capital infrastructure. Neglect of a sustained and planned approach to capital investment in economic and social infrastructure will have unavoidable deleterious effects. For example, emerging difficulties with urban housing require a fully integrated, planned and sustained response if the gap that now exists between the resource cost and price of such housing is to be eliminated; inaction results in unjustified penalties for house buyers. The same applies to public transport, where inactivity leads to increasing congestion costs.

The philosophy and approach to public sector capital investment need urgent and sustained reconsideration and development. A new emphasis on capital planning and on the funding and delivery of economic, social and productive infrastructure is required. Capital expenditure will have to be appropriately identified, reckoning only as capital such expenditure as genuinely merits the description – i.e., once incurred, it should yield value in cash or kind as income or services over a period of time.

Government has a pivotal role in proactive appraisal and planning of infrastructural needs and their provision. Infrastructural investments can have a very long lead time; because of their long-term nature and the ever-changing markets, effective capital investment policies need systematic attention and iterative adjustment over a sustained period. Once requirements are known, there should be no preconception in relation to supply and delivery. The most cost-effective arrangements for the consumer over the life of the project should be put in place for their supply. Such calculations must take into account the externalities – costs to the environment and to others – of the strategies devised. Competitive supply should be encouraged wherever possible. Where this is not possible, government must ensure, through either regulation or direct investment, that necessary infrastructure is provided cost effectively and that monopoly positions are not exploited to the detriment of industry, services and consumers. Privatisation should be considered where appropriate, but care should be taken where natural monopolies, access or essential services are concerned that such a course does not expose the consumer and the government to potential excess costs and, indeed, exploitation of monopoly positions. A final element of effective capital planning is ensuring that the necessary complementary administrative actions and support are in place, for example the designation of land use, appropriate taxation and investment policies, and the provision of supporting infrastructures at national and local level.

The current budget, too, faces a challenge of adjustment in the face of international competition and in the event of an economic downturn. The impact on social programmes might be mitigated over time if systematic provision were made for funding future welfare and pension liabilities. As regards other services which are paid for predominantly out of the public purse, such as health and education, demand management measures and reorganisation of supply are indicated.

An important element in public service provision is public service pay. The critical role played by national agreements over the last decade has deferred but not solved the question of appropriate market references and labour flexibility. The necessary changes should be achieved by negotiation. Otherwise it is likely that changes will be forced by the market or otherwise in a fashion ultimately detrimental to the public service and the community it serves. Adaptation to the market is the optimal and ultimately the only sustainable course.

Societal issues

The remaining essays in this book deal with a variety of other topics with which Ken Whitaker was involved. Hogan's essay not only is of historical interest but also highlights the significance of constitutional protections and illustrates how the central question of the balance between individual liberty and society was struck in the Irish constitution. Recurring civil friction in Ireland and throughout the world requires that an appropriate balance be devised in a free society. The constitution provides the ultimate safeguard against capricious or arbitrary action of administrators or politicians.

Gageby's essay on Northern Ireland illuminates the common humanity that binds, rather than the passions which divide, those who share this island. In a world where economic developments and globalisation are obliterating barriers between countries, where political developments are creating more integrated international structures, and where communications are rendering space and location less relevant, there is room to hope and work towards a situation where the animosity and suspicion which divided us and which appears increasingly dated can be replaced with a mutually beneficial dialogue and co-operation.

The experience and prospect of the Irish language and identity, a subject which has exercised many in Ireland since before our political independence, is comprehensively reviewed in Mac Cana's essay. And the final essay by Whelan contemplates the prospect of Ireland's sporting anadromous fish – salmon and sea trout. Salmon embraces sport, the environment, natural history and economics, and perhaps for this reason has engaged scholarly attention from the earliest times.

Conclusion

The Hardiman and O'Neill essay on science and innovation provides, in a sense, a common thread that unites all these concerns in the future. It addresses the phenomenon of change. The character of change is itself changing. The way we get information and the way we use it, the way new products are developed, and above all the speed of the transition from idea to product – these are defining characteristics of our present and our future. It would be fatal if, in Ireland or in Europe, we should convince ourselves that we have made all the necessary changes. Modern economic performance is a recurring event: success this year is no guarantor of success in the next. Success takes years of preparation, and while last year's efforts may stand to us, we can only compete if we keep in training. For the economy this means adapting, changing, learning and innovating – again and again and again.

The biggest challenge then is the challenge of change. It is essentially a challenge for the people. The government has an important role in encouraging and supporting change. Increasingly, government must facilitate and manage a process of change, anticipating necessary infrastructural investments and ensuring timely provision. At the same time it must ensure that the economy remains competitive in the global market environment.

Perhaps the defining difference between 1958 and the present is that, while in the 1960s and 1970s adaptation was seen as part of a journey on the road to free trade, the dynamic and speed of change are now such that adaptation and reorganisation are becoming the way of life rather than a step on the way. No aspect of our society is insulated against that accelerating tidal wave of information, technology and change. The importance which attaches to change in this new environment must be fully reflected in our institutions, in our policies and in our allocation of resources to innovation if we are to succeed. A continuing, creative, innovative response with a predisposition to change may be the elusive formula for success.

It is ironic that, in this era of openness and change, a climate of intolerance to non-conforming ideas has re-emerged in some quarters. Perhaps it should not surprise us that those whose ideas were once unacceptable should now apply a similar reserve to ideas outside their consensus. In particular, the perception of individualism as anti-social may carry the seed of its own destruction. It would be a tragedy if societal aims were misrepresented and applied as a means of infringing individual liberty and initiative, and the pursuit of independence of actions and ideas. That reaction, however modernist, is itself an impediment to necessary change.

Dedication

With these essays, therefore, we salute a colleague, a friend and a great Irishman. He is a man whose vision, training, warm humanity and unflagging zeal ensured that the administrative apparatus of the state was applied to the country's economic transformation at a critical juncture. It is fortunate that his ability and dedication were afforded the opportunity for such effective public service, and over such a long period. His contribution mirrors that ascribed to time in Yeats's poem 'To Ireland in the Coming Times':

> When Time began to rant and rage
> The measure of her flying feet
> Made Ireland's heart begin to beat;
> And Time bade all his candles flare
> To light a measure here and there:
> And may the thoughts of Ireland brood
> Upon a measured quietude.

Go mairfidh sé an céad!

Thomas Kenneth Whitaker: A Biographical Note

FIONÁN Ó MUIRCHEARTAIGH

Introduction

KEN Whitaker was born in Rostrevor in County Down on 8 December 1916. He was the son of Edward Whitaker, who was on the management staff of a small linen scutching and spinning mill known as Forestbrook. Edward Whitaker was first married to a teacher in the nearby Killowen national school. To this first marriage three daughters were born, the last of whom died in 1992. Following the death of his first wife, Edward married Jane O'Connor, the district nurse in Rostrevor. She was from County Clare. Ken and his sister Margaret (Peggy) were the happy result of that union.

The linen industry in which Edward worked experienced a slump after the First World War. As the future of Forestbrook was uncertain, he moved from Rostrevor to Drogheda in County Louth and took a position in the Greenmount and Boyne Linen Company. Ironically, Greenmount and Boyne eventually became a commercial casualty and was outlived by Forestbrook. Ken was shown early in life that there are no racing certainties, and that economic forecasting is not an exact science!

Growing up

Ken started his academic career in Rostrevor when he was four. His earliest memories are of being led to school by an older boy, Ben Dunne, who, years later, founded Dunnes Stores. Ben Dunne continued to help. At Ken's suggestion, he often became a generous but anonymous sponsor of artistic efforts. Works such as the film *Oileán* by Neville Presho (dealing with life on Tory Island) and paintings of Simon Coleman RHA benefited from such sponsorship.

Something of Ken's early years may be gleaned from his own notes and writings, especially an article which he wrote for the 1984 centenary issue of the *Drogheda Independent*. He was six years old when the family moved to Drogheda where they lived in Paradise Cottage. He has written that he doubts if he will ever again be as happy as he was in that earthly paradise! To grow up in Drogheda was appropriate for a young Whitaker. Apparently, the first Whitaker recorded in Ireland was bailiff of Drogheda in 1305 and, therefore, responsible for the municipal funds. In 1956, another Whitaker was to become bailiff of Merrion Street, as secretary of the Department of Finance, with responsibility for the public finances.

The Drogheda of Whitaker's youth may well ring a nostalgic bell for some. He was a Christian Brothers boy, with all that entailed. Conditions at school on the whole were good, but included a couple of rather grim years. In the secondary school there were outstanding teachers – the patrician Brother James Burke with his discerning taste in English prose and poetry, the shy scholar Peadar McCann whose enthusiasm for his charges during and after hours was undimmed by their merciless tormenting, and Brother O'Farrell who strove hard to build up the prowess of his pupils on the hurling field. These efforts were not in vain. Ken won a medal in a Louth Minor Hurling Championship but recalls no heroism, believing he was merely a sub!

The rigour of a Christian Brothers education was leavened with wider experience. Playing marbles along the kerb in Fair Street on the way home from school, nipping home and back again in the half-hour allotted to lunch, enjoying the life of the countryside when taking a five-mile walk after school – up the Ramparts, across the river at Oldbridge, and back on the Louth side into Drogheda. There he first took an interest in salmon, and the methods – legal and illegal – by which they were won. There he learned to shoot, and on one evening of slaughter shot seven cormorants. The bounty from the board of conservators paid for a day-trip to Dublin. His own account reveals how much in touch with nature he was in those schoolboy days:

> Walking along the Boyne was never without interest. Half-way to Oldbridge, you could wait until the semi-circle of draft net narrowed to hairpin shape in the hope of seeing a few salmon cast high up the bank in a last quick heave. Or you could watch the flocks of whirling starlings above the tall yellow reeds, or search for wild strawberries on the mossy crest of the wall which bounded the small wood just before the first lock of the old canal to Navan. You could follow the tow-path to a salmon weir where a round hide-covered coracle of ancient lineage was still being used. Every summer an exciting regatta was held on the stretch of river between the Viaduct and Tom Roe's Point; and late every autumn the tree-lined sweep of the Boyne above Oldbridge became a multi-coloured splendour. In those days, before the

prison gates began to close, one could experience Wordsworthian intimations sitting on the stump of the Obelisk or peering down the cold passage of the sanctuary of Aengus at Newgrange.

Culture, also, played a part in his formative years. Drogheda was well endowed with academic and music teachers. Ken was a choirboy and took piano and violin lessons. An annual opera, usually Gilbert and Sullivan, was staged by his violin teacher, Agnes McGough, and her sister. Ken and his fellow students were enlisted in the orchestra. Music, especially classical music, has remained one of the joys of his life.

It was in Drogheda, too, that Ken's interest in Irish and folklore developed. He searched out with friends any surviving traces of the language in the neighbourhood. Following spells in the Donegal Gaeltacht, the magic of which he recalls in an article in Irish 'Mise agus an Ghaeilge', reproduced in his book *Interests,*[1] an Irish-speaking youth club was formed. A dance was organised in the Mayoralty Hall, to which the girls' mothers also came as chaperones!

A further formative influence was the excellent library – the Carnegie library – which served as a reservoir of knowledge for the young man and for the town. Literature, history, archaeology and sporting activities were all elements in the formation of the quintessential public servant.

The public servant

In retrospect, it is interesting that the Constitution Review Committee of 1934 (the subject of a learned article in this volume) was meeting and reporting to President de Valera at the time Ken Whitaker was recruited to the civil service; 10 October 1934 was his first day in the civil service. There followed what even now would be considered a meteoric rise. Being placed first in the examination for clerical officer in 1934 was followed by similar successes in subsequent examinations for executive officer in 1935, assistant inspector of taxes in 1937, and administrative officer in 1938. As executive officer in the Department of Education he became, at age twenty, private secretary to the Minister for Education, Tomás Ó Deirg. His counterpart in the Department of Local Government was Brian Ó Nualláin, later to be known as Myles na gCopaleen. Who would then have foreseen that two major works would flow from their respective pens – *Economic Development* and *An Béal Bocht*!

It was in the Department of Education, too, that he met and fell in love with Nora Fogarty. They were married in August 1941, and had fifty-three happy years together, blessed by a family of five sons and one daughter.

When appointed administrative officer in June 1938, he was sent to the Finance Division of the Department of Finance where his first task was to draft memoranda for the government on the recommendations of the Banking Commission. Here he marshalled the arguments for following the majority view of the commission while traversing the recommendations in the minority reports; the subsequent government decision led to the establishment of the Irish Central Bank.

The Second World War improved promotion prospects for civil servants. In 1943 he was promoted to assistant principal, in 1947 principal, and in 1950 deputy assistant secretary. In 1953 he was appointed assistant secretary (equivalent to secretary in most departments), and then secretary in 1956.

During this upward climb he obtained by private study as an external student the BSc(Econ) and MSc(Econ) of London University.

Ken Whitaker was thirty-nine when appointed secretary of the Department of Finance. He was to serve in that capacity for thirteen years. The old order was changing, and Whitaker and his associates were to the fore in the movement towards a more purposeful development strategy. In his writings, the close partnership and unity of purpose between politicians and administrators are identified as of major significance. A number of guiding principles which informed this spirit are detailed in his book *Interests*. These thoughts would repay contemporary reflection.

In a volume of this kind it is not appropriate to attempt an assessment of his achievements. That is a matter for another day. But five areas merit particular attention:

- his commitment to excellent public service as an expression of patriotism
- the range of his contribution to key policy questions in the Department of Finance and at the Central Bank
- his contribution to dialogue with Northern Ireland
- his contribution to public service since his retirement
- his involvement with Irish language, folklore and cultural activities.

The role of the civil service

Whitaker's civil service was a service committed to excellence in the national interest. In his consideration of issues, there is a consistent search for what is right, an understanding of the difficulties of special interests, and a resolution to see the common good identified and acted upon. The staff recruited were selected on a competitive basis, and were, in a very real sense, *la crème de la crème*.

In *Interests* he outlines his views on the role of the civil servant, the role of the minister and relations between them. He quotes from a Department of Finance memorandum:

> It is the duty of civil servants to think all around the subject and give Ministers their unbiased opinions on matters referred to them when policy is being considered, and then when policy is decided on, to carry out that policy to the best of their ability, regardless of personal views.

On the civil servant's approach to flawed policies, he alludes to examples of successful and unsuccessful attempts to have government decisions changed before they solidified. The cases cited in Ronan Fanning's book[2] were, he notes, prompted by departmental rather than personal motives. Other happier cases are instanced where the department 'helped rescue Ministers from remaining prisoners of outmoded policies'.

Another basic principle of official relations in Whitaker's Department of Finance was that civil servants (like 'monks in a monastery') held their minister in great respect, irrespective of whether their personal relations were warm or reserved.

The role of the minister is also touched upon. In Whitaker's day the departmental function of ministers was seen as 'to decide rather than to argue'. They wrote little on official files. They were concerned with the practical aspects of government and demonstrated a mastery in welding together 'scraps of material into politically effective speeches'. The idea that a minister had to show 'who's boss' is characterised by Whitaker as a childish misconception untrue of any minister of quality. No Minister for Finance in his time as secretary suffered from such an inferiority complex.

The underlying philosophy was one of openness to ideas and experimentation, rigour of analysis, partnership with ministers and government, commitment to improvement and development of the economy and its infrastructure, and a systematic and performance-based approach to management in the public service. These themes still have a relevance for today's leaders, be they politicians, administrators, engineers, artists, economists, social workers or scientists.

Contribution to policy

Ken Whitaker's period of office at the Department of Finance is the bridge between the insularity and despondency that characterised the

Irish interwar scene and the present era of buoyant growth and confident expectations in a free-trade environment. *Economic Development* was the intellectual springboard of that transition. This work and the programmes which followed showed what enlightened politicians and administrators working together could achieve for the community. The national agreement processes of today are effective successors to that tradition.

Economic Development was initiated by Whitaker as soon as he was appointed secretary of the Department of Finance. He emphasised from the outset that it was a work of collaboration and his collaborators are named at the end of the introductory chapter. *Economic Development* recommended abandonment of the outmoded protectionist policy, adaptation to a free-trade world, encouragement of export-oriented expansion of industry and services, even if under foreign ownership, emphasis on productive investment in public capital budgets, and a more coherent, planned approach to national development. Whitaker's intuition as to 'the psychological value of setting up targets of national endeavour, provided they are reasonable and mutually consistent' was amply confirmed by the unprecedented economic progress of the 1960s.

Trade liberalisation

The liberalisation of trade was the first and probably the most crucial development. Central to this were the systematic efforts to transform Irish industry to make it competitive, the preparation of the economy for entry into the European Community, and, when that was postponed, the conclusion of the Anglo-Irish Free Trade Area Agreement.

The gradual dismantling of tariffs was complemented by a series of measures to encourage indigenous industry to adapt and export and foreign industry to invest. This was done through increased grants for investment projects and the extension of remission of tax on export profits. The policy of encouraging foreign investment was underpinned through repeal of the discriminatory Control of Manufactures Acts 1932–34. The government budget gave priority at the outset to the productive and potentially wealth and income generating elements of the public capital programme.

Economic and social balance

There were always critics of the apparent inattention to social policy in the new era of economic programming. Whitaker's view was clear:

  there is no conflict between what are termed 'socially desirable' and 'economic' objectives ... the permanent increase in employment associated with an expansion of real national output is to be preferred to the purely temporary increase which is all that non-productive investment, entailing a mere redistribution of existing incomes, can bring about.

Our actual development experience has provided the means for substantial social advances and enables us to plan confidently for further social, in association with economic, progress.

Other issues

Among the other memorable features of his service as secretary of the Department of Finance were:

- arranging terms for entry of Ireland into the International Monetary Fund (IMF) and World Bank (1957)
- visiting the capitals of the EC Six to promote Ireland's case for membership (1960)
- being the first chairman of the National Industrial and Economic Council (forerunner to the National Economic and Social Council)(1963–67);
- accompanying Seán Lemass on his first visit to Stormont (January 1965)
- leading the official team in the Anglo-Irish Free Trade Area Agreement talks (1965)
- negotiating the initial Ford Foundation funding of the Economic and Social Research Institute (1959–60).

Central Bank

Whitaker's tenure as governor of the Central Bank from 1969 to 1976 covered what he later described as a troubled septennium. His analysis of this period has been set down for some future historian in the archives of the Central Bank. But his retrospective article on his time at the Central Bank, combined with commentaries in the Central Bank's reports, leave little doubt of either the nature or the tenor of his efforts in those years.

The domestic threats to the integrity of the currency were assessed and monitored in the Central Bank's reports of the time. They are concerned with a confluence of unfavourable developments, including excessive public expenditure and borrowing, excessive credit creation and excessive income increases. The bank pointed in vain to the errors in fiscal, monetary and incomes policies over the period. It has been noted by Whitaker that while the Central Bank's unwelcome advice was usually heard in silence, it was in an atmosphere that was, at worst, neutral rather than hostile. The Central Bank's advice at that time rarely produced converts in government circles.

Whitaker retired in 1976, in his sixtieth year, on completion of his seven-year term as governor.

Northern Ireland

Northern Ireland has played a special part in Ken Whitaker's life. He was born in a lovely village in County Down before partition. He understands how deep and tangled are the roots of what he acknowledges to be a 'virtually intractable problem'. He has described himself as 'a peaceful and patient Irishman ... who hopes that the people of Northern Ireland will one day freely decide to join the people of the Republic in a new (agreed) Irish constitutional framework'. How to advance this ideal – and allay mutual distrust and unionist fears of Rome rule or Dublin rule – has always exercised his attention and concern.

When he moved to Drogheda, aged six, his earliest memory is of a wild-eyed man with a revolver running down the street as he tried to escape from the Free State forces. From his earliest days he was exposed to the richness and the energy of the two traditions. His many links and friendships with Ulster people and appreciation of their great talents were to make dialogue easier as the administrative, and then political, *détente* gathered momentum.

The historic visit to Stormont in 1965 of Seán Lemass as Taoiseach flowed from a friendship between Ken and Terence O'Neill, established in the context of IMF and World Bank meetings. There were elements of drama about that first visit to Stormont:

- O'Neill's invitation communicated orally to Ken in Dublin by Jim Malley
- Ken's consultation with Lemass and the prompt affirmative reply
- the tight secrecy of arrangements for the visit (even the Taoiseach's driver did not know in advance his destination that morning)
- the surprised but polite welcome by Northern Ireland ministers after lunch.

The immediate and widespread upsurge of goodwill throughout Ireland was heartening. Jack Lynch, as Taoiseach, repeated the visit early in 1967.

Two anecdotes concerning these visits illustrate the tragi-comedy of Northern Ireland. On the occasion of the first visit, and the lunch with

Terence O'Neill, Ken recalls that, with a glint in his eye, O'Neill tilted the label of the bottle towards him – Chateauneuf du Pape. This information would no doubt have further disturbed opponents of the visit. The sensitivity to papal influences is further illustrated by a story relating to Jack Lynch's visit. There was snow on the ground around Carson's statue at Stormont and two figures, clad in black, were silhouetted against the gleaming white backdrop. They were armed with snowballs. One was Ian Paisley. As Lynch and Whitaker alighted from the car they could hear Paisley roar in the clear air: 'No Pope Here'. Jack Lynch turned to Ken asking, in his soft Cork voice, 'Which of us does he think is the Pope?'

Because of his cross-border friendships, Ken was able to be of service to Jack Lynch as Taoiseach in the fraught years from August 1969 into the seventies. He prefers not to speak of his missions and encounters in those years, but he has deposited the relevant papers in the archives at University College Dublin.

His writings on the subject – in particular the articles reproduced in *Interests* – stress his aversion to violence and his advocacy of patient negotiation by the democratic parties:

> It is only by clinging to reason, by supporting the democratic process and all in these islands who observe it, by resisting emotional pressures and provocation, and by being prepared to soften rigidities, that progress can be made to a political settlement which is the only alternative to murderous anarchy.

Many years later, in September 1993, at an assembly of elder statesmen convened by RTÉ at Tinakilly House in County Wicklow (dubbed the 'Tinakilly Senate'), Whitaker would observe sadly that:

> Death and destruction do not seem to have the power to impel either side to enter genuine negotiation ... I believe it is time for the two governments to move from a benevolent watching stance to a more direct role in organising a political settlement.

The sequence of events since then is very much in that line, although progress has at times been painfully slow. Whitaker would wish to see 'the truly democratic parties make a serious effort to reach a realistic settlement, even on an interim basis'. By 'truly democratic parties' he means those who shun violence and accept the need for majority consent to constitutional change in Northern Ireland. His personal disposition is:

> I would be content to see a devolution of powers to a Northern Ireland

administration, subject to a strong guarantee of human rights, a devolution capable of enlargement by agreement but one which recognised both the need to qualify simple majority rule in the circumstances of Northern Ireland, and the legitimacy in the democratic politics of Northern Ireland of peaceful persuasion for (and against) constitutional change.

He appreciates the discomfort that faces the two traditions on their way to compromise, and would counsel governments and all concerned to take great care to soften, rather than reinforce, the inflexibility of the situation.

Life after 'retirement'

Retirement is a word which has little or no meaning in Ken Whitaker's lexicon. He would say that he has been refreshed and sustained by the opening-up of new areas of interest. Since his career in the public service, he has been a member of Seanad Éireann, the Council of State and various state and private boards, has chaired a number of important inquiries, has been chancellor of the National University of Ireland (NUI), has promoted overseas development aid and has been active in his support of, and involvement with, a wide variety of linguistic and cultural activities.

Participation in the democratic institutions of the state

In 1977, the year after Ken retired from the Central Bank, Fianna Fáil leader Jack Lynch was elected Taoiseach. The Taoiseach invited him, on the basis of complete political freedom, to be one of his Senate nominees. Whitaker's forthright, independent and, indeed, sometimes trenchantly critical but always reasoned contribution was recognised on an all-party basis in his nomination to the Senate by Taoiseach Garret FitzGerald of Fine Gael in 1981. He ceased to be a member of the Senate in 1982. More recently when President Mary Robinson was considering her nominees for the Council of State in 1991, Ken Whitaker was one of the seven – three men and four women – chosen.

Participation in public agencies/foundations

Among the positions he held subsequent to his retirement were:

- chairman, Bord na Gaeilge, 1974–78
- chairman, Salmon Research Agency, 1981–94 (continues as member)

- chairman, Agency for Personal Service Overseas, 1974–78
- chairman, council of Dublin Institute for Advanced Studies, 1980–95
- president, Economic and Social Research Institute, 1971–87
- president, Royal Irish Academy, 1985–87
- joint chairman, Anglo-Irish Encounter, 1983–90.

Participation in special inquiries

Ken Whitaker also chaired at least five major investigations for government or for individual ministers, most recently the Constitution Review Group 1995–96. This was an epic undertaking, completed, as requested, within a year. He was chairman of the Committee of Inquiry into the Penal System 1984–85, whose report, after being virtually neglected for years, is now receiving belated attention. He also chaired two important committees on fisheries for the Minister for the Marine. These were the Common Fisheries Policy Review Group 1991 and the Sea Trout Task Force 1993–94. His service as chairman of the Sentence Review Group 1989–94, a difficult brief at any time, gives another indication of the measure of the man. Ken was also appointed a member of the Dáil Constituency Commission in 1990 – an endorsement of his objectivity and impartiality.

Participation in education

As he approached retirement from the Central Bank, Ken was asked by the presidents of University College Cork, University College Dublin and University College Galway to be a candidate for the chancellorship of the NUI left vacant by the death of Eamon de Valera. Although not an NUI graduate himself, he received the overwhelming support of graduates in the subsequent election. He resigned in December 1996, having guided the university through a phase of unprecedented expansion and restructuring. In the new phase opened by the Universities Act 1997, the three constituent colleges and St Patrick's College, Maynooth receive recognition as universities in their own right, with virtual autonomy, but with the historical federal fabric preserved.

Participation in development agencies

In 1971, Professor George Dawson of Trinity College Dublin convened a meeting in his rooms to promote the idea of a distinctive Irish volunteer presence in the Third World to further sustainable development, as distinct from emergency relief. The outcome was the submission to government of a proposal drafted by Ken which, on assuming office in 1973 as Minister for Foreign Affairs, Garret FitzGerald progressed in government and parliament. The Agency for Personal Service Overseas emerged from this initiative and Ken became chairman for the first four years (1974–78), building from scratch an organisation of enduring national importance. As a senator, he strongly supported legislation for increased development aid.

Participation in private business

On his retirement from the Central Bank in 1976, Ken accepted invitations to join the boards of Guinness (Dublin and London) and the Bank of Ireland. He valued this experience as an education in how major undertakings are run, noting basic similarities with the public service but also some differences, notably the significant training benefit of inviting middle-line management staff to make presentations to the board and requiring them to deal on their feet with searching questions.

Cultúr agus Gaeilge

Is ar scoil ar dtús a chuaigh Ken i dtaithí ar an nGaeilge. Bhí paidreacha agus amhráin i nGaeilge ag a mháthair, a rugadh ach nár tógadh le Gaeilge i gContae an Chláir cé gurbh í an Ghaeilge príomh-theanga a tuismitheoirí. Thug togha múinteora, Peadar Mac Cana, bunús cuimsitheach dó sa mheánscoil i nDroichead Átha. Ag Feis Mhuirtheimhne, ghnóthaigh Ken scoláireacht chun freastal ar Ghaeltacht Thír Chonaill. Is go Coláiste Bhríde i Rann na Feirste, nach raibh tógtha ach le cúig bliana, a chuaigh sé sa bhlian 1931. San Alt 'Mise agus an Ghaeilge' is iad na smaointe is mó a ritheann le cuimhne Ken ná:

> Oícheannta na gcéilithe móra a mhair go maidin agus an cor seisear déag, a mhúin Séamus Ó Mealláin dúinn, á chasadh go haigeantach againn;
>
> An Sagart Ó Muireadhaigh ár ngríosadh chun damhsa le gach búirtheach as – 'Beirt eile anseo';
>
> 'Is iad mo chuid Gamhna na Gamhna Geala' nó 'A Shiúbháin Ní Dhuibhir' á chanadh aige féin;
>
> Hiúdaí Mhicí Hiúdaí, go ndéana an Rí a mhaith air, ag gabháil den phíob;
>
> Hiúdaí Pheadaí ag canadh 'A Bhríd Óg Ní Mháille';
>
> Na buachaillí i gcomórtas le chéile faoi na cailíní ba mhaith leo a thionlacan chun an bhaile ach a sáith cúthaileachta orthu san am chéanna. Ach lámh an

chailín a bheith i do láimhse, na méara snaidhmthe ina chéile, nó do lámh bheith thart fána com agus, b'fhéidir, póg amscaí a thabairt dí roimh scaradh léithe, a Dhia nárbh aoibhinn!

Ansin, ag triall go tuirseach thar carraigeacha loma go dtí Poll an tSnámha sula dtéimís isteach chun bricfeasta ag bánú an lae. Codladh trom go headra.

Nó an fuchsia faoi bhláth agus loinnir chorcra i ngreamhar an bhealaigh mhóir agus tú ag rothaíocht le fána go mall tráthnóna, ar amharc na farraige agus na n-oileán ... Draíocht agus díogras na hóige!

D'fhill Ken ar Rann na Feirste trí huaire sna triochaidí, agus thug triúr dá chlann leis ann i 1954. Chuaigh 'caint na ndaoine' i gcion air i dtithe Sheáin Mhicí Óig, Bhrianaí Hiúdaí, Chormaic, Frainc Bhig agus Joe Duffy! Thug sé cuairt ar Ghaeltachtaí eile nuair a bhí sé ar saoire lena chlann, ar an gCeathrún Rua, ar Charna, ar Bhaile an Sceilg, ar Mhúscraí, agus ar Iorras.

Bhi dúil ag Nóra, bean Ken, sa Ghaeilge freisin. Chaith sí tréimhsí i Rann Na Feirste sna triochaidí, ach níor casadh le Ken ansin í. De thoradh ar an meas a bhí acu beirt ar an nGaeilge, cuireadh bunús a gclainne ag foghlaim na teangan sa Ghaeltacht. D'fhreastal ceathrar acu ar Scoil na Leanbh sa Rinn. Is cúis áthais agus dóchais do Ken anois an Ghaeilge a fheiscint á úsáid agus á scrí ag a gclann siúd. Tá dóchas aige ná raghaidh an síol in éag.

Tá suim aige, freisin, i litríocht na Gaeilge. Cheannaigh agus léigh sé na leabhair nua-fhoilsíthe agus bhí árd-mheas aige ar iarrachtaí Sheán Ó hÉigeartaigh agus a bheanchéile Bríd as ucht a ndearna siad ar son na nua-litríochta.

Ó thaobh polasaí i leith na Gaeilge de, nochtann na meanraim atá foilsithe in *Interests* an dearcadh a bhí aige féin, agus an chomhairle a thug sé, i dtaobh athbheochan na Gaeilge. Fágadh faoi *An Páipéar Bán um Athbheochan na Gaeilge* a dhréachtadh. Chuidigh Séamas Ó Ciosáin leis. Foilsíodh an Páipéar Bán i mí Eanáir 1965.

Dhá bhun-phrionsabail thábhachtach a bhí ann, dar leis:

- polasaí an dátheangachais agus
- dearbhú nach mbéadh oiliúint cheart ar aon pháiste in Éirinn mura mbeadh an Ghaeilge foghlamtha aige nó aici ar scoil.

Tugadh le fios go soiléir nárbh é rún an Rialtais an Béarla a scrios ach an Ghaeilge a chaomhnú agus a húsáid a leathnú – polasaí ar bhain ciall agus dóchúlacht leis.

Níorbh é an Páipéar Bán an t-aon bhaint a bhí aige le raon na Gaeilge sa tseirbhís phoiblí. I bhfad roimhe sin, bhí sé ina bhall den choiste a shocraigh a raibh fágtha de mhuintir an Bhlascaoid a aistriú go dtí an mhórthír. Bhí sé ina bhall, freisin, de choiste a thug cuairt ar na Gaeltachtaí uilig i 1947 chun moltaí a dhéanamh faoin chaoi a bhféadfaí feabhas a chur orthu mar ionaid saoire.

Nuair a bhí sé sa Roinn Airgeadais, chuidigh sé le Séamas Ó Duilearga socraithe cuí a dhéanamh chun cnuasacht an Choimisiúin Bhéaloideasa a aistriú go Coláiste na hOllscoile, Baile Átha Cliath. Chaith se tréimhse cúig bliana déag mar chathaoirleach ar Chomhairle Bhéaloideas Éireann. Nuair a bhi sé sa Bhanc Ceannais mar Ghobharnóir chuir sé sraith altanna i nGaeilge i gcló i ráitheachán an Bhainc. Is le spéis a spreagadh i measc baincéirí agus lucht gnó i gcúrsaí Gaeilge a rinne sé seo.

An bhliain sular fhág Ken an Banc Ceannais, ghéill sé do achaine Aire Gaeltachta na linne – Tomás Ó Dónaill – bheith ina chathaoirleach ar Bhord na Gaeilge. Seo leanas cuid de na fadhbanna a bhí le sárú maidir le bunú an bhoird.

Cúis díoma dó chomh deacair agus chomh malltriallach a bhí sé foireann a earcú de bharr laincisí Choimisnéirí na Státsheirbhíse. Bhí air cur i gcoinne dianchóras smachta ar airgead a chaitheamh agus dúirt: 'Ba cheart go mbeadh iontaoibh as stuaim, díogras agus taithí na mball [baill an Bhoird] … má theipeann orthu aon ní fónta a dhéanamh taobh istigh de thréimhse réasúnta, tá sé de cheart ag an Rialtas bata is bóthar a thabhairt dóibh.'

Déarfadh sé féin gurab é an beart is éifeachtaí a rinne sé i leith na Gaeilge ná a áiteamh ar bheirt fhile a raibh sé cáirdiúil leo, Seán Ó Tuama agus Thomas Kinsella, an duanaire sin *Poems of the Dispossessed* a chur le chéile, mar go dtugann sé seo tuiscint do mhuintir na hÉireann ar an oidhreacht luachmhar atá acu si bhfilíocht na Gaeilge leis na céadta bliain anuas go dtí ár linn féin. Tá a chion féin ar an nGaeilge le brath ar a dhíograsaí is a thugann sé tacaíocht di – ag freastal go féiltiúil ar Scoil Gheimhridh Merriman ó bunaíodh í agus ar éigsí éagsúla eile, ag ceannach leabhar Gaeilge, agus ag taobhú le lucht a sábhála. Níl rud is fearr leis fós ná bualadh le cainteorí Gaeilge i measc phobal na tuaithe in Iorras nó áit ar bith eile ar fud na tíre. Bhí fhios ag an ngnáth dhuine go raibh cara sa chúirt aige a dhéanfadh a dhícheall chun an tradaisiún agus an teanga a chaomhnú agus a fhorbairt. Ba mhór an t-árdú meanmna é seo nuair a bhí meas ar an nGaeilge in ísle brí i measc an phobail i gcoitinne.

Cúis dóchais dó Raidió na Gaeltachta, Raidió na Life, agus le déanaí, Teilifís na Gaeilge. Cúitíodh go maith leis a shuim agus a shaothar ar son na Gaeilge. Deir sé linn 'Is saibhride go mór an spéis agus an sult a bhain le mo shaol an bhá sin leis an nGaeilge a músclaíodh i bhfad ó shoin i nDroichead Átha.'

Other activities

Ken's cultural and educational enthusiasms have not been confined to the Irish language. Down the years he has remained a student, with a particular interest in economics, archaeology and French literature. In 1946 he published a study of wartime finance in the US and the UK entitled *Financing by Credit Creation*. He wrote papers for the Statistical and Social Inquiry Society on Ireland's external assets, capital formation, saving and economic progress, and other topics. His role in *Economic Development* has already been mentioned. In 1983 a collection of his essays was published under the title *Interests*. His early-morning introduction to French in the Christian Brothers' School in Drogheda inspired a lifelong interest in French prose and poetry. He has been president of Alliance Française, and was honoured by the French government in 1976 by admission as a Commandeur of the Légion d'honneur. Honorary doctorates came from five universities, beginning with the DEconSc of the NUI in 1962. In the context of his scholarly interests, he has been president of the Economic and Social Research Institute and of the Royal Irish Academy (in its bicentenary year), chairman of the council of the Dublin Institute for Advanced Studies and member of the governing board of the School of Celtic Studies of that institute.

Conclusion

Ken Whitaker's family life has been very happy and fulfilling. Five sons and a daughter are all married and he delights in his twenty-two grandchildren. An increasing number of these are qualifying as graduates but the younger ones are still in beguiling infancy. Sadly, his wife Nora, who shared her grace and charm with him for fifty-three years, died in May 1994. Ar dheis Dé go raibh a hanam dílis!

Ken has declared that, for a reasonably balanced life, everyone needs to have one irresistible temptation, preferably not an immoral one. For Ken that temptation is fishing. This has virtually ousted golf in recent years and takes him down frequently during the salmon season to Mayo where he has converted an old schoolhouse on the fringes of the Gaeltacht. He has a scientific as well as a sporting interest in salmonids, having served on the committee of management of the Salmon Research Agency for many years and as chairman between 1981 and 1994. His public and private efforts to achieve better salmon and sea trout management policies in the national interest also continue. These efforts exemplify the unflagging character of his lifetime of patient, energetic and assiduous public service.

This biographical introduction to the Festschrift celebrating Ken Whitaker's first eighty years might appropriately conclude with the traditional Irish wish:

'Go mba fada buan thú.'

Fionán Ó Muircheartaigh

NOTES

1. T. K. Whitaker, *Interests*, Dublin: Institute of Public Administration, 1983.
2. Ronan Fanning, *The Irish Department of Finance, 1922–58*, Dublin: Institute of Public Administration, 1978.

Part I

Ireland, Europe and the World

1

Ireland and the Challenge of Globalisation

PETER SUTHERLAND

Globalisation

THE rapid integration of the world economy that is taking place today is not a new phenomenon. As historical economists have pointed out, it is in fact the resumption of a process which began in the middle of the last century but was interrupted and reversed from about 1913 until the end of the Second World War. In the intervening period central planning was adopted by a substantial part of the world economy while many other countries reverted increasingly to protectionist and interventionist policies. The liberalisation of trade and capital flows over the last fifty years has restored the world economy to a level of integration quite similar to that reached in the earlier period.

Today, however, what is remarkable about the process of integration of the world economy, which we usually refer to as globalisation, is the extraordinary scale and pace at which it is taking place. With the collapse of communism in the former Soviet Union almost every country in the world is now part of the global capitalist system. Both developing and transition economies are being rapidly integrated into the world economy. The liberalisation of trade and capital flows, reduced transportation and communication costs, innovations in business organisation and the increasingly rapid diffusion of technological progress across borders have greatly increased the ease with which national markets are integrated globally. As a result each part of the world is now inescapably affected by what happens elsewhere and the time-scale within which countries must adapt to changes in the global economy has been greatly reduced.

Trend in trade

The rapidly changing reality of the global economy is clearly reflected, for example, in the fact that the volume of world trade has expanded more rapidly than the volume of world output in nearly every year since the end of the Second World War. That ratio of trade to output has been increasing even more rapidly in the 1990s. According to the IMF's latest *World Economic Outlook,* the volume of world trade increased by over 9 per cent in 1995, more than double the growth in output. And although the gap narrowed in 1996, IMF forecasts show it will widen again in 1997–98. This trend indicates that firms everywhere are increasingly targeting global markets and are no longer relying on domestic markets alone.

Capital markets

Capital markets have also become more integrated. Gradual liberalisation since the early 1970s has seen gross capital flows soar, particularly in the past decade. According to the IMF, international transactions in bonds and equities in the major industrialised countries rose from less than 10 per cent of GDP in 1980 to over 100 per cent of GDP in 1995. Gross flows of portfolio investment and foreign direct investment (FDI) in the advanced economies more than tripled between the first half of the 1980s and the first half of the 1990s. The growing importance of international flows of FDI, which began to rise sharply in the mid-1980s with the total flow of FDI out of the advanced economies increasing more that fourfold between 1984 and 1990, is another clear reflection of the rapid expansion of the cross-border activities of multinationals and the globalisation of business. Since the slowdown in 1990–92 FDI has recovered strongly. Driving the recent rapid expansion of FDI is the fact that it is no longer confined to large firms. Even for small and medium-sized enterprises, production and distribution strategies increasingly span the globe as national and regional frontiers become less and less relevant for private sector decision-making.

Developing countries

The extent of globalisation is also reflected in the increased importance of transition and developing countries in the world economy. Growth rates in the developing countries have far exceeded those in the advanced economies. According to the IMF, in developing countries as a group GDP grew by 6 per cent in 1995 and 6.5 per cent in 1996. This compares with an average of 2.5 per cent for both years in the advanced economies. And besides increasing their share of world trade from 23 per cent in 1985 to 29 per cent in 1995 they have begun to deepen and diversify their trade linkages. Inter-developing country trade rose from 31 per cent of total developing country trade in 1985 to 37 per cent in 1995. This expansion, diversification and deepening of trade linkages has largely been the result of changes in trade and exchange regimes. Statist and inward-looking policies of protectionism and import substitution have been increasingly replaced by more outward-looking policies based on trade and capital market liberalisation. Indeed, there is strong evidence that convergence between developed and developing economies is closely linked to the introduction of more open trade regimes and other market reforms in developing countries. That is not to say difficulties have not arisen in both developing and transition economies in this process. However, those have been exacerbated by developed countries' policy of maintaining restrictions on imports in certain sectors such as agriculture, textiles and steel in which developing and transition countries have a comparative advantage.

GATT and WTO

The process of integration of the world economy was given a secure international foundation and underpinned by the successful conclusion of the Uruguay Round of GATT talks in December 1993 and the subsequent establishment of the World Trade Organisation (WTO) on 1 January 1995. Besides producing the largest tariff-cutting deal ever achieved, the conclusion of the Uruguay Round has also greatly expanded the range of economic sectors subject to multilateral trading rules. Agriculture and textiles and clothing, which since the 1950s had been gradually removed from the reach of the disciplines of the GATT, have been reintegrated into the multilateral system and agreements were signed on services and intellectual property.

In addition, the GATT system has undergone major institutional development through the establishment of the WTO and its improved dispute-settlement system. It is also worth noting that the WTO now has 126 members with another 30 countries, including China and Russia, wanting to join. This compares with 114 at the end of the GATT negotiations in 1993 and 92 in 1986 when the Uruguay Round began. Clearly free trade has never been more widely embraced in principle since the end of the Second World War.

Regional integration

It is no accident that the process of globalisation should be accompanied by the trend to strengthen and reinforce regional co-operation and integration. Individual countries recognise that they need to co-operate more closely and pool their shared interests in an era of global change. Significantly, nearly all members of the WTO also belong to one or more of the seventy-six free-trade areas or customs unions recognised by the GATT/WTO since its foundation and of these more than half have been established since 1990. Besides the EU, which of course has evolved well beyond the stage of being a mere free-trade area or customs union, the best known regional trading agreements are NAFTA (North American Free Trade Agreement), Mercosur (the Southern Cone Common Market in Latin America), ASEAN (Association of South-East Asian Nations), and APEC (Asia-Pacific Economic Co-operation). Although the WTO recognises these regional integration agreements as a step in the right direction if implemented according to certain criteria set out in Article XXIV of the GATT, there is concern that some agreements simply divert trade and investment away from third countries.

Demographic forces

However, there have been other developments, potentially a source of tensions, that will increasingly shape the international trade and economic environment. First, demographic trends in the developed and developing countries are markedly different. The global population, which has more than tripled this century, continues to increase at more than eighty million a year. Very low or zero population growth rates in the OECD countries are ageing the populations and bringing many attendant changes, not least of which are the financial implications for national pension schemes. As for the developing countries, over one-third of the population is under the age of fifteen and of the nearly two billion people who will be added to the world's population in the next twenty years, 95 per cent of them will be born outside the OECD area.

The consequence is that between now and the year 2015, the number of new jobs required to keep unemployment rates unchanged in the developing world will exceed the current populations of Western Europe and North America combined. Again the economic implications are manifold, including increased competition for capital and a continuing shift in competitiveness in labour-intensive activities to high population growth countries. Nor is it a coincidence that migration and the linkage between the pressures for migration from low-income countries and trade barriers in rich countries are moving rapidly up the international agenda.

Protectionism

Another significant development is that with the end of the Cold War competition has increasingly been refocused from the political–military sphere to the economic sphere with the result that national economic competitiveness has become the rallying cry. Of course, the notion of competition between countries and regions is rather simplistic in an era of greater global economic integration. Indeed, competition among enterprises is *the* issue in a global economy. Nonetheless, the concept of national champions has not lost its political appeal to some and it seems to include policy-making to a growing extent. In addition, as the interests that bound together traditional alliances have shifted, the cohesion that helped countries resolve economic problems can no longer be taken for granted, thus increasing uncertainty in the area of international economic relations.

Clearly the globalisation of the world economy presents national economies and policy-makers with new opportunities and new challenges. By accentuating competition it produces wide-ranging benefits from innovation, new product and service development, and greater specialisation in production. However, the reality of globalisation – and its implications for the future – is still far from being universally accepted. Business itself is not united in its welcome of the opportunities it represents or the rules that sustain it. For some sectors, especially those where protection and government assistance have been used to muffle the signals of international supply and demand, the global market is seen more as a threat than an opportunity. Such interests – and they exist in most countries – frequently devote the energy and resources that should go into restructuring and becoming competitive to a frantic and doomed effort to resist change.

Unfortunately, they find too often a sympathetic hearing from governments. Of course this reflects the lobbying power of old established industries which may be located in areas of high unemployment. It should be recognised by policy-makers that misguided political efforts to appease such sectional pressures impose high costs on consumers and export-oriented businesses. But, more generally, this phenomenon also reflects the confusion and anxiety that characterise societies and governments in the developed world today. The rapid erosion of old barriers between economic and political categories – and between nations – has outstripped the ability of established ways of thinking, and established political attitudes, to keep up. The results are a volatile and sometimes angry electorate and a tendency to look for simplistic solutions. The polemics of Le Pen in France have a certain seductive appeal and similar incendiary rhetoric can be heard in other European countries. What these arguments generally have in common is denial – denial of international economic integration, denial of the economic potential of the wider world, denial of the need to compete.

More often than not public debate on the phenomenon of globalisation is focused on the perceived negative aspects, in particular the effects of freer trade on employment and income distribution in advanced economies. The popular perception is that cheap imports from low-wage, developing economies are the cause of rising unemployment and falling wages among low-skilled workers and the decline of the manufacturing sector. However, a growing body of empirical evidence has shown that in fact globalisation contributes only marginally to unemployment or income inequality in advanced economies. According to the IMF economists Matthew Slaughter and Phillip Swagel, international trade accounted for only 10–20 per cent of the increased wage dispersion in industrial countries in the 1980s and 1990s. Instead, it appears that the increase in wage inequality has been driven principally by advances in technology that favour skilled labour.

It is also worth making the point that besides the economic advantage of freer trade to an economy such as ours, there is a moral issue at stake. Labour cost differentials largely reflect the different endowments and technological capacity of countries and are in fact one of the main sources of comparative advantage that developing countries have *vis-à-vis* their rich counterparts. As such they are the catalyst for new growth in poorer countries. There is evidence that as productivity levels converge between developing and advanced countries so too do labour costs. A concerted effort must be made, therefore, to reduce the scope of interest groups to point to such nominal cost differences as a legitimate rationale for protectionism.

Interdependence and autonomy

In addition, there is the widespread perception that the autonomy of national governments in the field of economic policy is increasingly restricted, at a considerable cost to national welfare, by globalisation. There is little doubt that globalisation has increased policy interdependence and reduced national policy independence. As advances in communications and transportation shrink distances between people, and each country's activities become more intertwined with those of other countries, it is inevitable that countries will find that there are increased external influences on what used to be considered purely domestic policies. Indeed, the range of policies considered as trade-related has steadily grown from measures applied at the border on imported products to policies whose trade effects are incidental to their main purposes, such as production subsidies, taxation, investment, anti-trust and technical standards and domestic regulations. New areas of attention include the protection of the environment and investment policy which are accepted as being part of the future trade agenda.

Rewards and penalties

However, it is wrong to perceive globalisation as a zero-sum game in which certain economies gain at the expense of others. I firmly believe that if national policies respond adequately and in time to the pressures for structural adjustment in patterns of production, investment, and foreign trade that are generated by increasingly integrated and competitive world markets, then all countries will be in a better position to exploit their comparative advantages, enhance their long-run growth potential, and share in the benefits of the expansion of the world economy. While globalisation may raise the costs of economic distortions and failure to introduce adequate reforms, it has also increased the potential rewards for sound, outward-looking policies. This is clearly illustrated if we consider the impact of the liberalisation of financial markets on fiscal policy. While the global capital markets reward sound fiscal policy with lower interest rates and reduced exchange rate risk premiums, profligate governments are swiftly punished with currency instability and rising interest rates. As Richard O'Brien of the Global Business Network has argued, a liberalised and globalised capital market helps to limit the abuse by national governments of their power to raise taxes, print money, and borrow. It might be said with some justification that financial markets tend to exercise discipline erratically. However, governments should not be tempted to respond to the excesses of financial markets by trying to restrict their power. Instead, governments would be better advised to conduct policy in such a way that it does not destabilise market expectations and to ensure that the markets are better informed.

The challenges facing Ireland

When T. K. Whitaker produced *Economic Development* in 1958 Ireland was at a crossroads. In significant respects the first three decades of Irish independence had been characterised by ever-greater isolation and Ireland was rapidly falling behind other European states in economic terms. A strong desire to attenuate the economic and political links with Britain, combined with the global economic conditions that prevailed in the 1930s, had led Ireland down the road of economic nationalism. An indiscriminate policy of protection that aimed to achieve self-sufficiency had swiftly transformed 'the last surviving example of a predominantly free-trading state' into 'one of the most highly protected in the world'. To use T. K. Whitaker's own words, Ireland had reached 'the dark night of the soul' in which people began to question the validity of national independence without economic development. To remedy this *Economic Development* advocated an economic policy of productive investment and free enterprise led by the private sector and encouraged a shift in Irish economic policy away from protection towards free trade and foreign investment in Ireland.

Working through the EU

Today, Ireland finds itself again at a moment in economic history of similar importance. After a long period of persistently high levels of unemployment and slow economic growth, the Irish economy is expanding at a rate that is unprecedented. And in the context of the globalisation process described above, an environment with low inflation, a declining deficit and record levels in important indices such as new car sales and housing starts indicates something of a revolution that could only be happening with the assistance of participation in European economic integration and indeed globalisation. It would be surprising if the Ireland of 1997 were not to bask in a certain sense of self-satisfaction at the state of its economy. However, we should not lose sight of the fact that these favourable trends have been achieved as a result of sound fiscal policy since the 1980s imposed by our own past failures and by some commitment over the years to improving Irish competitiveness, particularly as a location for foreign investment. These can only be maintained by rising to the new and dramatic challenges in global competition that have arisen out of the deeper and broader integration of the world economy that I have sought to describe.

So what should our response be to these challenges? How do they affect our situation as an island of only five million people in a corner of north-western Europe? How do they affect our attitude to and our common participation in the European Union? What can we do to respond to the challenge of globalisation so as to ensure the welfare and the prosperity of our people?

Significantly, Ireland's decision to emphatically embrace free trade coincided with greater economic integration elsewhere in Europe and the creation of the European Economic Community. Indeed Seán Lemass and T. K. Whitaker correctly identified membership of the EEC as a means to develop alternative opportunities for industry and services and to become less vulnerable to the fluctuations and performance of Britain. With the prospect of access to continental markets came the realisation that import substitution and protectionism could not be the basis of a viable national economic policy.

The rationale of that decision to join the EEC should not be forgotten today. The people of Ireland are indeed fortunate that they share common membership of the European Union. As the Uruguay Round came to a successful conclusion in 1993, I was acutely conscious of the influence and weight of the European Union as one of the largest trading partners for the rest of the world. Its negotiating strength was far greater than any one of the individual member states could ever hope to possess, even the largest among them. Sharing in the benefits of that strength was extremely important to the smaller countries and regions within the Union, including Ireland. Only an open, outward-looking Europe, confident in its internal coherence, will be capable of asserting its principles. Indeed, without the internal institutional framework that allowed the European Union to articulate and implement a common external economic policy, I am convinced that the Uruguay Round could not have been concluded successfully.

To their credit policy-makers in Ireland have increasingly realised that it is in our national interests to ensure that the EU functions effectively and helps the process of globalisation. Ireland is now in many respects part of the vanguard of member states driving forward the opening of the regional and world economies. For example, despite the obvious difficulties that the UK opt-out of EMU poses for Ireland, the Irish government has shown an unrivalled commitment to European monetary union both in relation to meeting the Maastricht Treaty convergence criteria and in its political support for the project. In addition, the Irish government is to be commended for its efforts, albeit in vain, to extend Community competence in international negotiations in Article 113 to new trade-related issues such as services, foreign direct investment, and intellectual property which are expected to dominate the WTO agenda for the foreseeable future. Failure to speak with one voice in these areas seriously reduces the EU's negotiating power which has contributed enormously to liberalising trade across the world and winning global access for European exports and investment. European integration is not an end in itself but an integral part of the much wider process of change in global competitiveness described above.

Adapting the state sector

Ireland's future economic prospects will depend to a great extent on our ability to adapt rapidly to this changing reality. Implicit in globalisation is even more competition. Sooner rather than later this will require the real structural adjustments that in some instances we have so far avoided. In particular, the size of the state sector will have to be reduced and labour markets rendered more flexible. The size of the state sector will inevitably be constrained by the strict fiscal rules which are an essential part of the Maastricht Treaty approach to monetary union. Moreover, it is now widely recognised that the high level of taxation on labour and income which has become necessary to finance the state is a significant drag on the competitiveness of the Irish economy.

Competition and the private sector

Membership of the European Union and the creation of the single European market have already had a positive impact on competitiveness in Ireland but a great deal still remains to be done in this area. The manufacturing sector which is exposed to international competition still relies substantially on tax relief to be competitive on foreign markets. And, according to the 1993 OECD economic survey of Ireland, anti-competitive practices are widespread in sectors such as food, transport, communications, and medical and health care which have long been sheltered from foreign competition.

The first Irish legislation to make anti-competitive practices illegal came into force in 1991, almost 100 years after the equivalent law, the Sherman Act, was introduced in the US. Essentially, the Competition Act extended the principles of EU competition law to the domestic economy and established the Competition Authority. However, EU legislation only prohibits anti-competitive practices that affect trade between member states and, therefore, cannot be relied on to check anti-competitive practices in subsectoral markets in a small economy like Ireland. Moreover, the Competition Authority, whose task it is to safeguard market competition in the private sector, was born without teeth, was inexplicably not allowed to initiate investigations independently, and, being overburdened with a backlog of cases, was severely underresourced. It was not until 1994 that this situation was partially rectified by an amendment to the Competition Act granting the Competition Authority greater resources and powers to initiate investigations. However, the amended Act does not specify the fines or penalties for non-compliance. The benefits that the rigorous enforcement of the Competition Act would have for the overall economy should not be underestimated. As I noted above, competition enhances market efficiency and ultimately reduces prices to the consumer which in turn releases consumer expenditure for growth in other markets.

Competition and the public sector

The public sector in particular suffers from a lack of competition. In 1993 the OECD warned that in the semi-state sector 'the principles of competition have been subordinated to more social and collectivist goals, leaving consumer interests at risk from relatively inefficient public sector monopolies and excessive regulation'. In addition, inefficiency in the provision of essential services by public monopolies adds to the costs faced by indigenous firms exposed to external competition and can seriously detract from Ireland's attractiveness as a location for inward foreign direct investment. In the long term this attractiveness must the founded on more than the offer of competing incentive packages and cheaper labour. The immediate introduction of greater competition and deregulation in these vital sectors would contribute significantly to improving efficiency and innovation in the economy as a whole.

Privatisation and investment opportunity

For this reason it is time that the question of privatisation was debated openly, free of the ideological bias that characterised the discussion elsewhere in the 1970s and early 1980s. Everywhere in the world, let alone in Europe, it is increasingly recognised that the state should not be running businesses. There may be arguments for some national monopolies, but they are few and far between. Semi-state or state enterprises with boards made up of political appointees (no matter how well motivated) and civil servants have been a recipe for inadequate commercial performance. This is particularly true when the state is also playing the role of regulator of the sector concerned. One has only to look at the prevarication by Ireland over the years in facing up to the regulation and demonopolisation of vital utilities required by EU directives to see the consequences of this symbiosis of regulator with owner. How can one justify the state running banks, hotels, a significant part of our entire public transport system, airports, telecommunications, and so on?

Even apart from the efficiency-enhancing effects of privatisation, the introduction of more substantial Irish companies to our stock exchange is badly needed. At present an excessive amount of our pension fund capital is invested outside Ireland. In relative terms we invest more of our domestic resources in company shares outside our own country than any other European Union state. Ultimately this represents a use of Irish savings to fund the investment strategies of companies elsewhere. However, the real question is why does so much of this money find its way abroad? Clearly pension fund managers are obliged to seek the best possible returns for the fund they manage. To accuse them of acting wrongly for this weighting of investment abroad is ludicrous. They are doing what they have to do to maximise return. Equities generally provide a higher return than bonds or other instruments. However, in Ireland we do not have the spread of companies to enable fund managers to give adequate weighting to the home market in their portfolio allocations. There are simply not enough stocks available, particularly in reasonably substantial companies.

Inward investment (FDI)

In contrast, Ireland's ability to attract inward investment in fast-growing, high-tech sectors has been a major factor in recent economic successes. At present there are over 1,000 foreign firms here which account for 45 per cent of total manufacturing jobs in Ireland, over 50 per cent of our industrial output, and more than 70 per cent of our industrial exports. They have created more than 100,000 jobs directly, most of which are high-wage knowledge-intensive jobs, and many more indirectly. However, an increasingly important aspect of globalisation is that the competition between locations where providers of capital can invest to obtain significant returns has been transformed and hugely expanded. With free movement of capital and the capacity to transfer huge sums instantaneously investors are no longer confined to investing at home. As investment is a prerequisite for growth, modernisation and especially employment, it is self-evident that we must continue to induce investors to invest in Ireland. This investment can come in different ways. Clearly foreign direct investment, as inspired by the activities of the IDA in particular, has been the cornerstone of the rapid industrialisation of our formerly agricultural society. This transformation has taken place largely since 1973. In the more recent past the success of the International Financial Services Centre also has been substantial and important. Apart from the obvious direct benefits of tax revenue and employment generated, Dublin has a new and consistent flow of business visitors that bring their own secondary benefits. These elements of our current economic success have not happened without cause. The attractions of an English-speaking country within the European Union have been vital elements in attracting and retaining what is often highly mobile investment. The beneficial tax regime permitted has also distinguished Ireland. However, it has a definite lifespan. Therefore, we should recognise that the current favourable economic conditions in Ireland can only be sustained through constant improvement in our own competitiveness. We cannot stand still. We are constantly evaluated against our competitors.

Investment in education

Another important element for the promotion of inward investment is human capital. It is vital that we provide a bank of individuals with relevant skills, particularly in computer technology. The fact that there is increasing evidence of a failure to have the necessary pool of individuals is an indictment of past policy implementation, particularly as many saw the issue in the 1980s and publicly commented on it then. Though we applaud the capacities of our young people who are much sought-after internationally, these capacities are the result of their application and not the policies of the state. We have underinvested in education: the proportion of our resources devoted to education is less than rather than more than the norm. In addition, we must ensure that teachers at all levels as well as being adequately rewarded are evaluated on performance and provided with updated skills over time.

Pension reform

Another area for concern is pension reform. This is an issue in Ireland as much as anywhere else in Europe even allowing for our different demographic profile. It is time we addressed the issues that are a major focus for economists and policy-makers elsewhere rather than pushing off the problem into the future and pretending it does not exist.

Agriculture

The changes wrought by globalisation have also begun to have an impact on the agricultural sector which is still of vital importance to the Irish economy. Although the GATT agreement on agriculture introduced only a modest degree of liberalisation, it provides a framework for the long-term reform of agricultural trade and domestic policies over the years to come. Above all, it represents an irreversible move towards the objective of increased market orientation in agricultural trade. Stronger rules should lead to improved predictability and stability for importing and exporting countries alike, but they will also mean new challenges.

It is important that policy-makers in agriculture and the farming community face up to the direction of agricultural reform. The review process beginning in 1999 will no doubt seek to strengthen the market orientation of international trade rules on agriculture. The process of liberalisation will not lose momentum. Apart from external pressures for reform from developing countries, central and eastern Europe, Russia and the countries of the former Soviet Union, internal constraints place a limit to the ability of even the richer areas of the world to finance open-ended support mechanisms that diverge from world market prices. Efforts to ensure budgetary and fiscal equilibrium in both the United States and an enlarged European Union mean that the days of unlimited market support are numbered. In addition, pressures for reform have increasingly come from consumers concerned with food quality and environmental interests opposed to the intensive and polluting farming encouraged by price-support mechanisms. The independence of mind and reliance on one's own efforts that traditionally have been associated with farming values in Europe are much appreciated. However, that notion of independence and self-reliance sits oddly with the massive subsidisation that has occurred in both the United States and Europe in recent decades.

Although some resistance to change can be expected from the agricultural sector, it is clear that in the future the general direction of agricultural policy will be towards greater liberalisation. This trend should be reflected in the reform of the Common Agricultural Policy (CAP) which the European Commission is expected to announce before the end of 1997. In the words of Ferdinando Riccardi (of Agence Europe), 'European agriculture is to be defended and protected, the CAP ... studied critically in order to remedy its flaws and curb abuse'. It is clearly unacceptable that massive overcompensation is still common in certain sectors under the CAP with the bulk of price support going to a minority of large farmers. Greater transparency in certain areas of EU agricultural expenditure is also necessary to correct persistent over-budgeting. Admittedly, anticipating agricultural expenditure for the year ahead is a difficult task. However, the recent decision to involve the Directorate-General for the Budget in the preparation of the guarantee section of the European Agricultural Guidance and Guarantee Fund budget must be seen as a step in the right direction.

In Ireland farming and the food and drink industry together account for about 17 per cent of GDP and employ almost 20 per cent of the workforce. It should be realised that failure to introduce adequate reforms to adapt to the competitive pressures of future liberalisation will condemn large parts of these sectors to decline. Inevitably, the longer adaptation is postponed the higher the economic and social costs of adjustment will be. Trade liberalisation offers greater opportunity to the resourceful. But if it is seen as a threat the opportunity will be taken up by someone else.

Certainly adjustment from a production-led commodity-type system to a market-led food-based system can be difficult, but it can also lead to greater competitiveness and new opportunities, as the example of New Zealand has shown. In this context of change, agricultural sectors which are excessively dependent upon price-support mechanisms will inevitably lose out. On the other hand, the new global markets offer great opportunities for those with innovative ideas, high-quality products and sound strategies to gain market share. The export prospects, for example, for high-quality foodstuffs such as can be produced in Ireland can only improve with the opening-up of markets in the fastest growing economies. Irish agriculture has to be ready to compete in these markets with higher levels of processing and value added, branding and use of Ireland's image of quality.

Standards, quality and the environment

In this context, food standards and quality and the environment have become vital issues for the farming and food-processing sector. The 1991 report by the Agriculture and Food Policy Review Group correctly argued that an increasingly environmentally friendly agricultural and food industry should be developed based on sustainable production processes, and that the highest internationally accepted food quality and safety standards should be adopted throughout the production chain from farm-level to the consumer. The quality and purity of Irish food products have had a major influence on the competitiveness of the agricultural sector in the past and will continue to do so in the future. Therefore, legislation must be strictly enforced to ensure that the quality and safety of Irish produce match the image that the sector wants to promote both at home and abroad. The negative impact of the BSE crisis on the consumer's perceptions should be a lesson to all in the industry.

The idea that compliance with increasingly stringent environmental legislation will erode cost advantages *vis-à-vis* countries with less stringent environmental legislation is short-sighted and should be discouraged. The report by the Agriculture and Food Policy Review Group rightly called for the environment to 'be brought into the mainstream of agricultural policy'. According to the report, because Ireland, in general, has a less polluted natural environment than most other EU countries, it is in Ireland's interests to support EU legislation promoting higher environmental standards. A high-quality environment can be a major source of competitive advantage, especially when marketing agricultural products abroad. Ireland's 'clean, green' environmental image has already been used effectively to promote food, drink and tourism exports and to claim premium prices, particularly in continental European markets. It should also be noted that these important Irish industries are predominantly owned by Irish entrepreneurs. A high-quality environment is also vital to the development of farm-based tourism which can be an important alternative economic activity, especially in disadvantaged farming areas.

Conclusion

Globalisation is a fact which we simply cannot ignore. It will increasingly shape the environment for business, for farmers, for traders and for individual participants in the economy and will also condition the choices open to governments in their management of the economy. To those who understand what it means to be globally competitive and are prepared for change, globalisation can bring handsome rewards. But those who ignore it do so at their peril.

For Ireland, the importance of international trade as a motor of renewed economic growth is clear. As a small open economy, trade is our lifeblood. Our exports amount to 63 per cent of our GNP and in recent years they have grown up to three times as fast as the economy as a whole. Six out of every ten jobs in the Irish manufacturing sector depend on export sales.

The fact that three-quarters of Ireland's exports go to other EU member states and about a third to the UK does not in any way lessen the importance to this country of trade with the wider world. On the contrary it makes it all the more important. The rest of the world is the market opportunity of the future. New opportunities are already emerging from the first wave of trade barrier reductions introduced by the members of the WTO. But growing attention must be paid to emerging markets in central and eastern Europe, east Asia and Latin America, which far from representing a threat to Irish or European industry should be considered as an opportunity for growth.

According to the Competitiveness Advisory Group's 1996 report, Europe has performed below its full potential in global trade compared with the US and Japan. The EU's share of total world exports has fallen by proportionally more than that of the US while Japan has held its share. This reflects the EU's failure to exploit export opportunities in the fastest expanding markets in south-east Asia. EU firms are still reluctant to invest in south-east Asia and have missed golden opportunities to develop infrastructure in other emerging markets such as China, India and Indonesia. Instead, the EU continues to rely on historical markets in Africa, central and eastern Europe and the Middle East, which have been growing at a slower rate. So do we in Ireland.

To adapt to the rapid change taking place in the global economy, policy-makers must be aware of the full implications that growing economic interdependence has for the notion of national sovereignty. No country, least of all a small country like Ireland, can claim to be able to fully control its economic destiny. Instead, Ireland's future lies clearly in an outward-looking Europe with the capacity to limit the risks and maximise the opportunities offered by the wider process of globalisation, of which European integration is an essential part. In particular, efforts to adapt to the single European market, monetary union and enlargement will enhance the overall, long-term competitiveness of the Irish economy and prepare firms for competition on a global scale.

The greatest challenge for Ireland's policy-makers today is how to manage the necessary adjustment and its inevitable costs. The prolonged use of what I call the 'dole and derogation' approach must be avoided. It should be clear to all involved that postponing the introduction of restructuring merely increases the cost of adjustment in the future.

Ireland's policy-makers must possess, above all, the ability to respond to new ideas and situations and to adapt their views in the light of new evidence, both qualities that are identified by Professor J. J. Lee in his history of twentieth-century Ireland as typical of T. K. Whitaker.

====== 2 ======

Challenges for Ireland in the Integrated European Union

ALAN W. GRAY

Introduction

THIS contribution considers the challenges for Ireland in the increasingly integrated European Union and identifies a number of priority policy areas. Before an analysis of these policy areas is undertaken this essay reviews the economic context. Some of the policy challenges suggested are primarily matters to be addressed at a national level, but a significant number relate to aspects of EU policy and raise the question of the appropriate respective roles of the EU and of member states in policy development; the essay presents an overview of this issue before preceeding to the analysis of the identified priority policy areas.

The economic challenges for Ireland reflect a number of vulnerabilities to continued growth in the economy. These include the possible increase in interest rates and greater instability in exchange rates arising from speculation in the pre-EMU period, and the potential divergence in the sterling–euro exchange rate in the post-EMU period. The recently announced reforms in the UK providing for greater in-dependence in the operation of the Bank of England may have implications for the extent of divergence between sterling and the euro. The implications for Ireland of the establishment of Economic and Monetary Union is a topic expressly covered in the contribution by Duisenberg. In this essay, the focus is on a number of other priority areas for policy development as follows:

- responsible policies concerning the public finances
- avoidance of re-emergence of cost inflation
- maintenance of a non-protectionist international trade environment
- supportive environment for foreign direct investment
- diversification of Irish trade

- removal of bottlenecks within Ireland
- maximisation of impact of EU funds.

Economic context

Ireland at the end of the 1990s is recording a remarkable economic performance. Real GDP over the past decade has on average been growing at around twice the OECD average and the imbalance in the public finances has been corrected. Interest rates have declined to historically low levels and there has been a continued buoyancy in exports. Ireland has, however, a large outflow from servicing the external debt and even more significantly from the dramatic growth in outflows of profit remittances/distributed profits from foreign-owned industry. For example, outflows of dividends, distribution of branch profits and inter-affiliate interest amounted to around £4,000 million in 1995. The current account of the balance of payments has, however, shown a significant improvement and has moved from chronic deficit to significant surplus, with a 1995 current account surplus of over £900 million.

Not surprisingly, given the growth in the economy, unemployment has declined, although it is still at a high level. Somewhat more surprisingly, given the rate of growth in the economy, inflation is lower than it has been since the 1950s. While this reflects the international openness of the economy and developments in our exchange rate, it is still noteworthy. Despite the impressive performance of the Irish economy, taxation and public expenditure remain very high. In addition, many groups in Irish society are experiencing very difficult economic conditions, and it should be recognised that GNP per head is still below the EU average and is likely to remain so for the rest of the decade.

Most economists would accept that it is hard to be certain of the significance of different possible explanations for the remarkable turnaround in the economy. The growth in the Irish economy has, without doubt, been influenced by a variety of factors, including fiscal correction and real exchange rate movements, as well as the significant inflows of current transfers, largely accounted for by EU Structural Fund payments, and favourable demographic trends. Also relevant have been the moderation in wage inflation and the rapid expansion of exports from the overseas manufacturing and international services sectors. All of these factors have fed into what has been a mutually supportive virtuous cycle of low-inflation growth.

Any understanding of what has been happening in the Irish economy and the challenges which we face in order to maintain this growth must take account of the buoyancy in exports which is reflected by the balance of payments surplus. Table 1 presents the trends in the estimated value of external trade over the past decade. The figures show that the surpluses on merchandise trade increased from around £750 million in 1986 to over £7,000 million in 1996. This reflected the extremely strong growth in the value of exports which rose from around £9,000 million in 1986 to nearly £30,000 million in 1996.

Table 1: Trend in estimated value of external trade (£m)

Period	Imports	Exports	Balance
1986	8,621.3	9,374.3	753.0
1987	9,155.2	10,723.5	1,568.3
1988	10,214.8	12,304.8	2,090.1
1989	12,284.3	14,597.0	2,312.8
1990	12,468.8	14,336.7	1,867.9
1991	12,850.8	15,018.9	2,168.1
1992	13,194.8	16,743.8	3,549.1
1993	14,884.7	19,829.7	4,945.0
1994	17,283.4	22,753.4	5,470.1
1995[a]	20,622.0	27,807.3	7,185.3
1996[b]	21,995.4	29,661.7	7,666.3

(a) Provisional
(b) Provisional estimates based on preliminary intrastat response levels – subject to revision.
Source: Central Statistics Office

This growth in exports has been significantly determined by the growth in exports from modern industry sectors, including electrical engineering, pharmaceuticals, computers and instrument engineering. In all of these sectors foreign-owned industry dominates. For example, in the case of electrical engineering, overseas industry accounts for over 87 per cent of output and in other sectors overseas industry accounts for over 95 per cent of output. The significance of the growth in exports from this small number of sectors can be seen from the figures in Table 2 which show the increasing importance of exports in sectors such as medical and pharmaceutical products and office and automatic data processing (ADP) machines. For example, medical and pharmaceutical exports increased from £193 million in 1986 to over £1,500 million in 1996.

The fact that the growth in the Irish economy is so dependent on exports and that these exports are dominated by overseas firms has important implications for the impact of EU and national policies on Irish performance. The significance of foreign direct investment is indicated by the fact that there are around 1,000 foreign-owned manufacturing and international services companies in Ireland which account for around 70 per cent of industrial exports.

Table 2: Estimated value of selected exports

	1986		1996*	
	£m	%	£m	%
Machinery and transport equipment	2,860.5	30.5	9,400.1	34.6
of which:				
Office and ADP machines	1,856.3	19.7	5,659.7	20.8
Electrical machinery etc.	406.1	4.3	2,094.7	7.7
Telecommunications etc.	141.7	1.5	562.2	2.1
Chemicals and related products	1,251.0	13.3	6,175.4	22.7
of which:				
Organic chemicals	620.0	6.6	2,942.4	10.8
Medical and pharmaceutical products	193.4	2.1	1,563.8	5.7
Food and live animals	2,194.4	23.4	3,845.0	14.1
of which:				
Live animals	235.4	2.5	124.3	0.5
Meat etc.	659.1	7.0	984.8	3.6
Dairy	470.0	5.0	711.4	2.6
Miscellaneous food products etc.	413.0	4.4	1,309.6	4.8
Selected traditional sectors				
Textiles	297.4	3.2	345.6	1.3
Clothing etc.	197.6	2.1	307.5	1.1
Furniture etc.	27.2	0.3	74.8	0.3
Footwear	13.5	0.1	25.4	0.1
Other products	2,546.6	27.1	7,028.0	25.8
Total	9,388.2	100.0	27,201.8	100.0

*January–November
Source: Central Statistics Office

Foreign-owned manufacturing is, however, less significant in terms of its direct employment contribution. As is highlighted in Table 3, Irish-owned manufacturing employs more than the foreign-owned sector and, not surprisingly, services employment dominates the Irish labour force. The significance of the local services sector implies that this sector may be of critical importance in influencing the overall competitiveness of the Irish economy and as the main area of employment opportunity.

Table 3: Components of Irish employment 1995 (000s)

Agriculture	139
Irish-owned manufacturing	128
Foreign-owned manufacturing	107
Internationally traded services	22
Local services	729
Miscellaneous industry	100

Sources: Central Statistics Office Labour Force Survey and Forfás Employment Survey

In identifying the future challenges for Ireland it is instructive to consider the geographic pattern of Irish exports as well as the overall sectoral trends. Table 4 shows that while nearly 70 per cent of the value of exports is to EU countries, the UK remains our single largest export market, accounting for nearly twice the value of exports to our second largest market (Germany). Many Irish-owned firms are particularly dependent on the UK export market and, given the more employment-intensive nature of Irish-owned industry, the employment significance of the UK market is greater than suggested by the export data.

Table 4: Estimated value of exports classified by country of destination (£m)

Country of destination	1996*
Great Britain	6,057.4
Northern Ireland	752.0
Austria	140.1
Belgium and Luxembourg	1,304.1
Denmark	358.3
Finland	152.2
France	2,314.0
Germany	3,547.8
Greece	160.1
Italy	999.1
Netherlands	1,835.3
Portugal	116.2
Spain	644.0
Sweden	497.3
EU – country not specified	2.7
Total EU	18,880.7
Switzerland	523.2
Japan	793.4
USA	2,585.8
Other countries	4,418.7
Total	27,201.8

*January–November
Source: Central Statistics Office

Respective roles of the EU and member states

The subsequent sections of this essay present a number of the key policy challenges for Ireland in the integrated European Union. What is interesting in considering these challenges is that many of them require decisions and support at EU level or are influenced by EU requirements or policies. These challenges for the Irish economy raise the issue of the

balance of the respective powers of the EU and of national governments.

One of the principles governing the respective role of the EU and
member states is the so-called principle of subsidiarity, which means that
the European Union must only do what cannot be achieved at national,
regional or local level. However, in a very wide range of policy areas,
national governments can no longer formulate policy unilaterally and
this is influenced or decided at EU level. The governments of member
states as a group in effect determine EU policy. While this may, or may
not, be a good thing, it is clear that member states have increasingly
relinquished, at least in part, many of their traditional powers over the
economy. In terms of macroeconomic policy, this has included ending
exchange rate controls and managing the public finances in conformity
with criteria set for countries wishing to join EMU.

The role of the European Union in a wide range of policy areas
suggests that exerting influence in the policy-making process of the EU
will be a key future requirement for Irish economic success. As a
member of the EU, it is important for Ireland not to take a narrow
short-term perspective of EU policies. It is essential that policies are
implemented which will ensure the growth and prosperity of the
European Union. This does not, however, imply that Ireland's economic
interest can be neglected: being good Europeans does not require this of
us. Enhancing the economic welfare of Irish citizens must be the
objective of Ireland in the EU.

There may be a need, therefore, to encourage some of the more
brilliant of Irish individuals to participate in EU policy-making, both
directly and indirectly. (The encouragement of individuals to join the
Irish public service, and their subsequent development, was one of the
many initiatives undertaken in the past by Dr T. K. Whitaker, and
perhaps analogous initiatives relating to EU policy may now be
required.) This could involve a system of encouraging secondment of
some of the best of our public officials to the European Commission, as
well as having implications for the Irish educational system in terms of
developing expertise in European law, economics and languages.

Public finance

Correction of the imbalance in the public finances has been a prerequisite for Irish economic growth. While the lessons of previous policy
errors are well known, there are potential dangers in this area, particularly if public expenditure programmes are planned on an assumption
of continued rapid growth. Specific responses to ensure a responsible

approach to the public finances are covered in other contributions, notably by Ó Muircheartaigh.

It is, however, important to emphasise the difficulty of adjusting public expenditure programmes, which could result in the re-emergence of large deficits and an expansion of public debt if there was an economic downturn. There have been significant changes internationally in how corporate organisations are structured to increase their flexibility and to reduce fixed costs in order to be able to respond to potentially less favourable conditions. Some of these changes to increase flexibility may have implications for the management of the public finances. Failure to adjust to a more variable cost structure has been behind many high-profile corporate liquidations in Ireland and internationally. It may be prudent to use this period of economic upsurge to build up reserves and enhance flexibility of response to less favourable circumstances. This could, for example, involve a greater degree of contracting within the public services. Also relevant are ongoing reviews to ensure the effective targeting of public expenditure programmes, some of which may not be either justified in terms of increasing the productive capacity of the economy or efficient in redistribution. Appropriate responses should also include shifting taxation to areas such as property and local taxation which are less influenced by economic growth. The overall level of public expenditure, and its implications for taxation, is a critical element in maintaining a competitive environment for foreign direct investment. This is considered later in this essay.

While managing the public finances is primarily a national economic issue, there are links with European policies, particularly as a result of the EMU criteria and the approaching reduction or end of EU Structural and Cohesion Funds, as well as the constraints on taxation policies.

Inflation and cost competitiveness

As indicated, factors explaining the growth in the Irish economy have been mutually supportive. Thus, for example, moderation in wage inflation, and its implications for cost competitiveness, has assisted the attraction of foreign industry, in both the manufacturing and the international services sectors, and has also contributed to the growth in exports and employment. All of these factors have, in turn, assisted in the correction of the imbalance in the public finances and the development of a low-interest environment which, in turn, has supported the growth in economic activity. While some exceptional pay claims are legitimate, recently there has been growing concern about the potential re-emergence of wage inflation, with an increasing number of groups looking for special pay increases, and/or a commission on pay, accompanied by actual or threatened industrial action. It is important that decisions are taken in relation to tax reform and other initiatives which would assist in a sharing of the benefits of economic growth. There is, however, a real danger that groups of employees attempting to improve their relative position could end up worsening their own position and that of other groups. The opening of the flood gates to special demands for pay increases would result in an increase in inflation, higher interest rates, higher taxation and lower levels of employment and economic growth. In the past productivity-adjusted wage settlements which were out of line with competitors had consequences for employment, inflation and the exchange rate. With Ireland's proposed membership of EMU, the full impact of a loss of cost competitiveness will be seen in reduced employment. Meeting the challenge of avoiding the re-emergence of wage inflation above the level of our competitors will be essential to the continued growth of the economy.

International trade environment

The maintenance of a non-protectionist and competitive international trade environment, both within the EU and internationally, is of particular significance for Ireland. Without such an environment there is little or no prospect of maintaining the growth of foreign direct investment and the buoyancy of exports. An open international trade environment, with resultant increase in world trade, is one of the most important determinants of Ireland's export performance.

The economic benefit to consumers of such an environment is the cornerstone of the economic rationale for the European Union. This rationale was highlighted in the first European Commission Report on Competition Policy where it was noted that 'Competition is the best stimulant of economic activity, it enables enterprises continuously to improve their efficiency, which is the sine qua non for a steady improvement in living standards.'[1]

Ireland should continue to insist that the EU presses for an increasingly open international trade environment. There is also a need within the EU to remove protectionist policies, including those relating to so-called problem sectors. This is of fundamental importance given that the main economic purpose of the European Union is to secure the benefits of economic integration within what is referred to as a single market system.

Many obstacles still remain to the achievement of a fully competitive EU market. These obstacles relate to problem industries, such as the motor and steel sectors, and also to the protectionistic policies, often *vis-à-vis* non-EU competitors, which apply in sectors as varied as tele-communications and textiles.

Employment in the motor industry is of major importance to many EU countries (much less so in Ireland although we have an important subsupply component manufacturing industry). The economic import-ance of the motor industry combined with the decline in competitive-ness compared to non-EU manufacturers, notably the Japanese, has led the EU to introduce a protectionistic trade policy and a rather inactive competition policy. Voluntary restraints on Japanese exports still apply and competition policy has included the introduction of a 'block exemption' to competition rules relating to the continuation of selective and exclusive car dealership arrangements. In the case of the steel industry, despite very large amounts of aid provided to the industry, the sector still has excess capacity and restructuring has been slow. There has also been protectionism in the form of anti-dumping regulations, which in the terminology of trade negotiations refer to interventions to provide effective protection for Community steel firms in the event of foreign exports adopting so-called unfair practices. In some cases, protection has arisen as a result of negotiations with foreign firms or governments leading to voluntary restraints in exports, often against the background of the threatened imposition of duties. In recent years a stricter application of competition rules has applied to the steel industry but the industry is still far from operating in a competitive manner.

On the grounds of economic efficiency there is need for a determined decision to tackle the problem, once and for all. EU policies which apply to problem industries should ensure that policies result in the necessary restructuring. Of course, an overly simplistic approach to this cannot be applied, and assisting firms, or economic regions dependent on such industries, to adjust must go in tandem with initiatives to create an open and competitive market. There is, however, some evidence that policies in many of these sectors may have delayed this restructuring by sheltering sectors from internal and external competition. A number of aspects of policy require change as follows:

- The EU should commit itself to an open competitive market in all sectors within a given time-frame. There should be a much closer integration of EU competition and trade policies with closer integration or co-ordination of policies between DGI (Directorate General for External Relations), which is responsible for trade policy, and DGIV (Directorate General for Competition), which is responsible for competition policy.
- Competition policy and an assessment of the overall economic

benefits to EU consumers should play a more forceful role in the determination of policy within this integrated approach. These policies should, in turn, be supported by appropriate adjustment initiatives, by way of either the Structural Funds or industrial policy initiatives.

Supportive environment for foreign direct investment

The significance of foreign direct investment and the associated buoyancy of exports from the so-called modern sectors in contributing to Irish growth was highlighted previously. A major challenge facing the economy will, therefore, be to maintain a supportive environment for foreign direct investment. Many of the elements in the achievement of this objective are within Irish control; these are outlined in the recent Forfás report[2] and are also reviewed in the contribution by Bacon in this volume. There are, however, two critical aspects of EU policy which could have a major influence, namely taxation policy and the enlargement of the EU. It is useful to consider each of these aspects and in particular to consider the issue of taxation policy in some detail.

EU and taxation

The role of the EU in determining or influencing Ireland's taxation policy may be a critical influence on our ability to attract significant inflows of foreign direct investment. While the EU's role in indirect taxation has been very significant, national governments have retained considerable flexibility concerning three key areas of taxation: income tax, property taxes and corporation tax.

There is an increasing move, however, for corporation taxation policy to be co-ordinated at EU or OECD level. How the future balance of decisions will lie, between the EU and member states, concerning corporation tax is likely to be of fundamental importance for Ireland and its ability to maintain a supportive environment for foreign direct investment. Ireland has a very low rate of corporation tax and, because of the transparency of this rate, has been the focus of much EU and international attention. An important question is whether member states should be permitted to compete for economic activity on the basis of corporate tax, as in effect they do on the basis of income taxes and other policies. This is particularly important given the fact that co-ordination of corporation tax rates at EU level may not be necessary for either a single market or for monetary union, although preferential tax regimes undoubtedly impact on investment flows. This issue is of importance because the spheres in which EU member states can act independently have become narrower and narrower. There is some recognition of the rationale for competition in terms of corporation tax but a somewhat arbitrary distinction is sometimes made between harmful and legitimate tax competition, without reference to the implications for regional policy and convergence.

A number of approaches are worth considering in thinking about the role of the EU in influencing, controlling or even determining the taxation policies in member states, including Ireland. This is likely to be one of the most important areas for future EU decisions and is one which has been given very little attention outside of the work done by specialists.

One approach would be for EU countries to agree a taxation system which would ensure that trade flows and resource allocations between countries are determined on the basis of the rate of return on the activity, prior to any tax influences. In theory, this would maximise economic welfare in the EU and facilitate the efficient allocation of resources, assuming that there were no distortions in the rest of the world. Such an assumption would of course be akin to highlighting the desirability of removing locks and alarms from homes in urban areas, on the assumption that there was no criminal activity. While correct in principle, it is of little value as a guide to decisions. In any case, it would require such a degree of loss of national fiscal sovereignty that it is very unlikely even in a medium-term perspective. Such an approach would also lead to unacceptable levels of geographic concentration of economic activity. This could further disadvantage peripheral and underdeveloped areas within the EU and would be against the objectives of EU regional policy. The Delors Report on Economic and Monetary Union, for example, stresses that progress towards EMU must be accompanied by policies to assist regional convergence.[3]

A second approach would be for EU and other countries to determine their tax systems unilaterally without any reference to the impact on revenue bases or economic activity elsewhere. This would not be sustainable in the present era of internationalisation of economic activity and extensive cross-border investment and trade flows.

A third approach would be for EU countries to retain significant sovereignty to design their own tax systems and rates of taxation, and for the international implication of this to be reflected in a network of bilateral international tax treaties, supported by an exchange of certain information between tax authorities. Other elements of this approach would involve the right of member states to implement domestic tax responses (consistent with their tax treaty obligations) to any perceived negative impacts arising from taxation policies in other countries. Of particular importance here would be the introduction of legislation such as CFC measures (control of foreign corporations). This broad approach is the basis for current international tax systems, but there are tendencies among some EU and OECD countries to move more in the direction of the first approach, outlined above, or at least to ensure a greater co-ordination of corporate taxation systems and the possible elimination of preferential tax systems which act as an incentive to locate economic activity in a particular country.

Such moves, however, raise the issue of why should countries within the EU not be free to compete on the basis of corporate and other taxation.

As well as moves to co-ordinate corporate tax systems, the EU has increasingly become involved in the harmonisation of indirect tax systems such as VAT and excise duties. In some cases this harmonisation is necessary to ensure free trade in the single market but in other cases the justification for EU co-ordination seems more distant. It would, for example, be entirely inappropriate for member states to attempt to put differential excise rates on imported, compared to home-produced, alcoholic spirits; but why member states should not be free to decide the level of taxation on a range of services from crèches to electricity is much less clear.

The above comments would suggest the need for a fundamental debate at EU level concerning its role in tax co-ordination. Perhaps there should be a presumption that this is a matter for national decision except where it acts as a barrier to trade. This is an area where Ireland's economic interests are likely to be significantly affected and thus should be the focus of high-level analysis and negotiation.

There is also a need for all aspects of national taxation policy to assist Ireland's competitive position for foreign industry. This includes personal income as well as corporate tax. With this in mind, there is a need to introduce an overall targeted limit for taxation. It is likely that taxation's share of GDP may have to decline significantly if Ireland's growth strategy is to remain effective.

Enlargement of the EU

Austria, Finland and Sweden joined the European Union at the start of 1995 and preparations are under way for the further expansion of the EU, in particular for the admission of Central and Eastern European countries. There is a prospect of a European Union of twenty-five or more members in less than ten years. The future economic impact on Ireland of EU enlargement is difficult for economists to predict with any accuracy. It is certain that the integration of economies at different stages of economic development with very different cost structures will have important implications for the Irish economy.

Of particular significance is the impact of the proposed inclusion of new members from Central and Eastern Europe. There are a number of fundamental implications for Ireland arising from the enlargement of the EU incorporating such countries. These include the implications for EU Structural and Cohesion Funds and for foreign investment and external trade.

If the inflow of EU Structural Funds to Ireland ceases at some stage in the future because our economic progress implies a sustainable economic strength for the economy, this would reflect success. This would be a different scenario to a position where such funds could end even if Irish growth falters, because the accession of low-income countries from Central and Eastern Europe would mean that Ireland's per capita income would be higher than the average for an enlarged EU. The accession of such countries will also present a low-cost challenge to Irish industry and agriculture.

The Central and Eastern European countries are currently attracting a strong level of foreign direct investment. The importance of foreign investment for the Irish economy suggests the need to assess the likely impact of the enlargement of the EU on the competition for our existing and potential overseas manufacturing and services plants. The enlargement of the EU will also open up opportunities for overseas investment by Irish firms as well as bringing new market opportunities for Irish exports. It is difficult to assess the significance of these countries as potential markets, but given the relatively low level of trade links to date and the pattern of expenditure in these countries, the impact on overall Irish trade may be relatively modest.

The above points would suggest that the potential impact of the enlargement of the EU is an area where much more detailed research would appear warranted in order to guide Irish input to policy at EU level. The fact that the enlargement of the EU will result in new challenges for the Irish economy does not imply that Ireland should be negative towards such a development. It is, however, essential that a realistic assessment of the scale of such a challenge is undertaken and that appropriate options and responses are identified. This will also have implications for Ireland's policy on the preferred pace and condition of enlargement of the EU, and the appropriate institutional reform within the EU to accommodate this development.

Diversification of Irish trade

The dependence of Irish exports on the UK market was highlighted in Table 4. This is particularly the case for indigenous industry. While the percentage of Irish exports sold in the UK market has declined significantly over the past decade, the UK is still the single most important market for both exports and imports.

The apparent diversification from the UK market is overemphasised because the growth in total exports owes so much to exports to other countries by the foreign-owned sector. For many indigenous companies there has been relatively little diversification of exports to non-UK markets.

Assuming that the UK does not join EMU, exchange rate instability between Ireland and its nearest and most important external market could result in a significant loss in competitiveness, with associated decline in exports and employment particularly in indigenous industry. The response to this will, of course, require marketing and cost changes within individual firms.

There would appear also to be a need for a more radical programme to assist individual companies to diversify from the UK market. This perhaps could include giving priority assistance to new indigenous industries to expand in non-UK markets and introducing a more significant targeted incentive programme to assist existing exporters to the UK to diversify to third markets. Authorities need to give more thought to means of allocating or smoothening out movements in the relevant exchange rate.

Removal of bottlenecks within Ireland

An important challenge for Irish economic policy is to ensure the removal of a number of bottlenecks to economic growth within Ireland. These include the following:

- lack of competition and barriers to entry in services
- potential skill shortages
- infrastructural gaps.

An analysis of the structure of the Irish labour force in Table 3 highlights the fact that most employment in Ireland is in the services sector. There is widespread acceptance that in many service areas in Ireland there are barriers to market entry and a lack of competition.

The European Commission has taken steps to create competitive and open market conditions for internationally traded services and for a small number of service sectors which are primarily domestically traded at present, for example banking and insurance. Assessments have suggested significant economic benefits for consumers in terms of lower prices and potential increases in economic activity. There are, however, despite the single market principle, extensive restrictive practices in a wide range of services in different EU markets. Within Ireland marked examples are such service activities as pubs, taxis and certain professions. The appropriate policy changes are absolutely clear and do not require detailed reports, or EU or national working groups: there should be no restrictions on market entry by national, EU or third-country firms, providing there is no abuse of market position.

It might be questioned why policies have been adopted which effectively restrict competition in services, if the economic case in favour of the removal of such restrictions is so strong. The answer may be that changing such policies results in losses which can often have a political influence. Holders of licences in sectors currently protected will face a loss, and policy considerations should focus on appropriate compensation. This could, for example, involve a system of charging for new licences on a declining scale over a number of years, with the resultant funds being used to compensate existing licence holders, or alternatively issuing an increased number of licences to existing holders for a number of years prior to the total liberalisation of the sector. It is, however, essential that such compensation arrangements are implemented within a context of a definite time-frame (for example three to five years) for abolition of such constraints to competition.

Ensuring competitive services is more appropriately a matter for national governments than for the EU but the fundamental issue is ensuring that, as we approach the new millennium, all restrictions designed to hinder competition in the service sectors are removed. This should be supported by a vigorous competition policy with high penalties for violators. As well as the potential welfare improvements, such action will improve the competitiveness of domestically traded services and enhance the potential for expansion of these sectors by stimulating demand. Given the increasing erosion of the difference between domestic and internationally traded services, this also has the potential to facilitate an expansion of international trade in services.

Skill shortages are likely to emerge in the Irish economy if the current rate of growth continues. There may be a shortage of technological or specialist skills in the internationally traded sector. There may also be a deficiency of language skills in relation to the growth of international services. There is, however, a common labour market in Ireland and demand in the larger non-traded sectors will impact on the exporting sectors. The potential skill shortages may, therefore, be more widespread and, as certain labour markets experience a rapid increase in demand, prices are likely to increase with potential implications for competitiveness.

The response to this must include resource-allocation decisions within the third-level and other educational sectors, but experience as well as training will be required in many cases. Enhancing skills and capabilities will become an increasingly important component of economic development in Ireland. This will need to reflect the requirements of high value added activities. The response in part to future skill requirements may be the attraction of skilled and experienced individuals from other countries. Recruitment should not be confined to the so-called 'wild geese'. This 'immigration' response has been a critical element of the economic development of most industrial countries at some stage. Because of Ireland's history of emigration and the poor historical performance of the economy, the attraction of overseas skills has not to date been seen as important. It is now, however, one of the potential benefits of participation in the EU, with its associated freedom of movement. There will be implications for income taxation policies. There may also be a case for greater use of the government's immigration scheme to attract skilled employees and not simply to attract passive finance (hardly in short supply in a country with no capital controls).

Infrastructural gaps are evident also in certain areas and could result in a constraint on economic growth. Many of these areas are being addressed by investment funded under the Structural and Cohesion Funds. The targeting of such funds on bottlenecks in Ireland's infrastructural network could produce high economic benefits. This is discussed further below. In other areas, such as the housing market, bottlenecks in the supply of land have resulted in higher site prices, with implications for housing inflation. Such bottlenecks should be addressed by appropriate planning and zoning decisions, for example by rezoning land for residential use or providing servicing to some of the land currently residential-zoned.

Maximisation of impact of EU funds

One of the factors contributing to the improved performance of the Irish economy is the inflow of EU Structural and Cohesion Funds. Precise measurement of the benefit is impossible but it seems likely that the long-term impact of such funds, if effectively spent, will be to raise Irish GNP by around 1 to 3 per cent, while the impact on growth over the short term may be somewhat higher. Given the scale of such inflows, the policy priority must be to ensure the maximum economic impact. There must be no acceptance that these funds represent 'free money'. Some of the current programmes may need adjustment to secure the highest potential returns.

EU funds are provided within the context of operational programmes which are designed to ensure a coherence between various categories of expenditure. These are, in turn, aggregated into an overall Community Support Framework. This approach has not only improved the effectiveness of the spending of EU monies but is likely to have assisted in the planning and evaluation of other public expenditure programmes. The role of the European Commission in influencing the approach to the planning and evaluation of expenditure programmes deserves more than a footnote in Irish economic history. Despite the progress which has been achieved on this basis, there may be merit in attempting a greater integration of EU Structural and Cohesion Funds with other national policies. How to achieve this, given the respective responsibilities of the European Commission and national authorities, is difficult to assess but the merits of further integration suggest that innovative thinking on how to make progress in this area is required.

The problem can be illustrated by reference to the EU funds for transport in Ireland. Under the Community Support Framework 1994–99 significant funds have appropriately been allocated to road investments. Despite the massive funds allocated to transport, it is taking much longer for people in the main population centre in Ireland to travel to and from work because of the increasing congestion on roads. If not addressed, this is also likely to act as a disincentive to establishing international services and other activities in Ireland. It would appear that there is something amiss in a situation where very large EU funds are invested in Ireland's transport infrastructure, with an implicit aim of reducing economic loss arising from the timing of transport journeys, at the same time as economic losses are clearly mounting due to increased congestion in the capital city. There are a number of aspects to this problem. Firstly, there is a need to improve the quality and usage of public transport and this has implications for a wide range of policy areas of which investment in public transport is only part of the response. There is also a need to accelerate investments in areas such as ring roads.

The second and fundamental explanation for the perceived inconsistency between the level of investment in transport and increasing congestion problems in Dublin relates to the need to combine the transport investment programmes with other national policies. For example, it would seem appropriate to use the taxation system to reduce congestion. This would involve higher road taxation and there may be merits in attempting differential taxation on the basis of such factors as whether motor users travel alone at peak periods into the city centre. There is a need for increased and perhaps differentiated taxation on city centre car park users and perhaps the tightening of benefit in kind rules on car spaces. There is a need to develop car parks outside of the city centre and to integrate these with public transport services. There is also a need to improve traffic management practices including advanced traffic management systems and traffic calming measures. A wide range of other responses is also required, including vigorous expansion of cycle, pedestrian and bus ways, consideration of the potential for alternative work schedules and encouragement of higher vehicle occupancy initiatives.

Conclusions

The Irish economy has recorded very strong economic growth over the past decade which is all the more remarkable given the underperformance of the economy in the previous decade. A review of the underlying determinants of this performance and the current characteristics of the economy suggests a number of priority areas for policy development as outlined in this essay. The proposals outlined include the following:

- The management of Ireland's public finances should be designed to accommodate a potential economic downturn. This could, for example, include the building up of reserves, increased contracting and the shifting of taxation to areas such as property and local taxes which are less influenced by economic growth.
- There should be an EU commitment to an open competitive market within all sectors within a given time-frame. This should be supported by a much closer integration of EU competition and trade policies.
- Ireland should lead a fundamental debate concerning the EU's role in tax co-ordination, perhaps with a presumption that this is a matter for national decision except where it acts as a barrier to trade.
- There is a need for national taxation policy to assist Ireland's competitive position for foreign industry. This includes personal income as well as corporate tax. There is a need to introduce an overall targeted limit for taxation. It is likely that taxation's share of GDP may have to decline significantly if Ireland's growth strategy is to remain competitive.
- Much more detailed research should be undertaken to assess the economic implications of enlargement of the EU in order to guide Irish input to policy at EU level.
- A more radical programme should be introduced to assist individual companies to diversify from the UK market. Authorities should also

give more thought to measures for allocating or smoothening out movements in the relevant exchange rate.

- There should be no restrictions to market entry by national, EU or third-country firms in the services or manufacturing sectors, providing there is no abuse of market position. This should involve the phased abolition of all licences which restrict market entry in areas such as pubs, taxis and certain professions. Within the context of a definite time-frame for abolition of constraints to competition, holders of existing licences should be compensated, for example by issuing an increased number of licences to existing holders.

- Potential skill shortages should be addressed by resource-allocation decisions within the educational and training sectors and by the attraction of skilled and experienced individuals from other countries. There may also be a case for use of the government's immigration schemes to attract skilled employees and not simply to attract passive finance.

- Infrastructural gaps resulting in constraints on economic growth should be addressed. This, for example, should include targeting of investment in infrastructural bottlenecks and, by appropriate planning and zoning decisions, easing the shortage of land for residential housing.

- There should be a greater integration of EU Structural and Cohesion Funds with other national policies. For example, transport investments to tackle congestion problems should be combined with taxation measures and improved traffic management initiatives.

The above proposals are designed to facilitate the continued expansion of the economy and the maximisation of Ireland's potential in the event of a less favourable external environment.

NOTES

1. Communauté Economique Européenne, *Premier rapport sur la politique de concurrence*, Bruxelles/Luxembourg, Avril 1992, p. 11.
2. Forfás, *Shaping Our Future: A Strategy for Enterprise in Ireland in the 21st Century*, Dublin: Forfás, May 1996.
3. Delors, Jacques, *Report on Economic and Monetary Union in the European Community*, Committee for the Study of Economic and Monetary Union, Luxembourg, 1989.

3

EMU and Ireland: Happy Together?

W. F. DUISENBERG

Introduction

EUROPE is about to see the accomplishment of a major political and economic feat: the establishment of Economic and Monetary Union (EMU). In early 1998, the European Council is to decide which countries will be allowed to join the euro zone from the very start of stage three in 1999. Ireland's prospects for passing the EMU test are excellent. With the Irish population long in favour of European unification, Ireland has already made an impressive move towards convergence in the course of its participation in the exchange rate mechanism (ERM) of the European Monetary System (EMS).

This paper is an attempt to weigh the pros and cons of EMU for Ireland. We will see that the advantages of EMU are to be found notably in the microeconomic realm, in the form of lower transaction and information costs, and less exchange rate uncertainty. On the liabilities side of the EMU balance, having to relinquish the exchange rate instrument as an adjustment mechanism in times of asymmetrical shocks is something Ireland may have some misgivings about. It is therefore of the utmost importance that EMU should be a stability community of sufficiently converged economies. The paper shows how, in this respect, the Irish experience could function as an illustrious example to the other member states.

Why EMU?

With the establishment of EMU and the changeover to the euro, the single market will have been completed. It is to have an anchor in a stability-oriented monetary and fiscal policy which is conducive to its well-functioning. After all, EMU will both reduce transaction costs and remove the uncertainty and political tensions which come from exchange rate unrest.

Elimination of transaction and information costs

The changeover to the single currency will eliminate two kinds of transaction costs: the costs which banks charge their customers for exchanging currencies and the costs incurred in hedging exchange rate risks. In its report 'One market, one money' published in 1990, the European Commission calculated that the Union as a whole stands to save somewhere between ECU 13.1 billion and ECU 19.2 billion (0.3–0.4 per cent of EU GDP) on transaction costs.[1] Based on the plausible assumption that the foreign exchange business represents at least 10 per cent of commercial bank income, the Economic and Social Research Institute (ESRI) has estimated that these savings for Ireland will be in the order of £75–142 million, depending on whether or not the UK also joins EMU.[2] These amounts may not seem excessive, but it must be remembered that even minor transaction and information costs may have a considerable impact on the economy.[3] After all, not only will transaction costs be materially reduced, but possibilities for price differentiation within the Union will also be drastically restricted, to the ultimate benefit of consumers all over Europe. In order to capitalise on these advantages, the national currencies will have to be replaced in all respects by the single currency. Irrevocable locking of the existing currencies alone will not do the trick, because they would still need to be exchanged, the concomitant costs being passed on to consumers. Empirically, the magnitude of bid/ask spreads proves almost totally insensitive to the degree of exchange rate variability.[4]

Elimination of exchange rate uncertainty

The elimination of exchange rate uncertainty may be seen as a major stimulus to external trade and investment in the European single market.[5] Better functioning of the price mechanism makes for a more efficient allocation of resources. Businesses may realise economies of scale in the larger, more transparent home market brought about by monetary union. Moreover, the investment climate will benefit when foreign exchange risk premiums are eliminated from interest rates formed in integrated money and capital markets. Another factor to be reckoned with is the political and economic consequences of exchange rate unrest. After all, exchange rate tensions undermine financial stability and hence the political foundation of the internal market. Any misgivings which the financial markets may have with regard to weak currencies will only be intensified if the monetary tightening needed to defend the exchange rate puts pressure on the budget, the employment situation and the financial sector in the countries involved. If major devaluations can then no longer be avoided, this will fuel the dismay felt by the EU partners at monetary policy being abused in aid of trade.

Once EMU has got off the ground, the competitive positions of the participating countries in the European market will have to be safeguarded by way of cost control because exchange rate realignments will have become obsolete. Member states with comparatively un-favourable wage movements will immediately see a deterioration of their competitiveness in the form of higher selling prices. As the euro, being a hard currency, will contribute to lower inflation through lower import prices, cost control should not be too hard to realise within EMU. It may be noted that countries such as Ireland and the Netherlands, whose wage developments have been relatively moderate for some time now, compare favourably with other member states in this respect.

Potential costs of EMU

The main drawback of EMU is that member states must relinquish the option of exchange rate adjustment *vis-à-vis* their partners. Just how objectionable a drawback this is depends on two factors. First of all, it depends on the frequency and size of country-specific shocks in the real economic sphere, the so-called asymmetrical shocks calling for adjust-ment of the real exchange rate. Secondly, the question is just how effective the nominal exchange rate still is as an instrument for bringing about the desired adjustment of the real exchange rate.

Asymmetrical shocks and the role of the United Kingdom

The geographical breakdown of imports and exports presented in Table 1 shows up the Irish economy's close ties to that of the United Kingdom. At the same time, Ireland's dependence on its big neighbour has diminished discernibly over the past few decades. Nevertheless, owing to this interwovenness, real shocks have at regular intervals made themselves felt which may be characterised as asymmetrical by comparison with the other ERM participants. Developments within the ERM since 1979 show that central rate adjustments of the punt were prompted largely by developments within the United Kingdom.

Table 1: Directions of trade – Ireland (% distribution)

	Exports of goods		Imports of goods	
	1979	1995	1979	1995
United Kingdom	46.4	25.5	50.0	35.5
Core EU countries[a]	28.5	35.6	18.2	14.7
Nordic EU countries[b]	2.3	3.9	3.6	2.4
Southern EU countries[c]	4.0	7.1	4.0	3.4
United States	4.9	8.3	8.5	17.7
Other countries	13.9	19.6	15.7	26.3
	100.0	100.0	100.0	100.0

(a) Austria, Belgium, France, Germany, Luxembourg and the Netherlands.
(b) Denmark, Finland and Sweden.
(c) Greece, Italy, Portugal and Spain.
Source: IMF, Direction of trade statistics

For about one-and-a-half centuries, Ireland operated a one-to-one ratio for the punt and sterling. This ratio was abandoned in 1979, when Ireland did, and the United Kingdom did not as yet, join the ERM. The Irish experience in the ERM may be roughly divided into three periods (Figure 1). During the first, from 1979 to 1987, it soon appeared that Irish participation in the EMS did not make for immediate exchange rate stability of the punt *vis-à-vis* the other currencies. In addition, the Irish authorities continued to be confronted by high and volatile capital market rates. Against the Deutsche mark, the punt was devalued seven times, the cumulative devaluation coming out at nearly 30 per cent. Under the influence of sagging oil prices and the ensuing depreciation of sterling, 1986 in particular became an *annus horibilis*. Within nine months, the punt was devalued three times (by a total of 14 per cent). However, with Ireland stubbornly abiding by its stabilisation programme, its currency managed to stabilise in the second period, between 1987 and 1992. The punt's position within the ERM was reinforced when sterling joined the mechanism in October 1990. The exchange rate stability achieved and successful budgetary consolidation made Irish debt certificates popular again with international investors, the Irish long-term interest rate even dropping to a level well below the comparable British rate.

However, in mid-1992, the Irish economy again had to face a number of unfavourable developments which were beyond the direct sphere of influence of its policy-makers. Waning economic activity in most of the Union was attended by increasing turbulence in the European foreign exchange markets. Having left the ERM, sterling plummeted, impairing Irish competitiveness. Renewed devaluation of the punt against the remaining participants in the ERM then became inevitable and was

Figure 1: Deutsche mark/Irish pound (monthly figures)

effected in January 1993 (10 per cent). Even after the fluctuation margins had been widened in August of that year, the punt continued to be subject to speculative pressures on various occasions. However, any weakening invariably proved to be temporary, and the punt is now again part of the hard core of ERM currencies.

Efficacy of exchange rate instrument

We have seen that the Irish economy regularly has to contend with asymmetrical real shocks which necessitate adjustment of its real exchange rate *vis-à-vis* the other ERM countries. Ireland has invariably opted to adjust the nominal exchange rate in order to bring about the desired adjustment of the real exchange rate. To what extent having to give up this option will prove to be a drawback when Ireland joins EMU depends on two elements: the efficacy and the viability of the current system of fixed but adjustable exchange rates.

The efficacy of the nominal exchange rate as an instrument for influencing the competitive position is contingent upon the relative openness of an economy and the incidence of real wage and price rigidities. In an open economy, devaluation will feed through to domestic price levels almost immediately by way of higher import prices. In the ensuing wage–price spiral, entrepreneurs and employees will attempt to pass inflation on to each other, an exercise which undoes the initial improvement of competitiveness and merely leaves them with higher inflation. For Ireland, this argument carries special relevance, given the exceptional openness of its economy (Figure 2). The significance of having to relinquish the exchange rate instrument also diminishes as EMU and the single market work as a catalyst on the flexibility of the labour market, especially in terms of (real) wage

Figure 2: Foreign trade of Ireland (% of nominal GDP)

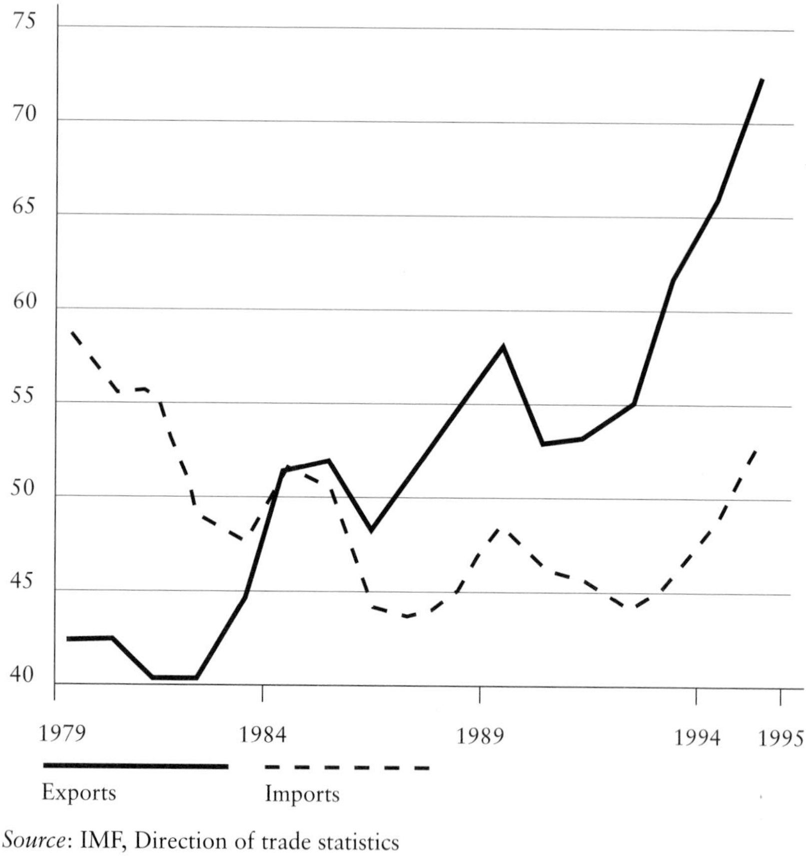

Exports   Imports

Source: IMF, Direction of trade statistics

determination. Finally, the efficacy of nominal exchange rate adjustments is also affected by the increased mobility of international capital movements. Countries with a tradition of slack monetary discipline and a tendency to resort to devaluation are watched anxiously by the financial markets, the result being greater exchange rate volatility and systematically higher interest rates.

The vulnerability of the Irish currency in the past has been a result of both external factors (major sterling depreciation) and (pre-1987) internal factors such as budgetary policies. The key to the effects on the Irish economy lies with the potential speed of adjustment of domestic prices and wages. If prices and wages adjusted instantaneously so that purchasing power parity (PPP) held even in the short run, then the choice of the exchange rate regime would be irrelevant. Employing a large-scale macroeconometric model of the economy, the ESRI has simulated the effects of asymmetric demand shocks on employment, wage rates and consumer prices under alternative exchange rate regimes including the scenario of Irish participation in EMU.[6] Corroborating a number of previous studies, this evidence suggests that PPP holds in the long run but that it typically takes 2–4 years for prices and wages to adjust to shocks. Nevertheless, while a more flexible exchange rate regime can reduce the adjustment costs to certain types of shock, the size of this reduction may be limited. In the case of a major sterling depreciation, up to half of the cost of adjustment probably could not be avoided, whatever regime is chosen. The simulations also highlight the fact that increased currency flexibility has a cost in terms of higher interest rates due to increased uncertainty, and that this may go a substantial way towards offsetting the benefits. All in all, it is suggested that the benefits to Ireland in participation in EMU are substantial, that these benefits are bigger with the UK also in the EMU, but that they are substantial nonetheless even with the UK out.

The question finally arises whether the current, alternative arrangement of fixed but adjustable exchange rates can be sustained in the longer term. This query is underlain by the observation already made by, among others, Whitaker in 1973 that financial integration, stable exchange rates and monetary policy autonomy are incompatible.[7] In an asymmetrical system such as the ERM, the relinquishment of national policy autonomy is a *sine qua non* for all participants but the anchor country, because in a system with n participants there are n–1 exchange rates to be fixed. Usually the remaining degree of freedom (independent monetary policy) falls largely and automatically to the large participant with the lowest rate of inflation, because, in terms of price stability, it is the only country with nothing (more) to gain from an exchange rate system.[8] Considering Germany's hegemony within the ERM, the 'n–1 problem' may seem applicable notably to small open economies such as those of Ireland and the Netherlands, but it applies no less to a member state more comparable to Germany in terms of economic size, viz. France. When cyclical developments diverge, this may constitute a regular bone of contention policy-wise, and hence be detrimental to the system's viability in the longer term. Exchange rate systems like the ERM should therefore be seen notably as transitional regimes on the road to complete monetary union. At the end of the day, the establishment of EMU is the best way of embedding the advantages of exchange rate stability in a permanent setting.

EMU as stability community

The need for convergence

For the participating countries, changeover to the single currency means giving up the option of exchange rate adjustments *vis-à-vis* their partners, which, especially in the Irish case, may not be completely without rhyme or reason. For the solidity of EMU to be warranted, the countries concerned will have to converge to a sufficient degree.[9] Any participant in EMU whose inflation rate is structurally higher than those of all the others will see a deterioration of its competitive position, and spreading unemployment. Pressure consequently might well be brought to bear on the European Central Bank to relax its monetary policy unduly, at the expense of price stability. Monetary and economic stability may also be thwarted by an ill-balanced policy mix. Price stability and sound economic growth are incompatible with major government deficits and debts. Today's budget deficit is usually tomorrow's tax rise, leading directly and indirectly to higher prices. Moreover, derailed public finances have, over recent years, repeatedly constituted a source of unrest in the financial markets.

It should be kept in mind that convergence is called for, not just before, but also after the start of monetary union. The Maastricht Treaty already provides for mechanisms making for sustained stability within the EU.[10] Consultations are currently under way in Europe about the actual shape to be given to these mechanisms in the third stage of EMU, to wit a so-called stability pact to underpin budgetary discipline and an exchange rate arrangement between the countries which do and those which do not take part in the monetary union from the outset, the ins and the outs. Both these mechanisms serve a purpose, first of all, in that they may contribute to greater cohesion within the single market, that is among all EU countries, be they in or out. Furthermore, sound public finance and monetary stability are in any case inextricably linked, as Ireland has demonstrated since 1987.

In order to prevent monetary policy within EMU from being thwarted in its quest for price stability, the Maastricht Treaty contains several macroeconomic criteria by which convergence can be measured. A country's inflation rate may be at most 1.5 percentage points above the average of at most the three best-performing countries. The capital market rate may be no more than 2 percentage points above the average of at most the three countries with the lowest inflation rates. A participating country's exchange rate must have moved for at least two years within the normal fluctuation margins of the ERM without having to be devalued. Government deficits are subject to an upper limit of 3 per cent of GDP. A higher deficit is permitted only if it is structurally declining and approaching the reference value, or if the excess is exceptional and temporary, and close to the reference value. Gross public debt may not exceed 60 per cent of GDP, unless its ratio is sufficiently declining and approaching the reference value at a satisfactory pace.

Irish performance

In early 1998, the European Council will decide, on the basis of figures for 1997, which countries are to join stage three in 1999. Irish prospects for passing the EMU test are excellent. During the years of participation in the ERM, Ireland has seen an impressive economic performance, the year 1987 forming a watershed (Figure 3). In that year, the government decided to undertake a drastic reduction of its financial deficit and to direct monetary policy more intensively at exchange rate stability. In a social pact, the government, farmers, employers and employees reached agreement on such matters as wage moderation.

Since 1987, outstanding results have been achieved with regard to public finance. By 1989 the deficit had already been brought down to a level below the Maastricht Treaty reference value of 3 per cent of GDP, where it has remained. This feat has barely been matched within the EU. Together with the low public deficits, the high economic growth rates have helped to reduce the Irish gross debt ratio substantially: from about 115 per cent of GDP in 1987 to around 75 per cent in 1996. These formidable achievements have not escaped the notice of the European finance ministers. Although the debt ratio is still above the reference value of 60 per cent of GDP, the situation regarding Irish public finance is not judged to be excessive as it is defined in the excessive deficit procedure.[11] The reason is that the ratio has been falling at a satisfactory

Figure 3: Irish convergence progress

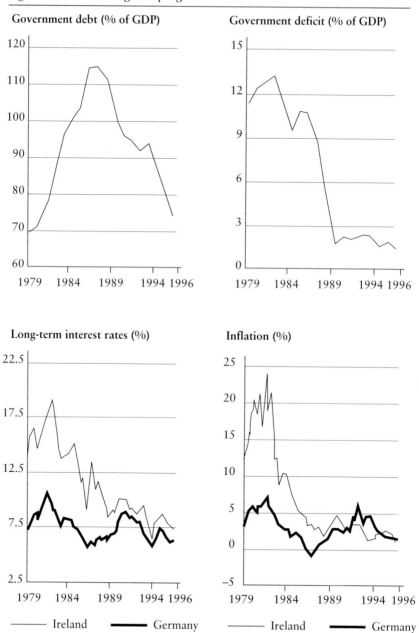

pace. Irish inflation, too, has been close to price stability, and is among the lowest in Europe. Capital market rates have also gone down considerably, not just in absolute terms, but also by comparison with long-term rates in Germany, which form the floor for many European countries. Finally, there is the punt's exchange rate, whose movements were already commented on in the previous section. Since 1987, the number of exchange rate adjustments has dropped materially.

In various respects, the Irish economic performance since 1987 is much like that of the Netherlands; from it several lessons can be learnt. The first is that restructuring the public finances need not have an adverse impact on economic growth. The drop of the Irish debt ratio by about 40 percentage points in the years 1987–96 went hand in hand with an average GDP growth rate of over 5 per cent. A comparable development has been in evidence in the Netherlands. In the period 1987–96, the Dutch public deficit was more than halved (from 5.9 per cent to 2.6 per cent of GDP). At the same time, employment expanded by an average of over 1.5 per cent per annum as compared with an EU average of 0.3 per cent. A comparable rate of expansion on average was recorded in Ireland in that period. However, as Ireland's working population increased more than proportionally (by an average of 1 per cent as compared with an EU average of 0.4 per cent), and economic growth was accounted for notably by the relatively labour-unintensive export sector, the unemployment situation unfortunately still cannot be termed satisfactory. Incidentally, neither can that in the Netherlands, in spite of the fact that its unemployment rate of about 6.5 per cent is about half that of Ireland. In the Netherlands, economic inactivity is reflected notably in the relatively large numbers of people receiving social security benefits of some sort.

The second lesson to be learnt from both the Irish and the Dutch experience is that restructuring operations should be attended by a policy of wage moderation as well as, in the case of small open economies, an exchange-rate-oriented monetary policy. Both contribute towards a stable economic climate and make for low inflation, allowing interest rates to remain comparatively low and ensuring sustainable economic growth rates.

Conclusions

With the take-off of EMU and the changeover to the euro, the single market will have been completed. A stability-oriented monetary and fiscal policy provides the single market with an anchor conducive to its well-functioning. A tentative comparison of the pros and cons for

Ireland shows that the pros are mostly microeconomic in nature, viz. lower transaction and information costs, and the elimination of the uncertainty and political tensions which accompany exchange rate unrest. The most important disadvantage of EMU is that member states can no longer adjust their exchange rates *vis-à-vis* partner currencies. Just how disadvantageous this is depends on the frequency and magnitude of asymmetrical demand shocks as well as on the efficacy of the (nominal) exchange rate instrument in achieving the desirable adjustment of the real exchange rate. In a small open economy such as Ireland's, this argument somewhat assuages the loss of the exchange rate instrument. In this respect, model-specific ESRI simulations have indicated that there are substantial benefits to Ireland in participation in EMU, that these benefits are bigger with the UK also in the EMU, but that they are substantial nonetheless even with the UK out.

When the exchange rate instrument is relinquished, there will, however, be a greater need for sufficient convergence of the member states' economic developments, both before and after the start of monetary union. In order to prevent monetary policy within EMU from being waylaid in its quest for price stability, the Maastricht Treaty provides several guarantees for convergence, the most well-known being the accession criteria. On the basis of these criteria, the European Council will decide in early 1998 which countries are to be in on monetary union from the very start. Ireland is well placed to pass the EMU test. With the Irish population long in favour of European unification, Ireland has already been able to make a remarkable leap towards convergence during the time it has participated in the ERM. Moreover, the Irish experience has shown that a policy of budgetary consolidation and wage moderation is conducive to a stable financial and economic climate with low inflation, low interest rates and sustained economic growth. In this respect, too, Ireland has set a notable example to the other member states.

NOTES

1. EC Commission, 'One market, one money', *European Economy* 44 (1990), p. 68.
2. Economic and Social Research Institute, *Economic Implications for Ireland of EMU*, Policy Research Series, Paper No. 28, Dublin: Economic and Social Research Institute, 1996, pp. 238–43.
3. G. Akerlof and J. Yelen, 'Rational Models of Irrational Behaviour', *American Economic Review*, Vol. 79 (1989), pp. 137–42.
4. C. Boyd, G. Gielens and D. Gros, 'Bid/Ask Spreads in the Foreign Exchange Markets', mimeo, Brussels, 1990.

5. A. C. J. Stokman, 'Effect of Exchange Rate Risk on Intra-EC Trade', *De Economist*, Vol. 143 (1995), pp. 41–54.
6. Economic and Social Research Institute, *Economic Implications for Ireland of EMU*, pp. 105–42.
7. T. K. Whitaker, 'Monetary Integration: Reflection on Irish Experience', in *Moorgate and Wall Street: A Review*, Dublin: Hill Samuel & Co., 1973, p. 14.
8. P. de Grauwe, *The Economics of Monetary Integration*, Oxford: Oxford University Press, 1994, pp. 105–16.
9. In fact Whitaker already pointed this out in 1974 when he noted, in connection with European plans for the establishment of an economic and monetary union as from 1980, that '... the unifying of monetary systems in the Community, and all that this implies in the way of central ordering of policies, is the ultimate step, something that can only take place when the various economies have attained a tolerable balance in their levels of development and individual trends of prices and costs are running nearly parallel'. See T. K. Whitaker, 'The Role of the Central Bank in the European Economic Community', *Central Bank of Ireland Quarterly Bulletin*, No. 1 (1974), p. 86.
10. Having joined EMU, member states continue to be subject to Article 104c, which states that excessive budget deficits must be avoided on pain of sanctions. Article 109m also continues to apply, prescribing that each member state treat its exchange rate policy as a matter of common concern. Finally, a disciplining effect is exercised by Article 103, governing the co-ordination of economic policies within the EU.
11. The excessive deficit procedure was first introduced in 1994, providing for the annual assessment of the member states' public finances. A member state not complying with the two convergence criteria on government deficits and gross debts is censured as having an 'excessive deficit'.

4

Public Expenditure in Ireland: Evolution and Prospect

FIONÁN Ó MUIRCHEARTAIGH

Introduction

IN Ireland in the coming years many of the old problems of economic management will be encountered, but in new contexts. None are older, nor more challenging, than the government budget – and particularly public expenditure. In the 1950s and 1960s, the strategy of refocusing public expenditure, first by creating the concept of the capital budget and second by giving priority to economic over social expenditures, was central to economic regeneration.

This essay addresses one pivotal dimension of modern economic life – public expenditure. The first half of the essay addresses the actual trends in the public budget since 1958. The ubiquitous long-run tendency of government expenditure to increase in Western economies is documented. The evolution of the Irish central government budget is examined and compared with the trend elsewhere in Europe. The size and composition of public expenditure, and the different priorities which have emerged at different times, are illustrated. The composition of the current and capital budgets is examined. Social expenditure trends are separately reviewed and compared with European experience. The second half considers budgetary issues for the future, viz. the size of public expenditure; the factors likely to influence the size of the public sector in the economy; the role of the capital budget and considerations in planning capital investment; key aspects of the current budget, including public service pay, the composition of the budget and the question of balancing the budget; and mechanisms for management, control and containment.

Why public expenditure?

This essay is not intended to provide the rationale for public expenditures. Nor will it deal with the estimated productivity of those programmes. Some reasons most frequently given to justify such expenditures are listed below. Some of these reasons were valid in the past, and some remain so. In the end, voters must decide whether or not these reasons are adequate. Equally, it might be expected that, with the growing economy, the development of incomes and markets would obviate the need for some of the interventions and programmes that were previously required. The outcome reflects a complex of political and social choices.

The following reasons are often given for public expenditure:

- necessity, e.g. national security
- provision of basic infrastructure required by society
- economic management
- social equity
- expenditures brought forward by democratic preferences.

Originally, the rationale for public expenditure was necessity, in particular the necessity to maintain law and order. The first essential for any state is that it is secure from external aggression. The second essential is that it is secure from internal aggression, and that there is a reasonable public order. This rationale is still clearly valid.

A second and related category of public expenditure concerns the provision of basic infrastructure and goods that might not be provided, or might be provided suboptimally, by the market system. Possibilities include the construction and improvement of roads and the provision of housing, water and sanitary services. It became clear that the market would underproduce certain public goods. Some health services, such as inoculation programmes, and environmental protection measures fall into this category.

A third set of reasons revolves around questions of aggregate demand management, which made countercyclical expenditures, and in particular capital investment and current budget deficits, popular in recessions. The corresponding cyclical budget surpluses in periods of rapid economic growth are considerably less popular!

Fourth, there are considerations of social equity. They include basic welfare programmes to cover contingencies such as old age, unemployment and ill health, and supplemental welfare programmes such as family supports and housing subsidies.

The fifth – and increasingly important – factor in public expenditure growth has been the influence of interest groups and individuals on social choice (Arrow, 1951) through the political system.

There are a number of factors, such as demography, labour force participation and EU funding, that are significant in relation to the evolution of expenditure. Important demographic changes include changes in the size of the population and its age structure. Demographic changes affect the dependency structure of the population and participation in the workforce. These factors have particular implications for the major social support schemes: health, education, pensions, housing and other social transfers.

Another potentially significant trend is the disengagement of central government from certain economic activities, such as steel, sugar, fertiliser and shipping, and the commercialisation in whole or in part of other activities within the state sector, e.g. An Post, Telecom Éireann and, most recently, the ports.

EU funding has increasingly influenced the shape of overall and incremental programmes in the government's budgets. The availability of European funds was often a key factor in whether programmes were expanded or frozen over the last decade. Public expenditure planning for the future will need to take account of the likely changes in European funding over the wide range of existing and emerging programmes.

The evolution of public expenditure

International experience since 1890

The growth of public expenditure in developed industrial countries over the last century is a worldwide trend. Ebrill (1996) has documented the growth of government expenditure as a percentage of GDP in industrial countries over the last century. Before the First World War government expenditure was less than 10 per cent and by 1939 it averaged 20 per cent. This growth continued: in 1960 it was 28 per cent, in 1980 it was 43 per cent and by 1996 it had reached 47 per cent of GDP.

These data are indicative, but the trend is incontrovertible. The average share of government expenditure in industrial countries continued to rise through to the mid-1990s.

Irish experience since 1958

This pattern of growth of public expenditure in Western economies is also characteristic of the Irish experience. Some relevant figures are presented in Table 1, which shows government budget expenditure and GNP for various years between 1958 and 1995. Government expenditure is defined here as net current expenditure out-turn plus the budget capital expenditure (public capital programme – PCP – plus non-programme outlays). These figures could be said to understate the share of the government in the economy, because the so-called appropriations-in-aid and Pay-Related Social Insurance (PRSI) contributions (£2.5 billion in 1995) are deducted from the expenditure figure. GNP and public expenditure are shown in 1995 money equivalent terms in columns 3 and 4 of the table. This gives a more comprehensible picture of the growth of national resources and of the government's budget in terms of absorbed purchasing power over the period.

Table 1: Growth in GNP and public expenditure in Ireland, 1958–95

	Current values		1995 values		Volume index	
	Public expenditure (1)	GNP (2)	Public expenditure (3)	GNP (4)	Public expenditure (5)	GNP (6)
1958	166	636	2,266	8,682	100	100
1970	585	1,658	5,002	14,175	221	163
1980	5,011	9,075	11,876	21,508	524	248
1985	9,376	16,611	12,490	22,128	551	254
1990	10,105	24,311	11,445	27,535	505	317
1995	13,300	33,801	13,300	33,801	587	389

Definitions of data:
Column 1: Public expenditure – net current expenditure and budget capital spending (£m)
Column 2: GNP current values (£m)
Column 3: Public expenditure 1995 values (£m, CPI inflator)
Column 4: GNP 1995 values (£m, CPI inflator)
Column 5: Index of real public expenditure (1958 = 100)
Column 6: Index of real GNP (1958 = 100)
Sources: Department of Finance, *Budget Booklets*, 1958–95; *Budgetary and Economic Statistics Booklet*, March 1997

Between 1958 and 1995, the real resources available to the community grew from £8.7 billion to £33.8 billion in 1995 money terms. This was an almost fourfold increase. The growth in resources absorbed by the budget grew from £2.3 billion to £13.3 billion, a sixfold increase. This very substantial absolute and relative growth in the size of government is the most striking aspect of public expenditure in Ireland during the period under review. Of the additional £25.1 billion available in 1995, £11.0 billion became part of the government budget and £14.1 billion was left with the private sector. On the basis of these calculations, and excluding appropriations-in-aid, for every pound of additional income that economic growth generated, 44p ended up being spent through the budget mechanism.

The inexorable rise in the absolute resources going to public expenditure was disturbed only once in the quinquennial periods reviewed in this paper. That was in the period 1985–90. Table 1 illustrates the time- span over which the public expenditure explosion was contained and then reversed. Following the very rapid increase in public expenditure between 1973 and 1980, it will be noted that, even with an almost stagnant national income between 1980 and 1985, government expenditure continued to grow but at a much reduced rate. It was only in the period 1985–90 that net government expenditure was actually reduced. The adjustment process endured between 1982 and 1989, with the most drastic measures being taken in 1987 and 1988, gives a measure of the difficulty of the process of downward adjustment in real government expenditure. Some steps taken at that time are described in Honohan (1992).

Against this background we will look more closely at the evolution of the central government share of expenditure in Ireland and its impact on the borrowing position, and this will be compared with the experience of a number of other European countries.

Ireland and European experience – government outlays

Table 2 presents some comparisons of general government outlays as a share of GDP in seven European countries during the period 1970–95. Data on general government outlays and general government financial balances are taken from the OECD's *Economic Review and Outlook* for various years.

Taking the percentage share of general government outlays in GDP as the measure, the inexorable upward drift is evident but the trend is abating. A modest general reversal of expenditure in the period 1985–90 should be noted. Since then, however, the overall upward trend has been resumed, and between 1990 and 1995 public expenditure as a share of GDP was contained near or below 1990 levels in only three of the seven cases considered: Ireland was one of these.

As far as Irish government outlays in the period are concerned, they were average in 1970 and above average in 1975 and 1980. However, since 1985 the share has fallen dramatically; during the general decline in 1985–90, the decline in Ireland was four times the average. General government outlays as a percentage of GDP in Ireland are now well below average for the countries considered here. While budget deficits generally expanded among European countries in 1970–75, the major slippage in Irish public finances occurred in these years. The error in later years appears primarily to have been the failure to address this position.

Table 2: Trend in general government outlays as a percentage of GDP in various European countries, 1970–95

	Belgium	Denmark	Finland	France	Germany	Greece	Ireland	Average
1970	41.1	40.8	30.0	38.5	38.2	–	39.6	38.0
1975	51.2	48.2	37.6	43.4	48.4	27.9	46.3	43.3
1980	58.6	56.2	38.1	46.1	47.9	30.6	48.9	46.6
1985	61.9	59.3	43.8	52.1	47.0	43.6	52.4	51.4
1990	55.0	58.6	45.4	49.8	45.1	46.6	41.2	48.8
1995	55.4	61.6	57.6	53.7	49.5	37.5	42.1	51.1

Source: OECD, *Economic Review and Outlook*, various years

Ireland and European experience – net borrowing

The evolution of the net borrowing position of these countries in the years 1970–95 is set out in Table 3. On average, this position deteriorated rapidly between 1970 and 1975, and continued to deteriorate until 1985. (Germany was an important exception; the figures suggest that it addressed this position decisively in the 1975–80 period.) Cuts in expenditure were quickly reflected in the borrowing requirement. Increases in public expenditure after 1990 in some countries led to renewed expansion of deficit funding.

And what of Ireland? In 1970, on the basis of these figures, government outlays here were in line with our European neighbours. Throughout the 1970s the net borrowing position in Ireland deteriorated, and between 1975 and 1980 the deficit as a proportion of GDP was three times the average for the other sample countries. By 1985 the absolute level was still very high, although by then it was down to twice the average of the countries considered here. The subsequent adjustment in Ireland was larger and quicker than in any of the countries shown, and by 1995 Ireland's net borrowing position was among the lowest of the countries documented in the table. Such international comparisons are always hazardous and must be treated with caution.

The figures suggest that even as borrowing began to turn down (or more accurately reach its practical limit), expenditure share was still growing (i.e. revenue share was rising) and the substantial decrease in the government deficit was achieved first by raising taxation and then by cutting the expenditure share. But it was the resurgence of economic growth, combined with the expenditure cuts, that made the reduction in the share of expenditure so spectacular (Honohan, 1992).

Table 3: Trend in net borrowing position of general government as a percentage of GDP, various European countries, 1970–95

	Belgium	Denmark	Finland	France	Germany	Greece	Ireland	Average
1970	−2.6	0.0	4.0	0.9	0.2	–	−4.3	−0.3
1975	−5.5	−1.4	5.8	−2.4	−5.6	−3.2	−11.9	−3.5
1980	−9.3	−3.3	2.9	0.0	−2.9	−2.6	−12.1	−3.0
1985	−8.7	−2.0	3.0	−2.9	−1.2	−11.9	−10.8	−4.9
1990	−5.4	−1.5	5.4	−1.6	−2.1	−14.1	−2.2	−3.1
1995	−4.3	−1.9	−5.7	−5.0	−3.1	−9.5	−2.5	−4.6

Note: Arithmetic average.
Source: OECD, *Economic Review and Outlook*, various years

The changing composition of government expenditure in Ireland since 1959

Total, current and capital budget shares of GNP

As Whitaker (1983, p. 84) explains, it was only in the estimates for 1950–51 that a division of supply (or voted) services into capital services and other services was first shown. This distinction developed throughout the 1950s and by 1958 had established a bridgehead in the annual budget. The actual share of the central government in the economy and the relative shares of capital and current expenditure are shown in Table 4.

Table 4: Capital and current budgets in Ireland, 1959–97, and their shares of GNP

	(1) Net current (£m)	(2) Capital (£m)	(3) Total (£m)	(4) GNP (£m)	(5) (2)%(3)	(6) (3)%(4)	(7) (1)%(4)	(8) (2)%(4)
1959	128	38	166	636*	23	26	20	6
1965	223	88	311	990*	28	31	23	9
1970	412	173	585	1,658*	30	35	25	10
1975	1,350	467	1,817	3,821*	26	48	35	12
1980	3,702	1,309	5,011	9,075	26	55	41	14
1985	7,615	1,761	9,376	16,611	19	56	46	11
1990	8,421	1,684	10,105	24,311	17	42	35	7
1995	12,029	2,633	14,662	33,801	18	43	36	8
1997	12,950	3,529	16,479	39,400	21	42	33	9

*GNP adjusted for budgetary financial year.
Note: The figures shown here for the capital budget are the figures shown in the budget tables for capital expenditure for the PCP and non-programme capital expenditure.
Sources: Figures for 1959–95 are from Department of Finance, *Budget Booklets*, 1959–95, Tables 2–3; figures for 1997 are from Department of Finance, *Budgetary and Economic Statistics Booklet*, March 1997.

The significant features for our purposes are where and when the growth occurred. The overall central government share, defined here as net current budget expenditure and public capital spending, grew strongly from 1959 to 1985, from 26 per cent to 56 per cent, more than doubling in that period. Subsequently, this trend was reversed, with the share declining from 56 per cent to 42 per cent in the period 1985–90, which represented a decline every bit as dramatic as the rise in the period 1970–75. The rapid growth in GNP was a significant contributory factor, but the containment of current public expenditure was the dominant influence. Growth of the budget share resumed in the early 1990s, and on this measure is now about 42 per cent of GNP. The resumed growth of public expenditure since 1990 has been accommodated by the exceptional rates of economic growth which have enabled the public expenditure share to be stabilised as expenditure increases.

The evolution of the capital and current budgets is described below for a number of subperiods:

- *1959–70.* While the capital and current budgets both grew as a share of GNP during the period 1959–70, the emphasis was on the growth of the capital budget. It expanded from 6 per cent to 10 per cent of GNP, while the current budget grew at a considerably lower rate, from 20 per cent to 25 per cent of GNP. Within the public budget, therefore, the relative importance of the capital budget increased in this period, with its share of the total budget increasing from 23 per cent to 30 per cent.

- *1970–80.* During the period 1970–80 the government budget grew rapidly from 35 per cent to 55 per cent of GNP. The relative importance of the capital budget declined as a share of the total budget (30 per cent to 26 per cent), but because of the growth in the government sector, the share of the public capital budget in GNP continued its upward trend (from 10 per cent in 1970 to 14 per cent in 1980). Current budget expenditure grew very rapidly over this decade, from 25 per cent to 41 per cent of GNP.

- *1980–85.* While the growth in the total government share stabilised in the 1980–85 period (growing only one percentage point to 56 per cent), this masked the continued growth of the current budget (from 41 per cent to 46 per cent of GNP, and 81 per cent of the total budget) and the continued decline of the public capital budget. The latter was evident not only in terms of its share of government expenditure (down from 26 per cent to 19 per cent) but also in terms of its share of GNP which had until then been rising (down from 14 per cent to 11 per cent).

- *1985–95.* Between 1985 and 1995 there was an enormous adjust-ment, the bulk of this occurring in the 1985–90 period. The share of the total budget in GNP declined 14 per cent between 1985 and 1990. Current expenditure fell from 46 per cent to 35 per cent of GNP in this five-year period and the capital budget fell from 11 per cent to 7 per cent of GNP. On average, since 1990 the growth of both current government expenditure and the public capital budget has resumed; however, as this has been in line with a resurgence of growth in the economy, the government/public sector share is only edging upwards. Nonetheless, it should be noted that despite a vigorous resurgence of economic growth and the availability of EU funds, the share of the capital budget in GNP is at levels comparable to the late 1950s and early 1960s.

Sectoral shares of current budgets

The changing sectoral shares of current budgets are considered over two periods, 1959–80 and 1980–96. This is because there is a change in 1980 in the presentation of figures in the primary source used here.

Table 5 shows the shares based on the main heads of current expendi-ture presented in the budget tables up to and including 1980. These are based on net expenditures, after appropriations-in-aid and PRSI contribu-tions are deducted from gross expenditures. They include expenditure on public service pay, which in view of its significance is separately tabulated.

Table 5: Proportionate shares of main heads of current government expenditure, 1958/59–1980 (%)

Category	1958/59	1965	1970	1975	1980
Debt service	20	19	22	18	21
Social services	37	34	35	45	42
Economic services	16	22	24	15	9
General services	20	18	14	16	15
Other expenditure	7	7	5	6	12
Total	100	100	100	100	100
Exchequer pay and pensions	32	32	27	33	36

Source: Department of Finance, *Budget Booklets*, 1959–80, Table 2

The categories defined were as follows:

- social services: social welfare, education, health
- economic services: agriculture, industry, transport, forestry and fisheries

- general services: post office, defence, justice and Gardaí, public service pensions.

Noteworthy points in the period 1959–80 are:

- debt service was essentially a constant proportion of the net current budget (this of course masks its rise as a proportion of GNP due to the rapid growth of the current budget share)
- the share of social services in the current budget declined at first, and then grew strongly between 1970 and 1975
- the share of economic services grew at first but fell substantially between 1970 and 1980 from 24 per cent to 9 per cent
- the share of general services declined between 1960 and 1970 and then stabilised
- exchequer pay and pensions are an important component of these services and the current budget; their share declined in the 1960s and grew substantially in the 1970s.

Data on current government expenditure categorisation in the budget booklets used as the source for this data changed in 1980. Essentially the sectoral categories were expanded with expenditure presented on a gross basis. This in effect increased the shares of those sectors which have significant appropriations-in-aid. This is reflected in the higher starting-point for the share of social services (Table 6).

Table 6: Proportionate shares of main heads of current government expenditure, 1980–96 (%)

Category	1980	1985	1990	1995	1996
Debt service	17	22	22	16	15
Economic services	8	9	7	7	7
Infrastructure	1	1	1	1	1
Social services	57	55	55	59	59
Security	8	7	8	7	7
Other expenditure	9	7	8	10	11
Total	100	100	100	100	100
Exchequer pay and pensions	35	28	30	31	32

Source: Department of Finance, *Budget Booklets*, 1980–96, Table 3

A significant feature of the current budget evolution since 1980 is the rapid rise in debt service in the first half of the 1980s and the subsequent and equally sharp decline in the 1990s. This decline has been largely absorbed by a further increase in allocations to the social services, and to the residual 'other expenditure' category which includes justice. Current funding of economic services has continued to stagnate or decline as a share of gross current expenditure.

The share of exchequer pay reached a peak around 1980, and then fell between 1980 and 1985 only to recover its share slowly in the following ten years. The size of the public sector pay share is most significant for the government's expenditures, and some of the related crucial issues are discussed later in this essay.

The capital budget and the public capital programme

The decline in the significance of the capital budget was illustrated earlier in this essay. This decline has a number of features which, for the future, are worthy of systematic consideration. The failure over the years to categorise clearly capital expenditure, and to elaborate clear criteria for such expenditure, does not facilitate such consideration. Within the overall declining emphasis on capital expenditure in the budget, several trends are worthy of note.

Exchequer and non-exchequer capital spending

The first notable feature of the government's capital spending is the distinction between exchequer and non-exchequer expenditures. Table 7 shows how the share of exchequer capital expenditures declined over the years, from almost three-quarters in 1959 to well under half in 1997.

Table 7: Composition of expenditure on the public capital programme, 1959–97

	Exchequer (£m)	Non-exchequer (£m)	Total PCP (£m)	Exchequer % in PCP	PCP in 1995 prices (£m)
1959/60	33	12	45	73	614
1970/71	124	70	194	64	1,658
1980	833	437	1,270	66	3,010
1985	976	713	1,689	58	2,249
1990	787	866	1,653	48	1,872
1995	1,268	1,365	2,633	48	2,633
1997[e]	1,579	1,950	3,529	44	3,361

[e]Estimate

Sources: Department of Finance, *Budget Booklets*, 1959 and 1970; *Budgetary and Economic Statistics Booklet*, March 1997 for the years 1980–97

There are a number of explanations for this change in share. With economic development there has been a greater demand for capital investments of a commercial character – energy supplies, telecommunications services, etc. – and increasingly these services have been commercialised and taken out of government departments, e.g. the establishment of An Post and Telecom Éireann. While there has been some limited use of privatisation, e.g. Greencore, not all movement has been in that direction. The now profitable and previously loss-making gas distribution industry (Cork Gas and Dublin Gas) has been national- ised through Bord Gáis Éireann.

The table also shows the variation in the level of real resources going into the capital programme over the years. These resources have fluctuated widely and have fallen back as a proportion of national income. The substantial increase during the 1990s (almost doubling between 1990 and 1997) has no doubt been driven by the need to provide economic, productive and social infrastructure as economic growth accelerates and by the need to provide matching co- responsibility funding for EU investments.

European funding

European funding has played a significant role in the renaissance of capital investment. Table 8 summarises receipts from the EU in the period 1975–97. It can be seen how the allocations in support of capital investment have grown, particularly during the 1990s through European Regional Development, Cohesion and Agricultural (FEOGA) Funds. The FEOGA guidance section would also include investment in forestry and farming. These European funds have not only complemented invest- ment, but also prompted and brought forward new and necessary pro- grammes. The planning of capital investment in the future will need to take into account changes in the availability of such funds.

Table 8: Breakdown of receipts from EU budget (£m)

	FEOGA (guarantee)	FEOGA (guidance)	European Social Fund	European Regional Development Fund	Cohesion Fund	Other	Total
1975	102	0.6	4	2	–	1	109
1980	381	32	47	46	–	55	561
1985	837	56	141	76	–	19	1,129
1990	1,287	94	129	225	–	7	1,741
1995	1,150	143	256	358	102	14	2,023
1997ᵉ	1,300	201	314	352	137	27	2,332

ᵉEstimate
Source: Department of Finance

Sectoral components of the public capital programme

The main sectoral components of the public capital programme during the period 1958/59 to 1995 are set out in Tables 9, 10 and 11.

Table 9: Main components of the public capital programme, 1959–95

	1959	1965	1970	1975	1980	1985	1990	1995
1. Sectoral economic investment								
£ million	11	32	56	174	473	384	502	955
Share (%)	29	33	32	37	38	23	31	36
2. Productive infrastructure								
£ million	18	42	70	134	436	701	796	1,032
Share (%)	48	43	40	28	35	41	49	40
3. Social infrastructure								
£ million	8	23	48	159	328	604	328	646
Share (%)	23	24	28	34	27	36	20	24
Total PCP								
£ million	38	98	173	467	1,237	1,689	1,626	2,633

Note: The years refer to budgetary years, i.e. 1959 is 1958/59, 1965 is 1964/65 and 1970 is 1969/70 while 1975 and subsequent years refer to the calendar year.
Source: The figures are taken mainly from the out-turn figures in Department of Finance, *Budget Booklets*, 1959, 1965, 1970, 1976, 1981, 1986, Tables 3 and 5, and PCP 1996 Table 3

Sectoral economic investment was given increased emphasis in the capital budget between 1959 and 1980; its share was cut severely in the mid-1980s, but has recovered in the 1990s to the levels of the 1960s and 1970s. Productive infrastructure investment, on the other hand, got less emphasis as a share of the total between 1959 and 1975. Thereafter the trend was reversed. Social infrastructure – largely schools, hospitals and housing – was fairly constant in its share of the capital budget between 1959 and 1970. Its share grew in the 1970s as the productive infrastructure investment was held back, declined in 1980, peaked in 1985 and has since dropped to its earlier level of about one-quarter of the capital budget.

Within this broad breakdown there have been interesting changes within the sectors. Table 10 shows an approximate breakdown of economic investment in the PCP. The most important change in the early period was the reversal of roles between agriculture and industry: where in 1958/59 investment in agriculture amounted to twice that in industry in the PCP, by 1970 industry had overhauled agriculture in the PCP, and by 1980 industrial investment was more than twice agricultural invest-

Table 10: Sectoral economic investment in the public capital programme, 1959–95 (£m)

	1959	1965	1970	1975	1980	1985	1990	1995
Agriculture	6	20	22	70	119	59	82	226
Industry	3	10	28	90	324	285	327	573
Tourism	0	1	3	1	4	12	41	66
Forestry	1	2	3	13	10	21	42	79
Fisheries	0	0	0	0	12	6	10	10
Miscellaneous	0	0	0	0	4	1	0	0
Total	11	32	56	174	473	384	502	955

Note: The years refer to budgetary years, i.e. 1959 is 1958/59, 1965 is 1964/65 and 1970 is 1969/70 while 1975 and subsequent years refer to the calendar year.
Source: The figures are taken mainly from the out-turn figures in Department of Finance, *Budget Booklets*, 1959, 1965, 1970, 1976, 1981, 1986, Tables 3 and 5, and PCP 1996 Table 3

ment. This pattern has been reversed since 1985, with the combined PCP expenditure on agriculture and forestry increasing at more than twice the rate of expenditure on industry. If PCP expenditure on forestry and agriculture are combined, their share of the capital budget has grown by 50 per cent since 1985. There has also been a significant increase in capital expenditure on tourism since 1985. What does this suggest, if anything, for the priorities for the future? These questions will be further considered in the concluding section.

Table 11: Productive infrastructure in the public capital programme, 1959–95 (£m)

	1959	1965	1970	1975	1980	1985	1990	1995
Energy	8	15	20	43	155	233	130	228
Transport	7	16	35	19	69	76	218	173
Roads and sanitary services	2	4	6	21	90	232	267	405
Telecommunications	1	6	8	50	122	160	181	225
Total	18	42	70	134	436	701	796	1,032

Note: The years refer to budgetary years, i.e. 1959 is 1958/59, 1965 is 1964/65 and 1970 is 1969/70 while 1975 and subsequent years refer to the calendar year.
Source: The figures are taken mainly from the out-turn figures in Department of Finance, *Budget Booklets*, 1959, 1965, 1970, 1976, 1981, 1986, Tables 3 and 5, and PCP 1996 Table 3

Social expenditure and current expenditure

Because of the increasing importance of current budget expenditure (see Table 4), and because social expenditure accounts for the major share of the current budget, it may be useful to consider the main components of social expenditure and their evolution using figures from the OECD (1995).

Table 12 shows trends in expenditure on social protection for a number of OECD countries, including Ireland, between 1960 and 1990. The growth of social expenditures in Ireland shadows that in a number of countries, and like a shadow follows behind the leaders. These figures suggest that the more affluent the country, the earlier the growth of the social protection budget. The most marked growth in Ireland was in the 1970s, when the share of social protection expenditures in GDP almost doubled. This can be explained by reference both to cyclical factors and to policy changes in social support programmes and expenditures.

Table 12: Trends in expenditure on social protection as percentage of GDP, various European countries, 1960–90

	1960	1970	1980	1990
Ireland	8.7	11.9	20.6	19.7
Denmark	–	19.1	26.0	27.8
France	13.4	16.7	23.9	26.5
Germany	18.1	19.5	25.4	23.5
UK	10.2	13.2	21.3	22.3
EU average[1]	10.1[2]	14.0[2]	21.6	21.7

[1] Unweighted. [2] Relates to wider OECD group.
Source: OECD (1995)

The breakdown of that expenditure between health and non-health is shown in Tables 13 and 14 respectively. Table 13 suggests that as a proportion of GDP social protection expenditures on health in Ireland were broadly comparable to those in the other countries shown. In 1980 Ireland had the highest proportion for the countries shown, but this has since fallen more into line with our European neighbours. The Irish health expenditure proportion would be substantially below that of countries where health expenditure is largely or exclusively in the private sector, such as the United States.

Turning to Table 14, Ireland's non-health social protection expenditures in 1990 were below the European average as a percentage of GDP, but not much. The overall figure masks important differences, however, as the proportion paid to the aged in Ireland was below the EU average, reflecting age composition. The proportion going to the non-aged (e.g. unemployed) was higher than in any of the countries considered here excluding Denmark.

Table 13: Public expenditure on health as percentage of GDP, various European countries, 1960–90

	1960	1970	1980	1990
Ireland	3.0	4.3	7.5	5.2
Denmark	–	5.2	5.8	5.2
France	2.5	4.3	6.0	6.6
Germany	3.1	4.2	6.3	6.0
UK	3.4	4.0	5.2	5.2
EU average	2.6	4.0	5.5	5.2

Source: OECD (1995)

Table 14: Public expenditure on non-health social protection as percentage of GDP, various European countries, 1960–90

		1960	1970	1980	1990
Ireland	Total	5.7	7.6	13.01	14.52
	Aged			6.18	5.85
	Non-aged			6.83	8.67
Denmark	Total	–	13.9	20.17	22.54
	Aged			8.69	8.12
	Non-aged			11.48	14.42
France	Total	10.9	12.3	17.89	19.87
	Aged			10.41	11.70
	Non-aged			7.48	8.17
Germany	Total	15.0	15.3	19.08	17.50
	Aged			11.08	9.90
	Non-aged			8.00	7.60
UK	Total	6.9	9.3	16.13	17.15
	Aged			9.17	9.72
	Non-aged			6.96	7.43
EU average	Total	7.5	10.0	16.06	16.46
	Aged			8.83	9.00
	Non-aged			7.23	7.46

Source: OECD (1995)

The general conclusion to be drawn is that the shares of social protection expenditures in GDP in Ireland in 1990 were not grossly out of line with European levels. However, comparison of health and non-health expenditures suggests at least the potential for larger demands on the public purse in the future. The ultimate impact of such services on public expenditure will depend on how they are provided in the future, the extent to which they are provided in the public and the private sector, how they are funded, the level of insurance in social protection programmes, and the age structure of the population.

Future prospect

The second half of this essay addresses key features of the future evolution of public expenditure. These are: the size of public expenditure and limiting factors; the role of capital expenditure; future considerations in current expenditure and its composition; and the development of mechanisms for management, control and containment.

The future size of public expenditures

The most striking feature of the public budget in Ireland since the publication of *Economic Development* in 1958 has been its growth: in that period nearly half of every extra pound of national income was channelled through the public budget. A fourfold increase in real income for the period 1958–95 saw a trebling of the resources available in private hands (from £6.4 billion to £20.5 billion) while public expenditure rose sixfold (from £2.3 billion to £13.3 billion). The level and size of government outlays and the growth experience emphasise the importance of the mechanisms by which public expenditure is determined and controlled. Both the general mechanisms of public expenditure determination and the mechanisms which regulate supply of and demand for particular public services will determine the future outcome. Is there a potential limit to public expenditure share?

The tendency for public expenditure to grow as a share of GNP is long established and has been generally noted. There is likely to be a limit to its share in practical terms. While the limit may vary from time to time and place to place, the last twenty years have demonstrated how that limit is approached, and the responses that have followed.

Generally, the clearest sign of the practical limit being approached is increasing recourse to borrowing for current as well as capital expenditure. A second classic response is to curtail capital expenditure and to apply the borrowing capacity to current needs by retaining or increasing borrowing. The third response is to raise taxes. Finally, the growth of debt and debt service payments and resistance to higher tax levels force an adjustment in public current expenditure. This, essentially, has been our experience.

There is clearly a limit to the sustainable share of public expenditure in national income, and there is clear evidence that this has been approached in the past. The experience of the period from 1972 to 1986 is an example of an unsustainable pattern. However, the experience of some economies in the recent past suggests that, for them, the limit may be as high as 60 per cent. That such a level is reached does not imply that it can be sustained without seriously damaging the productive capacity and future growth prospects of the economy. The absolute limit depends on the definition of public expenditure involved and the nature of the economy. The consequences of such high levels are poorly understood. A critical question for citizens and political leaders is what level is sustainable. In particular, a judgement must be made by electors and by government as to the level of expenditure that is consistent with continuing economic progress and the disciplines imposed by competitive evolution in the global economy. The 55 per cent share experienced in Ireland in the 1980s was manifestly inconsistent with acceptable economic advance. What is clear is that if taxation levels are uncompetitive, or if recourse to borrowing is made on a non-exceptional basis for current purposes, or if borrowing is used excessively for unproductive capital investment, economic growth at an adequate level will not be sustained in the medium term.

Factors likely to influence the expenditure share

Government expenditure is ultimately limited by the ability to finance and sustain it. In Ireland in the coming times downward pressures on taxes, borrowing and EU transfers – the three main sources of government revenues – are likely. The potential for any of these sources to increase their share of GNP in the present EU context is very limited. A further possibility is charges; this will be considered later.

The possibilities for increasing taxes are restrained by the consensus on economic policy contained in Partnership 2000, and in particular the aspiration of the social partners to reduce income taxation on low to middle incomes and to restructure PRSI to enhance employment. Capital and corporate taxation are likely to be constrained by increasing pressures on member states to provide a competitive environment for industry and services, and by increasing competition for internationally mobile investment and management, which is a central element of the current economic performance and strategy. Revenue possibilities of capital and company taxation are therefore limited.

Continuous borrowing for current purposes is not a sustainable option, nor is it consistent with participation in the EMU. If present plans are realised, and Ireland joins the EMU, the scope for fiscal discretion, particularly in relation to borrowing, will be all but eliminated. The Stability and Growth Pact will require a degree of balance in the budget, and is unlikely, in normal circumstances, to accommodate borrowing to meet expenditure aspirations.

A further source of public expenditure has been EU transfers. These transfers (the Agricultural, Social, Regional Development and Cohesion Funds) have been growing in absolute size. However, as national income grows, Ireland's exchequer contributions to the EU are also growing. Furthermore, those elements of the funds which are designed to help Ireland catch up are likely to decline, at least in proportionate terms.

These factors are likely to combine to exert downward pressure on the share of government in the economy.

These influences will, however, be offset to some extent by demands for the extension of social, health and education services. The change in emphasis in the government budget from capital to current may also carry potential implications for expenditure. If government capital expenditures continue to decline against the background of present growth rates, bottlenecks of an economic, infrastructural or social character may impede progress. While the opportunities for private capital and investment have been considerably expanded by economic progress, it is a moot point whether the retreat of the exchequer from capital investment is sustainable in the medium term if growth is to be maintained. The adequate provision of telecommunications infra-structure, for example, and a necessary emphasis on the timely and competitive availability of such facilities as outlined in the *Information Society Ireland* report (Information Society Steering Committee, 1996) carry clear implications for the provision of new and expensive infrastructure. A central role for government for the future is to ensure that, whatever strategies are pursued for capital investment, they are adequate to ensure the timely and economical provision of the necessary strategic and social infrastructures.

An economic downturn could also have implications for the public expenditure share. Normally, government social expenditures are countercyclical. In the event of an economic downturn, a growth in government transfer payments should be anticipated. With the decline in the capital component of the government's budget and an absence of contingency provisions (surpluses in good times), such growth can only in practice be met by cuts in other current expenditures or by increasing government expenditure. This suggests that more attention might be given to the pre-funding of cyclical liabilities of particular social schemes.

The approach to funding and charges will be an important factor in both the supply of and the demand for these services. The funding of pensions has been the subject of recent studies and has important implications for community transfers in the medium term. But the extent to which this will be addressed through public and/or private sector provision remains to be seen.

The out-turn in the medium term will hinge on political choices and on the extent to which decisions in economic management give priority, on the one hand, to considerations of competitiveness, and, on the other, to present as against future consumption.

The role of the capital budget

Apart from the size of the overall government budget, a key issue for the future of public expenditure will be the approach taken to the planning and funding of public capital requirements. Tables in this essay demonstrate the growing emphasis on current as against capital spending. The relative decline in exchequer funding of the capital programme is also noteworthy. One has the impression that capital investment has for too long been a hapless residual of the tussle for current funding within an overall exchequer constraint. An articulate and regularly reviewed and adjusted strategy, determined by government in conjunction with the social partners and supported in its formulation by the requisite experts, is required.

By the early 1990s the capital budget had reached an all-time low as a percentage of the total government budget (17 per cent) and of GNP (7 per cent) for the period 1959–96. It is ironic that while we celebrate with this volume the *démarche* of Ken Whitaker's *Economic Development* (1958), with its emphasis on capital as against current expenditure and economic or productive as against social expenditure, we have – in this period of unprecedented economic growth – swung the other way. It should be remembered, however, that overinvestment in the late 1970s and 1980s is only now being utilised. While there has been a resurgence of investment during the 1990s, infrastructural capital investment requires a consistent approach over long time periods. It is in the nature of the social consultative process that shorter term considerations (especially remuneration) receive the most emphasis. If this is so, a key priority for the government and the partners to social consensus will be to find an acceptable framework to ensure that capital provisions in the present are adequate to sustain economic performance in the future. That economic performance will depend, in no small measure, on the realism and timeliness of current decisions on capital provision and investment.

Within this context of a declining emphasis on public capital investment, European funding is increasingly important. With the advent of European funds and the Community Support Framework, the public capital programme has increasingly been formed in the context of objectives framed jointly with Brussels, and funded with European money. A major influence in these circumstances is that capital allocations are more easily available for some purposes than for others. In a sense the Community Support Framework has become an institutional substitute for domestic capital planning and programming. This is not, of course, entirely negative. European funds have in a very real sense served to prime the pump of the public capital programme since the mid-1980s, and at the time of the economic cutbacks of the late 1980s they were a critical factor in the retention of certain capital investment programmes.

For the future, a more rational basis will be required for determination of the levels and priorities of capital expenditure if sustained economic progress is to be assured.

The public capital programme has been an important component of national investment. It has contributed directly and indirectly to economic infrastructure, productive infrastructure and social infrastructure. In 1996, for example, the largest provisions were for industry, roads and housing, followed by telecommunications, energy, transport and agriculture. It has always been a key component of the expenditure of the building and construction industry. Yet the capital programme still lacks a definitive articulation of its primary purpose and objectives, and how these should be measured. Ironically, capital investment was more prominent in the budget debates of the 1960s than it is now despite the fact that, with the accelerating pace of change (technological and otherwise), it may be of more concern in the future than it was in the 1960s.

What should characterise the capital expenditure in the public capital programme?

A useful guide to this question is found in Ken Whitaker's essay 'Financial Turning-Points' in his book *Interests* where he quotes the Minister for Finance in 1967 as stressing the importance of 'reckoning as capital only such expenditure as genuinely merits the description. Expenditures which do not add to the national stock of capital, or must be repeated every year to maintain their effect, are suspect from this point of view.' But the ultimate guarantor of any capital investment is its productive nature – that once incurred it should yield value in cash or kind, as income or services, over a period of years.

The significance of public capital investment should be determined first and foremost by reference to its productivity. Provided the capital properly remunerates the investment made, it need not create a burden on the economy. This is only so if the investment is warranted in terms of demand and the income/revenues flowing from the use of the assets.

It is also necessary that the capital be provided in a cost-efficient fashion. This has implications for how the facility or service is provided. Desirable public capital expenditure should ideally have other characteristics. It should contribute to achieving a competitive basis for the economy, and it should take account of the anticipated economic and social need for such investment and of the extent to which these capital services are or can be efficiently provided by market mechanisms through the private sector at a competitive price.

Much of the current debate about public capital investment has been couched in ideological terms. In the past the public capital programme has been used as an instrument for development where private provision was inadequate or where the operation of the market would lead to underinvestment. It has not always been efficient. Provision by the market may be suboptimal because of long lead times in certain infrastructural investments, because of externalities, or because of deviations between individual and social benefits of investments. Investments in schools, housing, water, sanitary services, energy supply and particularly public transport are relevant in this context. While a larger and more affluent economy opens up the possibility for more private sector supply of services and social capital, the considerations which prompted public sector investment in major sectors such as energy, education, communications and transport have not disappeared, as is testified by the congestion on our streets and the availability and cost of high-capacity telecommunications links capable of supporting multimedia and interactive (broadband) applications for enterprises.

What principles should be applied to public capital planning?

The doubtful quality of some past investment decisions is no alibi for adopting a Rip Van Winkle posture on consideration of the economy's and society's capital requirements and how they might best be met. Rampant ideology of the left or of the right is likely to impair a rational outcome.

Four steps are suggested as an aid to a balanced approach for the future. These are:

- planning the appropriate scope for public capital investment and the supply of essential infrastructure and services
- introduction of competition and, in monopoly markets, regulation
- appraisal of public capital expenditure, both before and after the investment, and
- complementary administrative action and support.

Planning infrastructural capital requirements: Effective mechanisms to monitor public investment requirements in the 'strategic infrastructural heights' of the economy need to be put in place as a matter of course and subject to rigorous annual review. What areas require public investment, and what areas can be economically served by competitive forces? The pace of change is now such that five-year national investment programmes required to qualify for EU funds may need to be substantially reordered within the programme period. European and national priorities may diverge. Gaps may emerge in economic, social and productive infrastructure, and systematic structures need to be devised and reviewed to address these. The methodology and process for assessing the balance between programmes and the balance within programmes need to be re-examined and articulated. What role can and do the Irish government, the social partners, the EU and administration play in the allocation of funds between programmes, and is it satisfactory? Within programmes, are smaller programmes given adequate weight, e.g. public versus private transport, or ports versus railways? Within subprogrammes, there are further problems, e.g. in railway transport, the choices between mainline and urban transport systems.

The new multiannual planning system announced by the then Minister for Finance Ruairí Quinn in 1996 and developed in the 1997 budget context should be part of such a process. The stated aim is to put a strategic planning framework in place to agree overall spending limits over the medium term. It will need to be augmented by a wider process in which the EU, social partners and other experts have a role. However, public capital perspectives are essentially long term, and ultimately this is a matter for the government to judge in its pivotal role of defining and furthering the community's interest, as distinct from those of vested interests.

Introducing competition and regulating monopolies in the public interest: The second important aspect in the public capital programme lies in the supervision and regulation of public capital and monopolies. A priority for the better development of public capital is exploitation of the new opportunities which technology is affording for competition even in what were traditionally monopoly industries. The possible exploitation of monopoly positions in vital services is still a concern. In industries with the potential to exploit captive customers, a comprehensive competitiveness-monitoring procedure and independent and well-resourced regulators are a critical element in ensuring cost-competitive infrastructure and services; this is so, regardless of ownership. Derogation from EU regulations to protect domestic monopolies may serve the interests of neither the consumer nor economic development, and is no substitute for systematic pursuit of the disciplines of the marketplace with appropriate planning of timely provision of capacity.

Capital investment appraisal: The third essential measure is enhancement of the process of capital investment appraisal before and after public capital investment. The procedures of the Department of Finance in this regard, and the systematic evaluation of the EU structural funding mechanisms, have been beneficial at a project level, but comparison between various programmes remains problematic. There is ample scope for modification and improvement of the methodologies in use in the light of actual experience. In this context recent trends in public capital expenditure deserve attention. The resurgence of expenditures on agriculture and forestry is significant, as is the relative decline in the provisions made for energy and industry/services. Is this warranted in terms of the anticipated return or is there another explanation? The inclusion in the capital budget of the estimated returns to different capital expenditures might be a useful discipline.

Complementary administrative decisions: A further factor to be taken into account is the need for complementary administrative policies to maximise the return to the investments made. Thus if investment in housing, for example, is to be effective, the central and local authorities need to adopt consistent and complementary strategies in relation to zoning and servicing of land. Ideally, a share of the increment of value following such administrative action and investments should accrue to society. Other examples abound: investment in schools without equipment, teachers without retraining, armies without transport, and correctional facilities without rehabilitation makes limited sense. But this leads to a consideration of the current budget, which is the subject of the next section.

Conclusion on the capital budget

The capital budget in the past has provided some of the critical infrastructure which has made recent growth possible. Despite this positive role – and some expensive mistakes – there has been a less than comprehensive debate about the rationale and desiderata for public capital investment. On the supply side, a fully comprehensive approach to planning, evaluation and accounting for public capital investment remains to be agreed. On the demand side, there is an absence of a coherent and consistent philosophy in relation to both the terms on which public capital is provided and the strategy for provision of facilities and services where the absence of charges is likely to lead to wasteful demands for such facilities.

The growth of the market, new possibilities for competition in industries thought to be monopolies, and dismantling of regulations and monopoly structures – these developments open new possibilities in many sectors. The development of competition in air transport is a good example of how new entrants have, through competition, enhanced growth and performance.

The role of the public capital programme is deserving of more detailed attention in the planning process, with particular attention being given to identifying those types of investment which will yield a return on the investment and are, for whatever reason, appropriate objects for government investment. The trend of the capital programme should be based on the results of analysis, and not be the hapless residual of short-term pressures to accommodate expedient current expenditure demands.

The link between the public capital programme and national saving and investment will also need attention in the near future. Any downturn in EU funding will accelerate the urgency of this question. A further consideration for public capital investment is whether it should afford a mechanism to provide for contingent expenditures in the future through the accumulation of income-earning assets. Should the state make provision for pensions and other future liabilities by creating a real fund of income-earning assets? And what about provision for cyclical impacts – cyclical increases in unemployment, for example? Should provision for those liabilities be made by investing some portion of social insurance contributions in income-earning assets? Should such investment be at home or abroad? Income-earning assets would reduce the need for fresh borrowing in the future to meet contingencies that are likely to arise and which will otherwise require significant expenditure reductions or increases in taxes, or both.

The current budget

Consideration of the current budget suggests three dominant areas of spending – social welfare, education and health – as well as the ubiquitous issue of public sector pay. Social welfare, education and health are the subject of other essays in this volume.

Public sector pay

The public pay element, a third of all current expenditure, has a central importance not just for the future of the current budget but for the share of the public sector in the economy. This is because public services have such a large element of labour, e.g. teachers in education, medical personnel in the hospitals, soldiers in the army. The stable share over time (notwithstanding significant cyclical and other fluctuations) of public service pay in the budget understates its significance, because of the growth over time of the GNP and the share of the current budget in GNP (see Tables 5 and 6).

Three major considerations deserve attention for the future in relation to public service pay. First, there is the share of public sector pay in the economy generally. This is potentially significant because of the macro-economic impacts and in particular because it may restrict the government's ability to adjust and respond appropriately to economic problems. Second, there is the actual and potential influence of public sector pay on the efficiency of particular sectors, such as health, education and defence, where the pay element can account for a large share of the expenditure involved. *In extremis*, therefore, one could have teachers without adequate materials and equipment, an army without adequate transport, and nurses and doctors without adequate supplies to provide the most efficient service. Third, there is the comparability between various occupations in the public sector and the relationship of their remuneration with that in the private sector.

These questions cannot be answered easily, but a number of considerations might be relevant for the future. The first is a recognition that it is the service and not the servants that is the object of public policy, and that if the services are to be effective, their resourcing must be balanced. Trends in the labour intensity of services should be monitored with a view to ensuring that, within any overall budget constraint, the labour element does not absorb an undue proportion of the available resources. A second aspect is the comparability of the labour share of resources in this country in these services *vis-à-vis* that elsewhere. If this is substantially out of line with the practice in other countries, it requires attention if not adjustment. It has been suggested that this is a feature of both health and education expenditure. As for the vexed question of public sector/private sector relativities, these have over the past decade been largely determined within the social partnership process. In the years ahead, and in the absence of continuation or sustainability of such agreements, review of industrial relations procedures in critical services may be required. It will be essential that appropriate market-related references are established if competitiveness is to be maintained through the mechanism of such nationally negotiated agreements. Failure to address this issue directly is likely to force adjustment in other ways. In a world of increasing change and competition, timely adaptation and adjustment to the market is the only realistic sustainable course to prosperity for public sector workers. Here, too, the social partners will have to make difficult choices in the coming years.

Evolution of the current budget

This issue is embraced by the discussion above on the overall budget share. The demand for current services to be provided by the government is almost irrepressible. The extent to which such services can be expanded in a sustainable way depends on the degree of growth in the economy, and that in turn depends on the competitive status of the economy and the existence of the necessary physical and human capital to allow the growth to take place. The ultimate level of such services that can be provided will depend on the provisions made to enable that growth to continue. In the short to medium term there will be a clear conflict between current consumption and the sustainability of such consumption into the future.

Composition of the current budget

The third consideration for the current budget is its composition. Social services account for about 60 per cent of the current budget (see Table 6). As Finola Kennedy's essay in this volume shows, the categories of social welfare expenditures that have shown the most growth are the non-contributory categories. The opportunity arises now to provide for these liabilities in a more orderly fashion through the creation over time of funded schemes. Practice elsewhere should help inform such approaches. Economic services, including support services for industry, agriculture and tourism, have declined in importance in the current budget. Whether this lessened emphasis is consistent with a long-term high growth trajectory is another challenge for the coming times.

Balancing the budget

A final consideration for the current budget is the potential discipline which the Stability and Growth Pact may impose with the advent of EMU. Essentially this will constrain the conduct of the government budget, and it would be illusory to assume that, in the event of EMU going ahead, remaining outside EMU would insulate the government from the consequences of profligate budgetary behaviour. EMU will mean, however, that the restored balance between expenditure and resources is most likely to be a dominant feature of budgetary arithmetic in the Ireland of the coming times.

Mechanisms for management, control and containment

Mechanisms for management, control and containment involve a number of perspectives: first, mechanisms at national level; second, procedures at sectoral or company level; and third, economic signals to which citizens and consumers respond.

National mechanisms

As far as national mechanisms are concerned, there are four processes of particular relevance: the traditional estimates process; the dialogue of the social partners and consequent national programmes, e.g. Partnership 2000; the influence of the EU on the capital and the current budget; and the political–expenditure interface, in particular the operation of the political system in response to interest groups.

At the level of overall public expenditure, there is the increasing importance of social partnership in determining the role of government and the priorities of government expenditure. The operation of the democratic/political system has been an important factor in increasing public expenditure in the past. Whether and how this influence will be exercised to prioritise public expenditures on the one hand, and to contain the predations of special interests on the other, will be critical in the future. Attention to the capital requirement of the economy in a structured and prescient way will require a higher priority. The level of taxation, which has become a focus of late, will remain a priority. To retain the confidence of foreign investors and to contain taxation to a level compatible with maintaining a favourable and competitive environment for enterprise while simultaneously addressing social priorities and infrastructural challenges – that is the nature of the challenge to be faced. For the future, the magnitude of that challenge will need not just explicit recognition, but adoption of management and investment strategies consistently applied to those ends subsequent to informed consideration and debate.

Sectoral measures

At the sectoral level, there is the need for efficiency in the provision of services. This aspect has already been discussed in the context of the capital services and the provision of the capital budget. The government also provides extensive services of a current nature, and the provision and delivery of those services are matters of great practical importance. A number of recent initiatives deserve mention in this regard. The Comptroller and Auditor General (Amendment) Act 1993, the Public Service Management Bill and the Strategic Management Initiative are all directed, in one way or another, at improving the efficiency of public expenditure and the delivery of public services. While it is too soon to judge the success of these initiatives, the likelihood is that they will contribute to the more effective delivery of public services in the future.

Another important option open to government is the introduction of competition. This can be done through the privatisation of existing services and the introduction of new suppliers. Where this is not poss- ible because of the monopoly nature of certain industries, these should be subject to appropriate independent regulation. One important con- sideration which has arisen clearly in the context of the TV deflector controversy is that the conferring of exclusive rights is less amenable to adjustment in the case of private companies than in the case of publicly owned enterprises. As a general rule, where practicable and economic, competition is the best guarantor of effective supply; all monopolies potentially can abuse the consumer and are candidates for regulation or supervision to protect the consumer interest.

Economic signals, charges and public services

One feature of many goods and services provided is that they are not charged directly to the user. In a sense, they are perceived as 'free' to the user. All services have to be paid for by someone, and one of the keys to the control of public expenditure is to address systematically how differ- ent necessary goods and services should be provided for and funded. Adoption of such an approach would obviate the dislocation and disappointment, and indeed the inequity, which will follow the unavoid- able and arbitrary expenditure cuts that are inevitable in the absence of such an approach when economic fortunes change. Public expenditure crises can only be softened by advance economic planning for such con- tingencies and by the introduction of a sustainable and consistent approach to containment of the insatiable appetite for the misleadingly labelled 'free goods' and the general provision of other services supplied at public expense.

At the level of the individual service, there are several important questions: How is demand regulated? Should it be regulated? Are exist- ing arrangements those which are socially preferred? If so, how will they be paid for? This introduces the question of charges in relation to use, e.g. water charges, refuse disposal charges, university and third-level fees.

The wider use of charges would of course reduce in some cases the demand for services, and therefore the demand for the outputs of public expenditure. However, there has been little evidence to date of a comprehensive strategy of charges (e.g. toll roads), and there is a history of abolition of specific charges (e.g. rates, university and third-level fees), pushing the cost back to the general taxpayer.

The extent of the public budget will depend on both the goods that citizens demand and the resources available to government to supply them. The demand for goods depends crucially on the price that is charged for them. To the extent that government provides goods and services without charge this obviously increases the demand for them and for the resources to supply them. On the other hand, the introduction of charges or contributions would reduce demand for the product or service.

Then there is the consideration of funding: whether it is provided wholly or partly from taxation, whether and how it is subsidised, whether it is commercially provided, whether it is an entitlement or a transfer. These considerations are probably the essential elements in the framework for future consideration of public expenditure.

Conclusion

Public expenditure is the colossus of domestic economic policy. Directly under the control of government, its management remains the pivotal tool of economic management. For the future it requires ever-closer attention to ensure that the public expenditure strategy is optimised to achieve the community's economic and social goals in the most effective way.

This essay's review of the government budget suggests certain concerns for the future. First among these is the government's share in the economy. The jury is out on whether the share of public expenditure will be contained in the future but there is little doubt about the importance of this issue. The requirements of competitiveness and the voracious appetite for public expenditure are pulling in opposite directions. In his essay in this volume Peter Sutherland has stressed the significance for future economic performance of the ability to adapt and, *inter alia*, reduce the size of the state sector.

The inexorable growth of public expenditure was reversed in the late 1980s in Ireland, but since the early 1990s has been resumed. Furthermore, public expenditure has become increasingly current in character. Forces restraining public expenditure in the years immediately ahead include pressures of competition for internationally mobile investment, the provisions of the Stability and Growth Pact and the requirements of EMU, and voter pressure to reduce taxation. On the other hand, factors that are fostering public expenditure growth include not only the formidable interests of social equity and redistribution, but the myriad of pressure groups seeking special advantage at the expense of the tax-payer. More resources will be needed to deal with crime and to pay for increasingly costly health care, especially for the growing numbers of the elderly. The mechanisms of social, political and economic dialogue will need careful attention and development if society's interest in prosperous and sustainable development is to be achieved.

The reduced emphasis on capital expenditure in the government's budget is a striking aspect of this review. The role of government in relation to the medium to longer term capital needs of the economy will need more systematic attention in the future. Is the strategy of progressive relative disengagement of the exchequer from capital investment and provision sustainable if the opportunities of the present are to be harnessed to ensure the physical and human capital foundations for the early twenty-first century? Three conclusions are drawn in this regard. First, because of its long-term nature and its critical importance to economic progress, capital investment may require more and not less attention in the future. Second, much more attention is required to ensure more efficient delivery of the capital stock needed for national development through commercialisation of services, competition, privatisation as appropriate and regulation. Third, the social partnership mechanism may need to be adjusted to give greater weight to the planning and provision of the capital and infrastructure necessary for future development, whether sectoral, infrastructural or social in character. It is essential that the short-term requirements of consensus do not undermine its longer term sustainability. The link between government investment and national saving and investment also deserves particular attention in this planning framework.

The current budget has been dominated by the expansion of social support programmes and public sector pay. The growth in social programmes is analysed in some detail in Finola Kennedy's essay. The growth in public sector pay reflects, in large part, the employment content of services such as education and health. For the future it is likely that there will be more and not less demand for these services. The future role of the public service in their provision will ultimately depend on the flexibility and comparative efficiency and productivity of the service providers and on their ability to meet effectively the needs of the citizen/customer. Achieving the best results and value for resources invested, publicly and privately, should be the criterion for managing such expenditures.

An adverse change in economic fortunes will present a crucial test for the consensus approach to economic management. Nowhere will this challenge be more apparent than in the approach to any necessary adjustment of public expenditure and in the related area of taxation change. Careful strategic preparations should be made for the inevitable cyclical downturn, through retention of budget surpluses in good times, the establishment of income-earning asset funds or a systematic approach to providing for contingent liabilities. This should make the process of adjustment substantially less disruptive and painful.

Public expenditure must not be exempt from the model that has been successful in other areas – tolerance and openness to new and different ideas, especially ideas not shared by dominant political, social and administrative 'elites', and proactive encouragement of the capacity to question, challenge and construct new approaches and ways of thinking and operating. It would be ironic if the forces that combined so success-fully to achieve present prosperity were themselves intolerant of initi-atives and changes that may be necessary to sustain success in the future.

REFERENCES

Arrow, K. J. (1951). *Social Choice and Individual Values*, New York: John Wiley and Son

Ebrill, Liam P. (1996). 'Some Issues Concerning the Scale of Public Expenditure', paper delivered to the eleventh annual conference of the Foundation for Fiscal Studies, Dublin, October

Honohan, P. T. (1992). 'Fiscal Adjustment in Ireland in the 1980s', *Economic and Social Review*, Vol. 23, No. 3, pp. 285–314

Information Society Steering Committee (Forfás) (1996). *Information Society Ireland*, Dublin: Forfás

National Economic and Social Council (1996). *Strategy into the 21st Century*, Report No. 98, Dublin: National Economic and Social Council

OECD, *Economic Review and Outlook*, various years, Paris: OECD

OECD (1995), *New Orientations for Social Policy*, Paris: OECD

Whitaker, T. K. (1958). *Economic Development*, Dublin: Stationery Office

Whitaker, T. K. (1983). *Interests*, Dublin: Institute of Public Administration

5

The Organic Role of Taxation

MIRIAM HEDERMAN O'BRIEN

Introduction

CIVILISATIONS have been founded, sustained and ultimately undermined by their capacity to fund their administrations and their wars. The policy of extracting tribute in wealth rather than in lives marked the kind of culture which tended to survive and leave records for posterity. It may have coexisted with brutality but it offered a form of social contract between the governors and the governed which reached its European apex in the canons of Roman law. It has been absorbed into our concepts of citizenship and good government.

Modern taxes, defined as obligatory payments to the state, not directly related to benefits received and controlled by legislation, are descended from the duties, tolls and levies imposed on the governed since history began.

More recent examples of the effect of fiscal policy on society are found in both the development of republicanism and democracy on the one hand and the autocratic systems which they overthrew on the other. Popular history has impressed on us that not only was taxation (indirect) the proximate cause of the rebellion of the American colonies against England but that income tax (direct) was introduced into these islands as a temporary measure to pay for the war against the French. But the Franco-British war in America had a more profound effect on France and Europe than Anglophones are likely to remember. In *Citizens*, Simon Schama has used the definition of 'privilege' by tax exemption to provide a new understanding of the hostility against the nobility, the clergy and certain bourgeois office-holders enjoying immunity from taxes which flourished in Bourbon France.[1]

Citizens and governments in the latter part of the eighteenth century learned that punishments do not operate effectively against determined and widespread resistance. Whipping, branding, the galleys or even death by breaking on the wheel were not enough to stop the evasion of taxes or smuggling throughout Europe. Nor were the fruits of payment of taxes seen as conveying any particular benefit on taxpayers once a sufficiently large number of people declined to pay.

In the twentieth century even totalitarian regimes have respected the principle of a contract whereby a return is given for the wealth collected by the state. The extent of that 'return' may be unsustainable, or inequitable, or its nature may be masked, which will expose the regime to internal threat. But the obligation of the state towards its citizens is acknowledged in some form.

The idea of the taxpayer's *agreement* to pay is an essential element of a successful tax system. A contract between the state and its citizens about the way in which revenue is raised and spent is fairly explicit in democracy as we know it. Some political cultures carefully nurture the civic aspect of taxation. Such an approach is not historically part of the Irish tradition and an appreciation of the cost to the compliant taxpayer of those who evade their fair contribution is a recent and welcome development.

As far as faults inherent in any system of taxation are concerned, governments rely on a level of apathy on the part of the population. The electoral process however, even in countries which lack a particular civic commitment, ensures a constant and critical opposition to policies of taxation and expenditure. Unfortunately, such opposition is only rarely related to the objective flaws in the system. It is more closely allied to the strength of organised lobbies and the perceived electoral advantage in attacking taxation in any form.

'Acceptable' policies on taxation and expenditure reflect the priorities of the culture in which they operate. They are also driven by expediency. It has been found that a combination of taxes which relies on different sources of revenue is more satisfactory than a system which is based solely on one major tax, be it direct or indirect.

Revenue needs may lead governments to disrupt the equilibrium of taxpayers' contributions in areas where either it is difficult to measure the immediate effect or there is likely to be least political resistance. As a result, exceptions have to be introduced subsequently to ameliorate hardship or to drive policy objectives. These exceptions, in turn, re-distribute taxation and alter its impact. It is extremely difficult to withdraw fiscal privilege from categories of activity or special types of taxpayers. As a result, such privileges may be eroded but tend to remain in the system. Existing anomalies are used as an argument for introducing further anomalies, so that the clichéd 'level playing field' to which so many refer would resemble a deeply ploughed arena if all their pleas were granted. Fiscal privilege can only be effectively and fairly altered as part of a fundamental overhaul of the entire fiscal system.

A pure capitalist economy would have a skeletal tax system in tandem with minimalist public expenditure which would be limited to a strictly defined area of state activity, mainly defence. Examination of economies described as 'capitalist', however, shows a different picture.

The misuse of the term 'free market' to describe economies such as those of the US, Japan, Australia, New Zealand and most of Western Europe may give the impression that their markets are 'free'. The growth of regulation and of consumer and sectoral lobby-power together with the availability of technology to control access has made them strictly regimented and controlled markets. They are also competitive. Highly regulated and highly competitive economies create markets where the ability to comply with regulation (including the fiscal require-ments) and administrative efficiency become part of the competitive struggle.

The confusion created by the expression 'free market' has been compounded by repetition of the formula that the 'free market of itself brings about democracy which, in turn, leads to prosperity'. This formula was particularly popular with politicians such as Margaret Thatcher and Presidents Ronald Reagan and George Bush. Directed at countries formerly in the Soviet bloc, this simplistic doctrine, which would be unacceptable to the electorates of the leaders concerned, has been the source of many of the problems of the disenchanted citizens of Russia and countries to its east and west. Its promise of automatic political and economic success has a powerful appeal as an alternative to the control of all sources of wealth and production by the state. Unfor-tunately, it totally ignores the complex reality of competing freedoms and implicitly denies both the existence of a social contract between state and citizens and the increased need for taxation as the source of state funding in the absence of state ownership.

Taxation is the lifeblood of private enterprise: without it the state can-not even afford to provide security for its citizens unless it takes into its own ownership the main sources of national wealth.

Interaction of taxation and expenditure is at the heart of modern politics. The unacceptability of private affluence and public squalor (and vice versa) varies according to electorates but no democracy has yet accepted a completely market-driven economy. We live in 'mixed' rather than 'free market' economies and usually blame the proportions of that mix for any social or economic disadvantages which we perceive or experience. This helps to explain why fiscal fashions arise and become popular and eventually change.

The Irish tax system has evolved from the British model; it operates in the context of the rules and regulations of the European Union; it is expected to provide the funds to run the country and to pay for the social and political priorities of the electorate. Since Ireland became a member of the European Union its fiscal system has gained a European dimension – with regard to both taxation and the receipts of European funding.

As might be expected of a member of the OECD, the Irish tax system includes the usual mix of revenues: indirect taxation – value added tax and excise duties (customs revenue which was available prior to 1973 is now part of the European Union revenue flow and is also significantly in decline in the context of the development of the EU); direct taxation – income tax, social security taxes and corporation tax; capital taxes; property taxes, including a varying form of tax on residential property and rates on commercial properties (rates on residential property and on agricultural land as a form of local authority financing were abolished by government during the past twenty years); stamp duties; motor vehicle duties; health contributions and employment and training levies.

The framework and level of these components of the tax system have changed under successive governments and have been affected by factors ranging from failure to upgrade and modernise the rating system on domestic dwellings to the impact of free mobility of capital on the structure of capital taxation.[2]

Taxes have to be considered in tandem with the system of grants and allowances in almost every sphere of activity before the *effective rate of taxation* on any activity or source of income can be determined. This complex interrelationship pervades every modern economy, including Ireland.

As Ireland has evolved politically and had to compete internationally, its taxation system has had to face new demands. It has therefore been the subject of analysis, review, comment and change. There have been two independent enquiries into the Irish tax system, each appointed at a particular crisis in Irish fiscal and economic development.

Irish commissions on taxation

Mr Justice Cearbhall Ó Dálaigh chaired two commissions of enquiry relating to taxation: one into taxation on industry in 1953 (which reported in 1956) and the other into income taxation, appointed in 1957. The latter made seven reports to the Minister for Finance, the final report being submitted in 1962. These reports recommended, *inter alia,* substantial changes in the tax treatment of depreciation and capital allowances for industry and the introduction of Pay As You Earn (PAYE) for the taxation of wages and salaries. Most of the recommendations were adopted within two years of the publication of the reports.

The reports of the Commission on Income Tax were followed by two White Papers which dealt with the implications of the proposed changes, and this official response stimulated discussion and debate.

The Ó Dálaigh commissions were established at a time when Irish industry needed to prepare to meet the challenge of competition from abroad on the previously protected Irish market and when income tax had to be modernised to cope with the vastly increased numbers of taxpayers. They led to a much better system of taxation.

The improvements introduced as a result of the Ó Dálaigh commissions were eroded over the ensuing twenty years, mainly by annual impositions of unrelated and contradictory measures and by the perverse effects of inflation.

A Commission on Taxation under the chairmanship of Miriam Hederman O'Brien was established in 1980 against a background of serious voter unrest, large 'tax marches' of PAYE workers in 1979 and the erosion of real income gains through high levels of inflation. Its terms of reference specified an enquiry into the 'present *system*' (emphasis mine) of taxation to

> recommend such changes as appear desirable and practicable so as to achieve an equitable incidence of taxation, due attention being paid to the need to encourage development of the national economy and to maintain an adequate revenue yield.

The terms of reference addressed:

1. equity, or fairness with which to make the system acceptable
2. economic development with which to sustain the country and improve its prosperity
3. adequate revenue yield to enable the state to fulfil its obligations to its citizens.

The Commission on Taxation produced five reports between 1982 and 1985 as follows:

1. *Direct Taxation*
2. *Direct Taxation – The Role of Incentives*
3. *Indirect Taxation*
4. *Special Taxation*
5. *Tax Administration.*

No official response to any of the reports of the 1980 Commission on Taxation in the form of a White Paper on the subject of taxation was issued and the implementation of the recommendations of the five reports was uneven. This reaction is in contrast with the response to the Ó Dálaigh commissions' reports.

The thrust of the First Report, which dealt with all forms of direct taxation, personal and corporate, was to recommend a tax system which would deliver revenue according to the principles set out in the terms of reference. It identified the current system as 'unfair, muddled and complicated' and it made recommendations which, it claimed, would offer substantial improvements on all counts. It was radical insofar as it proposed a coherent system of direct taxation, with a single rate charged on all income arising in the personal and corporate sectors and a widening of the tax base. This approach was not widely followed in the subsequent debate which centred on details of its proposals.

The Second Report dealt with incentives in the direct tax system and set out criteria against which they should be monitored and judged. There has been some movement to streamline incentives in line with changing policy requirements in recent years but others have been introduced which would not bear scrutiny under the principles laid down by the commission.

Many reforms in the direction recommended by the Third Report on indirect taxation were adopted. The number and spread of rates were reduced and the tax base was extended. These changes were in line with subsequent regulations of the European Union.

The Fourth Report, dealing with special taxation (including local taxation) and taxation of special areas and activities (covering national property tax, taxation and the environment, mining and mineral development, and the taxation of charities), has been frequently cited in other studies since its publication in May 1985. The issues of local and residential property taxation were obscured by fundamental and unresolved questions about local government itself and a reluctance to tackle mandatory charges and other contentious matters in a coherent framework. The recommendations in these areas were not adopted. The commission approach to environmental taxes, on the other hand, which calls for an effective mix of taxation and regulation, has been broadly followed, particularly in the areas of heating and transport fuels.

The Fifth Report, dealing with administration, which recommended, *inter alia*, the introduction of self-assessment, has been largely adopted. The Revenue Commissioners implemented major improvements which some critics of the commission had claimed would never work in Ireland. As a result, the system of tax administration in Ireland has been transformed and now leads most of its EU partners (and competitors) in the fields of efficiency and good taxpayer relations.[3]

The trend of tax legislation since the 1980s has been shown to be somewhat erratic.[4] Corporation tax (the subject of the First and Second Reports) has been rationalised, largely as recommended, and its more unusual incentives have been attenuated while allowances have been aligned more closely to the concept of taxing the real return on investment, i.e. profit. The gap between the 10 per cent tax rate on profits from manufacturing, widely defined, and that on profits from other activity has been somewhat narrowed but the difference remains significant.

Many anomalies which formerly existed in direct taxation have been reduced or even removed but some new ones have been created. The chimera of adjusting the tax system to provide for all economic and social goals, including prosperity and full employment, remains in the political psyche. It is supported by the natural desire of special interest groups to lobby for favourable treatment through the tax system in order to achieve the maximum return for their members.

The conscious changes in the tax system, as enunciated by successive Irish Ministers for Finance, have been in the direction of improved efficiency and simplification, with a priority to decrease the relative burden on those at the lower end of the income scale.[5] One of the most stubborn obstacles to this end has been the interaction of the tax and social security systems, whereby simplifications in the income tax system are undermined by a system of Pay-Related Social Insurance (PRSI) which is complicated and has been shown to bear more heavily on those with lower incomes.[6] More efficient administration has been accompanied by an increase in the number of fiscal privileges, some small, some considerable, which have maintained the complexity of the system and have continued the high cost-level of compliance and administration.

Other changes have been dictated by the requirements of harmonisation within the European Union, particularly where regulations have prevented specially favourable treatment of indigenous enterprises or individuals over those from other member states.

Some of the less conscious tax changes have been influenced by outside forces, particularly the general climate generated by improvements in the fiscal systems of other countries.

One of the most significant changes, whether conscious or unconscious, has been the change in attitude to what is called the 'incidence of taxation', i.e. who bears the tax at the end of all the transactions which may be involved. The First Report commented that: '... except in the case of agriculture and business in the unsheltered sector, there may be considerable scope for the shifting of tax burdens in Ireland ...' There has been a much better appreciation in the past five to ten years of where the burden of any tax really lies and of the link between wages, income taxes and the level of other taxes.

Reports since the completion of the Commission on Taxation

Several serious studies undertaken since 1985 have either supported the general line taken by the Commission on Taxation or indicated measures which are broadly in agreement with its thrust. The National Economic and Social Council (NESC), representing the social partners, in its report *A Strategy for the Nineties* published in 1990 recommended reform of taxation as a central element of its proposals for strategic policy. It returned to the theme in *A Strategy for Competitiveness, Growth and Employment* published in 1993. The NESC reports stressed the need to combine social and economic needs with an acceptable level of equity in the tax and social systems. They recommended a wide tax base combined with a clearly targeted expenditure policy. Targeting should be done openly on the spending side and not through the creation of anomalies and hidden subsidies in the tax system.

Other reports were concerned with more specific areas of activity. In 1992, the Report of the Industrial Policy Review Group, chaired by Jim Culliton, contained a practical recipe for improving the effectiveness of the state-sponsored sector. It also advised that the tax system should be reformed in line with the recommendations of the Commission on Taxation in order to facilitate the other improvements which it identified as necessary.

The report of Forfás, the policy advisory and co-ordination board for industrial development and science and technology in Ireland (created after the publication of the Culliton Report), entitled *Shaping Our Future*, published in 1996, warned against complacency in the context of current revenue buoyancy. It addressed not only the level of taxation but also that of public spending. This naturally leads to consideration of taxation policy; the report recommended a further widening of the tax base for both direct and indirect taxes.

Eleven years after the Fifth (and final) Report of the Commission on Taxation, Forfás stated:

> A great many tax incentives have been introduced on an ad hoc basis, resulting in an overall system which lacks coherence, is difficult to administer efficiently and effectively, and promotes a thriving non-productive tax-avoidance 'industry'.

The Forfás report grasped the implications of its recommendations to reduce the higher rates of tax on corporate profits and personal income tax and duly addressed them. On the contentious subject of property taxes it said:

> While the issue is one of some controversy, the desirability of having a wider tax-base in Ireland and an improved system of local government financing makes it important to look at the whole area with objectivity and to consider some increase in property taxes, widely defined, in a way which relates taxation paid to the level of services provided and ability to pay.

Successive governments after 1985 cautiously accepted the *principles* of broadening the tax base and narrowing the range of incentives. Despite the support of these and other reports for tax reform, the emphasis continued to be on marginal redistribution of taxes. Implementation of tax strategy was uneven and individual areas of taxation continued to receive attention in turn, rather than together. There were many reasons for a piecemeal approach, some of which sprang from fear of the impact of what were considered far-reaching changes and others of which flowed directly from the traditional political party culture. Another contributing factor has probably been an assumption that tax concessions are 'costless' when compared with 'real expenditure'; they were therefore considered preferable.

The growth of democracy has not diminished the pressures exercised by organised groups on the legislature. On the contrary, it has strengthened the hand of the well-organised and the appeal of well-publicised demands over the needs of the community as a whole. The belief that tax can be 'fine-tuned' is attractive to special interests which would benefit from the 'tuning'. It spreads to political circles and is extended to trying to achieve a wide range of social, political and economic objectives which themselves possess inherent contradictions. Damage thus caused to the basic principles of equity and efficiency is then addressed by introducing remedial measures, which, in turn, add to the inequities and complexity of the tax system as a whole.

The political rhetoric of tax reform has receded in recent years as fiscal buoyancy has raised the possibility of realising the dream of every government – being able to increase expenditure while reducing taxation. The dream is heightened by the current flow of Structural Funds from elsewhere in Europe and no provision is made for when the funds start to flow in the opposite direction. Fortunately for our future, the prospect of Irish membership of a common European currency provides some element of constraint. The criteria to enter the 'Club' to which we aspire preclude a rising public debt in relation to GDP and help to enforce a measure of fiscal rectitude. Whether or not the euro materialises, Ireland must prepare for the twenty-first century when the level of external funds available will be lower and the services in place will have to be paid for mainly from national, internal sources.

Options for government

In the context of changes in taxation it is necessary to distinguish three approaches open to government:

1. alter, up or down, the general level of taxation
2. redistribute taxation, i.e. change the relative burden on certain categories of people and/or activities while maintaining the existing level
3. reform the tax system – which may or may not also involve the other two options.

Given the link which exists between the political process and taxation, no government will introduce deeply unpopular reforms unless forced to do so by external and drastic circumstances. Those who want improvements must, therefore, make proposals which are capable of winning acceptance from a wide constituency of interests among the electorate. It should also be understood, however, that such acceptance will be won only by a coherent strategy in which members of government believe.

The habit of legislating for the next election is ingrained but responsible politicians and administrators are extending the time-scale for fiscal strategy. The pressure for sound management and EU convergence supports this longer view. Under the provisions of the Stability and Growth Code, which will be required of member states entering the Economic and Monetary Union (EMU), Ireland (if it becomes a member) will be obliged to publish multiannual budgets. Even if this does not come about, there is little doubt that multiannual budgets and medium-term and long-term planning have been recognised in Ireland, as elsewhere, as necessary for effective state investment and efficient use of finite resources. To an increasing extent annual budgets are presented as part of a process of national fiscal strategy.

If it is accepted that the Irish fiscal system is flawed and that it is not merely neutral but actually inconsistent with some of the stated objectives of successive governments, it is necessary that it should be corrected. I have looked as widely as possible, but in vain, to find a serious study or analysis which supports the present Irish tax system as a vehicle for progress. Taking this negative search in conjunction with the conclusions of the studies mentioned above (plus many similar which have not been included for reasons of space), one is entitled to hope that responsible civil servants and other ministerial advisers will address the current situation and advise government and the public accordingly.

There are three options for Irish governments over the next five years:

(a) to follow a trend of adjusting taxation at the margins. This would involve minor changes and improvements but would not alter the components of the tax system or their relative impact.
(b) to pursue a consistent fiscal policy on an incremental basis. This would require a more explicit approach to gradually changing taxation (and expenditure).
(c) to identify aspects of comparative advantage in an effective, efficient national tax system and introduce them as part of a comprehensive overhaul or as (b) above.

If one takes the view that government actually wants to reform, i.e. improve, the tax system, then government must identify the reasons for such a policy. If the reports referred to earlier are correct, the shortcomings of the Irish tax system are handicaps which inhibit a progressive social policy and an efficient economic environment. This is quite a compelling reason for tackling tax reform. In addition, where government embarks on a major policy initiative, such as strengthening local government for example, the implications will require a change in the allocation of tax revenues and, more fundamentally, the raising of such revenues. Taxation should therefore be approached as a *system* so that changes or even improvements in one area will not lead to anomalies or distortions in another.

The political dilemmas of taxation

'Tax reform' is often used as an inaccurate description for tax reduction or tax redistribution.

Two constraints may make true tax reform difficult: the desire to have no 'losers' as a result of change and the need to ensure adequate revenue yield. When revenues are buoyant it is certainly easier to introduce tax reform by cushioning 'losers' in the inevitable redistribution and maintaining exchequer yields. It is also easier to reform if there is a dramatic crisis and the tax system has to be urgently, albeit painfully altered.

In order to ensure that the change contemplated is a real improvement on the existing system, reforms must be based on the implicit contract which I identified at the beginning of this essay.

The terms of reference of the Commission on Taxation identified three aspects of taxation which have to be reconciled in any democracy. The tax system should:

1. be seen to be fair
2. be efficient
3. produce enough revenue to enable government to fulfil its stated policy objectives ('adequate revenue yield').

Fairness has two components. The first is that those in similar circumstances should have to pay similar amounts of tax. This is the reason why tax privileges, since the time of the French revolution, have had such an unsettling effect on citizens. The second is a widely held perception that those who have significantly more wealth or income should pay appropriately more than those with the average or less. This perception underlies the principle of a 'progressive' tax system. It is not as self-evident as the first element of fairness but it is widely adopted in democratic societies.

Because the tax and expenditure systems are so interconnected in modern economies, the ultimate evaluation of the equity of a tax system must be based on the combined impact of revenue and expenditure policies. Failure to take this approach will result in erroneous comparisons, mistaken analysis and flawed argument. The expenditure system is a better vehicle to impart the desired degrees of progressivity and responsiveness into the fiscal system than is taxation (except for the imposition of a straightforward higher rate at the highest levels of income and wealth).

If a tax system is relatively *simple* it is also fairer: first, because it is easier to see its 'incidence' or who really bears the burden and secondly, because it will not place high compliance costs on ordinary taxpayers. It seems reasonable that the requirements of the revenue authorities should not be on a different plane of complexity to the effort needed to generate the income on which the tax is assessed.

Efficiency in the tax system avoids the misallocation of resources and imposes minimal dead-weight costs. It requires that tax measures should fulfil the aims for which they are intended. If a provision is intended to help those at the lower end of the income scale and actually gives a greater benefit to those at a high level it is inefficient from a policy point of view. Another element of efficiency, as of equity, is the operation of the system in a manner which does not place undue burdens of cost on the administration or on the taxpayer. The third element is that the tax system should not distort business and personal decisions in a way that diverts energy and resources into activity which is favoured by the tax system rather than into enterprise which is conducive to sound social and economic development.

What level of revenue is *adequate*? This is the issue on which govern-ments decide and political parties rise and fall. The fiscal system must allow for changes in external and internal circumstances and for differ-ent political views on the correct balance between public and private funding. It should not be operable only at a particular level of taxation or in the context of a particular level of public expenditure. It must be sufficiently stable and coherent to allow business and individuals to plan with some degree of security and yet be sufficiently flexible to accom-modate changes needed for economic or political reasons.

Efficiency and progressivity in income tax

Single rates of direct and indirect tax are remarkably efficient. They can be operated in tandem with a progressive expenditure system in a manner which ensures that whatever income and wealth distribution objective is desired can be achieved.

There is, however, a strong political commitment in many demo-cracies to an element of progressivity in the personal tax system itself. This is translated into varying rates of income tax as a means of dis-tributing more of the tax burden to the higher end of the scale of income and wealth and into heavier taxes on inheritances. As the rates become higher and more numerous the exemptions become larger and more complex.

The First Report of the Commission on Taxation in 1982 identified the unfairness and inefficiency of varying rates of taxation operating on a narrow tax base. The key finding of the commission was that imposing progessive rates of income tax made the adoption of a comprehensive income tax base impossible to achieve. High nominal rates of income tax did not produce effective distribution of income in Ireland or in other countries. It is therefore necessary to find a system which will combine:

- a wide tax base
- efficient operation
- some element of progressivity.

The present Irish tax system favours some forms of savings and invest-ments much more than others. Questions have been asked as to whether these are the types of savings and investments which most benefit the community and the economy, and whether they would have been the most appropriate for the savers and investors concerned if they had not been subject to tax privileges. The answers have rarely been an enthus-iastic endorsement of the current system.

Is it possible to combine a single rate of income tax, based on a very wide tax base, with a higher rate of tax on higher levels of income and wealth, leaving greater choice to taxpayers as to the forms of savings and investments which they favour? It is – but it is difficult to find a suitable name for such a system.

If there were a single rate of income tax on all income, with a comprehensive definition of income and agreed tax credits, the present higher rate of income tax could be transformed into an 'x' tax on incomes above a certain level. The 'x' tax, however, would only apply to income which was consumed and not to savings or investments. The 'x' tax would, therefore, supplant the existing higher rates of income tax, progressive taxation of gifts and inheritances, and the special tax treatment of some kinds of savings and investments. The 'x' tax would work roughly as follows:

- Income tax at a single, relatively low rate would be paid on all income, including capital gains, and the taxpayer would claim the tax credits allowed.
- Taxpayers with incomes deemed to be high enough would pay an additional amount of 'x' tax on all income above the determined threshold which was not invested or saved. Savings and investments would be shown each year and the 'x' tax would be paid whenever such savings and investments were realised and consumed.

It is not possible to give a full explanation of such a structure in a brief account such as the present one. (The issue and the problems of transition are explored in the First and Fifth Reports of the Commission on Taxation.)

The introduction of such a tax (akin to the 'cash flow income tax' in the US and the 'direct expenditure tax' described by Sven Olaf Lodin, quoted and adapted by the Commission on Taxation) would bring about fundamental improvements both in the efficiency of the Irish tax system and in the relation between taxation and the development of the economy. High earners would be enabled to accumulate capital to start a business or invest in enterprise without having to have recourse to complex tax avoidance which inhibits their initiative. Employers would be able to pay high achievers in salaries rather than in complicated schemes which are only remotely linked to real performance.

If the introduction of an 'x' tax led to 'oversaving' (an unlikely scenario but one which has been put forward as an argument against it), the situation could be adjusted by reducing the rate of the tax and the incentive to save.

Under such a system, political and economic debates would focus on the single rate of income tax, the level of tax credits and the distribution of revenue. The 'x' tax would bring in an element of progressivity into the system, while maintaining a simple and efficient administration for the vast bulk of income and the majority of taxpayers. It would be possible to align the rate of tax on personal and corporate income and thereby eliminate some of the anomalies which now exist between income earned in different ways.

A single rate of income tax, with an 'x' tax on high levels of wealth and income, would provide the wide tax base, efficient operation and the element of progressivity which have been identified as being important for an effective tax system.

In the context of membership of the European Union, which closely regulates indirect taxes and incentives, the competitive advantage of an efficient tax system with low costs of compliance and administration, incorporating a higher rate with an inherent bias towards enterprise and investment, would be considerable.

A remaining problem is finding an appropriate name for the 'x' tax. 'Direct expenditure tax', which is used in the literature and by the Commission on Taxation, confuses the public. One of its advocates in a wider form, Professor James Meade, won a Nobel Prize for his work. The person who finds a better name for the concept deserves at least fame and possibly fortune.

The competitive aspect of taxation

Countries in the early stages of economic development are often urged, usually by potential outside investors, to keep some taxes as low as possible in order to attract mobile capital and management expertise. It is only at a later stage that the problems of the sectors which have to make up the revenue shortfall become so acute that the strategy has to be revised. Finally, recognition is given to the need to operate a coherent tax system which rewards investment of time and energy into productive enterprise rather than tax avoidance.

The Forfás report *Shaping Our Future* set out the principles to 'create the optimum environment for enterprise development'. These include the following:

- the tax system should facilitate economic growth and employment creation
- the tax system should be fair so as to inspire public confidence and gain the necessary social cohesion that is essential for economic development

- tax bases should be as wide as possible
- the tax system, as a minimum, should not make it more difficult for firms to compete in domestic and international markets
- as a starting-point, the tax system should be neutral and incentives should be introduced only for good reasons in key areas in a way in which the benefits exceed the costs
- the balance of taxation should be shifted as far as possible from production in order to encourage employment and investment.

At times these principles may conflict but they establish a useful framework within which to construct a tax system that promotes enterprise which is competitive against European and international suppliers of goods and services.

The Irish tax system has certain advantages. Foremost among these are:

- a sophisticated and technologically advanced tax administration
- a tax administration which responds in a constructive fashion to genuine difficulties
- a reputation for favourable treatment of specialised areas of activity such as financial services and film-making which attracts the attention of those seeking a new location for such activities.

The Forfás report pointed out that:

> The tax system will need to adapt, more quickly than in the past, to changing economic circumstances. Ireland has, with certain exceptions, tended to react to developments in other countries rather than be pro-active. In the future, efforts should be made to ensure that:
>
> - Modern legislation is brought in quickly to cover emerging developments
> - An efficient system of advance rulings is introduced to provide greater certainty in tax treatment
> - More weight is accorded to the need to keep compliance costs low.

Where tax administrations take care with issues such as the tax compliance requirements for taxpayers, they can improve the quality of small and medium business as a significant if sometimes unexpected bonus. Good reporting procedures improve the information available to business, and a proper definition of profit can prevent new enterprises from making disastrous business decisions. A working partnership between the revenue authorities and taxpayers can become the basis of mutual learning to the benefit of enterprise and employment. This, in turn, gives a new understanding of taxation as a tool with a competitive edge.

The implications for democracy of integrating fiscal policy into social, economic and political decisions

There have been many changes affecting fiscal policy since the 1980s. Freer movement of capital, for example, has become a constraint on national fiscal autonomy. Dramatic developments in information technology have opened up options previously regarded as administratively impossible.

As far back as 1978 the National Understanding negotiated by the social partners factored in tax reductions in order to conclude a national agreement to achieve wage moderation. This approach to wage stability and inflation control has continued and was followed in the 1996 negotiations on the latest in a series of national agreements, Partnership 2000, with largely beneficial effects.

As changes occur, some sources of tax revenue are closed off and others are opened up. The new scenarios focus attention on links between revenues and their objectives and between tax revenues and the way in which they are spent. The linkage is vital if we want to strengthen the democratic credibility of our economies.

Under modern conditions, the power of the strong lobby groups needs to be counterbalanced by explanations of policy which appeal to the electorate on the basis of common sense and the common good. Roger Douglas, who as Minister for Finance successfully introduced the most radical reforms into the New Zealand system, explained that in order to bring about fundamental improvements, government must:

(a) be convinced that there is a serious problem
(b) know what it wants to do to rectify it
(c) introduce reforms in its first budget after election
(d) ensure that unpalatable measures are spread widely and can be followed by widespread benefits.

If this recipe is followed he promised that the advantages would begin to flow within two years, in time to win the next election. To introduce reforms piecemeal was to court defeat as each sector affected would concentrate on attacking government for the loss of its comparative advantage and commentators would identify anomalies which still persisted in other areas.

There are, however, two factors which militate against such a programme for Ireland. The first is the view that the Irish tax system is not so bad after all and that its improvement would not confer any particular competitive advantage on the economy as a whole. The second is a reluctance to decide on a policy of change which would require substantial explanation to the electorate. If the view of the Irish tax system as benign or, at worst, neutral is correct there is no need to change. If that view is not correct, we will face the next century with a self-inflicted handicap at the heart of our economy.

As a member of the European Union, Ireland has a say in the fiscal component of EU policies on a wide range of important issues ranging from the environment to freer trade. It would be reassuring to hear Irish policy-makers propound fiscal regimes which would benefit all member states, including Ireland. It would be even more heartening to learn that we led the field with an integrated approach to issues such as internal and external transport and the consumption of energy for example. These are areas in which we have a vital interest because of our geographical position and economic interests. There is a great deal more work to be done on the taxation of energy in all its forms in order to find the appropriate mix of tax and regulation which we need to achieve economic development without impoverishing future generations.

As the member states move more closely together, particularly in the context of EMU, it will become more difficult to vary direct or indirect tax rates. Since Ireland has opted to abolish any form of residential property tax (other than stamp duty which arises only on the transfer of second-hand houses), it has removed a potential source of tax income retained by other member states. We are therefore effectively indicating that we can match their expenditure without one of their sources of revenue.

This country is experiencing the most prosperous period in its history and is responsible for making the best use of this prosperity. At present it must be said that, despite the improvements noted here, the tax system does not enjoy full public confidence that it is fair. On an objective perusal of the system, tax bases are too narrow, particularly as regards income tax and VAT.

There are too many incentives, some of them pushing in opposite directions (e.g. house purchase and house rentals). The proliferation of incentives makes it difficult for taxpayers to know their entitlements, for government to assess their impact and for those who do not gear their business to maximise their tax gains to compete with those who do.

Because the 'tax wedge' (i.e. the difference between the gross and nett return after all obligatory payments of taxes, social security and levies have been paid) is still heavy on low and medium wages, it bears disproportionately on production and employment.

Since there will be little or no taxation of residential property, other than stamp duties, other taxes will have to be increased if the current tax revenue falters or if there is an increased need for expenditure. Given the constraints on the levels of capital and indirect taxation, this leaves government with the options of increasing income tax and/or imposing charges or levies.

The administrative and compliance costs of the tax system should be further reduced since they are a nett cost to the economy.

The tax system needs to be examined with intellectual rigour and honesty and to be tackled with courage. Such rigour and courage would constitute our greatest competitive advantage in the coming years. They would also reinforce the contract which exists and should be seen to exist between the Irish citizen and the state.

NOTES

1. Simon Schama, *Citizens: A Chronicle of the French Revolution*, Harmondsworth: Penguin, 1989.
2. For a description of the Irish tax system see Frances Ruane and Francis O'Toole, 'Tax Measures and Policy', in J. W. O'Hagan (ed.), *The Economy of Ireland: Policy and Performance of a Small European Economy*, Dublin: Gill & Macmillan, 1995.
3. Frank Cassells and Don Thornhill, 'Self Assessment and Administrative Tax Reform in Ireland', in Cedric Sandford (ed.), *Key Issues in Tax Reform*, Bath: Fiscal Publications, 1996.
4. Francis O'Toole, 'Tax Reform in Ireland Since the Commission on Taxation', *Journal of the Statistical and Social Inquiry Society of Ireland*, Vol. XXVII, Part 1 (1993–94), pp. 85–123.
5. John Kay, 'Tax Reform: A Perspective Longer than the Life of One Parliament', in *Papers of the Ninth Annual Conference of the Foundation for Fiscal Studies*, Dublin: Foundation for Fiscal Studies, 1994.
6. *Planning for Progress – Tackling Poverty, Unemployment and Exclusion*, Dublin: Justice Commission of the Conference of Religious of Ireland, 1997.

6

The North: Ruminations

DOUGLAS GAGEBY

THE North is, to many in the twenty-six-county Republic, simply a problem; maybe, it is barely an Irish place.

But the North includes some of the most beautiful country in the whole of the island, and its people are as warm and welcoming as anywhere else in the whole of the thirty-two counties.

Yet it has, in the course of even this century, been the scene and cause of horrors, crimes against humanity.

In 1996 people in the Republic were jolted by the Neil Jordan film *Michael Collins* into recognising the violence that had been part of life in the years around 1922 and the foundation of the Irish Free State.

It is not true to say that force settles nothing, but civil war always degrades and demeans, especially when women and children are the victims. Patrick Pearse and his colleagues in 1916 surrendered to spare the civilian population of Dublin further loss of life.

Perhaps we are moving slowly into an era where there dawns the conviction that the problem with the North is less in lines drawn on maps than in bringing people to see that living together, peaceably, respecting each other's traditions should be the first and main objective.

Let no one on this island forget that the problem of today, in the North, did not start with 1969.

In the terrible year of 1935, when rioting broke out in Belfast on a huge scale, with many deaths, there was one cool calm healing voice, often raised.

It was from John Frederick MacNeice, then Bishop of Down. He said: 'We are here, in the providence of God, Protestants and Roman Catholics, side by side in a small country. It must be that we are here not to destroy one another, but, while we have opportunity, to help one another, and to remember always that to all who bear Christ's name, there has been committed a ministry of reconciliation.'

The same man said: 'I call Ireland our beloved country. No man is to be more pitied than the man who has no country, or the man who is not sure what his country is.'

These were the words of a generous man, calling not for an exclusive nationalism, but for a generous patriotic spirit, a simple love of country. He was one of the few voices of the Protestant side in the thirties to warn of the tensions and of the desperation building up in Belfast before the devastating riots and killings of July 1935.

His was a great voice of liberalism and compassion, especially of compassion. He was not popular in those circles where political conformism in regard to unionism was held to be almost an article of Christian faith. He was born in Omey Island, County Galway.

It is hardly necessary to quote the bishop to assert that Irish men and women of every stripe and of every sect or no sect at all love the land of their birth; love it and express love of it. Or their corner of this island, at any rate. Patriotism, I think, begins with the parish or even the townland. Love that, and much follows.

The bishop was also saying in many of his sermons and speeches: Do not despise anyone, do not reject anyone. For to despise anyone is to degrade that person. We have seen how in Germany of a few generations ago, Jews and other categories were first despised, their human qualities derided, then on to dehumanising them, calling them subhuman creatures, of a lower order. Not indeed 'people like us'.

Only under intense propaganda to that end could the intelligent and artistically gifted German people have been led to acquiescing in, or at least turning their eyes away from, mass bureaucratic slaughter.

I do not for a minute think that the Irish people could be brought to such a state of mind, but to despise and reject and deride is far enough down the slippery slope to go.

We have seen in recent times in the North derision being expressed about other people's religion. That too is a slippery slope.

We are good at forgetting. We are good at emphasising our differences rather than seeking out and cultivating an appreciation of all that we have in common. Often we *like* to forget.

People talk of the Pan-Nationalist Front, the Pan-Unionist Front. Do we hear of the Pan-Christian Front?

And how much, at our very worst, are we alike, North and South. When factionalism breaks out over some religious or social question, we like to forget that the orthodox Catholic view, or even the right-wing Catholic view, is so similar to the more vociferous Northern Protestant view.

For example, the furore in the Republic in the early nineties about the X case and abortion was paralleled by the demonstrators from the Protestant side in the North agitating on the streets of Belfast against the setting up of Brooke Clinics for sexual instruction.

And we were good at forgetting until quite recently – or rather not forgetting, simply blindly overlooking – the fact that so many Irishmen from what is now the Republic fought in the First World War and in the Second World War. Collins died in the arms of Emmet Dalton, who had served in the British army.

You may say that ecumenism has produced some laudable organisations and purposeful leaders, but in a country where the Christian gesture of a clergyman in wishing his opposite number, a Catholic priest, a Happy Christmas, as happened a few years ago, can provide a ticket out of Ireland, where a congregation can be gunned down in its own church building, when killings hand to hand are so frightful that the perpetrators are known as the Butchers – how about the teaching and performance of the churches?

Only the ecumenism of individual effort seems to matter.

Not long before he resigned his bishopric to take up a theological teaching post in Britain (1 April 1973) the then Church of Ireland Bishop of Clogher the Right Rev. Dr Richard Hanson said that all the major religious denominations in Northern Ireland had long ago bartered their integrity and independence to political ideologies in return for the support of their people. 'The churches themselves are now one of the main sources of sectarianism, if only they would realise it', he said.

He declared that, by and large, whether the Orange Order intended it or not, it did stand for religious division. And he pointed out that his own church, the Church of Ireland, was deeply involved in that Order: 'Of the forty-three clergy in my diocese, about 50 per cent are members, and 99 per cent are prepared to take Orange services. It is not because they sympathise with the Order, but some of them are simplistic enough to see their action as a form of human sympathy which gets them closer to their people. Their theology is something that no rational man could believe.'

Some of the churches in his diocese, he said, ran up Orange flags in July. But he was not in a position to take them down. 'I am a typical church leader, impotent.'

As to the power and place of the Orange Order, here is a small example. Terence O'Neill, some time later, told me that on the morning of the famous Lemass visit to Stormont in 1965, no one outside his close circle of advisers at Stormont knew. But he did inform one person just hours before the arrival: he telephoned the Grand Master of the Orange Order informing him of what was happening.

Lemass was accompanied by Ken Whitaker, who has been at the centre of so much accomplishment in Irish life that volumes could be, and will be, written about him.

I said earlier that only the ecumenism of individual effort matters.

We don't need to abandon our own beliefs. We don't need to step out of our normal persona to go to meet our fellow man. And it is not just a matter of studying the other versions of history apart from our own. It is a matter of finding out what goes on in the other person's mind. What he or she fears. What makes the people on the other side proud of their inheritance. What they resent in yours.

Don't regard this as doing good, if it embarrasses you, but you owe it to yourself from the point of view of intellectual curiosity. Don't take the myths. Seek out the person. The myths on your side about the other side can be the motive for some lunatic gunmen to cut loose. Again, look to the build-up in Germany of lies about the Jews, lies about the Poles, as inferior races.

What makes you think that God favours your sect or tribe over the others? That you are more one of God's creations than they are? That attitude is not only presumptuous, odiously exclusive; it could be blasphemy. And it is often murderous.

Both those who call themselves republicans and those who call themselves Protestant unionists are very far from the theme of the Young Irelanders 150 years ago, and the urge for peace among them and the common bond of being Irish.

Thomas Davis wrote:

> What matter that at different shrines
> We pray unto one God?
> What matter that at different times
> Your fathers won this sod.

There were certainly planters in the seventeenth century. There were planters when the Celts displaced or disposed of the earlier inhabitants of this island. Many who were called planters were lords, in a backstreet in Belfast, of about 4 square yards behind the house, where the privy and the coal (when they had coal) were situated.

Bishop MacNeice's 'beloved country' is indeed a fascinating country with a fascinating diversity of people. It is a country of great humanity and generosity. This is hard to accept if you live in conditions which so many people in the North have lived in for so many years. But it is so.

And yet in the North there are those who know only 'their own kind'. I don't want to live my life entirely among 'my own kind', i.e. people of my own religion. And as a Protestant living in the Republic I do not regard myself as a minority man. I am one of the totality of the people of this island.

I said before that the people of the North are among the most hospitable of people on earth. I remember when *The Irish Times* started, in the sixties, to enlarge its coverage of the North, we wondered how reporters from the Southern side of the border would feel about being asked to go to Belfast for a long spell. The answer is that there was a queue for the jobs. They loved Belfast, they loved the people. They wondered why they hadn't heard this side of the North before.

Protestants in the North worry about the 'Romanism' of legislation in the South and in the South generally. The truth is that all of us on this island are, or have been, thoroughly soaked in religion. Protestant and Catholic. I remember in Belfast when one of the most frequent questions put to you, sometimes even by people you didn't know well, was 'Are you saved?' None of their business, you might think. Being saved, running one-man religions, is the North's answer, if you like, to the extreme orthodoxy of some of their Catholic neighbours.

Things are changing. Perhaps not as much as we think. But if you look into the unionist mentality, the number one persona with which unionists are concerned is not the Queen of England, or the Prime Minister of England, but the Pope. The Pope is ever-present. I remember a Protestant journal which used to explain that the Pope and Stalin were at one in planning the downfall of Protestant Ulster.

Violence did not start in 1969. My father and mother had brought me to Belfast from Dublin in 1922, my father returning to the city he had left about twenty-five years before because, as he said, he never had enough to eat in his father's house. My father liked to walk home after work. He called, on his way, into a pub or two. When we lived in Alliance Avenue, now in Ardoyne, he would come via the Crumlin Road or Old Park Road. Every few days he would casually say that some poor devil had been shot in such and such a place; that a pub had had its windows smashed; that a house had been set on fire; that a policeman had been attacked at another place – all the time incidents throughout the twenties and thirties which barely were worth mention in the papers.

In the earlier days in Belfast, our house bordered on miles and miles of green fields. I remember once being awakened suddenly in the night by the sound of feet running along the pavement. I woke up, then one of the footsteps softened, going onto the grass. The second stopped short. 'Halt or I fire', said a loud voice, just under my window. A shot rang out; I heard no cry or a second shot. I went asleep. I didn't even ask next morning what it was about. It wasn't a nightmare.

Belfast, in those days, was a place of dreadful hunger and deprivation. Men used to pass our house in thin blue suits and white chokers; pale, many consumptive, they walked in a circle from The Bone, Havana Street, around our avenue and back, some trailing whippets. Thin, ill-nourished men. As bad as any conditions in the Irish countryside of the previous century.

This was one of the awful legacies of industrial Belfast, perhaps one of the contributing factors to so much of its ferocity.

Have we worked our way through much of the planned and casual savagery of the last few generations in the North?

John Hume in his recent book *Personal Views: Politics, Peace and Reconciliation in Ireland* tells us: 'No instant package will wipe away the damage done over the centuries. But I am absolutely certain that the agreement will eventually emerge. The healing process must begin. The old prejudices and hatreds will progressively dissolve. The new Ireland of the twenty-first century will emerge out of that process. It will not, in all likelihood, conform to any of our traditional models.'

Does anyone believe in an instant solution? I doubt it. 'Brits Out'; and what of 'Irish Out' of Britain, our sons and daughters and nephews and nieces we have sent over there because they couldn't find work here? Or who, just fed up in the North with the old wrangles and old labels, simply quit?

The truth is that it is possible to break or loosen or ease political ties between the islands, and I believe that will come, but we will never disentangle the social and familial threads arising from so much emigration.

I remember in County Galway a man came to work on a house I was staying in. He spoke Irish and good English with his own western accent. His young grandson, about eight or nine years old, who was with him, spoke pure Cockney.

A few years ago a Northern Ireland civil servant made a study of forms of association between groups of islands and countries. I don't re-member the details, but do remember that the solution which might emerge could go under the acronym of IONA – Islands of the North Atlantic.

If there is a will for an easier association between these islands, with dual citizenship or any other safeguards for those who require such, lawyers and diplomats can work out the technical details. If there is a will, that is, and perhaps a little inspiration – perhaps a Christian inspiration.

We are as entitled as are the people of England to peace on our own island.

We had a short burst of working together in the North during the power-sharing executive in 1974. Both unionist and nationalist elements in that government knew that it worked, and spoke out saying that it worked. Brian Faulkner, formerly the ogre, became the trusted and hard-working friend and colleague of men who could hardly believe the transformation they were experiencing – within themselves as well as within the men they were proud now to hail as comrades.

We had better see to it that we do not make any more miscalculations like the one that brought down that wonderful adventure.

And one miscalculation can be that the gun, at some stage, will tip the balance. It won't, from either side here, or from Britain. Many of the people who sided with the forces which wiped out that power-sharing experiment must have had doubts since. We are looking for an Ireland with respect for diversity on the lines that Davis and his comrades sought for, so very long ago.

Back to the man from Omey Island who took a bold look into the future. Talking of the people of Belfast he said: 'I have known them long and loved them much. I long to see Belfast the freest place in Ireland. May there be given to us a version of our city, as it might be, a city of justice, a city of plenty, a city of peace, where all success should be founded on service and all honour given to nobleness alone ...'

A personal and green note. When Jimmy O'Dea, that great comedian and observer, if not historian, of our people, came to Belfast, he used to bring down the roof of the old Empire Theatre with this last line to one of his sketches. 'Sure', he would say, 'isn't the grass in County Antrim as green as it is in Kerry.' Thunderous, continuous applause.

I always wanted to go back stage and say 'Mr O'Dea, in Antrim it's greener.'

Part II

Challenges of Social Policy

7

The Course of the Irish Welfare State

FINOLA KENNEDY

Introduction

IN 1996 there were 870,000 recipients of a weekly social welfare payment in Ireland. When adult and child dependants are taken into account 1.5 million people, or 41 per cent of the total population, benefited from a weekly social welfare payment. There had been an increase of 140,000, or nearly 20 per cent, since 1990, just six years previously. Forty-six years previously, in 1950, there were 330,000 recipients of social welfare payments; recipients and dependants amounted to 21 per cent of the population. While expenditure on social welfare in 1950 was just 5 per cent of gross national product (GNP), in 1995 total expenditure on social welfare amounted to £4.2 billion; it accounted for 29 per cent of gross current public expenditure and 12.4 per cent of GNP. The growth in both the number of recipients and expenditure testifies to a greatly enlarged welfare state. In addressing the future of the welfare state, this essay proceeds in three stages. Firstly, it examines the growth of the welfare state in Ireland. Secondly, it highlights how the core assumptions on which the provision of payments in the welfare state is based – namely the norm of full employment, and a traditional family structure with a breadwinner male and dependent wife and children – have changed. Thirdly, in the context of the changes presented, the essay focuses on the main challenges to social welfare policy at the beginning of the twenty-first century, taking account of our membership of the European Union.

Growth in the welfare state

For the purposes of this essay attention centres on those services provided under the aegis of the Department of Social Welfare during the fifty years of its existence since its establishment on 22 January 1947.

These services form the core of the Irish welfare state. During those fifty years (up to the 1997 general election, when Dermot Ahern was assigned the newly titled portfolio of Social, Community and Family Affairs), thirteen men and two women have held the Social Welfare portfolio, six of them on more than one occasion, and in the case of one minister, Dr Michael Woods, on five occasions. There have been nine Fianna Fáil ministers, four Labour Party ministers, one Fine Gael minister, Gemma Hussey, who held the portfolio for thirteen months, and one Democratic Left minister, Proinsias De Rossa. These ministers, as members of their respective governments, have held ultimate responsibility for the development of social welfare provision, the most obvious manifestation of the growth of the welfare state in Ireland.

The payments made by the Department of Social Welfare fall into two broad categories: social assistance and social insurance. Social assistance payments are means tested while social insurance payments are based on a contributions system. The 1908 Old Age Pensions Act first provided for old age pensions payable at 70 years, subject to a means test, while in 1911 the National Insurance Act introduced compulsory social insurance for unemployment and sickness benefit. The assistance and insurance services developed slowly during the first half of the century. Innovations included the introduction of unemployment assistance in 1933, widow's and orphan's pensions in 1935 and a universal scheme of children's allowances in 1944. By 1947, when there were a total of 295,000 recipients of social insurance and social assistance payments, the great majority, 81 per cent, received assistance payments (Table 1). By 1966 payments were equally divided between insurance and assistance. The relative importance of insurance grew until the insurance share reached close to 60 per cent in the late 1970s. Since then it has dropped back and was at 47 per cent in 1996 (Table 1).

Table 1: Recipients of social insurance and social assistance payments and relative shares, selected years, 1947–96

	Insurance		Assistance		Total	
	Number	%	Number	%	Number	%
1947	56,926	19.3	237,748	80.7	294,674	100
1966	170,090	50.0	170,044	50.0	340,134	100
1976	292,876	57.8	213,619	42.2	506,495	100
1985	350,230	56.8	266,054	43.2	616,284	100
1995	405,727	48.3	433,906	51.7	839,633	100
1996	413,825	47.3	460,510	52.7	874,335	100

Source: Commission on Social Welfare (1986); Department of Social Welfare (1996)

Since the first compulsory social insurance scheme was established in Germany in 1883 social protection has become a fundamental facet of European societies (Ferrera, 1996). The term 'welfare state' appears to have been first used by Archbishop William Temple, in a pamphlet entitled *Citizen and Churchman* in 1941 (Gregg, 1967). The following year, the Beveridge Plan, which became the charter for the welfare state in the UK and had considerable influence in Ireland, was published. The concept underlying the Beveridge approach was a citizenship model aimed at providing a minimum level of income for all. A core assumption in Beveridge was a full employment norm, that is an unemployment rate of 2.5 to 3.0 per cent of the workforce. Protection was offered for old age, illness and other contingencies, including unemployment, which was assumed to be of finite duration. A second core assumption in the world of Beveridge was the centrality of a breadwinner male with dependent wife and children (Pedersen, 1995). In the continental model of the welfare state there was somewhat more emphasis on insured employment as the source of benefits. Thus the guiding principle of the Bismarckian statist corporatist model of welfare was that 'workers are guaranteed benefits and a substitute income calculated from their previous earnings in return for the payment of employment related insurance contributions' (Hantrais, 1994). The influence of the continental model is apparent in the Social Charter, 1989, which aims to provide a social dimension to the Single European Act of 1986. The Social Charter is mainly concerned with the rights of workers. In the continental model the role of social insurance contributions, which constitute a higher percentage of total state revenue on the continent than they do in Ireland, is absolutely pivotal.

Increase in recipients

In 1950 the number of recipients of weekly social welfare payments amounted to 330,000. Twenty years later, in 1970, when the number of recipients passed 400,000, the inventory of payments, although growing, still comprised, in the main, old age pensions, widows' pensions, supplementary welfare allowance and unemployment payments. In the mid-1990s, with record rates of economic growth, the number of social welfare recipients is more than twice as great as twenty-five years ago.

It may be argued that the fruits of economic growth have permitted a vastly extended social welfare network. However, given the fact that since 1970 the lion's share of the growth in social welfare has been accounted for by two fully state-funded assistance schemes – unemployment assistance and lone parent's allowance – a paradox exists: rapid economic growth has been accompanied by a great increase in dependency on state welfare payments. The rapid growth in unemployment assistance reflects a very marked growth in the long-term unemployed while the growth in the lone parent's allowance largely reflects the increase in solo mothers and, more recently, separated persons. The increased reliance on social assistance occurred contrary to the expectations of the Commission on Social Welfare which reported: 'The proposals for a widening of the social insurance base should lead to a situation where social assistance plays a more residual role within the social welfare system' (1986, pp. 10–11). The reverse has been the case.

Table 2 shows the number of recipients of weekly social welfare payments by scheme since 1950, while Table 3 shows the share of the increase in total recipients accounted for by certain schemes between 1970 and 1996. As can be seen from Tables 2 and 3, two-thirds of the increase in numbers of social welfare recipients during the period 1980–96 was accounted for by unemployment assistance, lone parents and deserted wives, while in the years 1990–96, nearly 20 per cent of the increase was accounted for by lone parents. It is quite possible that there is some linkage between the growth in unemployment and the increase in the number of single mothers, who constituted the largest group of lone parents, as the growth in unemployment has meant that for increasing numbers of men the 'breadwinner' role has not been a realistic possibility.

Table 2: Number of recipients of weekly social welfare payments by scheme, 1950–96

Scheme	1950	1960	1970	1980	1990	1995	1996
Old age pension (contributory) (1960)	–	29,124	46,549	65,401	74,470	69,179	67,988
Retirement pension (1970)	–	–	3,518	31,981	48,475	65,761	69,740
Old age pension (non-contributory)	156,638	124,548	113,570	130,077	118,223	102,984	101,624
Pre-retirement allowance (1990)	–	–	–	–	6,104	15,023	14,151
Single woman's allowance (1974)[a]	–	–	–	3,142	2,187	–	–
Blind person's allowance[b]	–	–	–	–	–	2,476	2,450
Disability benefit	32,196	42,604	54,372	65,208	52,765	41,830	42,460
Invalidity pension (1970)	–	–	11,619	16,868	34,068	42,092	43,046
Injury benefit (1967)	–	–	936	1,378	577	658	690
Interim disability benefit (1987)[c]	–	–	–	–	1,804	1,006	1,010
Disablement benefit (1967)	–	–	1,861	4,801	7,241	8,977	9,364
Death benefit pension (1967)	–	–	104	356	473	500	502
Disability allowance[d]	–	–	–	–	–	32,699	37,054

Table 2: Number of recipients of weekly social welfare payments by scheme, 1950–96 (cont.)

Scheme	1950	1960	1970	1980	1990	1995	1996
Widow's pension (contributory)	15,558	32,917	53,238	69,985	84,011	94,713	96,107
Widow's pension (non-contributory)	27,095	23,797	16,898	11,195	17,877	19,108	19,046
Deserted wife's benefit (1973)	–	–	–	2,873	10,462	14,284	14,738
Deserted wife's allowance (1970)	–	–	1,284	2,920	1,793	2,125	2,138
Prisoner's wife's allowance (1974)	–	–	–	182	9	8	6
Unmarried mother's allowance (1973)	–	–	–	5,267	–	–	–
Lone parent's allowance (1990)[e]	–	–	–	–	25,231	45,779	50,557
Maternity benefit/allowance	n/a	3,080	8,371	18,489	4,656	3,889	4,592
Health and safety benefit (1994)	–	–	–	–	–	17	19
Adoptive benefit (1995)	–	–	–	–	–	6	10
Orphan's allowance (contributory)	1,078	416	538	872	723	765	808
Orphan's allowance (non-contributory)	874	267	147	177	144	299	340
Supplementary welfare allowance	33,448	18,668	16,498	16,558	12,572	16,552	19,513
Family income supplement (1984)	–	–	–	–	6,569	11,398	11,847
Carer's allowance (1990)	–	–	–	–	1,240	6,917	8,298
Prescribed relative's allowance (1969)	–	–	1,859	2,832	1,323	–	–
Unemployment benefit	20,493	31,905	36,413	63,598	63,118	62,050	62,751
Unemployment assistance	40,076	26,218	23,614	50,178	144,739	200,587	184,031
Smallholders' unemployment assistance (1965)	–	–	17,949	20,639	12,657	9,904	8,756
Rent allowance (1982)	–	–	–	–	1,109	746	699
Total	327,456	333,544	409,338	584,977	734,620	872,332	874,335

(a) Single woman's allowance is now included with pre-retirement allowance.
(b) Formerly included with old age non-contributory pension.
(c) Formerly included with injury benefit.
(d) Disability allowance is a replacement for disabled person's maintenance allowance – DPMA – which the Department of Social Welfare took over in 1995.
(e) Composition of lone parent's allowance in 1996: unmarried parent 37,506; separated 11,268; widowed 1,685; prisoner's spouse 98.

Source: Department of Social Welfare. For schemes not in existence in 1950, the date of their introduction is given in parentheses.

The importance of the widow's contributory pension in the increase in the number of social welfare recipients is directly related to the abolition of the earnings ceiling for insurability in 1974 and the associated growth in the fully insured workforce (Table 3). A widow's contributory pension is available on the contributions of either the husband or the wife and it only requires contribution for three years. If the earnings ceiling had not been abolished, many of those in receipt of a widow's contributory pension today would not have qualified, as their husbands would not have been covered by full social insurance. The importance of disability allowance in the growth in the number of social welfare recipients reflects both administrative change, whereby the Department of Social Welfare has become responsible for the allowance, and an increase in the number of recipients.

Table 3: Share of increase in total number of social welfare recipients accounted for by certain schemes, 1970–96 (%)

Scheme	1970–96	1980–96	1990–96
Widow's contributory pension	9.2	9.0	8.7
Deserted wife's benefit/allowance	3.4	3.8	3.3
Lone parent's allowance	10.9	17.5	18.1
Unemployment benefit	5.7	–0.3	–0.3
Unemployment assistance	34.5	46.3	28.2
Disability allowance	–	–	26.5
Other	36.3	23.7	15.5
Total	100.0	100.0	100.0

Source: Department of Social Welfare

Increase in cost

The cost of welfare services has been growing steadily. Apart from the rise in public debt, the biggest contributor to the rise in the overall public expenditure/GNP ratio since the Second World War has been social welfare. The bulk of the increase in the social welfare ratio to GNP occurred in the crucial decade of the 1970s when the ratio rose by four percentage points from 7.6 per cent to 11.5 per cent of GNP. It rose further to 14 per cent of GNP in 1986 but fell back to 12.4 per cent in 1995. Table 4 shows the breakdown of social welfare expenditure in 1995. It includes expenditure on child benefit, which is paid monthly, as well as all the weekly social welfare payments and some miscellaneous payments which are paid at different intervals. In 1995 the distribution of social welfare expenditure under the different headings was somewhat distorted by the payment of almost £200 million, or 5 per cent of the total, on equal treatment payments. When expenditure on these payments and on administration is excluded, almost 80 per cent of expenditure is accounted for by the four contingencies of unemployment, old age, illness and widowhood. Expenditure on unemployment payments amounted to 28 per cent of the total (excluding equal treatment payments and administration); £800 million was spent on unemployment assistance and £200 million on unemployment benefit. Included in these figures are £131 million on child dependant allowances. Over £270 million was spent supporting more than 60,000 lone parents and deserted wives (£194 million and £77 million respectively).

Table 4: Expenditure on social welfare, 1995

Scheme	Expenditure (£m)	As % of total	
		Excluding equal treatment payments and administration	Including equal treatment payments and administration
Unemployment	1,061.1	28.0	25.4
Old age	1,056.6	27.9	25.3
Illness	447.6	11.8	10.7
Widows/widowers/orphans	402.6	10.6	9.6
Child benefit	300.9	7.9	7.2
Lone parent's allowance	194.3	5.1	4.6
Supplementary welfare allowance	119.5	3.2	2.9
Deserted wives	76.8	2.0	1.8
Maternity benefit	27.3	0.7	0.7
Family income supplement	21.3	0.6	0.5
Carer's allowance	20.0	0.5	0.5
Other various	62.0	1.6	1.5
Equal treatment payments	194.6	–	4.7
Administration	193.7	–	4.6
Total excluding equal treatment payments and administration	3,790.2	100.0	–
Total	4,178.5	–	100.0

Source: Department of Social Welfare, *Statistical Information on Social Welfare Services, 1995*

Table 5 shows income support payments for children in 1995. It includes £305 million spent on child benefit which is paid monthly (and therefore not listed in Table 2, which relates to all weekly payments), together with expenditure on child dependant allowances, which are paid to social welfare recipients with dependent children, and family income supplement (both of which are covered by Table 2).

Table 5: Income support for children, 1995

Payment	Number of children	Expenditure (£m)	Average annual expenditure per child (£)
Child benefit	1,066,000	305.3	286
Child dependant allowances	515,000	320.5	622
Family income supplement	32,078	23.0	717

Source: Expert Working Group (1996)

Size of payments

The size of weekly social welfare payments in June 1997 varied from £78 per week for the old age contributory and retirement pension to £65.40 per week for short-term unemployment assistance and supplementary allowance. In 1986, the Commission on Social Welfare recommended that social welfare payment rates should at minimum be 'of the order of £50–60 per week in 1986 terms', which is equivalent to £69.20–83.00 in 1997 terms. Only the old age contributory pension and retirement pension payment rates exceeded the lower end of that range in 1986 and only the widow's pension and deserted wife's benefit rates have reached that level (£69.20) since then. The increases in the 1997 budget brought all social welfare payments to a minimum of 95 per cent of the £69.20 rate with the bulk of payments being at least 98 per cent of that rate. Invalidity and carer's payments reached the target level in 1997. In the National Anti-Poverty Strategy published in 1997 (Ireland, 1997), there is a commitment by government to raise social welfare payments to the minimum recommended by the Commission on Social Welfare by 1999, in line with Partnership 2000.

An Economic and Social Research Institute (ESRI) study, published in December 1996, suggests a minimum adequate income range of between £68 and £96 per week for a single adult (Callan et al., 1996). The study, which uses a number of methods to measure minimum adequate income, highlights the complexity of the issue. On a comparative basis the study finds that 'Irish social welfare rates are generally more generous relative to average earnings or income than those in the UK, but if anything below the average for EU countries as a whole' (Callan et al., 1996, p. xiii).

Key ideas

In attempting to clarify the main strands of thought, the key ideas, in the development of the welfare state in Ireland, two in particular stand out. These are the shift towards a minimum income guaranteed by the state and the equal treatment of men and women. Both have implications for the future.

A minimum income

Prior to the spread of welfare state policies, social thinking in Ireland in regard to income provision could be summarised by the directive principles of social policy contained in Article 45 of the 1937 constitution. These in turn were in keeping with papal encyclicals of the time which stressed the independence of the family unit and the breadwinner from the state. The 1949 White Paper, *Social Security* (Department of Social Welfare, 1949), was haunted by the spectre of malingering and moral degeneration through 'dole' payments to the unemployed. Throughout the 1940s, 1950s and much of the 1960s policy towards 'intervention' by the state in the social sphere was cautious. The introduction of children's allowances in 1944 for the third and each subsequent dependent child was innovative in that it was a universal scheme, paid irrespective of means, and fully financed by the state. A critical barrier was breached in the field of public expenditure with the announcement of free post-primary education for all, which was introduced in 1967 by the Minister for Education, Donogh O'Malley. This copperfastened a number of earlier initiatives taken by Dr Patrick Hillery when he was Minister for Education. However, it was not until the 1970s that state engagement in the social sphere became very clearly marked. The years 1973–75, immediately following Ireland's entry to the EEC on 1 January 1973, were pivotal in terms of the subsequent development of the welfare state in Ireland. While the immediate fiscal fruit of EEC entry was the freeing of funds for government spending in other areas, due to substantial savings on agricultural subsidies, there was widespread political support for increased social spending, especially in the Labour Party. Prior to the 1973 general election the Fine Gael and Labour parties issued a Statement of Intent promising increased social spending. Following the election the Fine Gael–Labour coalition government fulfilled its promises.

A striking illustration in the health expenditure area was the increase in the number of people with a medical card as a proportion of the population. The share rose from 33.9 per cent in 1973 to a record high of 41.4 per cent in 1977. It fell to 36 per cent in 1979, and was just below 36 per cent in 1995. On the occasion of the introduction of the Social Welfare estimate in the Dáil in 1974, Frank Cluskey, the Parliamentary Secretary to the Minister for Social Welfare, Brendan Corish, explained the government's commitment to an expanded state welfare system. He quoted with approval from a statement on social policy of the Council for Social Welfare of the Catholic hierarchy: '... the principle of a guaranteed income related to the cost of living index, for each household, whatever the circumstances, ought to be accepted'. This represented a defining moment in social policy as emphasis was now firmly placed on the right to a minimum income guaranteed by the state, as distinct from the previous policy emphasis on the right to provide for one's own livelihood as set forth in the directive principles of social policy in the constitution. The notion of a minimum income represented an endorsement of Beveridge. It is a more limited concept than that of a basic income as discussed in the *Report of the Expert Working Group on the Integration of the Tax and Social Welfare Systems* (Expert Working Group, 1996) and in the work of the Conference of Religious of Ireland, *Towards an Adequate Income for All* (1994).

In the same Dáil speech in 1974, Frank Cluskey displayed pride in the growth in social welfare expenditure which he claimed had increased by 100 per cent on the previous year, while the staff of the Department of Social Welfare had grown by 20 per cent, to 2,800 people. (It was 4,300 in 1996.) Cluskey pointed out that, since the coalition government had come into office fifteen months earlier, payments had been introduced for unmarried mothers, for single women over 58 years, for adult dependants of old age non-contributory pensioners, and for families of long-term unemployed. An important change introduced in 1974 was the removal of the income ceiling for insurability. This would have very significant long-run effects for eligibility for contributory pensions and benefits. At the stroke of a pen the number of insured people increased by 19 per cent to 970,000 in the year ended March 1975. A range of pay-related benefits was also introduced. These were subsequently phased out by 1995. In 1975 the total net estimate of the Department of Social Welfare was nearly double that of 1974. Nothing less than the elimination of poverty became the goal of policy, and with that end in view the Advisory Committee on Pilot Schemes to Combat Poverty was established.

The shift towards the notion of a minimum income guaranteed by the state, as distinct from the opportunity to provide for one's needs through employment, was grounded both in ideology and in changing economic and social realities. The directive principles of social policy in the constitution, referred to earlier, state:

The state shall, in particular, direct its policy towards securing:

> That the citizens (all of whom, men and women equally, have the right to an adequate means of livelihood) may through their occupations find the means of making reasonable provision for their domestic needs.

This principle, which stresses the rights of individuals to provide for their needs through their occupations, is quite different in emphasis from the quotation from the Catholic Bishops' Council for Social Welfare used by Frank Cluskey regarding a minimum income whatever the circumstances. The shift in ideology is important in understanding the evolution of social policy. It represents a shift from Catholic social teaching of the 1930s expressed in contemporary encyclicals and enshrined in the 1937 constitution, which stressed the primacy of citizens to provide for their own needs, in practice the family farm unit in the rural economy and the family breadwinner in the urban setting, towards a more socialist post-Vatican II emphasis in keeping with the principles of the Beveridge Plan and, significantly from an Irish perspective, endorsed by the encyclicals of Pope John XXIII. The Irish hierarchy moved from a position which emphasised selectivity, subsidiarity and self-supporting families to one which endorsed guaranteed state provision, independent of workforce attachment. Evidence that politicians were influenced by church teaching at that time is found in a number of sources, for example the Fine Gael *Just Society* document which was published in 1965 and which stated that 'most people in public life will state their acceptance of the teachings contained in the Papal Encyclicals'. As well as an ideological shift, the shift towards a minimum guaranteed income was grounded in practical realities. Rising unemployment meant that large numbers of people were unable to provide for their own needs, while the growth in non-traditional family structures meant that the breadwinner role was often not fulfilled for other reasons.

Equal treatment of men and women

In the company of Beveridge and Catholic Church teaching, the Treaty of Rome has been a powerful influence on the evolution of the welfare state in Ireland. The European Union is fundamentally a political and economic reality, and social policy has been related closely to working conditions and has operated mainly as ancillary to economic policy. Yet Article 119 of the Treaty of Rome, which includes the principle of equal pay for men and women, probably has had more impact on social welfare policy in Ireland than any purely domestic initiative. Article 119 states:

Each member State shall during the first stage ensure and subsequently maintain the application of the principle that men and women should receive equal pay for equal work.

For purposes of this Article, 'pay' means the ordinary basic or minimum wage or salary and any other consideration, whether in cash or in kind, which the worker receives, directly or indirectly, in respect of his employment from his employer.

Article 119 together with the subsequent Equality Directive led to equal treatment of men and women in the workplace and in the social welfare system. This helped to transform the entire basis of the welfare state from one in which married women were seen automatically as the economic dependants of men. In the social welfare system the duration of unemployment benefit to which women were entitled was increased and access to unemployment assistance for married women in their own right was introduced in 1986. By 1995, the number of married women in receipt of unemployment assistance had grown to over 13,000, while over 20,000 married women were receiving unemployment benefit. Delays in implementing the Equality Directive led to court cases, which resulted in the payment of almost £200 million in outstanding equality payments to women in 1995. The equal treatment of women with men may possibly be regarded as a step on the road towards the individualisation of payments. An aspect of this is evident in the fact that adult dependants, generally women, can opt to receive the dependant allowance directly in certain circumstances.

Shift in the basis of the welfare state

No sooner was the welfare state well established in Ireland, specifically with the explosion in social welfare provision following entry to the EEC, than precisely at that point both labour market conditions and family patterns, on which the basis of the welfare state was predicated, began to change in a radical manner. The key changes were, firstly, the steady rise in unemployment and, secondly, changes in family patterns which included a decline in the popularity of marriage, an increase in marriage breakdown, an increase in births outside marriage and an increase in the labour force participation of married women (which is both a family and a labour market change).

Table 6 shows how the unemployment rate has changed in Ireland, the EU and the UK since 1973. Since Ireland joined the EEC the unemployment rate has more than doubled, rising from 5.7 per cent of the labour force in 1973 to 11.7 per cent in 1996. Record highs were reached in the early 1980s. Over the same period the unemployment rate throughout the EU has risen more than threefold from 2.6 per cent to 10.9 per cent. Since 1993 the Irish unemployment rate has fallen by four percentage points while the EU rate has remained static. At this rate of decline the Irish rate could be down to the EU average by 1998 (Kennedy, 1996). The UK rate has also been falling since 1993; in 1996 it was 8.2 per cent, which was well below Ireland and the EU average. While a debate is in progress regarding the relative merits of the Labour Force Survey and the Live Register measures of unemployment, the Live Register is of great significance for the schemes under the Department of Social Welfare. In January 1973 the total on the Live Register was 75,700 (62,100 men and 13,600 women). By November 1995 the total had increased by 200,000 to 275,000 (175,000 men and 100,000 women).

Table 6: Unemployment rates for Ireland, the EU and the UK, selected years, 1973–96 (%)

	Ireland	EU	UK
1973	5.7	2.6	3.0
1980	7.3	6.4	6.4
1985	17.0	10.5	11.2
1990	13.3	8.1	6.9
1993	15.6	10.9	10.4
1995	12.3	10.9	8.4
1996	11.7	10.9	8.2

Source: Kennedy (1996). The data are based on, or consistent with, Labour Force Survey data. The increases in the unemployment rates would be greater, and the decreases smaller, if Live Register data were used.

Table 7 shows some of the changes in family patterns which have occurred since 1971. One in five households is now a one-person household compared with one in six in 1971; one in three married women is in the workforce compared with one in twelve in 1971; and nearly one in four births is out of wedlock compared with less than one in thirty in 1971, while one in three of all first births is now out of wedlock. In 1994 over 90 per cent of all births to teenagers were to single women and over 50 per cent of births to women aged 20–24 years were to single women (Fahey and Fitz Gerald, 1997). The changes in family patterns which occurred in Ireland from the second half of the 1970s and into the 1980s had occurred at an earlier period in other European countries. For most European countries the postwar years, until the mid-1960s, represented the 'Golden Age of Marriage' (Kuijsten, 1997; van de Kaa, 1987). Then, from the mid-1960s until the mid-1970s there was a sharp drop in first marriage rates, with some stabilisation in the 1980s.

In Ireland the 'Golden Age' only dawned in the 1960s; it persisted into the early 1970s and has since faded rapidly. Most other European countries were experiencing the postponement of marriage and the 'Dawn of Cohabitation' when Ireland was entering the 'Golden Age'. Since 1980 in Ireland young people have been postponing marriage and the average age at marriage has been rising. Furthermore, of those marriages which have taken place there has been a sharp increase in marriage breakdown.

Table 7: Certain social indicators, 1971 and 1995

	1971	1995
Percentage of women aged 20–24 years who were married	31.1	8.4*
Percentage of women aged 25–29 years who were married	68.9	51.7*
Percentage of married women in the labour force	7.5	34.0
Percentage of total births outside marriage	2.9	22.2
One-person households as percentage of total	14.2	20.2

*1994
Source: Central Statistics Office

Future of the welfare state

The achievements of the welfare state in Ireland, although very considerable, have fallen short of expectations. In view of the much higher levels of unemployment and the close association between poverty and unemployment, there is an understandable loss of faith in the capacity of state expenditure policies to comprehensively solve social problems. Over the past twenty-five years, economic growth and welfare state growth have been strongly underpinned by transfers from the EU – a net £20 billion since Ireland joined. There is cause to reflect on what could happen if the European well runs dry for Ireland.

Disenchantment with the welfare state as well as pressure for tax cuts and fears about competitiveness are leading to restrictions on social welfare expenditure in several countries. In the UK the end of the welfare state, as it has been known for the past fifty years, is foreshadowed in proposals made by both the Conservative and Labour parties for the increased use of private insurance, for example. The state is moving towards the role of regulator rather than that of provider. Evidence of social welfare trimming abounds in continental European as well as Scandinavian countries. One of the most striking moves signalled is a shift away from widows' pensions based on the status of widows as dependants of their deceased husbands; while this is a logical enough outcome of the drive towards equal treatment of men and women, it is also quite an ominous one from the point of view of traditional households with one partner in the workforce and one a full-time carer in the home. In Ireland, however, such a move remains on a distant horizon as widowers' entitlements to pensions are brought into line with widows' entitlements to pensions and a provision has been introduced whereby insurance entitlements are safeguarded for those who care full-time in the home for children under 12 years. Apart from a renewed emphasis on the detection of fraud, there is little evidence of a hardening of attitudes among the social partners towards welfare in Ireland. The National Anti-Poverty Strategy states that in 1994 one-third of the population were living on disposable incomes which were below 60 per cent of the national average and that 9–15 per cent of the population live in conditions of 'persistent poverty' (Ireland, 1997, p. 3).

The European Union and restructuring the welfare state

The Treaty on European Union 1992, signed at Maastricht, included an agreement on social policy, the Social Chapter, which was signed by all the member states except the UK. Because of the close economic links between Ireland and the UK, the emergence of different social security regimes in the two countries would be a cause for concern. The Social Chapter widened the remit of the EU to look at social exclusion, that is, poverty, marginalisation and related issues. At present the intergovernmental conference which is reviewing the Treaty on European Union is considering possibilities for an extension of the social dimension which might be incorporated in a future treaty. The EU as a whole has a very poor record on employment, with even the richest members experiencing severe unemployment despite good growth rates. The challenge of 'jobless growth', a striking EU phenomenon, is increasing pressure on the welfare state throughout Europe. Since Maastricht, unemployment has been recognised as the key economic and social problem in the EU. A central problem for the Union is how to maintain competitiveness and at the same time provide for social protection in the light of the enormously higher labour costs in the EU than in Eastern Europe, the developing world and China. In addition to the labour market situation, the transformation of traditional family patterns and the associated ageing of the population are important issues throughout the EU as they are in Ireland (Ferrera, 1996). Within this context, which is broadly similar throughout the EU, three areas are identified as critical for social welfare/social protection planning in the coming years. These are:

(i)   the balance between social protection and competitiveness
(ii) demographic changes, and issues relating to changing family structures, in particular young and old dependency
(iii) poverty strategy, including adequacy of payments.

The remainder of this paper will concentrate on the second and third of these issues. The first issue, the balance between social protection and competitiveness, includes a discussion of the role of Pay-Related Social Insurance (PRSI) and a number of other matters raised in the report of the Expert Working Group on the Integration of the Tax and Social Welfare Systems (Expert Working Group, 1996). It includes a discussion of taxation and incentives, and whether PRSI would be better treated as part of general taxation, as suggested by the Commission on Taxation, or should be reformed to enhance its role as specifically related to social insurance. It is worth remembering that social insurance contributions play a vital role in all the European welfare systems. In Luxembourg, for example, they amount to 20 per cent of GNP and the rate of unemployment there is only 3 per cent. Luxembourg is, of course, not typical in that it does not maintain an armed force nor does it have any universities or pure research institutions. The Department of Social Welfare has published an important discussion document, *Social Insurance in Ireland* (Department of Social Welfare, 1996), which deals with the balance between social protection and competitiveness.

Demographic changes

Throughout the European Union there will be significant demographic changes over the next twenty to thirty years, in particular the ageing of the population. Life expectancy will continue to increase, by one year every five years (European Commission, 1994). According to the most recent Central Statistics Office (CSO) projections, the population aged 0–14 years in Ireland could fall by between 22 and 40 per cent by 2026 (Central Statistics Office, 1995). The number of children is projected to fall from almost 950,000 in 1991 to between 565,000 and 735,000 in 2026. The population aged 65 and over is likely to increase by 70 per cent by 2026. The increase in the elderly population will not become marked for another ten years, until after 2006. At present there are approximately 405,000 persons aged 65 years and over. This number will rise quite slowly to 440,000 in 2006 but over the following twenty years the number is projected to rise substantially by around 250,000 to 690,000 in 2026. An interesting projection is the relatively large number of elderly women as they continue to outlive men by a substantial margin. It is estimated that, of the projected total aged over 65 years in 2026, some 396,500, or 58 per cent, will be women. Forecasting the child population is a much more difficult task than forecasting the elderly as it depends on a range of assumptions regarding fertility, marriage and migration which may vary to a considerable extent.

As shown in Table 8, the over 65s will account for 17–19 per cent of the population, and be equivalent to 26–29 per cent of those defined as in the economically active ages between 15 and 64 years, in 2026. The extent of labour force participation by the age group 15–64 will be critical in determining the ratio of the over 65s to the labour force. The CSO estimates that by 2006 those aged 65 years and over may be equivalent to between 43 and 45 per cent of the labour force. While female participation, mainly of married women, in the workforce is rising, there is a clear trend, projected to continue, for both males and females to defer entry into the workforce until well after age 15 years due to extended participation in education. At the same time there is another clear trend, also projected to continue, of declining participation in the labour force, due to earlier retirement, of both males and unmarried females aged 55 years and over. The number of people on pre-retirement allowance (PRETA) has risen very steeply from 6,100 in 1990 to over 15,000 in 1995 (Table 2). PRETA is payable at age 55 to those who give up work. It could be regarded as a disguised form of unemployment assistance, but there is no requirement to sign on the Live Register to obtain PRETA, and, while it is really governed by unemployment rules, the recipient receives a pension book.

Table 8: Ratio of those 65 years and over to total population, to population aged 15–64, and to labour force, 1991 and 2026 (%)

	1991	2026
Ratio to total population	11	17–19
Ratio to population aged 15–64	18	26–29
Ratio to total labour force	30	43–45*

*2006; because of the complexity of factors affecting the labour force, 2006 is the latest year for which the CSO has made estimates.
Source: Central Statistics Office (1995)

In the EU as a whole, it is noteworthy that the percentage of working age men *outside* the labour force rose from just 8 per cent in 1968 to 22 per cent in 1993. For women, the trend was reversed, falling from 58 per cent to 44 per cent over the same period. These factors, together with the increase in the number of persons aged 65 and over, explain the sharp projected rise in the ratio of over 65s to the labour force. The CSO has made no separate projections of the ratio of persons age 65 and over to the *employed* portion of the total labour force; by how much it would be higher depends on the balance between employment and unemployment. However, it is possible that within the first two decades of the next century there could be one pensioner for every two persons at work. The rise in Ireland's old age dependency ratio (i.e. those aged 65 and over as a percentage of those aged 15–64) to between 26 and 29 per cent by 2026 will still leave it well below other European countries such as Germany and France with ratios projected to exceed 30 per cent, but Ireland will be following rapidly in their direction. In 1995 expenditure on old age and survivors' pensions as a percentage of gross domestic product was 5.7 per cent in Ireland compared with 10.8 per cent in the UK, 12.1 per cent in Germany, 12.7 per cent in France and 15.4 per cent in Italy (European Commission, 1995).

A key question for those responsible for social welfare expenditure is to what extent will increases in income support for the elderly, primarily pensions, be offset by a decline in support for children and the un-employed, as well as by an expansion in the numbers in employment and the growth in social insurance contributions. Reflecting on the econ-omic context of the projected decline in overall dependency in the decade immediately ahead, Walsh stressed the need to 'avail of the opportunity presented by the declining dependency ratio over the coming ten to fifteen years to accumulate assets that will maximise the eventual return to the nation when the burden of old dependency begins to increase' (1996, p. 7). This could be helped by maintaining the current level of employee/employer social insurance contributions and/or main-taining the level of the exchequer contribution, instead of reducing both as has been done in recent years. A move could be made from Pay As You Go financing of pension liabilities to a funded system in part or in total.

State expenditure on the young and old, and other groups, extends far beyond income support payments made by the Department of Social Welfare. For example, expenditure on education is particularly impor-tant in relation to the young, while expenditure on health is a significant element in state support for the elderly. People aged 65 years and over have twice as many GP visits per year as have the population as a whole, while there is a particularly high usage of health services by the over 75s (Nolan, 1991). Broader questions than those posed here are therefore relevant in the overall public expenditure picture. For example, could savings on education be available for geriatric care?

Child income support

Given the projected sharp decline in the number of children in the population, it might be assumed, other things being equal, that sub-stantial savings would be forthcoming in the area of child income support. However, other things are not equal and the most important factor here is the continuing rise in births outside marriage and the associated rise in solo parenting. Added to these trends is the increasing rate of marriage breakdown reflected in the rise in lone parent's allowances paid to separated people. No attempt has been made to measure the financial implications for the Department of Social Welfare budget of the number of divorces which may occur now that divorce legislation is in place. During the 1995 divorce referendum campaign the Department of Social Welfare estimated that the incremental cost would be minimal. To judge by the experience of other countries, however, divorce has definite public expenditure consequences.

While the total young dependency ratio continues to decline, the share of child dependency likely to be borne by the state is increasing steeply. The rise in births to single women, particularly young single women, is likely to necessitate a significant increase in public expenditure. If births outside marriage continue at the present level, there could be approximately 180,000 extramarital children in the dependent age group by 2010, though not all of these would be dependent on state support. As shown earlier (Table 4), the state spent over £270 million on income support for lone parents and deserted wives in 1995. In reply to a question in the Dáil on 4 October 1995 the Minister of State at the Department of Social Welfare, Bernard Durkan, stated that in 1995, an estimated £300,000 would be contributed by 232 liable relatives, mostly fathers, towards the upkeep of their families. In further discussion, he said that a very high proportion of liable fathers were on social welfare and it was futile to pursue them, as they lacked the ability to pay. It seems likely that this situation will continue. In the opening days of 1997, the Minister for Social Welfare announced new rules whereby lone parents will be able to earn up to £115 per week without any diminution of their social welfare payments. Above that level payments will taper off until they are stopped completely at earnings of £230 per week. The idea behind these provisions is to encourage lone parents into the workforce.

The future size of state child income support depends, therefore, on more than a simple headcount of children. A number of factors are relevant. These include the number of children born out of wedlock and the proportion of those children not supported by a breadwinner; the level of unemployment and the number of children of unemployed people; the amount of family breakdown requiring income support for children; the extent of low pay, where family income supplement is required as a supplement to earnings; as well as policy in regard to child benefit. It is likely that, even as the overall number of children in the population declines substantially, the family circumstances of a larger percentage of children will require additional income support.

Pensions

The prospect with regard to pensions seems much clearer than with regard to child income support. Projections of increases in the numbers of elderly suggest that there will be substantial increases in pension costs as we move into the next century with a very marked rise occurring between 2006 and 2026. The National Pensions Board (NPB) made projections of the cost of social welfare pensions between 1990 and 2035 in 1990 prices (National Pensions Board, 1993). The cost projections were based on lower population estimates of those aged 65 years and over than the 1995 CSO projections used in this paper. The NPB estimates did not take sufficient account of the improvement in mortality over the past decade. Based on their more conservative estimates of growth in pensioners, the NPB projected that expenditure on social welfare pensions, including retirement, old age, survivors and invalidity, would increase by 19 per cent in real terms between 1990 and 2005 and by 39 per cent between 2010 and 2025. The NPB estimated that, if the pension contribution rate for employees, employers and the self-employed remained unchanged, the exchequer share of the total cost of pensions would remain relatively unchanged until 2021, but would increase by 223 per cent over the following twenty-five years.

It may be argued that the NPB assumptions regarding labour force participation and unemployment are somewhat pessimistic given the improvement in the economy since 1993 (Fahey and Fitz Gerald, 1997), but there is no gainsaying the fact that social welfare pension costs are set to rise very steeply after 2010, regardless of the state of the economy. While overall employment is rising at present, the changing nature of that employment has implications for pensions. The number of part-time, temporary and contract jobs is increasing as distinct from full-time, single career span, jobs. If this trend continues it will mean that an increasing proportion of the workforce will have difficulty building up adequate pension entitlements. In the context of the current debate regarding PRSI it should be stressed that social insurance funding in Ireland is on a Pay As You Go (PAYG) basis. Any dilution of PRSI contributions would further limit policy options while any move from a PAYG system to a funded system would lead to increased emphasis on the contributory principle.

The issue of how to pay for social security pensions is engaging the minds of a number of prominent economists at the present time, including Martin Feldstein. In his recent Richard T. Ely lecture, Feldstein states: 'Reforming the Social Security retirement program is an issue of enormous practical importance. Yet it remains the missing piece in American policy analysis' (1996, p. 1). Feldstein says that the outstanding social security liability in the United States is three times as large as the official national debt, and that the tax rate required to pay each year's pensions is growing steadily. He argues that the current unfunded system in the US distorts the supply of labour, and that returns would be higher with a funded system. Similar arguments might be applied in the Irish case, and while efforts are being made to address the pensions issue, more remains to be done. The jury remains out on the question of the impact on national savings of increasing privatisation of pensions (Hughes, 1996), and of the overall rise in age dependency (Roseveare et al., 1996).

Unemployment payments

For some time a debate has been in progress regarding the relative merits of the Live Register and the Labour Force Survey as measures of unemployment. This has arisen because of the large and growing disparity between the numbers on the Live Register and those classified as unemployed in the Labour Force Survey. The difference between the two measures was insignificant in 1986 but has grown steadily since then, especially in the last few years. The disparity between the two measures varies markedly for men and women. Until 1990 the figures for male unemployment were almost identical according to the two measures, while the difference for women between the two measures has been growing since the mid-1980s. In 1995 the difference between the number classified as unemployed according to principal economic status in the Labour Force Survey and the number on the Live Register was 85,000, of which 48,000, or 56 per cent, were women, predominantly women aged over 25 years. Thus while women comprise 36 per cent of the total Live Register, they account for 56 per cent of the discrepancy between the Live Register and the Labour Force Survey.

Hitherto, in explanations of the difference between the two measures, attention tended to focus on women to explain a large proportion of the discrepancy. A CSO note on the matter in December 1991 stated:

> The principal drawback with the [principal economic status] measure is that it involves a degree of subjectivity on the part of the respondent. For example, married females without a job, who are actively seeking work and available for work, regularly classify themselves as 'engaged on home duties' rather than 'unemployed'.

In September 1996 the CSO published a summary of the results of a study of the difference between the two measures (Central Statistics Office, 1996). The CSO findings received considerable publicity, and

while the CSO did not use the word fraud widespread claims regarding
fraud were made in the public domain. Whatever the true position is,
the test regarding social welfare expenditure will be how much money is
retrieved as a result of alleged past fraud, as well as how much is saved
through the prevention of future fraud. This will determine how much
becomes available for income support under all headings, including the
190,000 who were definitely unemployed according to the Labour
Force Survey in 1996.

In addition to the general economic situation, a number of qualifying
rules and regulations are clearly very important for the definition of
those eligible for payment on the Live Register. As can be seen from
Table 9, the share of women on the Live Register, particularly women
over 25 years, has grown steeply since 1986, while the share of men has
fallen. As a result of equal treatment the duration of unemployment
benefit for married women was extended from May 1986 while equal
treatment for women in relation to unemployment assistance came into
force in November 1986. Before then married women were effectively
precluded from claiming unemployment assistance. In 1996, the majority, that is 34,500, of the total recipients of unemployment benefit were
women, and two-thirds of these were married. It is possible that a
proportion of these women were working out their entitlements following childbirth and prior to withdrawing from the labour force for a
period. Of the 56,000 women receiving unemployment assistance,
13,000, or one-quarter, were married. In addition to changes in the
rules regarding married women, changes in the rules regarding part-time
workers and young people have had an impact on numbers. The
extension of social insurance to part-time workers from April 1991
means that they would generally qualify for payments from January
1993, while changes regarding young people mean that they may now
qualify for unemployment assistance in certain circumstances, even
when living with their parents.

*Table 9: Males and females aged under 25 and 25+ as a proportion of
the Live Register, end year 1981, 1986, 1995 and 1996 (%)*

	Males			Females		
	Under 25	25+	Total	Under 25	25+	Total
1981	16.9	59.3	76.2	8.7	15.1	23.8
1986	19.4	54.3	73.7	11.2	15.1	26.3
1995	15.7	48.1	63.8	11.2	25.0	36.2
1996	13.6	48.6	62.2	10.1	27.7	37.8

Source: Central Statistics Office, Live Register Analysis, various years

Unemployment and poverty

From the large volume of research on poverty in Ireland the most striking feature is, not surprisingly, the close association between poverty and unemployment. The risk of poverty is intensified in households where there are large families and an unemployed household head. Of the 275,000 on the Live Register in 1995, 94,500 (58,000 men and 36,500 women) had dependent children. A large majority had less than three children, but 17,500 had more than three children. The Child Poverty Action Group in Britain stated in its 1996 annual report that 'poverty is caused by not having access to decently paid employment. It is also the result of the extra costs of having a child, or a disability. Poverty is particularly acute when these two factors combine' (Child Poverty Action Group, 1996).

The link between unemployment and poverty is recognised in the government's National Anti-Poverty Strategy, *Sharing in Progress*, which was launched in April 1997. The formulation of the strategy, over a period of two years, involved an unprecedented level of consultation with voluntary and community groups and with individuals experiencing poverty. The consultation was carried out on a country-wide basis. The strategy sets out a framework within which poverty will be tackled over a ten-year period with an overall objective to reduce by half the number of people identified as consistently poor by 2007. Targets have been set under five headings: educational disadvantage, unemployment, income adequacy, disadvantaged urban areas and rural poverty. The challenge now is to establish a series of concrete actions across all government departments to work towards the realisation of the targets over the lifetime of the strategy. Within the Department of Social Welfare attention has focused on income adequacy and the ESRI has published a thorough review of the adequacy of payments in light of the recommendations of the Commission on Social Welfare (Callan et al., 1996).

A key question for social planners is whether poverty should be tackled through employment creation or through a minimum social welfare payment or through a combination of both. This issue clearly goes beyond the present remit of the Department of Social Welfare. In 1987 the department took an important initiative when the Minister for Social Welfare, Dr Michael Woods, introduced the JobSearch scheme. For the first time in its history the Department of Social Welfare took responsibility for helping to shift recipients towards employment and away from social welfare dependency, while at the same time closing off some possibilities for fraud. The JobStart scheme, initiated by Minister for Enterprise and Employment Richard Bruton in 1996, operates between FÁS, the Department of Enterprise and Employment and the employment exchanges to encourage employers to take on long-term unemployed workers. While take-up of JobStart has not been strong to date, the Department of Social Welfare's 'Back to Work Allowance' scheme and the two-year PRSI holiday for employers have been effective. It may be remarked that in several European countries the areas of social affairs and employment are combined in a single ministry. Value judgements, as well as practical possibilities, are involved in the balance between attempting to increase job opportunities and providing minimum income support. An inspiring motto is that adopted by the Northside Partnership, 'From Welfare to Work' (Northside Partnership, 1996), but ultimately the possibility of adopting this as a national as distinct from a regional or district motto depends on the actual existence of jobs as well as the proper balance of incentives.

Conclusion

This paper has examined the growth in the scope and scale of the services provided by the Department of Social Welfare since it was established fifty years ago. It has shown how the key assumptions on which the welfare state was based – full employment and a traditional family structure – have altered. The main questions for the future spring from these changes. In view of the increase in old age dependency and the decline in young dependency, combined with a marked change in the composition of young dependency, how can social protection for the dependent age groups be secured most effectively? Most challenging of all, what more can be done to engage the unemployed in meaningful activity and draw them into active social and economic participation? What is the optimum balance between state income support guarantees and employment projects? At the administrative level, do the links between the Departments of Social Welfare and Enterprise and Employment need to be strengthened?

As the Department of Social Welfare completes its first fifty years it faces new challenges. Social welfare expenditure has grown to levels undreamed of when the department was established. Yet poverty persists. It is time to take stock and reflect. It is time to clarify the guiding principles on which the system is to be based in the future. Clearly resources are limited. The capacity to tax is limited. But it is not just a question of financial constraints. No state, irrespective of its wealth, can meet all welfare needs. The richest nations contain some of the most deprived people. Family networks, no matter how altered the family is, are vital. There is a need to recognise the contribution of those working outside the labour force as homemakers and carers whose work is ignored in traditional national accounting measures. There is a need to maximise their contribution, and that of the active retired who have departed the labour force. There remains a profoundly important role for voluntary groups of all sorts.

In a paper entitled 'Economic Planning in Ireland' delivered on 11 February 1967 to a Workers' Union of Ireland seminar, Dr T. K. Whitaker remarked, 'The day-to-day decisions of government, no less than those of individuals, tend too often to respond to the pressures, the needs, the provocations and the opportunities of the moment. Good management demands the longer view.' As usual, Dr Whitaker got to the heart of the matter. The size and complexities of the social welfare system in Ireland are such that considerable emphasis is, and must be, placed on the day-to-day delivery of services. But good management of the welfare state services requires that a longer term view be taken. The Planning Unit in the Department of Social Welfare strives to fulfil this function, and I can testify personally to the commitment and hard work of the members of the unit. In addition there has been substantial work undertaken by review groups such as the Expert Working Group on the Integration of the Tax and Social Welfare Systems, and a large volume of high-calibre research undertaken by the ESRI, the Conference of Religious of Ireland and others. What is missing is the linking together, in a coherent and cohesive manner, of a plan for the welfare services and their funding in the years ahead. No doubt, given the resources, the Planning Unit could draw up such a plan. The unit might also draw on outside expertise, but it is my belief that the emphasis should now be placed on devising a strategy based on the wealth of valuable research already in existence. It is hoped that this essay may help to focus on some of the salient issues which such a strategy must address.

ACKNOWLEDGEMENTS

Special thanks are due to Brian Ó Raghallaigh of the Department of Social Welfare for his help. I also wish to thank Fionán Ó Muircheartaigh, Patrick Lynch and Kieran Kennedy for their comments on an earlier draft of this paper. Deirdre Carroll of the Department of Social Welfare also made very helpful comments, and she, as well as Elaine Soffe, Cathy Barron and others in the department, helped with the supply of data. I am very grateful to the following who helped in relation to particular points: Tim Callan, John Fitz Gerald, Gerry Hughes, Brian Nolan and Brendan Walsh. The most recent data on recipient numbers refers to 1996, while the latest audited expenditure figures available refer to 1995.

REFERENCES

Callan, Tim, Brian Nolan and Christopher Whelan (1996). *A Review of the Commission on Social Welfare's Minimum Adequate Income*, Policy Research Series, Paper No. 29, Dublin: Economic and Social Research Institute

Central Statistics Office (1995). *Population and Labour Force Projections 1996–2026*, Dublin: Stationery Office

Central Statistics Office (1996). *Unemployment Statistics: Study of the Differences between the Labour Force Survey (LFS) Estimates of Unemployment and the Live Register*, Dublin: Central Statistics Office

Central Statistics Office, *Live Register Monthly Area Analysis*

Child Poverty Action Group (1996). *Annual Report*, London: Child Poverty Action Group

Commission on Social Welfare (1986). *Report of the Commission on Social Welfare*, Dublin: Stationery Office

Conference of Religious of Ireland (1994). *Towards an Adequate Income for All*, Dublin: Conference of Religious of Ireland

Department of Social Welfare (1949). *Social Security: White Paper Containing Government Proposals for Social Security*, Dublin: Stationery Office

Department of Social Welfare (1996). *Social Insurance in Ireland*, Dublin: Department of Social Welfare

European Commission, (1994). *European Social Policy – A Way Forward for the Union: A White Paper*, Brussels: European Commission

European Commission (1995). *Social Protection in Europe*, Brussels: European Commission

Expert Working Group (1996). *Report of the Expert Working Group on the Integration of the Tax and Social Welfare Systems*, Dublin: Stationery Office

Fahey, Tony and John FitzGerald (1997). *Welfare Implications of Demographic Trends*, Dublin: Oak Tree Press in association with Combat Poverty Agency

Feldstein, Martin (1996). 'The Missing Piece in Policy Analysis: Social Security Reform', Richard T. Ely Lecture, *American Economic Review*, Vol. 86, No. 2 (May), pp. 1–14

Ferrera, Maurizio (1996). 'New Problems, Old Solutions? Recasting Social Protection of the Future of Europe', paper read to the European Social Policy Forum, Brussels, March

Gregg, P. (1967). *The Welfare State*, London

Hantrais, Linda (1994). 'Comparing Family Policy in Britain, France and Germany', *Journal of Social Policy*, Vol. 23, No. 2, pp. 135–60

Hughes, Gerard (1996). 'Would Privatising Pensions Increase Savings?', *Irish Banking Review*, Spring, pp. 28–42

Ireland (1997). *Sharing in Progress: National Anti-Poverty Strategy*, Dublin: Stationery Office

Kennedy, Kieran A. (1996). 'Irish Unemployment in a European Context', *Irish Banking Review*, Winter, pp. 2–14

Kuijsten, Anton (1997). 'Variation and Change in Family Forms in the 1980s', forthcoming article

National Pensions Board (1993). *Developing the National Pension System: Final Report of the National Pensions Board*, Dublin: Stationery Office

Nolan, Brian (1991). *The Utilisation and Financing of Health Services in Ireland*, General Research Series, Paper No. 155, Dublin: Economic and Social Research Institute

Northside Partnership (1996). *From Welfare to Work: Area Action Plan 1996–1999*, Dublin: Northside Partnership

Pedersen, Susan (1995). *Family, Dependence and the Origins of the Welfare State: Britain and France, 1914–1945*, Cambridge: Cambridge University Press

Roseveare, Deborah, Willi Leibfritz, Douglas Fore and Echard Wurzel (1996). *Ageing Populations, Pension Systems and Government Budgets: Simulations for 20 OECD Countries*, Paris: Organisation for Economic Co-operation and Development

van de Kaa, Dirk J. (1987). 'Europe's Second Demographic Transition', *Population Bulletin*, Vol. 42, No. 1, Washington DC: Population Reference Bureau.

Walsh, Brendan (1996). *Some Economic Implications of the Ageing Irish Population*, Working Paper 96/2, Dublin: University College Dublin

8

Irish Prisons: Alternative Strategies in Overcrowded Times

LIAM RYAN

There is nothing more difficult to carry out, nor more doubtful of success, nor more dangerous to handle than to initiate a new order of things. For the reformer has enemies in all those who profit by the old order, and only lukewarm defenders in all those who would profit by the new.

Machiavelli, *The Prince*

IN 1985 the Report of the Committee of Inquiry into the Penal System, largely under the guidance of its chairman, Ken Whitaker, proposed a substantial set of reforms for Irish prisons. There were three main recommendations in the report: that a Prisons Board be established to manage the day-to-day running of the prisons; that the numbers in prison be substantially reduced by using prison only as a last resort; and that basic living conditions in prisons should correspond to those available to people on the outside with an average disposable income. It was part of the philosophy of the Whitaker Committee that 'people were sent to prison as punishment not for punishment' and that the deprivation of liberty was in itself an adequate penalty.

After eleven years, during which various governments had clearly set their faces against the principal recommendations, the Minister for Justice in November 1996 announced plans for the establishment of a Prisons Board. The case for the devolution of prison functions from the Department of Justice was forcefully made in the Whitaker Report which stressed that necessary changes in the prison system could be more readily brought about through an independent agency. However, in the intervening years, the problems of the prison system which Whitaker sought to remedy have grown ever more acute. The chronic crisis of overcrowding in Irish prisons is so great that it threatens to undermine the criminal justice system. The establishment of a Prisons Board will do little to change the system while the overcrowding continues. Meanwhile, the forthcoming change in the bail laws, which makes it much more difficult for those on remand to obtain bail, will add to the pressure and add to the estimated 5,000 'revolving door' releases a year due to lack of prison space.

The Whitaker recommendation to curtail the use of imprisonment was so central to the reforms proposed that the possibility of a continuing increase in prison numbers was not envisaged. It is ironic that as the government sets about implementing one of the main Whitaker reforms it should completely ignore the other. Plans are well under way to increase the number of prison places from 2,300 to 3,000 by the end of 1998. In the recent election, Fianna Fáil called for an increase of 2,000 places and for an implementation of a 'zero tolerance' policy which would send offenders to jail for even the more minor of crimes.

Some comparisons

As crime rates and the seriousness of crimes increase, correspondingly most Western countries have experienced huge increases in committals to prison. In the United States and in England prison populations have doubled over the past thirty years. In 1975 in Ireland there were 3,052 committals to prison. By 1995 the number of committals had reached 9,844. Between 1990 and 1995 there was an increase of 54 per cent in total committals annually, a 20 per cent increase in committals to longer sentences (over two years) and a 52 per cent increase in committals for serious offences. Some 53 per cent of the sentenced population in 1996 were serving sentences of two years or more, while 60 per cent of the sentenced prison population were serving sentences for violent crimes.

Given the level of overcrowding in Irish prisons it is surprising to learn that of the total of 9,844 committals in 1995, some 3,644 (37 per cent) were remand prisoners not subsequently convicted by the courts. Admittedly, their stay in prison was brief but clearly they should not have been there at all. Imprisonment is irrevocable in that time spent in prison cannot be restored. Prison also imposes a stigma and a burden on the prisoner's family, as well as on the prisoner, no matter how short the period of custody.

While the Irish prison system is at present committed to a policy of expansion of prison places, and while Irish courts are handing down stiffer and more frequent sentences, it must be noted that Ireland has one of the lowest rates of imprisonment in Europe, about 59 prisoners per 100,000 of population. Ireland has also the lowest proportion of female prisoners, on average about 2 per cent of total prisoners compared to a European Union average of about 5 per cent. In comparisons with our nearest neighbours in Northern Ireland and Scotland, Ireland's reliance on imprisonment appears modest. The average daily number of

prisoners in Scotland in 1996 was 5,630 compared to 2,100 in Northern
Ireland and 2,200 in the Republic. The rate of imprisonment per
100,000 inhabitants (1994 figures) was 58.6 in the Republic, 109 in
Scotland and 117 in Northern Ireland. In the USA the rate in 1992 was
an amazing 455, by far the highest proportion for any country.

Despite these favourable comparisons, the Irish prison system is
approaching a crisis situation largely due to overcrowding in antiquated
Victorian institutions. The Victorian era created the large institution not
to treat society's problems but to preserve society from its problem
people by locking them away. The large-scale mental asylum, the poor-
house, the workhouse, the orphanage: all now have passed into history
but society's faith in the Victorian prison remains firm. The prison
system of Ireland, as of most Western countries, remains set on a
relentless expansionist course despite the fact, as pointed out by the
Whitaker Report, that extra prison places penalise the taxpayer as much
as the prisoner. The cost of custody of a prisoner per year in the
Republic at £46,500 is surpassed in Europe only by that of Northern
Ireland where the cost reaches a staggering £63,800.

Andrew Rutherford, an outspoken critic of contemporary British penal
policy, believes that it is possible to break the expansionist mould but that
a real change of direction requires an informed and sceptical view of
prisons by the public and their political representatives. He states that
'most contemporary prison systems are expanding through a combination of drift and design. Criminal justice administrators perpetuate the
myth that the prison system is swept along by forces beyond their control
or influence. The convenient conclusion is announced that, given
increased rates of reported crime and court workloads, it inevitably
follows that there is no alternative other than for the prison system to
expand further' (1984, p. 171). He concludes that, in large part, criminal
justice administrators are the architects of the crisis with which they are
now confronted. If this is so, then perhaps the first step in reform is to
replace the administrators, as the Irish system is now doing. But is it
likely that the new Prisons Board will adopt the Whitaker philosophy of
a reduction in prison numbers and how realistic is such a policy at the
present time in Ireland? To answer this question we must first look at the
origin of present policies and see if there are alternatives to overcrowded
prisons and the high cost of incarceration.

The prison as punishment

Until the nineteenth century imprisonment had been little used as a form
of punishment. It had instead been mainly a holding place where

prisoners were kept while awaiting trial, transportation or execution, or for debts to be paid. As the use of the death penalty, floggings and physical mutilations waned, the punishment role of the prison increased. As French sociologist Michel Foucault notes, with the arrival of the prison the focus of punishment shifted from the body to the soul. Once it had arrived, it was difficult to remember what had preceded it or to imagine what might replace it: 'it banished into oblivion all the other punishments ... it seemed to have no alternative, as if carried along by the very movement of history ... and although, in little over a century, this self-evident character has become transformed, it has not disappeared. We are aware of all the inconveniences of prison, and that it is dangerous when it is not useless. And yet one cannot see how to replace it. It is the detestable solution, which one seems unable to do without' (Foucault, 1979, p. 232).

Prisons have been seen as serving many purposes – deterrence, prevention and curbing of crime, reform and rehabilitation of the criminal, payment of a debt to society – but over the past hundred and fifty years the prison system has served primarily as a punishment for those convicted of a criminal offence. The effectiveness of prison as a means of reform or of reducing crime has been questioned since the mid-eighteenth century; Henry Fielding, writing about houses of correction in 1751, stated: 'whatever these houses were designed to be, or whatever they at first were, the fact is that they are at present, in general, no other than schools of vice, seminaries of idleness, and common bearers of nastiness and disease' (quoted in Rutherford, 1984, p. 8). Yet faith in the prison as an appropriate form of punishment for the wrongdoer has never waned and is today more widely held than ever.

Two major changes with their roots in America have led to the view that 'only prison counts' and that advocating anything less is to be 'soft on crime'. Barry Goldwater was the first to make 'law and order' an issue in the 1964 US presidential election and ever since conservative politicians have criticised opponents as 'soft on crime' while arguing that stricter punitive policies, featuring much greater use of imprisonment, will create a safer society. The 'short, sharp shock' treatment for young offenders, the California 'three strikes and you're out' policy that required life sentences for people convicted of a third felony, and the New York 'zero tolerance' policy are all examples of this accepted wisdom. More recently, President Bill Clinton has felt it necessary to 'take crime away from the Republicans' by his support for tougher sentences, more capital offences, and increased funding for prisons and police. The lesson has not been lost on some Irish politicians who are beginning to adopt law and order electoral strategies.

A second American impact on prison policies comes from the elaborate experimentation with 'intermediate sanctions' since the early 1980s. The apparent failure of many of these programmes has left reformers disillusioned and has convinced conservatives that there really is no alternative to the harsh punitive regime of the traditional prison. Electronic monitoring of probationers and parolees, systems of day fines and week fines, boot camps (short-term prisons featuring hard labour in lieu of longer sentences), community service sentences, intensive supervision probation programmes, day-reporting centres and many similar experiments with intermediate sanctions have not proved to be more cost effective than prisons; neither have they proved more successful in reducing recidivism or crime. Good intermediate sanction programmes proved expensive to operate; many others failed because they were poorly implemented, with insufficient planning, finance or support.

However, according to Professor Michael Tonry of the University of Minnesota Law School, these programmes failed because the political will to implement them did not exist. He concludes that: 'if we have the political will we can operate intermediate sanctions that save money, reduce prison populations, and avoid unnecessary disruption to the lives of offenders and their families, and all without sacrificing important public interests in public safety. The only question is whether we will soon have the political will' (Tonry and Hamilton, 1995, p. 13).

An English experiment in electronic monitoring

Electronically monitored home detention remains one of the most frightening and fascinating of intermediate sanctions. Introduced in the USA in 1985, pilot schemes in electronic monitoring (EM) spread rapidly and by 1990 there was a daily monitored population of 12,000 spread across all fifty states. To some it heralded the arrival of the Orwellian new age of surveillance; to many beleaguered criminal justice administrators it offered a solution to overcrowding and overstretched budgets. It has not provided the magic solution but it does remain an underused alternative that may some day counter society's capacity to incarcerate.

A pilot project in electronic monitoring was set up in England and evaluated during 1989–90 involving a total of fifty people on bail: seventeen in Nottingham, fifteen in North Tyneside, and eighteen at Tower Bridge. In all cases EM was used as an alternative to imprisonment. It became immediately clear that home detention with EM was not equally suitable for all types of people. It may have been suitable for mature, responsible people with a family and employment, but those on the pilot projects tended to be young and unemployed, and many lacked the self-discipline required to cope with its demands. Of those monitored, twenty-nine absconded or were charged with a new offence; there were a total of 217 alleged time violations, and all fifty viewed the long curfews of up to sixteen hours as particularly oppressive. The experiment was discontinued when the six-month pilot scheme ended.

George Mair, principal research officer in the Home Office Research and Planning Unit, had this to say of the scheme: 'The evaluation of the pilot projects showed that EM is not a quick and easy answer to penal problems, but it is primarily because of lack of money that EM is not currently in use as a criminal justice tool in England and Wales. The use of electronic monitoring for offenders may yet be resuscitated; it certainly has not disappeared from the penal agenda' (Mair, 1995, p. 120).

Lack of Irish initiatives

The Whitaker Report proposed two mechanisms for reducing the prison population: an increase in remission from 25 per cent to 33 per cent of sentence and greater use of non-custodial alternatives for the majority of petty offenders. Clearly, these mechanisms were intended to be illustrative rather than exhaustive, and the report did point to the singular lack of initiatives taken by authorities in the Irish prison system since independence. This same point is made forcefully by Paul O'Mahony in *Crime and Punishment in Ireland* where he finds a complete failure to respond creatively to the unique aspects of the Irish situation. He sees the fact that we tend to look to Britain, rather than to smaller countries such as Denmark or Norway, for new initiatives in the criminal justice area as a serious indictment of our system and its failure to look for original solutions to our unique problems. He concludes that his study of Irish prisons 'has emphasised the unique conditions found in Ireland in many areas relating to crime and punishment. Ireland's culture, community values, and profile of crime and punishment are highly distinctive, despite many important similarities and affinities with neighbouring countries. However, most of the Irish legal and penal structures date from the time when Ireland was ruled from Westminster and are based on models which probably never were particularly suited to the local conditions and certainly are not now' (O'Mahony, 1993, p. 239).

Denmark has been far more adventurous in designing its own customised prison system than any other European nation, and it has set the standard for all the Scandinavian countries. While it is necessary to stress that, in the management and treatment of offenders, no ideas no matter how brilliant they might seem to their authors can be transferred intact from one country to another, yet fruitful comparisons can be made and many lessons learned in looking at the Danish system. Denmark lies in the average group of European countries in its use of imprisonment. It currently has 68 inmates per 100,000 inhabitants, slightly higher than Ireland. What makes Denmark unique is that it has best lived up to the principle of using prison only when strictly necessary. While crime in Denmark has doubled during the past twenty years, the prison capacity has not been extended at all.

Before examining whether the Danish system might not serve as a model for Ireland, there are some important considerations to be kept in mind. One is that the potential prison population in the two countries is likely to be quite different. In Ireland, as in Britain, despite some well-published exceptions, prisons are largely filled with the poor, the disadvantaged, the underclass and 'losers' of our society. The vast majority of Irish prisoners are young men, who have multiple convictions, usually against property or the person, and are no more successful at crime than they were in school, in work, in their own families or anywhere else. Denmark, by and large, does not have this category of offender. It has largely eliminated its underclass because rather than tolerate a dualism between state and market, between working class and middle class, its social democrat politicians pursued a welfare state that would promote an equality of the highest standards, not an equality of minimal needs as pursued by welfare regimes in Ireland or Britain. In brief, the Scandinavian countries set about creating a much more egalitarian society than did the remainder of Western European nations.

The Danish prison system: a model for Ireland?

As in the Whitaker proposals for reform of the Irish penal system, the Danish system is based on two fundamental ideas: that imprisonment, by the very deprivation of liberty, is a punishment in itself, and that prison be used only as a last resort. In Denmark, before the courts impose a prison sentence they must consider all other sanctions of a less radical nature. The legislature has continually adjusted the maximum and minimum penalties for stated crimes, and the use of alternatives to imprisonment has been greatly increased, notably conditional sentencing, probation, parole and fines, and community service orders. Denmark has stayed with traditional alternatives and not gone down the US road of excessive faith in computerised technology or novelty solutions.

In Denmark, the two fundamental ideas serve as a basis for three principles of normalisation, openness and responsibility within the prison system.

Normalisation means that one seeks as far as possible to approximate life in prison to the conditions in the outside world. This means that every decision and rule must be controlled, not by habit or tradition or what is practicable, but by the principle of: how would this be done in the outside world? If there are reasons for doing it differently in prison, these must be specified and justified. In Denmark, this means that the norm is to place people in an open prison; approximately two-thirds of prison places are in open prisons. There is no segregation of young and old, male and female, experienced criminals and newly convicted, unless clearly necessary. Inmates retain their civil rights such as voting in elections, having their own furniture in their cells, wearing their own clothes, the right to phone or write to those outside, and the right to a family life and conjugal visits. The only right that is curtailed is freedom of location.

Openness in the Danish system is an attempt to prevent the prison being a total institution in Erving Goffman's meaning of that phrase. No matter how liberal, life in prison is always formally managed, a daily rhythm of fixed rules, fixed hours and minutes of constant and irritating supervision. This is why the Danes believe it is so important to open prisons to the outside world. Visits from next of kin are permitted even daily. Visits are without control except for efforts to control drug smuggling. Leave of absence is permitted on every third weekend from open prisons, and even from closed prisons when a quarter of sentence has been served. Leave for special purposes such as weddings or birthdays is normal. Inmates are also free to participate in free debate in the press, and most have televisions and phones in their cells provided they pay for them themselves.

Responsibility is an attempt to break the overpaternalistic aspect of prisons and an endeavour to give the inmate a sense of responsibility, self-respect and self-reliance. As William Rentzmann, deputy director general of Danish Prisons, explains: 'Prisons traditionally have a large number of "hotel" services. We wake inmates in the morning, serve their breakfast, take them to work, serve their lunch, do their cleaning ... and get them to bed early. Naturally, there are good reasons for doing this, in particular preserving order and discipline in the prison' (Rentzmann, 1992, p. 11). The Danish system tries to break this mould in the belief that if prisoners are given responsibility for their own cooking, cleaning and hygiene, responsibility for their own treatment, they end up being responsible. Self-administration rather than staff administration has become the goal of the system.

While clearly in the Danish system there are stricter prisons for more serious offenders, one may well ask what element of punishment remains for the vast majority of inmates. William Rentzmann provides the Danish answer: 'the most important answer to this question is provided by the European Prison Rules themselves ... imprisonment is by the deprivation of liberty a punishment in itself. The prison services, we who work in this field, must not add additional suffering to the deprivation of liberty. The restrictions we impose on the inmates' daily lives, the deviations we make from ordinary civil rights, must be necessary to maintain the deprivation of liberty or to keep discipline. All other limitations will be in conflict with one of the key principles of the European Prison Rules' (Rentzmann, 1992, p. 11).

What can be achieved?

Ken Whitaker had already developed his own personal philosophy of the role of imprisonment long before he saw the Danish experiment at first hand. His Danish experience merely convinced him that his ideas were practicable and could be implemented in the Irish system while acknowledging that national prison systems move along different tracks and will inevitably be at different stages of development.

Already there is a new openness in the Irish prison system. There is great public interest in prisons, and both the Department of Justice and prison governors have acknowledged that there is nothing to hide and nothing to be gained from maintaining the prison as one of the last great secretive institutions in society. The arrival of the journalist and the television camera within the prison walls has compounded the public in its ambivalence about the purpose of imprisonment and the way we use imprisonment as punishment. On the one hand there is a call for tougher prison sentences, for more extensive use of imprisonment and for ending the 'revolving door' of early release. On the other hand there is severe criticism about inhumane prison conditions, about the over-crowded prison system and about the fact that it has clearly failed as a method of deterrence or of preventing increasing crime rates.

The new Prisons Board will effectively have its hands tied if it cannot control the level of intake into prisons. The Department of Justice's five-year plan, *The Management of Offenders,* envisaged the provision of an additional 210 prison places 'while taking such steps as are necessary to ensure that the prison population does not drift above the 2,200–2,300 level' (Department of Justice, 1994, p. 7). Already this rhetoric bears little resemblance to the reality. What Andrew Rutherford has called 'the new gaol fever' has taken hold of the Irish system and its indiscriminate use of imprisonment bears testimony to the fact that prison is considered the 'normal' punishment for crime and that other alternatives are considered only when the prison system is in crisis. A significant reduction in prison numbers will be possible only if the new Prisons Board, firstly, is convinced of the wisdom of the Whitaker philosophy; secondly, has the ability to influence the courts and the entire criminal justice system; and thirdly, has the capacity to tackle the issue of an annual bill of £20 million in overtime payments and the understandable anger of prison staff faced with the possibility of sizeable loss of earnings.

Imprisonment as a punishment in itself has developed only over the last two hundred years and has expanded in a very ad hoc manner that had little to do with notions of justice or the purpose to be achieved. Probably, there is no humane way that one human being can lock up another and, consequently, the question will always remain: what do prisons achieve? Or does everyone in prison now have to be there? The Irish prison system has seldom looked beyond the British system for inspiration, nor has it been in the forefront in testing new initiatives or seeking original solutions to Ireland's unique problems. In implementing the Whitaker recommendation of establishing an independent Prisons Board it is hoped that the Irish system will also have the will and the wisdom to seek to implement the other two main recommendations: reduction of prison numbers and the 'normalisation' of life within the prison walls.

ACKNOWLEDGEMENTS

I am grateful to the Department of Justice for supplying statistics on the Irish prison system.

REFERENCES

Coyle, Andrew (1994). *The Prisons We Deserve*, London: HarperCollins

Department of Justice (1994). *The Management of Offenders: A Five-Year Plan*, Dublin: Department of Justice

Foucault, Michel (1979). *Discipline and Punish: The Birth of the Prison*, London: Penguin Books

Mair, George (1995). 'Electronic Monitoring in England and Wales', in Tonry and Hamilton (1995)

O'Mahony, Paul (1993). *Crime and Punishment in Ireland*, Dublin: Round Hall Press

Rentzmann, William (1992). *Prison Information Bulletin*, Council of Europe, No. 16, June

Rutherford, Andrew (1984). *Prisons and the Process of Justice*, London: Heinemann

Tonry, M. and K. Hamilton (1995). *Intermediate Sanctions in Overcrowded Times*, Boston: Northeastern University Press

Von Hirsch, A. and A. Ashworth (1995). *Principled Sentencing*, Boston: Northeastern University Press

9

Primary and Second-Level Education in the Early Twenty-First Century

ÁINE HYLAND

A society which rates highly spiritual and moral values and seeks to develop the mental and physical well-being of its people will devote a substantial part of its resources to education. There are, in addition, social and economic considerations which reinforce the claim of education to an increasing share of expanding national resources. Improved and extended educational facilities help to equalise opportunities by enabling an increasing proportion of the community to develop their potentialities and raise their personal standards of living. Expenditure on education is an investment in the fuller use of the country's primary resource – its people – which can be expected to yield increasing returns in terms of economic progress.
Second Programme for Economic Expansion, 1963[1]

THE *Second Programme for Economic Expansion*, published in 1963, had major significance for education in Ireland. This was the first public acknowledgement by government that expenditure on education was an investment in the nation's future. Taken with a number of other documents dating from the first half of the 1960s, it charted a new direction for Irish education. In the early 1960s, government spending on education in Ireland was estimated at 4.1 per cent of GNP.[2] Even the most optimistic projections did not envisage an increase of more than 0.6 of a percentage point in subsequent decades: the 1965 *Investment in Education* report suggested a rise to 4.7 per cent by 1970/71 – an increase which was described by the report team as 'substantial'.[3] Today government spending on education is about 8 per cent of a very much larger GNP.[4] Writing in a 1996 issue of *Administration*, Martin O'Donoghue, a member of the Investment in Education team in the 1960s, wrote:

I imagine ... that we would have regarded an 8 per cent share as being 'riches beyond the dreams of avarice' or – on a more down to earth note – more than adequate funding to support any necessary reforms or developments in the educational system.[5]

166

There was a considerable increase in the number of full-time students in education in Ireland at primary, second level and third level between 1965/66 and 1994/95, as Table 1 shows.

Table 1: Number of full-time pupils by level, 1965/66 and 1994/95

| | 1965/66 | | 1994/95 | |
	Number	%	Number	%
Primary	504,865	75.5	499,282	51.4
Second level	142,983	21.4	375,457	38.6
Third level	20,698	3.1	96,681	10.0
Total	668,546	100.0	971,420	100.0

Source: D. Thornhill, Talk to Primary Principals' Conference, Cork, October 1996

In 1965 there were 668,000 pupils in full-time education. Thirty years later the figure was approaching one million. In 1965 more than three-quarters of the pupils were enrolled in primary schools and just over 20 per cent were enrolled at second level. Thirty years later, only half of the pupils were enrolled at primary level and the proportion at second level was almost 40 per cent.

Government expenditure at primary and second level has also increased dramatically, as Table 2 shows.

Table 2: Government expenditure on education per pupil by level, 1965/66 and 1994/95 (£, constant 1995 prices)

	1965/66	1994/95
Primary	425	1,425
Second level	850	2,225
Third level	2,375	3,750

Source: D. Thornhill, Talk to Primary Principals' Conference, Cork, October 1996

In 1965, exchequer current expenditure at primary and second level totalled £18.9 million and £9.7 million respectively. In 1995, the corresponding figures were £696.5 million and £825.6 million. Expressed in constant 1995 prices, government expenditure per student at primary level in 1965 was £425 whereas by 1995 it had increased to £1,425. At second level government current expenditure per student in 1965 was £850; it had risen to £2,225 by 1995. And although average pupil–teacher ratios in Ireland continue to be high by OECD standards, particularly at primary level, there has been nevertheless an appreciable decrease in the pupil–teacher ratio particularly at first level – from

33.6:1 in 1965 to 24.3:1 in 1993 to 22:1 in 1995. The decrease has not been as marked at second level where the ratio fell from 20:1 in 1965 to 18.1:1 in 1993.[6]

As we look forward to the twenty-first century it is interesting to speculate on how the education system at primary and second level will develop and to ask ourselves whether the investment level of the past thirty years will continue and what the outcomes of this investment are likely to be. The publication of the government's White Paper on education, *Charting our Education Future,* in 1995 and the relative openness and transparency of national policy-makers make this task a good deal easier than the task which confronted our predecessors thirty years ago. This paper will consider primary and second-level education in Ireland in the early decades of the twenty-first century under the following headings:

- the demographic situation and its likely effect on school enrolments
- the role of schooling in combating social exclusion
- curricular changes, including new approaches to teaching and learning
- implications of change for teachers – initial training, induction and incareer development
- administrative considerations.

Implications of demographic change for schooling

The last thirty years saw considerable fluctuation in the demographic situation. *Investment in Education* projected an average of about 65,000 births per annum in the early 1970s rising to 72,000 in the later years of that decade.[7] What the report could not have envisaged was the significant immigration of the 1970s, with the result that the population had risen by about 25 per cent by the late 1970s. The annual birth figures also increased, culminating in a peak of 75,000 births in 1980. From 1981 onwards the annual number of births declined steadily and by 1994 had fallen to 48,000. The resultant fall in the child population in the past fifteen years has already had a significant effect on pupil enrolments at first and second level and will continue to do so for the foreseeable future. The most recent pupil projections for primary education suggest that enrolments could fall from the current 480,000 to 360,000 within the next twenty years. Enrolments are also projected to fall at second level. Currently there are about 375,000 pupils enrolled at second level; in twenty years' time the figure could be less than 300,000.[8]

It is of some relevance that official second-level figures currently include about 18,000 pupils enrolled in vocational courses at second level, almost all of which are post-Leaving Certificate courses. Within the past two years the Department of Education has finally recognised a category of 'further education', and while this new sector is still in something of a limbo, it is likely that its reality will be given more formal recognition within the next two decades. Other factors which make it somewhat more difficult to project enrolments at second level include the recent introduction of alternative tracks within the senior-cycle programme. The introduction of Transition Year as a right for all students has been widely welcomed. In the current year (1996/97) almost three-quarters of second-level schools are offering Transition Year as an option, and this has resulted in an increase in student numbers at second level. Currently, 80 per cent of the relevant age cohort remain on in school until the end of senior cycle and the White Paper on education stated that 'the target is for at least a 90 per cent completion rate [at senior cycle] by the end of the 1990s'.[9] With the introduction of the Leaving Certificate Applied in 1996, a new and different programme is now available for those students for whom the established Leaving Certificate is not appropriate or satisfactory. The Leaving Certificate Vocational Programme provides a high-status, more vocationally oriented Leaving Certificate, as recommended by the Culliton Report in 1992.[10] These two initiatives are already attracting significant numbers of students and it is likely that the 90 per cent target for senior-cycle completion will be reached by the end of this decade.

Combating social exclusion

The *Report of the Constitution Review Group* points out that there is a much greater awareness in the 1990s of the implications of educational inequality than there was in the past. It suggests that the implications of the failure of the education system to cater adequately for the needs of the less advantaged are serious – for the individual, the economy and society – and it states:

> Because of the central role which knowledge plays in determining the generation of wealth, it is extremely important that all people have access to education, and can participate and benefit from it so that they are not precluded from the process of wealth generation in society. As the Annual School Leavers Surveys conducted by the Department of Labour show, there is a positive correlation between the level of education attained and employment opportunities and those who leave school without any formal credentials are severely disadvantaged in the labour market.[11]

The accelerated pace of change in the 1990s and the demands that this has placed on the education system have been widely acknowledged. Schools are continually challenged to meet the changing demands posed by economic, political and social change. While the Irish education system is believed to provide a sound academic basis for many young people who aspire to higher education and to entry to the professions, there is increasing concern that it is failing to address the issue of underachieving and non-achieving pupils who account for up to 20 per cent of the age cohort. A number of reports including the White Paper on education and the Operational Programme for Human Resources Development 1994–1999[12] have identified the need to broaden the education system in order to:

- deal effectively with school failure
- improve retention rates and combat early school leaving, and
- strengthen the vocational and enterprise dimension in second-level schools.

In spite of increasing investment in education, educational inequality resulting from social and economic disadvantage remains a problem. The *Report on the National Education Convention* points out that the individual and social costs of educational failure can be great and that prevention costs are relatively insignificant when measured against the prospective costs of correcting educational failure through welfare, health and perhaps justice services.[13]

In spite of the many changes in the education system during the past decades, some of the more intransigent problems still remain to be resolved. A 1997 report by the National Economic and Social Forum estimates that approximately 1,000 young people drop out of full-time education while still at primary level, 3,000 leave without any qualifications, 7,500 leave with only the Junior Certificate and a further 2,500 leave with the Junior Certificate and some subsequent vocational qualification but without a Leaving Certificate.[14] Long-term unemployment rates for early school-leavers are depressingly high – up to 50 per cent for some categories. The 1995 EU White Paper on education and training focuses particularly on this problem. It states:

> There is a risk of a rift in society between those that can interpret; those who can only use; and those who are pushed out of mainstream society and rely on social support: in other words between those who know and those who do not know.[15]

It goes on to state that 'a special effort has to be made for the most vulnerable sections of the population, particularly in the urban areas hardest hit by unemployment'. It recognises that 'naturally everything starts at school which is where the learning society has its root' and concludes: 'School has to adapt but nevertheless remains the irreplaceable instrument of everyone's personal development and social integration.'

Need to support the disadvantaged

There has been increasing recognition in recent years of the need to provide additional state support for disadvantaged groups within the education system. There is also an acknowledgement of the need for early intervention to identify and support children at risk of failure. The following list from a 1996 article by Clancy includes some current and recommended programmes within what he refers to as the 'intervention agenda':

- pre-school early start programme
- home–school community liaison programme
- designation of disadvantaged areas
- early identification of educational underachievement
- remedial teachers
- targeted reduction of pupil–teacher ratios
- school psychological service
- enhanced capitation grants for designated schools
- setting of explicit policy targets for:
  - reduction of educational failure
  - participation of children of the travelling community
  - participation in higher education of students from disadvantaged backgrounds
- Youthreach
- Vocational Training Opportunities Scheme (VTOS)
- quota of reserved higher education places for those from disadvantaged backgrounds
- higher education access programmes
- links between third-level colleges and designated second-level schools.[16]

Clancy points out that pre-school intervention has been identified as an area which should get priority. He also states that there is strong support for the innovative home–school community liaison project.

Criteria have been established by which certain schools have been designated 'disadvantaged' but most disadvantaged pupils are still in normal schools. However, the weight of research seems to support current government policy of targeting additional resources at designated schools, and the 1995 publication *Educational Disadvantage in Ireland* by Kellaghan et al. puts forward nine specific recommendations for consideration in formulating national policy relating to schemes of assistance to schools in designated areas of disadvantage.[17] These recommendations include proposals for very specific targeting of a limited number of schools in which there is a high concentration of pupils from disadvantaged backgrounds. Under the recently announced 'breaking the cycle' initiative the Minister for Education has already adopted this policy and it will be interesting to see within the next decade or so what the result of this policy will be. Other suggestions – including one that the intervention should be comprehensive and co-ordinated – are also being implemented, well-resourced support structures have been put in place, and linkages are being developed with the Operational Programme for local urban and rural development in order to tackle the problem on a multifaceted basis. It will be important that all of these initiatives are carefully monitored as there is a danger that strategies to deal with disadvantage will result in penalising effective schools and rewarding ineffective ones.

Children of the traveller community

The education of children of the traveller community continues to be a serious problem in Ireland. The participation rates of traveller children at all levels of the educational system are 'unacceptably low for a democratic society'.[18] It is estimated that there are about 5,000 traveller children of primary school age in the state, 4,200 of whom attend primary schools. Of these, about 1,800 are in ordinary classes and the rest are in either special classes or special schools.[19] In the White Paper on education, the government has stated as a policy objective that all traveller children of primary school age should be enrolled and participate fully in primary education according to their individual abilities and potential within five years. It also states that traveller children will be encouraged to enjoy a full and integrated education within the school system and that the placement of these children in special schools and classes will be done only on the basis of special educational need.[20]

At second level the problem is more serious, with the current participation of traveller children being very low. The 1995 *Report of the Task Force on the Travelling Community* pointed out that whereas significant improvement has occurred in both the standard of and access to second-level education for the general population in the past thirty years, this improvement has had little or no impact on the traveller population.[21] While no definitive statistics exist in relation to the enrolment of traveller children at second level, it is estimated that only approximately 100 traveller children aged 12–15 years attend mainstream second-level schools out of the estimated 2,000 children eligible to do so.[22] The White Paper on education states that the overall policy objective is that within ten years all traveller children of second-level, school-going age will complete junior-cycle education and 50 per cent will complete the senior cycle.[23] However, this objective is unlikely to be reached without great difficulty. The highly competitive structure of second-level education as it has evolved in recent decades militates against children with learning difficulties, including traveller children. They find it particularly difficult to cope with the organisational structure of our second-level schools, especially the inhospitable practice of moving from teacher to teacher and from room to room as is usually required by a subject-based approach to curriculum. Government policy in this regard will not be successful unless there is a determined commitment on the part of school authorities to respond creatively to the challenges which will inevitably arise in relation to the education of traveller children.

Children with special educational needs

A further area which will require commitment and determination on the part of school authorities is the education of young people with special educational needs – those young people who during the past thirty years or so were enrolled in special schools, for example schools for mildly and moderately handicapped pupils. Government policy is that a continuum of provision should be provided for children and young people with special educational needs. Such provision could range from occasional help within the ordinary school to full-time education in a dedicated centre or unit, with students being able to move from one type of provision to another as necessary and practicable.[24] Such a policy has already begun to be put in place at primary school level, and at second level a small number of schools in Dublin and Cork are recognised as designated schools for students with physical, visual or hearing impairment and they have been given additional teachers and support personnel. Most of their students can be included in normal classes for most of the curriculum and they sit the public examinations, some with special concessions. The *Report of the Special Education Review Committee* concluded:

By and large this model of provision works well and enables the student with the disability to benefit to the greatest extent possible from attendance in an ordinary school. It is a model which could usefully be extended to other areas of the country.[25]

However, because of the geographical spread of pupils with special needs, it may not be as easy in practice to ensure a continuum of provision as outlined in the White Paper for pupils outside the city areas.

A further issue which will become more pressing during the coming decades will be the provision of suitable education for profound and severely handicapped young people. Until recently, educational provisions for these children were limited if not non-existent. However, a 1993 decision of the High Court ruled that such children have a right to an appropriate education.[26]

Curricular changes, including new approaches to teaching and learning

The subject choices of current second-level students differ in many respects from the choices made by their parents thirty years ago, as Table 3 shows. As can be seen from the table, there were significant differences in the proportion of pupils taking Latin to Leaving Certificate level between 1964 and 1994. In 1994 less than 1 per cent of boys took Leaving Certificate Latin compared to nearly 90 per cent thirty years earlier. There has also been a substantial increase in the numbers taking modern European languages. The emphasis within the language syllabi has also changed during the period, with a much greater emphasis on oral language today than there was in the past. This emphasis will increase in the coming decades as there is a commitment in the White Paper on education to increase the proportion of Leaving Certificate marks for oral and aural competence:

> The policy objective will be to move towards a position where 60 per cent of the total marks available will be awarded for oral and aural competence in the Irish language and in modern European languages. ... Furthermore, second-level schools will be encouraged to promote a wide range of languages, including Spanish and German.[27]

A number of cross-curricular areas of study have also been introduced in recent years. These include various Pastoral Care, and Social and Health programmes.

In the coming decade further curricular changes will occur. All schools will be required to introduce Civic, Social and Political Education at junior cycle from 1997/98. This will be an examinable subject, and will replace the old Civics programme which had not been overhauled since its introduction in the 1960s. A new cross-curricular programme in Relationships and Sexuality Education will also be introduced in 1997/98. Within the coming decade, two subjects which have been marginalised in many schools in the past because of their non-examinable status are likely to become exam subjects. These are Religious Education and Physical Education. These subjects will require an innovative approach to assessment and certification, and discussions are currently taking place with teachers and management about possibilities in this regard.

Table 3: Percentage of second-level students studying selected subjects at senior cycle – Leaving Certificate programme by gender, 1964 and 1994[a]

	Boys		Girls	
Subject	1964	1994	1964	1994
Applied Mathematics	10.9	3.4	0.0	0.4
Art[b]	1.8	14.6	18.2	21.4
Biology	n/a	36.0	n/a	64.9
Botany	2.2	n/a	8.6	n/a
Business Organisation[c]	n/a	34.8	n/a	39.4
Chemistry	31.7	15.4	4.8	13.2
Classical Studies	n/a	1.3	n/a	0.7
Commerce	22.0	n/a	13.9	n/a
Construction Studies	n/a	25.1	n/a	1.1
Domestic Science	–	n/a	60.3	n/a
Drawing/Technical Drawing	29.0	30.0	17.5	1.4
Engineering	n/a	19.9	n/a	0.8
English	99.7	99.0	100.0	99.1
French	21.0	52.5	64.4	69.6
General Science	5.2	n/a	4.7	n/a
Geography	80.9	45.1	89.6	36.8
German	1.9	17.4	2.7	22.0
Greek	8.6	0.03	0.0	0.0
History	64.3	30.4	73.1	26.0
Home Economics[d]	n/a	9.9	n/a	56.7
Irish	99.3	95.9	99.4	97.2
Latin	88.3	0.5	38.5	0.2
Maths	99.3	99.1	82.3	98.8
Music[e]	0.6	0.7	1.7	3.2
Physics	28.8	29.4	2.0	9.4
Physics and Chemistry	7.2	4.1	4.7	1.5
Physiology and Hygiene	1.0	n/a	41.8	n/a

(a) The Leaving Certificate programme was offered only in secondary schools in 1964.
(b) The figures for Art in 1994 include both the Design and the Craftwork option.
(c) As well as Business Organisation, Accounting and Economics are also offered in senior cycle.
(d) Home Economics includes both Social and Scientific, and General.
(e) Music includes both Syllabus A and Syllabus B.
Source: Table compiled from *Investment in Education – Report of the Survey Team*, Dublin: Stationery Office, 1965, p. 276, and Department of Education, *Statistical Report, 1993/94*, Dublin: Stationery Office, 1996

At primary level, there has been no substantive change in the curriculum guidelines since the so-called 'New Curriculum' was introduced in 1971. However, this is shortly to change; the National Council for Curriculum and Assessment is currently putting the finishing touches on a revised curriculum which is expected to be introduced into all schools before the end of the decade.[28] This revised programme will retain the fundamental child-centred approach of the current curriculum but will restructure the curriculum to facilitate the early identification of children who are falling behind, particularly in the areas of literacy and numeracy. It will place greater emphasis on oral skills in English and on a more practically orientated approach in Mathematics. A more specific Science programme will be introduced and the Irish language curriculum will be radically revised. The new programme will also include an expansion of the Arts education curriculum, with a greater emphasis on the appreciative aspects of Visual Arts. Finally, a new programme in Social, Personal and Health Education will be introduced.

The teacher as facilitator

In bygone times, schools and teachers were repositories of knowledge. They were regarded as the fount of knowledge to which empty vessels would come in order to be filled. Together with the local priest and the doctor, the teacher was looked up to and respected as an educated person to whom others could turn for advice. While the status of teachers in Ireland remains high, they are no longer on the pedestal of the past. Although they may no longer be regarded as the main repositories of knowledge, I believe the key role of teachers in the education of young people will continue into the twenty-first century. Their role will not however be that of purveyors of knowledge; rather they will be facilitators and providers of opportunities for learning – supporting, motivating and encouraging young people to learn for themselves.

The theory of multiple intelligences

In this regard it is pertinent to refer to recent research in the United States on the theory of intelligence and its implications for teaching and learning. The classical view of intelligence suggested that there was a single form of logic and a single form of thinking. This view influenced the development of curriculum as far back as the ancient Greek education systems which emphasised logic, rhetoric and geometry – skills which stressed linear abstract reasoning. Such a curriculum was maintained into the Middle Ages and through the Renaissance when the era of modern scientific investigations began. Scientific psychology, which dates from the mid-nineteenth century, was built on the view that intelligence was closely linked to skill in abstract thinking.[29]

However, research in the 1980s by cognitive psychologists, particularly in the United States, has put forward a different view of intelligence. The central point emerging from this research is that there is not just one underlying mental capacity, but rather a variety of intelligences working in combination. This theory of multiple intelligences is based on a synthesis of evidence from diverse sources. Its main proponent is Howard Gardner, who regards the intelligences not as physical entities but 'only as potentially useful scientific constructs'. He sees intelligence as 'not a thing but rather a potential, the presence of which allows an individual access to forms of thinking appropriate to specific kinds of content'. In his early work in the 1980s, Gardner proposed that there were at least seven intelligences and in his more recent work he adds an eighth:

- linguistic – the capacity to use words effectively
- musical – the capacity to perceive, discriminate, transform and express musical forms
- logical/mathematical – the capacity to use numbers effectively
- visual/spatial – the ability to perceive the visual/spatial world accurately
- bodily/kinaesthetic – expertise in using one's whole body to express ideas and feelings
- intrapersonal – self-knowledge and the ability to act adaptively on the basis of that knowledge
- interpersonal – the ability to perceive and make distinctions in the moods, intentions, motivations and feelings of other people
- naturalist – the ability to recognise and classify the numerous species of one's environment.[30]

Although the intelligences are set out separately in Gardner's literature, he makes the point that in life one never finds intelligences operating in isolation. All roles and products involve a combination of intelligences.

Implications of the theory of multiple intelligences for the curriculum

Multiple intelligences theory offers a useful framework for curriculum design in schools. If people possess at least eight intelligences, then their educational experiences should provide opportunities for all of these to be developed and should recognise the potential for accessing knowledge through various intelligences. The educational culture in this country, as indeed in most Western countries, and consequently our educational system tend to emphasise linguistic and logical/mathematical intelligences, while bodily/kinaesthetic, interpersonal and intrapersonal intelligences in particular are often neglected and marginalised.[31]

It is increasingly recognised that young people learn more effectively when they are actively engaged in the process of planning, doing, reviewing, recording and target setting.[32] The White Paper on education emphasises the value of active learning methodologies at all levels.[33] One way of enabling students to take more control of their learning is to help them to understand themselves as learners, to appreciate and value their strengths and to identify their weaknesses. Multiple intelligences theory can be used as a way of helping young people to understand their own learning process, to recognise and value their strengths, and to identify ways in which they can build upon these while developing the areas which are less strong.

There is no blueprint for a multiple intelligences classroom, especially not in this country where the theory has only begun to be adopted. There are many suggestions for classroom practice from experience in the United States but these will need to be adapted to meet the needs of Irish teachers and pupils.[34] A number of possibilities have been suggested, including the planning of lessons to provide different gateways to learning particular topics or concepts. It might also be useful to consider the increased use of colour, music, movement, and audio and visual aids in the classroom (access to new information technologies would facilitate this). Another approach might be to help individual students to develop their own individual profile, outlining their own strengths and weaknesses in different intelligences and devising strategies and approaches to use and build on their various strengths.

Reform of assessment

Since curricular reform and assessment reform are so closely inter-related, curricular reform should not be undertaken without reference to assessment reform. If our educational goals promote a broad range of outcomes and recognise a wide variety of educational achievements, these goals should be reflected in an equally broad assessment policy. Assessment drives the curriculum, and this is true particularly in Ireland because of our historical tradition. When government funding first became available for secondary education in 1878, the money was distributed to schools on the basis of the results of their pupils at public examinations. In more recent years, pressure from the Leaving Certificate points system has contributed to an assessment-driven approach to teaching and learning.

Traditional patterns of assessment tend to reward intellectual/cognitive aspects of achievement and the subjects in which these forms of achievement are pre-eminent. They only recognise a fraction of the multiple intelligences described by Gardner. There are increasing arguments for expanding and developing the traditional patterns of examination and assessment with which we are familiar. Gardner has referred to intelligence-fair assessments in his writing. Other US educationists refer to authentic assessment as those forms of assessment that reflect real-life situations and challenge pupils' ability to test what they have learned in those situations.[35] Authentic assessment has the following features:

- it is based on actual forms of what we want pupils to be good at (e.g. reading, writing, speaking, creating, doing research, solving problems)
- it requires more complex and challenging mental processes
- it acknowledges more than one approach or right answer
- it emphasises uncoached explanations and real products
- it has transparent criteria and standards
- it involves trained assessor judgement.

The White Paper on education pays particular attention to the significance of appropriate approaches to assessment. It acknowledges that assessment and the uses to which it is put influence teaching methods and the wider school environment. It points out that assessment procedures should be comprehensive enough to test the full range of abilities across the curriculum and to evaluate all the elements of learning.[36]

It is generally accepted that the current Junior Certificate examination does not adequately support the achievement of the full range of curricular objectives as set out in the new Junior Certificate programme. This is recognised in the White Paper where it is stated that 'an essential shift in emphasis from external examinations to internal assessment will be implemented in the future and ... new assessment methods will include projects, orals, aurals and practical work'.[37] The development of appropriate approaches to authentic assessment is one of the challenges which face educational planners and decision-makers during the coming decades. The issue has already been addressed to some extent by those involved in devising the assessment of the Leaving Certificate Applied and the link modules of the Leaving Certificate Vocational Programme. Portfolio assessment is an important component of the Leaving Certificate Vocational Programme. Authentic assessment approaches are also used for the Leaving Certificate Applied where a range of 'tasks' are identified and assessed. The Junior Certificate Elementary Programme also includes innovative approaches to assessment, including profiles of achievement noted and recorded over a period of time.

It will be important during the next decade or so that employers and those involved in determining entry criteria for further and higher education institutions look seriously at these new and innovative approaches to assessment and be fair and open-minded in their appraisal of them. It would be a pity if new modes and techniques of assessment were dismissed or rejected out of hand, simply because employers and others were unprepared to reconsider their traditional approaches to selection and were unwilling to give young people an opportunity to prove that a different approach to learning and assessment might well be as successful as what we have become familiar with – if not more so.

Implications of change for teachers – initial training, induction and incareer development

There has been a sharp increase in recent years in the professional needs of teachers arising not only from curricular changes but also from a significant broadening of the role of the teacher. This broadening role encompasses:

> Not only the instructional, the custodial, the inspirational and the disciplinary but extends into practically all spheres of life with teachers acting as agents of physical, moral, and spiritual development, emotional and mental health and social welfare.[38]

Among the factors creating new demands on teachers in the education system are the following:

- changes in economic, technological, social and cultural aspects of society requiring new teacher methodologies and curricula
- falling numbers of pupils and the concomitant reduction in the need for new teachers resulting in a stable, ageing profession
- the broadening role of teachers in terms of school administration and management, and in terms of meeting growing demands in such areas as parent–teacher relationships, pastoral care and counselling, and coping with pupils with learning difficulties and with pupils from socially deprived backgrounds
- the personal development needs of teachers to meet the demands of changing role and expectation.[39]

The *Report on the National Education Convention* recognises that 'the quality, morale and status of the teaching profession are of central importance to the achievement of desired reforms in the decades ahead'.[40] The report refers to the importance of supporting a policy which views the teaching career as a continuum involving initial teacher education, induction processes and incareer development opportunities available periodically throughout a teacher's career. While each of these points of support is important, it may well be, as stated in the OECD report *Schools and Quality,* that 'at a time of declining student numbers and declining recruitment through initial training, investment in inservice education is manifestly the most effective way of improving the quality of teaching generally'.[41] Another recent OECD report *Schools under Scrutiny* has noted that improved initial teacher training and inservice teacher training is one key method of raising standards in education but comments that governments are sometimes reluctant to launch big inservice programmes because of the cost and because they may not reach the staff who really need to improve.[42] This may be one of the biggest challenges to educational policy-makers during the coming decades – how to address in a comprehensive way the needs and aspirations of talented and well-educated young teachers as they progress through their careers. A 1993 report from the National Economic and Social Council notes that, rather than being viewed as a facility provided at times of dramatic change, inservice teacher training should be an accepted regular constituent part of teacher education. It recommends that

> necessary changes in organisational and other arrangements must be effected to enable this to happen. This is of particular importance given the relatively low turnover in teaching staff. The teaching profession cannot be expected to continue delivering a quality service ... if [teachers] are not equipped with the necessary skills to do so.[43]

EU funding of almost £40 million has been obtained for incareer development in this country during the period of the five-year plan for 1994–99. A major programme of inservice has been initiated and new models and approaches to teacher inservice have been put in place in the context of this funding. A particularly successful approach has been that taken in the context of the Transition Year programme. Under this initiative a national team of six teachers have been released for a two-year period and this team, with the assistance of regional co-ordinators, have put in place a nationwide support process for teachers involved in Transition Year. This model of inservice is school focused, i.e. the national and regional co-ordinators work with the teachers within the context of either an individual school or groups of schools. They advise and support the teachers and help them to devise appropriate and relevant curriculum and assessment approaches for their individual schools. Similar models are being implemented for teachers in curricular areas such as Relationships and Sexuality Education and Civic, Social and Political Education at junior cycle. Initial evaluation reports suggest that this approach to incareer development is effective and it is likely that this model of inservice will be more widely used in the coming decade. The strengthening of the education centre network is another major plank for inservice development; EU funding is being used to increase the number of full-time centres and to develop a more permanent infrastructure for them. Many of the problems relating to difficulties of access, inappropriateness of models of inservice, etc. are now being tackled and feedback from teachers suggests that satisfaction levels with the current approaches are reasonably high.

The introduction of a revised primary school curriculum in the near future will necessitate a major programme of inservice for primary teachers and it is likely that the approach to this programme will build on good practice and on the innovations introduced for second-level teachers in the recent past.

Administrative considerations

Possibly the most visible and potentially controversial area of change in education in the coming decade will be the administrative area.

There has been criticism in recent years of the overcentralised approach to educational administration in Ireland. The 1993 Green Paper on education, *Education for a Changing World,* indicated that the Department of Education intended to divest itself 'of its excessive involvement in day-to-day administration of the education system'.[44] The *Report on the National Education Convention* stated that:

> The highly centralised character of educational administration has also fostered a culture of dependency with an overreliance placed by institutions on the department's role, which may have resulted in the sapping of self-reliance and innovative approaches at local level.[45]

Joe Lee, in his major work *Ireland 1912–1985,* made a similar point when he wrote 'A big question mark hangs in any case over the appropriateness of highly centralised "planning" in the fields of education and health' and added: 'In many advanced countries, responsibility for both these activities lies, in varying degrees, with local and regional authorities.'[46]

While many people's perception of our education system is of a highly centralised bureaucracy, a 1995 OECD/CERI report found that decision-making in Irish education is in fact more school focused than it is in any of the other thirteen countries surveyed. The survey identified four possible levels of decision-making – school, lower intermediate level, upper intermediate level and central government – and found that Ireland has the highest proportion of decisions taken at school level – 73 per cent – with New Zealand a close second at 71 per cent.[47] Table 4 shows the situation in each of the fourteen countries surveyed.

Table 4: Proportion of decisions taken at decision-making levels in fourteen OECD countries (%)

	School	Lower intermediate level	Upper intermediate level	Central government
Austria	28	8	26	28
Belgium	25	50	25	–
Denmark	41	44	–	15
Finland	40	47	–	13
France	31	–	35	33
Germany	33	42	18	7
Ireland	73	8	–	19
New Zealand	71	–	–	29
Norway	32	45	–	23
Portugal	40	–	3	57
Spain	28	26	13	33
Sweden	48	48	–	4
Switzerland	10	40	50	–
United States	26	71	3	–

Source: OECD/CERI, *Decision-Making in 14 OECD Education Systems*, Paris: OECD, 1995, p. 40

The report points out:

In Ireland and New Zealand, the school's importance in the decision-making structure is similar to that for private education. In Ireland's case this is partly due to the fact that public sector schools belong to religious establishments, which enjoy a broad measure of autonomy as regards resources and management of non-teaching staff.

In the vast majority of the countries surveyed, the school takes between 25 per cent and 41 per cent of decisions and there is a fairly even sharing of decision-making between institutional, local, regional and national levels. The lack of intermediate structures in Ireland has meant that educational decision-making is polarised at the institutional and the central extremes.

This imbalance is likely to be redressed shortly, with the setting up of ten regional education boards. The rationale for these education boards was summarised in the White Paper on education as follows:

- The need for greater awareness of and sensitivity to the needs of local and regional communities in order to improve the quality, equality, efficiency and relevance and flexibility of delivery of all educational services.
- The value of further involvement and empowerment of local and regional communities, in addition to their current and continuing involvement at school level.
- The desirability of releasing the Department of Education from much of its current involvement in the detailed delivery of services to schools, in order to allow it concentrate on the development and monitoring of the education system at national level.
- A realisation that the demands of educational provision cannot, in many instances, be met at the level of the individual school.[48]

Draft legislation to set up education boards has recently been published and will shortly be laid before the Houses of the Oireachtas. It is proposed to transfer 'substantial co-ordination and support service functions' to these boards while ensuring at the same time that they will not 'impinge on areas of responsibility and discretion proper to individual school boards'.[49]

The transfer of some functions from the Department of Education to the new education boards will, it is hoped, free up the department to 'concentrate on higher level administration and policy oriented tasks' as recommended in the OECD report *Review of Educational Systems – Ireland* in 1991.[50] The role of the department will be changed to focus on strategic planning and policy and on the execution of those activities most efficiently conducted at national level. This is in keeping with the government's 'vision for Ireland' as presented in the coalition government's policy agreement *A Government of Renewal* (1994) and reiterated in *Delivering Better Government – Strategic Management Initiative*, published in May 1996:

> In the lifetime of this Government, we pledge ourselves to the reform of our institutions at national and local level to provide service, accountability, transparency and freedom of information. In so doing, we are committed to extending the opportunities for democratic participation by citizens in all aspects of public life.[51]

While the establishment of regional education boards will provide a framework for the devolution of educational decision-making, the new boards will need to tread carefully to ensure that they maintain the co-operation of the various partners in education, particularly the churches.

The symbiotic relationship between church and state in education is one which most Irish people take for granted, but when the OECD examiners visited Ireland in 1990, they found that this relationship was 'the most intriguing factor for the external observer'. They wrote:

> The State would not contemplate subverting the authority of the Church in educational matters either by usurping any of its functions or by introducing measures that it would be likely to find unpalatable. Change is only feasible through discreet negotiations and an unspoken search for consensus . . . it is a question of the State not embarking on a reform affecting the school system as a whole without the implicit or explicit assent of the Church and where applicable other interest groups.[52]

During the coming decades a combination of falling school rolls and a reluctance on the part of the state to usurp any of the functions of the church in education is likely to lead to tension and clashes about the suitability of the Irish education system for all our young people. Ireland is no longer a homogeneous society in terms of culture, religion, race or ethnicity (if indeed it ever was). There is an increasing recognition of pluralism as an important underlying educational principle, and this recognition is evident in the White Paper on education. An aspiration to pluralism is praiseworthy but it raises problems in a context where virtually all primary schools are owned and controlled by the churches. Table 5 shows that in 1992/93 only ten primary schools (multidenominational) were not church-owned schools.[53] That figure had increased to fourteen (one of which is an all-Irish school) by 1996/97.

Table 5: Number and type of primary schools, 1992/93

Category	Number of schools
Catholic	2,988
Church of Ireland	190
Presbyterian	18
Multidenominational	10
Methodist	1
Jewish	1
Muslim	1

Source: Department of Education

An increasing proportion of the population belong to religions which do not own or control schools or describe themselves as having no religion. In the 1991 census of population the proportion in these two categories together with those who chose not to declare a religious affiliation came to almost 6 per cent of the overall population.[54] In other words, approximately 30,000 children of primary school age do not belong to the churches which own and control schools. In addition, there is evidence that, given the choice, a significant proportion of Catholic and Protestant families would prefer their children to attend religiously integrated or multidenominational schools.

During the past two decades, fourteen multidenominational primary schools have been set up by parents who wish to have this option for their children. Most of these schools are oversubscribed and have long waiting lists. But some parents are now taking the view that it should not be necessary for groups of parents to trudge the tortuous and expensive route of setting up (privately owned) multidenominational schools and that the state, either directly or through regional boards, should provide such schools as is done in all other EU countries.[55]

The *Report of the Constitution Review Group* addressed issues such as these in its treatment of education and religion, and stated that these and similar problems have been avoided to date largely by ad hoc and pragmatic responses in particular situations.[56] However, the report is of the view that, with an increasingly diverse and rights-conscious society, these problems can no longer be ignored. It points out that 'Many of these difficulties are attributable to the fact that, unlike other countries, there is not a parallel system of non-denominational schools organised by the State which would cater for the interests of minorities', and adds:

> The present situation, therefore, presents a potential conflict of rights to which there is no satisfactory answer. The conflict lies between the rights of the child (exercised through its parents) not to be coerced to attend religious instruction at a publicly funded school and the right of denominational schools in receipt of such public funding to provide for the fulness of denominational education through the medium of an integrated curriculum and other measures designed to preserve the religious ethos of a particular school.

In view of the increasing tendency of individuals to have recourse to litigation for adjudication of their constitutional rights, it seems likely that within the next decade or so the issues discussed here will come before the courts, and decisions made by the judiciary could have significant implications.

Conclusion

It has been possible in this paper to focus on only a small number of the issues which are likely to arise in relation to primary and second-level education in the coming decades. Issues which have not been addressed include the implications of the dramatic decrease in the child population for school rationalisation and amalgamation. In parallel with this decrease, there is a growing demand from parents for a wider choice of schooling for their children. This issue came to public attention in July 1996 when the Minister for Education refused to sanction a number of proposed new Gaelscoileanna at primary level. The demand for all-Irish schools is a relatively recent phenomenon but it will be difficult in coming decades for governments to meet the growing demand for Gaelscoileanna and multidenominational schools while simultaneously presiding over the closure of adjacent denominational schools. This issue is currently being addressed by the Commission on School Accommodation Needs but there is not likely to be an easy solution in the immediate future.

Other issues which this paper has not considered include the implications for secondary schools of the decline in religious vocations. Thirty years ago, about half of the teachers in secondary schools were priests or members of religious orders or congregations. By 1990 the proportion had fallen to 12 per cent, and it is likely to be less than 5 per cent by the turn of the century.[57] Thirty years ago the principalship of virtually all Catholic secondary schools was held by a priest, a brother or a nun. Today, about half of the principals are lay men or women and the number is increasing year by year. The ad hoc management approaches of the past are being superseded by more professional models of management. Negotiations are currently taking place to set up middle-management structures in all schools of an adequate size.[58] Internal management structures will be paralleled by a more structured, accountable and transparent management approach by the schools' boards of management. This will be manifest through published school plans and annual reports, and through the development of whole-school inspection in all schools – a move which is not likely to occur without some controversy.[59]

I am confident that the Irish schools of the twenty-first century will maintain and improve the generally high standard that has characterised Irish education in the past decades. We are no longer as naive as some of our political masters in the 1950s who smugly reassured themselves that Ireland had the best education system in the world.[60] Today there are international agencies which provide indicators of comparative educational performance across a number of countries.[61] While Ireland does not come out at the top of the league, its performance is creditable particularly when one notes the position of Ireland in the league of comparative indicators of resource input.

At the end of the day, we must always remember that education is about people – good structures and physical resources are a help in delivering a good service but nothing can replace a caring, able and committed teacher. The following quotation from the White Paper on education is an appropriate note on which to end this paper:

> The quality, morale and status of the teaching profession are of central importance to the continuing development of a first-class education system in the decades ahead ... Teachers have made an enormous contribution to Irish society. The profession's standing has also been recognised internationally. It is important, therefore, that the career of teaching continues to attract talented people and that it proves professionally rewarding to those who follow it.[62]

NOTES

1. *Second Programme for Economic Expansion*, 1963, quoted in Á. Hyland and K. Milne (eds.), *Irish Educational Documents*, Vol. 2, Dublin: Church of Ireland College, 1991, p. 36.
2. M. O'Donoghue, 'Investment in Education – Context, Content and Impact', *Administration*, Vol. 44, No. 3 (Autumn 1996), p. 23.
3. *Investment in Education – Report of the Survey Team*, Dublin: Stationery Office, 1965, p. 398.
4. D. Thornhill, Talk to Primary Principals' Conference, Cork, October 1996.
5. O'Donoghue, 'Investment in Education', p. 23.
6. Thornhill, Talk to Primary Principals' Conference.
7. *Investment in Education*, p. 27.
8. Commission on School Accommodation Needs, *Report of the Technical Working Group on Rationalisation of Vocational Education Committees*, Dublin: Commission on School Accommodation Needs, 1996, p. 70.
9. *Charting our Education Future*, White Paper on Education, Dublin: Stationery Office, 1995, p. 44.
10. Industrial Policy Review Group, *A Time for Change: Industrial Policy for the 1990s*, Dublin: Stationery Office, 1992.
11. *Report of the Constitution Review Group*, Dublin: Stationery Office, 1996, p. 346.
12. *Operational Programme for Human Resources Development 1994–1999*, Dublin: Stationery Office, 1995, p. 100.
13. J. Coolahan (ed.), *Report on the National Education Convention*, Dublin: Stationery Office, 1994, p. 106.
14. *Early School Leavers and Youth Unemployment*, Dublin: National Economic and Social Reform, 1997.
15. *Teaching and Learning: Towards the Learning Society*, EC White Paper on Education and Training, Brussels: European Commission, 1995, p. 25.
16. P. Clancy, 'Investment in Education – The Equality Perspective: Progress and Possibilities', *Administration*, Vol. 44, No. 3 (Autumn 1996), p. 38.
17. T. Kellaghan et al., *Educational Disadvantage in Ireland*, Dublin: Educational Research Centre, 1995.
18. Coolahan (ed.), *Report on the National Education Convention*, p. 127.
19. *Report of the Task Force on the Travelling Community*, Dublin: Stationery Office, 1995, p. 173.

20. *Charting our Education Future*, p. 26.
21. *Report of the Task Force on the Travelling Community*, p. 184.
22. *Ibid.*, p. 185.
23. *Charting our Education Future*, p. 57.
24. *Ibid.*, p. 24.
25. *Report of the Special Education Review Committee*, Dublin: Stationery Office, 1993.
26. *O'Donoghue v. The Minister for Education*, 1993; judgment of Mr Justice R. O'Hanlon.
27. *Charting our Education Future*, p. 61.
28. *Comhairle*, Newsletter of the National Council for Curriculum and Assessment, December 1996.
29. H. Gardner, M. L. Kornhaber and W. K. Wake, *Intelligence – Multiple Perspectives*, Fort Worth: Harcourt Brace, 1995.
30. H. Gardner, *Multiple Intelligences: The Theory in Practice – A Reader*, New York: Basic Books, 1993.
31. Sheelagh Drudy and Kathleen Lynch, *Schools and Society in Ireland*, Dublin: Gill & Macmillan, 1993, pp. 236–9.
32. V. Chamberlain, B. Hopper and B. Jack, *Starting Out the MI Way – A Guide to Multiple Intelligences in the Secondary School*, Bolton: D2, 1996.
33. *Charting our Education Future*, p. 58.
34. See for example, T. Armstrong, *Multiple Intelligences in the Classroom*, Alexandria, Va.: ASCD, 1994; B. Campbell, *The Multiple Intelligences Handbook: Lesson Plans and More*, Stanwood, Wash.: Campbell and Associates, 1994; B. A. Haggerty, *Nurturing Intelligences – A Guide to Multiple Intelligences: Theory and Teaching*, Addison-Wesley Publishing Co., 1996.
35. A. Hargreaves, L. Early and J. Ryan, *Schooling for Change*, London: Falmer Press, 1996, pp. 112–39.
36. *Charting our Education Future*, pp. 59–60.
37. *Ibid.*
38. OECD, *Review of Educational Systems – Ireland*, Paris: OECD, 1991, p. 91.
39. CHL, *Review of Professional Development in Teaching*, Report commissioned by the NCCA, Dublin: CHL Consulting Group, 1991.
40. Coolahan (ed.), *Report on the National Education Convention*, p. 85.
41. OECD, *Schools and Quality*, Paris: OECD, 1989, p. 77.
42. OECD, *Schools under Scrutiny*, Paris: OECD, 1995, p. 39.
43. National Economic and Social Council, *Report on Education and Training Policies for Economic and Social Development*, Report No. 95, Dublin: National Economic and Social Council, 1993, pp. 219–20.
44. *Education for a Changing World*, Green Paper on Education, Dublin: Stationery Office, 1992.
45. Coolahan (ed.), *Report on the National Education Convention*, p. 15.
46. J. J. Lee, *Ireland 1912–1985: Politics and Society*, Cambridge: Cambridge University Press, 1989, p. 677.
47. OECD/CERI, *Decision-Making in 14 OECD Education Systems*, Paris: OECD, 1995, p. 40.
48. *Charting our Education Future*, p. 165.
49. *Education Bill, 1997*, Dublin: Stationery Office, 1997.
50. OECD, *Review of Educational Systems – Ireland*, p. 41.
51. Government of Ireland, *Delivering Better Government – Strategic Management Initiative*, Dublin: Stationery Office, 1996.

52. OECD, *Review of Educational Systems – Ireland*, p. 38.
53. This table was presented by the Department of Education at the Roundtable Discussions on the Governance of Schools in 1994.
54. *Census of Population 1991*, Vol. 5: Religion.
55. See Á. Hyland, 'Multi-Denominational Schools in the Republic of Ireland 1975–1995', in M. Lemosse (ed.), *Education et Religion dans les Iles Britanniques: Dieu à l'École*, Nice: CYCNOS, Vol. 13, No. 2 (1996), p. 42.
56. *Report of the Constitution Review Group*, p. 386.
57. Figures from the Conference of Religious of Ireland.
58. *Revised Teachers' PCW Proposals*, December 1996.
59. *Education Bill, 1997*.
60. S. Ó Buachalla, *Education Policy in Twentieth-Century Ireland*, Dublin: Wolfhound Press, 1988.
61. See for example OECD, *Education at a Glance*, Paris: OECD, 1995.
62. *Charting our Education Future*, p. 121.

10

Third-Level Education in Ireland: Change and Development

JOHN COOLAHAN

A backward look

THE role of higher education has become recognised as a central one in the economic, social and cultural life of society in countries of the developed world. This role has been increasingly emphasised in Ireland in a range of public documents. Public confidence in the investment value of higher education received external endorsement by the OECD *Economic Survey on Ireland*, 1995, when it stated:

> On the basis of the current system of financing higher education and current income and indirect tax rates, the rate of return to government would appear to be around 12 per cent, which is higher than the rate of return on government bonds and the long-run private rate of return on equities.[1]

It also noted that 'the social rate of return would appear to be somewhat higher than this'.[2]

Within a generation, the profile of higher education in Ireland has changed dramatically. It is just thirty years since the Commission on Higher Education published its long-awaited report. The commission's assessment of the existing situation in higher education painted a rather dismal picture. It criticised the piecemeal character of the system and the lack of planning machinery. It considered that increasing numbers of students, low entry standards and inadequate staffing and accommodation placed academic standards in jeopardy. The commission was not impressed by the level of postgraduate studies and research where it found 'the insufficiency of staff, equipment and accommodation has been especially frustrating'. It criticised the academic appointment procedures and the constitution and administrative structures of the higher education institutions.[3] Overall, the commission considered the inadequacies as 'so grave as to call for a concentrated effort to remove

191

them'.[4] While the commission referred to 'increasing numbers of students', the *Investment in Education* report of 1966 highlighted that only about 4 per cent of the school leavers' cohort studied progressed from second-level to university education and, of these, it demonstrated a massive social imbalance whereby 85 per cent of places in university were held by students from the top three categories of the occupational matrix devised by the researchers.[5]

Building from this very weak base of the mid-sixties, policy measures were implemented over the succeeding three decades which transformed the structure and character of higher education in Ireland. Among key features of the changed configuration of higher education were the establishment of a strong binary tradition whereby the regional technical colleges (RTCs), the Dublin Institute of Technology (DIT) and the national institutes for higher education (NIHEs) in Limerick and Dublin formed the strong pillars of the extra-university sector. The designation of the NIHEs as the University of Limerick and Dublin City University in 1989, the first universities established in independent Ireland, did not impair the binary approach. The Higher Education Authority (HEA), set up in 1968 with significant responsibilities for higher education, but particularly for the university sector, and the National Council for Educational Awards (NCEA), set up in 1971 with academic responsibilities for the extra-university sector, were to be pivotal institutions in this developmental and expansionary era. The diversification provided by many new higher education institutions was matched by the expansion of established institutions and by many new and restructured course offerings.

Table 1 sets out an overview of the general pattern of full-time student participation from 1965 to 1995. A further 12,000 students were enrolled on a part-time basis in 1995/96. The age cohort transferring to tertiary education increased to 50 per cent in 1994/95. The proportion of students registered at postgraduate level in the university sector in the nineties has been steady at about 16 per cent of the total student body.

The impressive expansion in the provision of diversified forms of higher education placed heavy demands on the national exchequer. The current expenditure increased from about £10 million in 1965 to £430 million in 1995. The capital expenditure from public sources increased from £11 million in 1965 to £36 million in 1995.[6] The OECD figures in *Education at a Glance*, 1995, indicate that expenditure in Ireland on higher education, as a percentage of total expenditure on education, is close to the OECD average, at 24 per cent.

the DIT and RTCs forming the second prong. In its appraisal of the situation in 1992 the Green Paper concluded that 'it is important that the distinctive missions of the two sectors should be maintained and fostered', while it urged that links between the universities and the RTCs be improved to better serve regional needs.[11] The binary issue was discussed at the National Education Convention and its report recorded strong pressure from the RTC sector against any 'capping' of its degree-level work but also noted concern by others of a danger of 'academic drift' by this sector to the disadvantage of the colleges' mission.[12] The White Paper came down unambiguously on the maintenance of the binary system stating:

> The diversity of institutions and the separate missions of the two broad sectors will be maintained to ensure maximum flexibility and responsiveness to the needs of students and to the wide variety of social and economic developments.[13]

The report of the HEA Steering Committee (June 1995) also favoured the retention of a binary tradition stating:

> The Committee fully endorsed the maintenance of a diversified system of higher education to meet the varying needs of students, of society and of the economy.[14]

It urged the extra-university sector to develop its distinctive role in the area of technician training, the 'practical' orientation of its programmes, the engagement with applied research and experimental work in product development, and the regional focus of its work. While recognising the difficulty in projecting forward with accuracy in this area, the Steering Committee recommended that the percentage of the total number of students in the extra-university sector should increase from 40 per cent in 1994/95 to 44 per cent by the year 2000.

While such endorsements of the binary system are significant, it seems clear that the future will see more pressure from the extra-university sector for greater status within the higher education system. The Dublin Institute of Technology has been pressing for some years for the right to award its own degrees. In November 1995 an international review team was appointed by the HEA to evaluate the quality assurance procedures in the DIT. In its report in June 1996, the review team recommended that the DIT be given degree awarding powers with effect from the 1998/99 academic year.[15] On 12 December 1996 the Minister for Education announced that she intended to make an order to confer degree awarding powers on the DIT from the

1998/99 academic year, within the policy framework set out in the White Paper. In the context of the debate in the Oireachtas on the Universities Bill, the DIT lobbied strongly that it be awarded recognition as a university under section 9 of the bill. However, the Minister for Education has not agreed to this but promised a review committee to advise on relevant issues. Some of the RTCs were also pressing for university status. The HEA Steering Committee had recommended that the title of RTCs be altered to 'regional technical institutes'. In January 1997 the Minister for Education conferred this title on Waterford Regional Technical College, and, predictably, this caused quite a furore in some other RTCs which considered their claims to such status to be equally good. In response to this, the minister appointed a representative committee to advise her on the future nomenclature and status of RTCs.

Internationally, there are also trends towards blurring the distinctions which have, in the past, operated within the binary concept of higher education. A recent OECD thematic comparative review of the early years of tertiary education stated:

> The real issue is not rigour in distinguishing types of programmes, institutions and sectors but how best to meet the widely ranging needs of students for different levels and links to tertiary education ... To place the student at the centre of the analysis and to ask what is required to meet students' needs and expectations, and, by extension, those of society, is to approach the matters of demand, structure and provision from a rather different standpoint than was presented hitherto.[16]

Even if, in the future, the boundaries between the binary sectors become more blurred in Ireland, it will be important that the needs of individuals and society are met by a broad range of diversified courses and that transfer bridges are available between the sectors which facilitate students.

Of great significance for the extra-university sector was the statement of government policy in the White Paper to establish an Irish national certification authority, TEASTAS, which would be 'responsible for the development, implementation, regulation and supervision of all non-university third-level programmes, and all further and continuation education and training programmes'.[17] The NCEA is to be reconstituted as a sub-board of TEASTAS. The Minister for Education established an interim TEASTAS authority in September 1995. If TEASTAS succeeds in its objectives, it should bring a valuable coherence to the whole area of awards and certification which will be important in both national and international contexts. In its *First*

Report (January 1997) TEASTAS emphasised the potential for two-way transfer within the binary system:

> The Board believes that the possibilities for access, progression and mobility are likely to significantly increase in the future through greater two-way transfer of students between universities and institutions within the TEASTAS framework.[18]

It recommends that the university interest be represented in TEASTAS at board level and on the boards of studies that are to be established.

The changed role of the HEA set out in the White Paper also presages new developments for the framework of higher education. The remit of the HEA is to be extended, on a phased basis, to all publicly funded third-level colleges including the DIT and RTCs. The composition of the HEA will be restructured in new legislation. Among its extensive responsibilities 'across the whole sector' will be:

> ensuring, within agreed policy parameters, a balance of level, type and variety of programmes among the various institutions, including an appropriate balance between certificate, diploma, degree and postgraduate work, as well as relevance to the occupational and skill needs of the economy.[19]

This emphasises that, while the binary approach is being maintained in government policy, the comprehensive overseeing role of the HEA, as envisaged above, is intended to ensure appropriate balances in course provision aligned to the needs of the economy.

Participation

With 50 per cent of the age cohort proceeding to some form of higher education, the issue of future planning of participation is a matter of major public policy. The introduction of free fees for full-time undergraduate students in 1995 is likely to fuel greater demand. At present, a numerus clausus system operates for many professional faculties and gives rise to increasing levels of competitiveness, based on points attained in the Leaving Certificate examination. In more open access faculties problems of overcrowding occur, high student–teacher ratios exist and pressure is placed on libraries, student support services etc. Rapidly expanding enrolments bring concomitant demands on current and capital expenditure for higher education. A further complication exists when the distribution of public expenditure on higher education is seen as regressive due to the selective participation by social class. Nevertheless, the return to the government on public expenditure on higher education was calculated in 1995 at about 12 per cent. The duration of courses in Ireland tends to be less than in many other countries and drop-out and failure levels appear to be relatively low. The employment prospects for graduates are good, with shortages being recorded in a number of fields. The expansion in demand for and provision of higher education is a phenomenon being experienced in all developed countries. As a recent OECD comparative study states:

> Not so long ago, tertiary education was a distant goal for a small minority; now participation in some form of education at tertiary level is moving towards the norm. This is a remarkable change whose significance has yet to be fully realised ... Participation in tertiary education reflects current cultural aspirations of and for youth, the growing interest of adults in systematic learning to advanced levels, and the emergence of a knowledge-based society in which prolonged education becomes a social norm.[20]

In Ireland considerable attention is being paid to projecting future student enrolment trends in higher education and to the composition of the student body. As the White Paper noted, despite the impressive increase in participation in higher education over recent years, Ireland's participation rate 'lags behind that in most other European countries'.[21] Past projections of participation have tended to be passed out in reality. For instance, the Green Paper's figure of 100,000 full-time students for the year 2000 has already been exceeded. At the National Education Convention the Department of Education raised its projections to 115,000 by 2000 with a further growth to 122,000 by 2005.[22] The report of the HEA Technical Working Group in 1995 projected a figure of 111,500 for 2000 rising to 125,400 by 2010.[23] Of course, varied elements go into the calculations and many of these are captured in the following statement of the HEA Steering Committee report:

> The Committee concluded that further expansion of higher education enrolment was warranted and required in view of social demand, public expectations of enhanced provision, social and economic aims, longer-term benefits, international comparisons and the need to address socio-economic and regional disparities as well as inadequate provision for those with disabilities, and for mature students.[24]

The Steering Committee's projections were more modest than those of the Technical Working Group and ranged from 112,000 in 2000, to 119,000 in 2005 and 120,000 in 2010. The representative of the Department of Finance was unable to agree with these figures, regarding them as too high. In February 1997, at the instigation of the Department of Finance, the government appointed a new committee, with strong representation from government departments, to prepare new projections for future provision of higher education. However, in view of the impulsion for greater participation in higher education, due to many reasons, it is difficult to see how reduced projections could be realistic.

A very significant policy concern in recent years is access to higher education, irrespective of social class, age or disability, for all who have the capacity to benefit from it. In his most recent (1995) study of access patterns Patrick Clancy states:

> Notwithstanding the persistence of high levels of socio-economic group inequality, it is evident that, when we compare the present findings with those of earlier surveys, a significant reduction in inequality has occurred.[25]

However, inequality persists and Clancy goes on to note that the more prestigious the sectors and field of study, the greater the social inequality in participation levels. The *Report on the National Education Convention*, the White Paper and the reports of the HEA Technical Working Group and the Steering Committee all focus a lot of attention on the problems of various disadvantaged groups in relation to higher education. Special initiatives are being undertaken to improve access for those from socio-economically deprived backgrounds and for students with special needs due to disabilities. All institutions are required to prepare and publish policies to promote gender equality in higher education. Particular attention is also being given to improve participation by 'mature' students. The Steering Committee projected an increase of such students from 3.7 per cent of the total number in 1994 to 6.2 per cent by 2000 and subsequently to 16 per cent by 2010. To achieve this there is a need to change the funding arrangements for part-time students who make up a large part of the mature student category. Such a policy would also be in tune with the desire to provide second chance education as part of a new strategy on lifelong learning, successfully promoted during the Irish presidency of the EU in 1996.[26]

The potential of distance education and of information technology for higher education purposes is likely to be further developed and utilised in the next century. Increasingly, people are availing of distance education courses provided by the Open University, the National Distance Education Centre at Dublin City University and agencies such as the Institute of Public Administration. A more active policy on outreach centres by established institutions opens up new possibilities for people whose geographical location hitherto impeded their participation. Modern technology, the regional character of many education institutions and centres, the presence of new institutions such as private colleges, ease of communications and the traditional Irish desire for learning bode well for the future of Ireland as a learning society.

Postgraduate students are a category which has received little attention in the various reports and policy statements of recent years. At present, all types of postgraduate students combine to form about 16 per cent of total enrolment. The HEA Steering Committee projections favour the retention of this proportion. Its report provides little or no discussion on the matter, but suggests that the issue should form one of the topics for a comprehensive study on aspects of higher education. This is the minimum which the issue deserves. It would seem that in the concern to provide greater access to initial forms of higher education insufficient attention has been given to the postgraduate sector. The support systems for postgraduate students, particularly in the humanities and social sciences, are very inadequate. Irish society may lose out a great deal by the relative neglect of postgraduate studies and research as postgraduate students are at the cutting edge of developments in their subject areas. The depth of study and analysis involved, particularly at masters and doctorate level, should be of major benefit to participants and to society. Good quality understanding, analysis, communication, leadership and innovation are crucial in a knowledge-based society, and postgraduate study and research provide a training ground for their nurture. It is important for the future well-being of society that postgraduate work gets greater priority in higher education policy.

Teaching and learning

The large expansion of student numbers in recent years has put a strain on the higher education institutions in terms of maintaining quality of performance and international acceptability of graduate output. Yet, as noted by the HEA Steering Committee, the quality of the intake of students is at its highest level ever and the percentage of students graduating with honours from degree-level programmes has increased from 30 per cent in 1965 to 72 per cent in 1992. Irish graduate students tend to achieve very well in postgraduate courses in well-regarded international universities. The evidence of international employers also indicates good quality among Irish graduates. Nevertheless, it is realised that the capacity of the system is already stretched and that further expansion needs to be supported by the necessary level of investment. The average student–teacher ratio in Irish universities is 22:1. Many students experience difficulties in library and other facilities, while the annual capital equipment grants fall miserably short of what is required.

Ireland, like many other countries, lays stress on quality features of higher education and policy-makers are concerned to ensure that it is manifest. A range of initiatives is under way which, on accumulation, is likely to have significant influences on the traditional manner in which higher education institutions have conducted their teaching and learning. Among these changes is a shift towards modularisation and semesterisation of courses. As the Green Paper put it:

> What is envisaged is the development of a comprehensive system of modularisation and credit transfer across the third-level sector, building on existing initiatives nationally and internationally.[27]

Modularisation and credit transfer are seen as promoting student mobility within and between institutions at home and abroad, facilitating access, facilitating mature and second chance students and enhancing continuing or recurrent education. Many Irish institutions already operate, or are in the process of developing, modular patterns of course provision, and this trend is likely to continue. Moves towards interdisciplinary and cross-faculty courses are also taking place.

In this era of mass higher education the issue of teaching in higher education has come more to the fore. The recent OECD comparative study stated:

> the need to make teaching more transparent, for evaluating its quality, for procedures to support and improve it and for recognising success and effectiveness, is gaining acceptance everywhere.[28]

In Ireland, the *Report on the National Education Convention* pointed to:

> the need for a development programme which will assist third-level staff in improving their teaching skills.[29]

This recommendation was adopted in the White Paper which stated that:

> The putting in place of a comprehensive programme for the development of teaching skills for third-level staff will be a priority.[30]

Such a programme is now in operation. All state-supported third-level colleges have staff development programmes in operation. A very wide range of courses is on offer, many of them designed to improve styles of teaching and assessment for various categories of teaching staff. Evidence of teaching ability is now also taken into consideration for promotion purposes.

There is a concern internationally that not only should quality be promoted but it should be seen to be operative in higher education. Hence the drive towards quality assurance as part of a general climate of accountability. The White Paper sets out the intended policy clearly:

> Quality auditing systems will continue to be developed by the institutions under the overall direction of the HEA. These will focus on:
>
> - the cyclical evaluation of departments and faculties by national and international peers, preceded by internal evaluation by the department or faculty;
> - arrangements for the implementation and monitoring of evaluation findings;
> - the development of appropriate performance indicators, including national and international comparisons.[31]

Since 1995 the universities have been conducting pilot evaluations based on internal review and external peer evaluation. These assessments include student feedback on the overall quality of their learning experience. These quality assurance initiatives have been conducted under the auspices of the Conference of the Heads of Irish Universities and are financially supported by the HEA. As the process of quality assurance develops, the universities will be keen to retain the guiding role with regard to the procedures employed, seeing these as linked to the proper academic role of the institutions. This would seem to be secured under section 32 of the Universities Act, although the HEA is given the right to review and report on the effectiveness of the evaluation procedures employed. The extra-university sector is also engaging in academic appraisal exercises. Both the initiatives on staff development and the quality assurance procedures are creating a new and more open climate within the higher education institutions and a general realisation seems to be taking hold that these are developmental processes for such institutions operating in modern conditions.

Research

As with other areas of higher education policy, the issue of research has come under close scrutiny in a range of reports and policy documents in recent years. The Green Paper signalled changes in policy emphases. The National Education Convention recorded considerable disagreement with some of these emphases and made a number of alternative recommendations. The White Paper adopted some of these but held off on a more explicit policy on research until it received the outcomes of a number of studies being conducted on the theme. Among key policies set out in the White Paper were that the unified teaching and research budget to colleges will be continued, that additional funding for research will be provided in a separate budget open to competitive bidding, most basic and strategic research will be conducted in the universities, while the focus of the extra-university sector will be on applied, regionally oriented research. Each institution will be required to develop and publish an explicit policy on its approach to research.[32]

The report of the HEA Steering Committee only dealt lightly with the topic. In 1995 the STIAC Advisory Council took a strategic view on how science and technology could be more utilised for the benefit of Irish society.[33] This was followed in 1996 by a White Paper on science and technology. In April 1997 a new Advisory Council was established. As another paper in this volume deals specifically with the role of science and technology in modern Ireland, the topic does not get detailed treatment here. However, one agrees with Vincent McBrierty when he remarks:

> Debate on the role of research in education invariably focuses on the sciences by virtue of their undeniable strategic importance, whereas scant attention is paid to the arts. Such an approach denies the complex inter-relationship between the two sectors. Nevertheless, many of the arguments invoked in support of research in the sciences, particularly basic research, are no less valid for the arts.[34]

In the legitimate concern to promote research in science and technology, for a variety of purposes, society would be making a strategic error in ignoring or largely neglecting the role of research in the humanities and social sciences. Looking to the future, it will be important to sustain efforts by involved parties to ensure that a better balance is struck in research policy, and this will not be an easy task. In this context, one welcomes the recent statement of the HEA:

> The social, intellectual and cultural value of research must be given the same recognition as the economic and financial value. Research in basic science and in the social sciences and humanities is no less vital for the development of an innovative, outward-looking, and creative society than is research that is more immediately oriented to product and business development.[35]

Research in Irish higher education has traditionally been very under-funded. In 1982 public funding amounted to only about £12 million. Over the subsequent decade, it grew to about £48 million, largely due to EU funding which, in turn, tended to dictate the nature of the research being undertaken. Capital funding for research purposes has been very inadequate while the ongoing provision of about £2 million per annum for research equipment can legitimately be viewed as derisory in contemporary circumstances. The debate at the National Education Convention deprecated the low level of funding for research and the gross undervaluation of the importance of higher education research for Irish society. It also urged a more explicit national policy on the funding of research. A strong recommendation also emerged that national research councils should be established for the natural sciences and for the humanities and social sciences.[36]

In the light of concerns such as these, the HEA commissioned the CIRCA Group to carry out a study of an unprecedented character. It attempted a comparative international assessment of the organisation, management and funding of university research in Ireland and Europe. Its report was presented to the HEA in December 1996. Its findings are likely to have major implications for future research policy and deserve to be highlighted. In its comparative assessment of Irish research the report states:

> In terms of quality, many areas of Irish university research now appear to be at or above world levels. . . .
>
> Against a background of chronic underfunding, it is quite remarkable that the Irish universities have managed to improve both their research output and their contribution to industry and services in Ireland. . . .
>
> Considering the scientific, social, cultural and economic contributions of university research, it is apparent from our analysis that there is something seriously amiss with public policy towards the support of higher education research in Ireland.[37]

As regards funding, the report states:

> Public funding of higher education research in Ireland is among the worst in the OECD . . . There is virtually no financial support for basic science, little post-graduate support and very inadequate funding structures.[38]

Not surprisingly, in view of the tradition of gross underfunding, when the CIRCA team examined the management, planning, organisation, evaluation and reporting mechanisms for research in Irish universities it found that these lagged behind best practice in the European universities which the team visited. As well as its recommendations for increased funding for research and new structures for its distribution, most of the CIRCA team's recommendations emphasised the need for Irish universities to strengthen the organisation and management of university research. Many academics would not agree that more rigorous management of research is likely to improve its range or quality, although there is scope for improvement in planning, co-ordination, support, reportage and dissemination of the research. The report recognises that Irish colleges are opposed to separating funding for teaching and research in their bloc grants, despite some international trends. But the report suggests that this should happen. Should this be pushed too hard as a policy position it is likely to cause considerable tension in the years ahead. The report supported the proposal of setting up two research councils, the further development of a dynamic interface with industry and services, and the establishment of inter-university and multi-disciplinary collaboration.[39]

The middle nineties may come to be seen as a turning-point regarding research in higher education. If a coherent policy is not devised with a much greater public investment in such research, allied to new organisation and accountability procedures, then it would seem that a strategic opportunity will have been lost with long-term deleterious consequences for Ireland in 'the learning society of the future' when the creation, organisation and dissemination of knowledge will be crucial.[40] The analysis, diagnosis and prescriptions have been made. What is required is the political, public and collegiate will to give the research issue the priority which is required.

Internationalism

A trend of recent decades which is likely to be further developed in the future is the greater internationalism of the higher education sector. From an earlier position of considerable insularity of attitude and limited international contact, the situation has altered greatly. In line with Ireland's stronger profile on the international stage, through EU membership and its role in other international political, academic and cultural bodies, the higher education sector has participated in a variety of arrangements with higher education institutions in many countries in recent years. The presidents of Irish universities have taken a prominent role in the Confederation of European Union Rectors' conferences which have helped them to keep abreast of thinking within the EU on higher education issues and also to make inputs to the shaping of attitudes on university matters. They also participate in the European Rectors' Conference (CRE) which is a pan-European body. CRE held its international conference in 1993 in St Patrick's College, Maynooth. The theme of the conference, 'Human Resources at the University', was revealing of new concerns in university discourse.[41] Leaders in the extra-university sector have also been active in international engagements with their peers. Through sabbaticals and exchange programmes, Irish academics have been very proactive in benefiting from international experience. They have also been well to the fore in international academic associations and at international conferences within their disciplines. As noted above, their research output and its quality is well regarded internationally. Irish academics have been drawn upon a good deal by international bodies, such as the OECD and the World Bank, on academic consultancy projects in many countries. Aligned to the strong tradition of emigration, considerable numbers of Irish scholars go abroad to work, sometimes on a permanent basis, sometimes to garner experience and return to a post in Ireland. The scale of this international interaction is highly beneficial to individuals, to institutions and to society.

One of the major stimuli for international academic co-operation has been the various EU schemes for the promotion of research. A condition of approval and financial support in most schemes is the involvement of researchers from a number of member countries. These schemes have brought Irish academics into productive working relationships with their European peers. The process of the planning and execution of joint schemes has fostered close co-operation and encouraged the exchange of insights and expertise. Irish institutions also form part of a grouping of international institutions which offer joint courses. These have helped to bring students, as well as staff, into close working and learning relationships. On a wider level, Irish students have been availing of opportunities under the Erasmus and Socrates programmes, and other EU exchange schemes, to spend periods of their studies in foreign institutions, and foreign students have been coming in large numbers to Irish colleges. Mutual recognition of qualifications is progressing within the EU and the operation of the ECTS credit transfer scheme facilitates student transfer between courses. Thus, in many ways, the international dimension has come much more to the fore than formerly and is reminiscent of the great tradition of old European universities which hosted students from many nations. The opening out of our institutions to the wider intellectual and academic world has had many benign outcomes and the future holds much promise in this regard.

Interaction between higher education personnel in both parts of the island of Ireland has also developed. Following the Irish Universities Act of 1908 and the partition settlement of 1922, relationships became very tenuous as Queen's University Belfast tended to look to England for its linkages and political allegiances, and tensions in general did not favour co-operation. This has changed considerably in recent years with many linkages and shared undertakings being established between institutions, North and South, that are vibrant, self-confident and outgoing. Symbolic of this relationship was the establishment of the Conference of Rectors of Ireland (CRI) in 1992, in which the heads of the universities in

Northern Ireland and the Irish Republic meet and confer on issues of mutual interest. Another significant step in improving co-operation was the earlier initiative of the Northern Ireland Economic Council and the National Economic and Social Council (of the South) when they commissioned a study, held a conference and published a report entitled *Higher Education in Ireland: Cooperation and Complementarity.*[42] Nowadays students from both sides of the border participate freely in courses which attract them in higher education institutions in both parts of Ireland, and close relationships exist between academics who interact in a variety of capacities. Ireland, North and South, is an attractive destination for many categories of foreign students, and a more proactive marketing approach has been developing, particularly in disciplines such as medicine and business studies. Something of the tradition of the 'island of scholars' is alive and well in our land.

Concluding comment

As one reflects back over the space of a generation, one cannot but be struck by the quiet revolution, the transformation which has taken place in Ireland's higher education system. There now exists a diverse, thriving, self-confident sector with many gifted thinkers, teachers, researchers and administrators. Bearing in mind the constraints of limited resources in the past, a considerable degree of partnership has existed between the institutions, the Department of Education and bodies such as the HEA and the NCEA. There has not been an absence of vision and courage in moving forward. The new institutions which were established have been very successful. While being open to learn from external experience, Ireland has forged its own way forward, infused by its own cultural style of doing things. The higher education institutions are bulging with bright, energetic students, the first generation in Irish history when one out of every two school leavers is entering tertiary education.

The role of the higher education institutions, particularly the universities, has been greatly altered and expanded. The old emphasis on teaching with limited research has changed whereby teaching is still regarded as central but with new emphases and, indeed, new status. The research role has been expanding greatly and is of world standard. If the correct strategic decisions and investments are made, the research area seems destined for significant breakthroughs in the years ahead. The consultancy role has developed in a variety of ways and academic personnel are seen as closer partners to policy-makers than used to be the case. Relationships with industry and the commercial sector have become more interactive and mutually supportive. A noted feature of the previous era was the ignoring by industrial/commercial interests of the higher education sector in terms of sponsorship and investment. This has been altered and higher education institutions have benefited from a more enlightened approach, albeit sometimes not without cost to the institutions or their leaders' time and energy. The sector has become much more internationalised in its outlook and activities.

We are now at the beginning of a new era of restructuring and change in higher education. Having seen the foundations of this new era laid, one of Ireland's most distinguished public servants, Dr Ken Whitaker, who as chancellor of the National University of Ireland for twenty-one years was close to many of the developments outlined, retired from his position as chancellor on 31 December 1996. The university over which he presided is itself being restructured, ninety years after its establishment. Its four main colleges will operate with a greater degree of institutional autonomy, but plans have been laid so that the National University, as an institutional framework, will adopt new and developing roles in support of its colleges and of higher education generally. It too should have an exciting future.

While acknowledging the significance of the achievements of recent decades, one of the most reassuring features of the work of the middle nineties has been the complete absence of complacency or of a 'resting on the oars' mentality. Rather, existing and new challenges are being faced. This paper has sought to highlight what some of these are and how we are going about them. In conclusion, one is not reiterating these except to emphasise a few. The broad cultural and social role of higher education will be more critical in the open, pluralistic and media-influenced society of our times. The issue of equality of access and participation remains as a significant challenge. The area of second chance education as part of a lifelong education philosophy will loom large. The role of the university with regard to incareer professional education and training will need to be extended further. Postgraduate and research policy require much greater in-depth attention. The hope is that the new tranche of EU Structural Funds will continue to invest in human resource development and allow Ireland to benefit from further investment in its education provision. In this lies Ireland's best hope for a distinguished and prosperous future within the learning society which is now being shaped.

NOTES

1. OECD, *Economic Surveys: Ireland*, Paris: OECD, 1995, p. 61.
2. *Ibid.*, p. 110.
3. Commission on Higher Education I, *Presentation and Summary of Report*,

Dublin: Stationery Office, 1967, pp. 22, 23.

4. Commission on Higher Education, *Report*, Vol. 1, p. 121.

5. *Investment in Education*, Dublin: Stationery Office, 1966, pp. 172–6.

6. Government of Ireland, *Charting our Education Future*, Dublin: Stationery Office, 1995, p. 90.

7. Peter Scott, *The Meanings of Mass Higher Education*, Buckingham: Society for Research into Higher Education and Open University, 1995, pp. 168–79, and Malcolm Skilbeck, 'The Role of the Humanities', in Eda Sagarra and Mireia Sagarra (eds.), *The Dancer and the Dance: Trinity Quatercentenary Symposium*, Dublin: Trinity College Dublin, 1993, pp. 88–97.

8. Government of Ireland, *Education for a Changing World*, Dublin: Stationery Office, 1992, p. 183.

9. *Ibid.*, p. 203.

10. *Charting our Education Future*, p. 87.

11. *Education for a Changing World*, p. 197.

12. John Coolahan (ed.), *Report on the National Education Convention*, Dublin: Stationery Office, 1994, pp. 92–3.

13. *Charting our Education Future*, p. 93.

14. *Report of the Steering Committee on the Future Development of Higher Education*, Dublin: Higher Education Authority, 1995, p. 29.

15. 'Report of the International Review Team on Quality Assurance Procedures in the D.I.T.', 1996, pp. 22, 23.

16. OECD, *Thematic Review of the First Years of Tertiary Education: Comparative Report*, Paris: OECD, 1997 (forthcoming), p. 28.

17. *Charting our Education Future*, p. 85.

18. TEASTAS, *First Report*, Dublin: TEASTAS, 1997, p. 13.

19. *Charting our Education Future*, p. 94.

20. OECD, *Thematic Review*, p. 9.

21. *Charting our Education Future*, p. 89.

22. *Report on the National Education Convention*, p. 91.

23. *Interim Report of the Technical Working Group*, Dublin: Higher Education Authority, 1995, p. 4.

24. *Report of the Steering Committee on the Future Development of Higher Education*, p. 14.

25. Patrick Clancy, *Access to College: Patterns of Continuity and Change*, Dublin: Higher Education Authority, 1995, p. 154.

26. Education Committee of the EU Presidency Paper, 'Strategy for Lifelong Learning', December 1996, and John Coolahan (ed.), *Increasing Participation: Proceedings of the Irish National Conference on Lifelong Learning*, Dublin: TEASTAS and St Patrick's College Maynooth, 1996.

27. *Education for a Changing World*, p. 186.

28. OECD, *Thematic Review*, p. 45.

29. *Report on the National Education Convention*, p. 94.

30. *Charting our Education Future*, p. 104.

31. *Ibid.*

32. *Ibid.*, p. 107.

33. STIAC Advisory Council, *Making Knowledge Work For Us: A Strategic View of Science and Technology*, Dublin: Stationery Office, 1995.

34. Vincent McBrierty, 'The University and Research – Aims, Conditions and Resources', in *The Role of the University in Society*, Dublin: National University of Ireland, 1994, pp. 79–93, p. 79.

35. Statement of HEA contained in report of the CIRCA Group, 'A Comparative International Assessment of the Organisation, Management and Funding of University Research in Ireland and Europe, p. 3.
36. Report on the National Education Convention, p. 97.
37. CIRCA Group, A Comparative International Assessment, pp. ii, iii.
38. Ibid., p. iv.
39. Ibid., pp. xvii–xix.
40. European Commission, Towards the Learning Society, Brussels: European Commission, 1995, p. 2.
41. Andres Bartlan (ed.), Human Resources at University, Geneva: European Rectors' Conference, 1993.
42. Northern Ireland Economic Council and National Economic and Social Council, Higher Education in Ireland: Cooperation and Complementarity, Dublin and Belfast: National Economic and Social Council, 1985.

11

Irish Health Policy in Perspective

MIRIAM M. WILEY

Introduction

WHEN the Department of Health was established in 1947, state grants accounted for just 16 per cent of total health service costs. As the health services were being expanded under successive pieces of legislation, including the Health Services (Financial Provisions) Act 1947 and the Health Act 1953, the responsibility for financing was shifted from local rates to the central exchequer (Wiley, 1997). It was not until the White Paper in 1966 (Department of Health, 1966), however, that it was finally proposed that ultimate responsibility for health service financing should rest with the state. It was recognised that such a shift of responsibility would warrant changes in the administration of the services, and these were given effect in the Health Act 1970. The Irish health system which emerged from these initiatives now accounts for one of the largest items of government expenditure. In 1996, non-capital expenditure on the health services from central exchequer sources accounted for 6.8 per cent of GNP. In addition to this commitment of public expenditure, about one-quarter of total expenditure on health is derived from private sources.

The health system which currently places such heavy demands on government resources will first be described here. This will be followed by an analysis of recent strategic initiatives proposing reform of the system. Finally, the challenges looming for health service provision into the next millennium will be reviewed.

The Irish health care system in the 1990s

While the White Paper of 1966 provided the vision, the legislative structure for the present Irish health system originated in the Health Act 1970. Under this legislation, a regionalised system of health service provision was introduced with the establishment of eight regional health boards. The operation of these boards is built around three core programmes: the general hospital programme, the special hospital programme and the community care programme. Health boards also enter into agreements with a wide range of voluntary organisations, particularly those caring for the mentally handicapped, for the provision of designated services.

When the health boards were being established in 1971, the voluntary public hospitals were maintained outside of this structure. Many of these hospitals traditionally have been run by religious orders and function as teaching hospitals; others are incorporated by charter or statute and work under lay boards of governors. Most of these hospitals are located in Dublin and other large centres of population.

The relative importance of each of the expenditure programmes can be assessed from the estimates of public expenditure presented in Table 1 for the period between 1980 and 1994. The general hospital programme has consistently been the largest programme and currently accounts for half of all public health expenditure. While the community care programme as a whole accounted for 27 per cent of public expenditure in 1994, this includes 11 per cent attributed to the General Medical Services (GMS) scheme covering general practitioner services and pharmaceuticals for medical card holders and 2 per cent for the drug subsidisation schemes. The special hospital programme accounted for close to one-fifth of public health expenditure in the same year.

Table 1: Public health expenditure by programme, 1980–94

					1994	
Programme	1980 (£m)	1984 (£m)	1990 (£m)	1994 (£m)	% of total	% of GNP
General hospital	393	593	801	1,147	50.1	3.7
Special hospital	153	252	320	438	19.1	1.4
Handicapped	60	113	152	223	9.7	0.7
Psychiatric	93	139	169	216	9.4	0.7
Community care	150	254	383	613	26.8	2.0
Health	90	147	231	371	16.2	1.2
Welfare	47	90	127	201	8.8	0.6
Protection	13	18	24	40	1.7	0.1
Support	35	58	71	93	4.1	0.3
Total	731	1,157	1,575	2,291	100.0	7.3

Source: Department of Health, 1996

One of the fundamental tenets underlying the Irish health system is that the one-third of the population with the lowest income have full eligibility for all health services which are provided free and funded out of general taxation. The remaining two-thirds of the population have limited eligibility; they must pay privately for general practitioner and pharmaceutical services but are entitled to public hospital services on payment of a modest statutory charge.

The Irish health service is predominantly a tax-funded system. While approximately 85 per cent of total health expenditure was derived from public sources in the 1980s, this has since declined to the current level of around 75 per cent. Approximately one-quarter of total health expenditure now consists of expenditure from private sources, particularly health insurance companies and household expenditure on general practitioner visits, pharmaceuticals and private hospital stays. Table 2 provides an overview of how the public sources of health service funding have changed since the early 1970s. The abolition of the contribution from local rates in the mid-1970s was balanced by an increase in central exchequer funding from 80.5 per cent in 1973/74 to a high of 94.5 per cent in 1977. With the increase in additional sources of income – particularly from the earmarked health contribution, EU receipts, the National Lottery and local income – the central exchequer contribution to public health expenditure dropped to 82.4 per cent in 1996. The increase in local income from the early 1980s may be mainly attributed to the introduction of user charges for public health services in 1987.

Table 2: Sources of funding for public health expenditure, selected years, 1973/74–96 (%)

Funding source	1973/74[a]	1977[a]	1980[b]	1996[b]
Exchequer	80.5	94.5	87.9	82.4
Rates	13.9	–	–	–
Hospitals Sweepstakes	0.6	0.5	–	–
Health contributions	3.8	4.0	6.4	8.7
EU receipts	1.2	1.0	1.5	2.1
National Lottery	–	–	–	0.8
Local income	–	–	4.2	6.0
Total	100.0	100.0	100.0	100.0

Source: (a) Hensey (1979)
      (b) Department of Health, 1996

The overall funding level for the health services is determined in negotiations between the Department of Finance and the Department of

Health, which provides annual budgets to the eight regional health boards for the provision of public health services. These budgets are determined by demographic factors, commitments to service provision and the general economic guidelines applied to the operation of the public service as a whole. These guidelines have particular reference to pay, which is the largest component of health expenditure. No specific measure of 'medical need' is built into the budgeting framework. Service provision is assumed to be a response to service needs and thus to reflect medical need. As previously noted, the voluntary public hospitals have been maintained outside of the health board structure and funding for these hospitals is negotiated individually with the Department of Health. In addition to service delivery agencies, a number of corporate bodies and registration boards are supported by the Department of Health. These include such bodies as the Blood Transfusion Service Board, Comhairle na n-Ospidéal (the Hospital Council) and the Health Research Board.

While the dual categorisation of eligibility within the Irish health system is reasonably straightforward, what makes the system more complex is the fact that both public and private services may be secured from the same providers. The majority of general practitioners and hospital consultants provide services to both public and private patients; pharmacists serve the public and private sectors; and the major public hospitals have public and private beds. In addition, depending on the nature of their contracts, hospital consultants may practise in both public and private hospitals. The close relationship between the public and private sectors is the result of explicit government policy which has historically supported the development of a 'mixed' health care system in Ireland (Department of Health, 1994). The policy of supporting the provision of public and private services from the same source is intended to ensure that the same high quality services are available to all, regardless of income, though the absence of appropriate empirical data means that this proposition has not been adequately tested in the Irish context.

An additional distinguishing characteristic of the Irish system is that the private, health-insurance-based sector historically has operated as part of the broader state health system. The Voluntary Health Insurance Board (VHI) was established in 1957 as a semi-state organisation for the provision of private health insurance in Ireland. This initiative was intended to enable the 15 per cent of the population who did not have entitlement to free public health services at the time to make financial provision for their health service needs, and particularly to insure against the higher costs associated with hospital care. It was against this background that health insurance premia were originally allowable against income tax at the marginal tax rate. While access to public hospital services was extended to the entire population in the late 1980s, health insurance premia continue to be allowable against income tax, though the deduction has now been reduced to the standard tax rate.

With the exception of a number of small occupation-based schemes, the VHI has operated as a virtual monopoly for the provision of private health insurance since its foundation. The number of VHI subscribers has increased consistently since its establishment. From a level of 100,000 in the early 1960s, it grew to 0.5 million in the mid-1970s and the 1 million level was exceeded in 1983. Over 1.3 million people (approximately one-third of the population) are currently insured with VHI.

With the passing of the Third Directive on Non-Life Insurance for the European Union, however, the government was required to introduce legislation allowing competition within the private health insurance market. The Health Insurance Act 1994, which came into effect on 1 July 1994, is the legislative basis for the regulation of the Irish private health insurance market and the introduction of competition within this market. This legislation was given effect by the supporting regulatory framework agreed by government in March 1996.

Community rating, open enrolment and lifetime cover are now mandatory requirements for all health insurers operating within the Irish market. Under the 1994 legislation, each individual will pay the same premium for a given level of health insurance cover, irrespective of age, sex or health status. Open enrolment means that all health insurers are required to accept applications for membership from all individuals aged under 65 and that, once enrolled, membership cannot be terminated or renewal refused. The regulations provide for maximum waiting periods in respect of pre-existing medical conditions and for the operation of a system of risk equalisation within the health insurance market. Under this system, an insurer with a higher than average risk profile will receive a transfer of funds from the system while those with a lower than average risk profile will pay into the system. Currently, BUPA Ireland Ltd is the only major international health care company to offer health insurance on the Irish market, though there are suggestions that other companies may enter this market in the future.

Strategic health initiatives

Within the past decade, various initiatives have been launched by the Department of Health to address problems arising in relation to the health care system. The first such undertaking got under way in 1987 with the establishment of the Commission on Health Funding as a direct response to the real cuts in public health expenditure being applied in the mid to late 1980s. The commission was given the task of examining the financing of the health services with the objective of making recommendations 'on the extent and sources of the future funding required to provide an equitable, comprehensive and cost-effective public health service and on any changes in administration which seem desirable for that purpose' (Commission on Health Funding, 1989, p. 1).

With regard to health service funding, the commission's recommendation was that this should continue to be primarily tax-based. A key conclusion of the commission's deliberations was that 'the solution to the problem facing the Irish health services does not lie primarily in the system of funding but rather in the way that services are planned, organised and delivered' (p. xi). Following on from this conclusion, an essential recommendation was that the administration of the health services should be restructured, with the minister and the department discharging policy and legislative functions and the overall management of the health services being transferred to an executive authority. While this proposal has not been implemented, a broadly similar framework involving a redefinition of the role of the Department of Health and the rebirth of the health boards as 'health authorities' has also been proposed in the most recent strategy document published by the Department of Health (1994).

This strategy document *Shaping a Healthier Future* was intended to build upon the recommendations of the Commission on Health Funding and the earlier strategy document *Health – The Wider Dimensions* (Department of Health, 1986) to provide a new policy framework for the development of the health services in Ireland. The launch of *Shaping a Healthier Future* in 1994 was intended to facilitate a 'reorientation of the system towards improving the effectiveness of the health and personal social services by reshaping the way that services are planned and delivered' (Department of Health, 1994, p. 8). This reorientation is to be based on the key principles of equity, quality of service and accountability. Three distinct dimensions for action have been specified:

- *the services*: prevention, treatment and care services are to focus more on improvements in health status and quality of life and to place more emphasis on the provision of the most appropriate care
- *the framework*: management and organisational structures are to provide for more decision-making and accountability at regional level, together with the application of better methods of performance measurement

- *the participants*: there should be greater sensitivity to the right of the consumer to services which respond to needs in an equitable and quality-driven manner in addition to a greater recognition of the key role played by service providers.

The strategic overview presented in *Shaping a Healthier Future* is accompanied by a four-year action plan for the period 1994–97. This action plan covers a wide range of service areas including health promotion, primary care services, services for women, children and special needs groups, acute hospital services, and food and medicine control. The extent to which public health expenditure is intrinsically linked to overall government economic policy is indicated by the fact that when the resource commitment necessary for the implementation of the specified targets is addressed, it is stated that 'The Government will aim to provide over the next four years the resources for the development needs identified in the Action Plan which is incorporated in this Strategy, while observing the budgetary policy set out in its Programme for a Partnership Government' (Department of Health, 1994, p. 12).

Shaping a Healthier Future also pursues the theme of health system reorganisation originally proposed in the *Report of the Commission on Health Funding* (1989). As previously noted, the public voluntary hospitals are still funded directly by the Department of Health, independently of the health board structure. As the majority of these voluntary hospitals are located in the Dublin area, this means that the Eastern Health Board has minimal involvement in the provision of acute hospital services within its region. The parallel provision of acute hospital services through the health board structure and the public voluntary hospitals has been considered to result in some fragmentation of the system and differences in efficiencies within the sector (Wiley and Fetter, 1990; Dublin Hospital Initiative Group, 1991). It has been acknowledged by the Department of Health that the direct funding of some voluntary agencies 'impedes the proper co-ordination and development of services at local level. In particular, it hampers the development of links between community and hospital services, and between statutory and voluntary agencies' (Department of Health, 1994, p. 33).

In responding to these problems, the Dublin Hospital Initiative Group and the Hospital Efficiency Review Group in 1991 recommended the establishment of a regional hospital authority in Dublin which would be independent of the existing health board structure (Dublin Hospital Initiative Group, 1991). This proposal is advanced further in *Shaping a Healthier Future* where it is indicated that as part of a general reform of health system organisation, 'The Eastern Health Board would be replaced by a new authority which would have comprehensive responsibility for all health and personal social services in the Eastern region' (Department of Health, 1994, p. 30). With a view to the implementation of this commitment, the Department of Health in 1996 announced the establishment of a high-level task force to address the organisational and administrative arrangements necessary for the transition to the proposed new structures over the following two to three years. In a separate but related initiative in 1996, the Department of Health also announced the establishment of a Management Development Strategy with the objective of improving health care and population health through a strengthening of the management capacity in the health and personal social services.

Challenges for the future

With a view to planning for the future development of the health care system in the context of increasing financial and social integration in Europe, a Dutch government committee published an important report on choices in health care in 1992 (Ministry of Welfare, Health and Cultural Affairs, 1992). The reasons put forward as to why choices in health care may become more demanding are equally relevant in the Irish context and include the following factors: (1) increased life expectancy and declining birth rates have contributed to the ageing of the population in general; (2) the rapidity of technological and scientific advancement means that the pressures for health system expansion will be ongoing; and (3) controlling health expenditure presents a continuous challenge.

In attempting to develop a structured response to these challenges, the Dutch government committee suggested that the available range of choices has a number of common elements, including the financing and efficiency of the health system, and the approach to making decisions regarding care delivery more explicit. This categorisation of the choices pending for the future development of the health services provides a useful framework within which to consider the priority issues expected to arise in the Irish context. The financing of the system will therefore be briefly considered here, followed by a review of the question of efficiency.

There is no 'right' answer to the question of what level of resources should be invested in a health system. The resource investment in the Irish health services annually is a political decision. It therefore seems reasonable to assume that society's priorities for the investment of productive resources are reflected in this decision. As the state assumes increasing responsibility for health service provision, the community comes under pressure to provide access to an expanding range of services. When faced with ever-increasing demand for health services therefore, the difficulties incurred in committing higher proportions of tax-funded revenue to the health services are a critical constraint on health system expansion. In attempting to assess the future resource requirements for the Irish health system, a historical review of variations in the level of health expenditure may be helpful.

Table 3 shows the percentage change in health expenditure as a proportion of GNP for the five decades since the establishment of the Department of Health in 1947. Up to the most recent decade, the general trend in evidence is an increase in the proportion of GNP devoted to health care. The level of the increase can be seen to vary, with the first decade of the Department of Health's existence being associated with the greatest increase in health expenditure as a percentage of GNP. For each of the four decades between 1947 and 1986 the proportion of GNP devoted to health expenditure increased by over 30 per cent. For the most recent decade, however, there is a dramatic reversal of this trend with the proportion of GNP devoted to health expenditure being reduced by 6.8 per cent over the 1987–96 period.

Table 3: Public health expenditure as a proportion of GNP: changes in the five decades since 1947*

	Health as % of GNP		
	Beginning of period	End of period	Percentage change in health expenditure as % of GNP
1947[a]–1956[a]	1.7	2.9	+70.6
1957[a]–1966/67[b]	2.9	3.8	+31.0
1967/68[b]–1976[b]	3.8	6.0	+57.9
1977[b]–1986[c]	6.0	7.7	+30.0
1987[c]–1996[c]	7.3	6.8	−6.8

*The data presented here are intended to show broad changes in trends over the period and should be treated with caution as approaches to compiling this series may have changed over time.
Source: (a) Hensey (1959)
      (b) Tussing (1985)
      (c) Deparment of Health, 1996

A different picture emerges if, instead of taking the establishment of the Department of Health as the starting-point, calendar decades are assessed. With this approach, the expansionism of the 1970s is clearly in evidence as the proportion of GNP allocated to health increased by 56.8 per cent, from 4.4 per cent in 1970/71 to 6.9 per cent in 1979. During this period, public spending increased substantially and health service eligibility and availability were also expanded. The 1980s sharply contrasted with the previous decade, however, as a public expenditure crisis and economic recession were associated with a reduction of 16 per cent in the proportion of GNP allocated to health expenditure from 8.1 per cent in 1980 to 6.8 per cent in 1989. In contrast, the 1990s has developed as a period of greater stability in the proportion of GNP devoted to health expenditure. While this decade began with close to 7 per cent of GNP being devoted to health, this increased to a high of 7.6 per cent in 1993. There has been a general downward trend since then to the point where 6.8 per cent of GNP was allocated to health in 1996. The net result of these changes is that since the beginning of this decade there has been a 2.6 per cent reduction in the proportion of GNP devoted to health.

When looking behind the pattern of changes in the health to GNP ratio in the 1990s compared with the 1980s, a substantially different picture emerges. The review of gross non-capital health expenditure in current and constant terms presented in Table 4 for the 1980–96 period indicates that while health expenditure remained fairly stable in constant terms throughout the 1980s, it has generally been increasing since 1989. Despite the continuing increase in health expenditure throughout the 1990s, the exceptional growth in the Irish economy in the latter part of this period has meant that the share of GNP devoted to health has declined since 1993.

Table 4: Gross non-capital public health expenditure, 1980–96

Year	Gross non-capital expenditure (current, £m)	As % of GNP	Gross non-capital expenditure at constant 1990 prices (£m)
1980	732	8.13	1,537
1981	858	7.90	1,495
1982	999	8.02	1,488
1983	1,091	8.02	1,470
1984	1,155	7.82	1,434
1985	1,245	7.92	1,465
1986	1,303	7.76	1,476
1987	1,324	7.32	1,455
1988	1,339	7.07	1,440
1989	1,425	6.83	1,473
1990	1,576	6.97	1,576
1991	1,752	6.92	1,698
1992	1,956	7.33	1,838
1993	2,161	7.57	2,003
1994	2,291	7.49	2,074
1995	2,446	7.29	2,162
1996	2,459	6.79	2,143

Source: Department of Health, 1996

When assessing potential future commitments to health expenditure, the experience of the past two decades would suggest that future investment in the health services would be expected to continue to reflect the general well-being or otherwise of the Irish economy. We have seen that in difficult economic circumstances, particularly in the 1980s, health expenditure levels were held fairly constant, while in the growing economy of the 1990s health expenditure has been increasing. Given that public health expenditure as a proportion of GNP has been held below 8 per cent since 1984, this upper limit seems likely to prevail for the foreseeable future.

The question of health system efficiency relates to the return achieved on the resources deployed. While the achievement of optimal efficiency is an important operational objective for all sectors within the health system, the fact that the hospital sector constitutes the largest programme of health expenditure means that the efficiency of this sector has been the subject of particular investigation (Commission on Health Funding, 1989; Wiley and Fetter, 1990). In considering how the efficiency of this sector could be improved, the Commission on Health Funding recommended the use of global budgets based on predetermined service levels for the funding of hospitals. It was further recommended that the calculation of these budgets should be based on an assessment of the activity level implied by the hospital's agreed role and catchment area, and the case-mix-based cost indicated by the level of service provision (Commission on Health Funding, 1989). In addition, it was suggested that techniques such as diagnosis related groups (DRGs) or other case-mix measures should be used to determine the level of funding required for the service level agreed.

The establishment of the National Case-Mix Project by the Department of Health in 1991 was a partial response to this recommendation, in addition to being prompted by the recognition that 'the principal problem in promoting equity and clarity in the way the Department of Health funds hospitals lies in the difficulty in measuring hospital workload in a manner that is equally meaningful to both clinician and funder' (Department of Health, 1993, p. 3). A report of a research project supported by the Department of Health demonstrated that the DRG case-mix classification system could be successfully applied to Irish hospital discharge data (Wiley and Fetter, 1990). The Department of Health then proceeded with the development of a system within which hospital workload measured by DRGs could be related to resource allocation for acute hospital services. For the first time, in 1993 the budgets for the largest acute hospitals incorporated a case-mix adjustment within the allocation process (Wiley, 1995). With the application of this adjustment, the most inefficient hospitals receive some financial penalty while the more efficient hospitals receive a financial reward, though the adjustments would have to be considered marginal in the context of the overall hospital budget.

If the commitment to the health services from national resources remains fairly stable, and the pressures for the expansion of service provision increase, it is to be expected that the demands for greater efficiency in all service areas will also increase. While the efforts applied to date at improving efficiency within the hospital sector are welcome, these must be considered the beginning of what should be a longer term strategy. The proposed reorganisation of the Eastern Health Board region is also a partial response to variations in efficiency standards observed where hospitals are funded from different sources. Structural reorganisation will, however, take some time and may not, in itself, be an adequate response to the problem of differential efficiency at the hospital level. If efficiency is to be improved throughout the hospital system and the health services as a whole, it will be necessary to ensure that the deployment of resources is clearly related to output targets. The expanding pressure on resources within the health sector therefore means that service providers increasingly will be required to make more informed choices about resource deployment.

The Department of Health's strategy document *Shaping a Healthier Future* has outlined targets to be achieved in designated service areas over the 1994–97 period. As the end of this target period approaches, it is to be expected that the achievements over the course of the period, together with revised targets for the future, will be prepared by the Department of Health. In preparing a service plan to take the Irish health services into the next millennium, in addition to service areas previously identified in relation to avoidable and treatable morbidity, a number of additional areas will require consideration. The expansion of state responsibilities for child care and protection and the increase in the number of older people in the population mean that these population groups will in the future require special consideration with regard to service provision. While it has previously been noted that improvements in efficiency levels will necessitate that resource investment is more directly related to output targets and their achievement, improvements in the effectiveness of the health services are no less important. The pursuit of this objective will require that the conduct of medical audit becomes more routine and outcome targets for individual services are explicitly specified.

As the single market takes effect in health as in other areas of the economy, the increased potential for mobility may in future mean that geographical boundaries are less relevant for service delivery purposes.

In these circumstances, the relationship between medical need and access will have to be more clearly defined. An associated development is reflected in the increasing empowerment and rising expectations of health service consumers. Improved and more comprehensive forms of communication between service providers and consumers will be required as consumers will also be expected to make more informed choices regarding resource deployment for health service use.

The ethical issues posed by advancements in technology, service techniques and pharmaceuticals should not be underestimated. The increased potential for extending life at both ends of the life cycle and developments in genetic engineering and such areas as organ transplantation pose serious questions regarding the ethical standards which will be considered acceptable in a societal context. These questions can only be adequately addressed where development of a community health service is pursued as a partnership between all the participants, including service providers, consumers, financiers, managers and administrators.

Conclusion

As the end of the twentieth century approaches, the health care systems of all Western developed nations, including Ireland, harbour an inherent pressure to expand as advances in research, technology and pharmaceuticals enhance the capability of the services to combat disease and to extend and improve the quality of life. This pressure for expansion, however, must be contained within a very real cost constraint as the level of resources which any society can commit to the health care system, over any other system, is limited. As the blueprint for the development of the modern Irish health service, the White Paper in 1966 demonstrated impressive foresight, and a number of its key conclusions continue to be as relevant today as they were three decades ago. The following statement with regard to the development of the services in the latter decades of the twentieth century continues to be relevant to planned development into the next millennium:

> if the burden of our health services on the limited numbers who will have to pay for them is to be tolerable, then their development must be planned so as to ensure the utmost efficiency and economy in their administration and so as to avoid expenditure on services (or extensions of services) not demonstrated to be reasonably necessary (Department of Health, 1966, p. 26).

In analysing the strengths and weaknesses of the Irish health system in the 1990s, *Shaping a Healthier Future* recognises the importance of the prevailing political and social consensus for the development of an adequately funded, high-quality and equitable public health system. Additional attributes noted include the well-qualified, committed and caring staff, the strong voluntary sector and the mix of public and private services fulfilling complementary roles. The weaknesses which are seen to persist within the system, however, include the fact that the main causes of premature mortality have not been adequately addressed, many services are not targeted towards the achievement of specific goals, and co-ordination, organisation and management within the system generally are less than adequate (Department of Health, 1994).

While the action plan presented in *Shaping a Healthier Future* can be expected to assist in overcoming some of the current problems within the system, one four-year plan could not be expected to transform the system completely. As the planning cycle underlying the Department of Health's current strategy comes to an end, it seems reasonable to expect that a start is about to be made on a revised strategy. In the development of an updated plan, consideration should be given to some of the longer term strategic issues previously noted as being relevant to health system development, in addition to the shorter term planning targets which constitute the current action plan. While planners may correctly consider certainty an elusive commodity, we can be sure that in health system development choice will always be necessary in an environment where expanding needs compete for limited resources. As difficult choices undoubtedly loom ahead, it is essential to maintain the political and social consensus regarding the principles of health service development which has been so essential to the advancement of these services to date. If the Irish health system is to be safely guided and protected through to the next millennium, a good starting-point would seem to be acceptance of the principle that the health services will continue to be developed on the basis of a community-oriented approach within which the interests of equity and solidarity are considered priority objectives.

REFERENCES

Commission on Health Funding (1989). *Report of the Commission on Health Funding*, Dublin: Stationery Office

Department of Health (1966). *The Health Services and their Further Development*, Dublin: Stationery Office

Department of Health (1986). *Health – The Wider Dimensions*, Dublin: Department of Health

Department of Health (1993). *Casemix Manual*, Dublin: Department of Health

Department of Health (1994). *Shaping a Healthier Future: A Strategy for Effective Healthcare in the 1990s*, Dublin: Department of Health

Dublin Hospital Initiative Group (1991). *Report of the Dublin Hospital Initiative Group*, Dublin: Stationery Office

Hensey, B. (1959). *The Health Services of Ireland*, 1st edn, Dublin: Institute of Public Administration

Hensey, B. (1979). *The Health Services of Ireland*, 3rd edn, Dublin: Institute of Public Administration

Ministry of Welfare, Health and Cultural Affairs (1992). *Report of the Government Committee on Choices in Health Care*, The Netherlands

Tussing, A. Dale (1985). *Irish Medical Care Resources: An Economic Analysis*, General Research Series, Paper No. 126, Dublin: Economic and Social Research Institute

Wiley, Miriam M. (1995). 'Budgeting for Acute Hospital Services in Ireland: The Case-Mix Adjustment', *Journal of the Irish Colleges of Physicians and Surgeons*, Vol. 24, No. 4, pp. 283–90

Wiley, Miriam M. (1997). 'Financing the Irish Health Services: Transition from Local to Centralised Funding and Beyond', in J. Robins (ed.), *Reflections on Health*, Dublin: Department of Health (forthcoming)

Wiley, Miriam M. and Robert B. Fetter (1990). *Measuring Activity and Costs in Irish Hospitals: A Study of Hospital Case Mix*, General Research Series, Paper No. 147, Dublin: Economic and Social Research Institute

Part III

Sectoral Economic Development in Ireland

12

Economic Opportunities for the Twenty-First Century

PETER BACON

Introduction

THIS essay sets out the rationale and thrust of policies required to realise economic opportunities in the coming decade and more. It draws heavily on *Shaping Our Future: A Strategy for Enterprise in Ireland in the 21st Century*. This study was published in May 1996 by Forfás, the policy advisory and co-ordination board for industrial development and science and technology in Ireland. It is a particularly relevant report in the context of the present volume, since it also provides a contemporary counterpart to the process of planning initiated by T. K. Whitaker and his fellows in the late 1950s and early 1960s. In that regard there are three important points of comparison and contrast which are worth making.

Firstly, by comparison with those early endeavours, the breadth, scope, perspective and diversity of resources and skills drawn upon to compile the Forfás report were enormous. The goals too are more ambitious – to halve the rate of unemployment, double living standards and raise the quality of life for all those living in Ireland. *Economic Development* was concerned 'to highlight the main deficiencies and potentialities of the economy and to suggest the principles to be followed to correct the deficiencies and realise the opportunities, indicating a number of specific forms of productive development which appear to offer good long-term prospects'.[1]

Secondly, while there are noticeable differences between the two approaches there is a fundamental common thread which the two share, namely, that the establishment of explicit goals, the rigorous assessment of current circumstances and a logical and co-ordinated approach to policy formulation can facilitate the realisation of these goals. 'In the context of a programme of economic development extending over five years or longer, it would be easier not only to avoid inconsistencies between individual decisions but also to secure acceptance of decisions which, presented in isolation, might arouse strong opposition.'[2]

Thirdly, *Economic Development* was set against a background of stagnation. The starting-point of *Shaping Our Future* is a recognition that we are living through a period of profound change and transformation that is rearranging the shape of Ireland's society and its underlying economic base. The nature of production, trade, employment and work in the coming decades will be very different from that of today. The ingredients of economic success in the new environment of the future will not at all be the same as those required at present or that were relevant in the past. Yet the basic economic objectives of society remain the same: the achievement of growing living standards with low rates of unemployment.

The recent trend of strong achievements

While the full potential of the economy has not yet been realised, the experience of the last decade and a half demonstrates that sustained progress can be made, sometimes in the face of a difficult international environment. The Irish economy today is in better shape than it has ever been. The number of people at work is at the highest level since independence but significant progress on unemployment remains outstanding. The enterprise sector is strong and that strength is growing. A review of progress in the past fifteen years in Ireland's main macroeconomic indicators shows what has been achieved, both in absolute terms and relative to the EU-15 (see Table 1).

In the first half of the 1980s growth of the economy was weak. While GDP expanded in line with the EU, GNP barely increased in the five years 1982–86, compared with the EU average increase of 2 per cent per annum. Employment fell and unemployment accelerated. The balance of

Table 1: Ireland's relative economic performance, 1982–95 (average annual percentage changes)

	1982–86		1987–91		1992–95	
	Ireland	EU	Ireland	EU	Ireland	EU
GDP growth	1.8	1.7	4.7	3.0	5.1	1.5
Inflation	10.8	8.0	3.2	4.6	2.3	3.7
Unemployment rate (%)	14.3	9.1	15.8	8.5	15.5	10.6
Current balance (as a % of GDP)	–7.0	0.1	0.4	–0.3	6.0	–0.3
Government borrowing (as a % of GDP)	–12.0	4.8	–3.1	–3.4	–2.3	–5.4

Source: Shaping Our Future: A Strategy for Enterprise in Ireland in the 21st Century, Dublin: Forfás, 1996

payments was in persistent and substantial deficit. The effects of un-competitive price performance, high real interest rates and a large and unsustainable fiscal imbalance were reinforced by a generally weak international economic environment. The policy response, over a sustained period from the early 1970s, was inadequate to the needs of the economy.

In the next five years, 1987–91, major progress was made. There was a rapid reduction in the fiscal imbalance from 1987. With that, interest rates began to fall and inflation subsided. Strong economic growth recommenced, averaging 4.7 per cent per annum, which was significantly higher than the EU average of 3 per cent. Employment in the non-agricultural economy rose by over 14,000 per annum. In the private sector, the rate of increase was even faster, 18,000 per annum. This experience was in sharp contrast to the previous five years, when non-agricultural employment fell by more than 7,000 per annum. The rise in unemployment was halted and gradually commenced falling.

These positive developments have been sustained to date. Growth in GDP averaged 5.1 per cent per annum during 1992–95. Employment growth in the non-agricultural economy accelerated to 39,000 in the twelve months to April 1994 and further to 50,000 in the next twelve months. Of this cumulative increase of 89,000 some 60,000 arose in the private sector. However, faster increases in the labour force have meant that unemployment is slower to fall. Nevertheless, the drop of 34,000 in the two years to April 1995 is encouraging. Inflation continues to be low and the balance of payments is in substantial surplus.

Ireland's annual fiscal deficit is now amongst the lowest in the EU, whereas in the early 1980s it escalated to an unsustainable level. The transformation has been dramatic, although the level of public debt outstanding, as a proportion of GNP, is still amongst the highest in the EU.

Sensible economic policies, pursued on a sustained basis for about a decade, have brought about a fundamental strengthening of the economy. A sustained rise in living standards has been achieved and the gap with Europe has been narrowed. Employment growth, driven largely by the private sector, has accelerated strongly. More recently, the rate of unemployment has shown the first signs of a significant fall: the future will tell if this progress can be sustained.

Taking a longer term perspective, the transformation that has occurred appears dramatic. In the past forty years or so, since Whitaker's *Economic Development*, real GNP per capita has tripled. The economy has been transformed. Over one-third of the labour force was engaged in agriculture in the late 1950s compared with around 10 per cent now; moreover, that sector was very underdeveloped in the 1950s compared with the modern one of today. Enormous improvements have occurred in the standard of housing, and the country has the highest rate of home ownership in the EU. In 1956 there was one car to every six households. Now there is one to every 1.2 households. The number of telephones and television sets per household has shown similar dramatic increases. Participation in education and access to health services have also increased very substantially.

Ireland is now on a much higher growth path than it was in the past. Good economic foundations are in place and continue to be laid. The general strategic policy stance of successive governments has been well chosen. The enterprise sector has, once more, become the engine of economic and employment growth. As a result of strong expansion in manufacturing and services, Ireland's economic growth performance is outstripping most other EU countries.

With the right policy framework for the future, Ireland can achieve a major leap forward, to much higher living standards and low rates of unemployment. Unless the opportunity presented by the recent strong economic performance is grasped, the full potential of the economy, again, will not be realised. There are risks that recent achievements will give way to complacency. That, in turn, would lead to slippage from the current high growth path. The right strategy and policy framework can propel the economy forward. In order to do so it must be informed by an understanding of the major forces for change shaping the future.

Forces shaping the future

Identifying and addressing the issues posed by the forces for change that are reshaping the global economy are more relevant to future success than dwelling on the effectiveness of past achievements. What are these forces for change and what threats and opportunities will they present?

The impact of technological change

A revolution is taking place in information and communications technologies. Numerous studies show that these technologies are resulting in a dramatic transformation of many aspects of economic and social life, including working methods and relations, the organisation of companies, the focus of training and education, and the way people communicate with each other. They are bringing about major gains in productivity in industry, and in the quality and performance of services. A new 'information society' is emerging in which the services provided by information and communications technologies will underpin human activities.

Another source of technological change arises from developments in biotechnology. Modern biotechnology comprises a growing range of techniques, processes and procedures. Developments in this area are not likely to give rise to new industries in the same way as are developments in information technology, but they can substitute and complement existing technologies, thereby giving rise to the possibility of new products and production processes in a range of existing industries. (The likely growth sectors of the future, resulting in part from technological change, are portrayed below.)

Advances in technology are resulting in changes to organisation structures and the production techniques used by enterprises. The distinction between 'goods' and 'services', already blurring, will become even less distinct because so much of the value provided by the successful enterprise will entail services: the specialised research, engineering and design services necessary to solve problems; the specialised sales, marketing and consulting services necessary to identify problems; and the specialised strategic, financial and management services for intermediating the first two.

In manufacturing, instead of large, compartmentalised plants with high levels of specialisation, the new 'ideal plant' will integrate and link a variety of functions. Thus design, management, production and marketing have already begun to become part of an integrated system. Flexibility and diversity will become crucial. Instead of producing large quantities of identical units, the output of manufacturing firms can now be more diverse, responding to new consumer demands for a greater diversity of higher quality products.

Instead of hierarchical structures, the demand for flexibility is dictating a much more decentralised structure within firms. In this new environment group-working, for example, will become much more common, and each individual worker will have much more responsibility.

In the future, firms will survive and succeed by being able to meet the unique needs of particular customers, by moving from high volume to high value. Whether the industry is engaged in manufacturing or providing services, old or new, mature or high tech, the pattern will be similar. Business will be successful both because customers are willing to pay a premium for goods and services that exactly meet their needs and because these high-value businesses cannot easily be duplicated by high-volume competitors around the world.

Competition among high-volume producers will continue to compress profits on everything that is uniform, routine and standard – that is, on anything that can be made, reproduced or extracted almost anywhere on the globe. Successful business in advanced nations will move to higher ground, based on specially tailored products and services. The new barrier to entry will be neither price nor volume but, increasingly, the skill in finding the right fit between particular technologies and markets. Growth, therefore, will increasingly centre on specialised knowledge. In high-value enterprises, profits will derive not from scale and volume, although in some industries these will remain important, but from continuous discovery of new linkages between needs and solutions.

Another feature of the changing industrial structure is that it is reaching across the globe in a way that is making national boundaries increasingly irrelevant. Firms are becoming part of a global web of economic activity. Some of these firms are part of multinational corporations, others may be partners in an international joint venture, others still may be stand-alone enterprises. All are increasingly interdependent on international economic relationships. The move to a single market in Europe – allowing goods, services, labour and capital to move freely within the EU – and the next step, a single currency, can be seen as mechanisms which remove barriers and obstacles that national borders impose on this emerging global economic web. As more and more goods and services move around, a country's capacity for sustaining growth in the longer term will be determined by its ability to trade internationally in the products of the future.

Trends in international trade and shifts in the world's economic centre of gravity

The composition of international trade is changing, reflecting these influences. Within agriculture, trade in bulk commodities is declining in importance relative to more complex, value-added foods; within industry, intra-industry trade is growing in importance relative to the exchange of finished products; and relative to both agriculture and industry, trade in services is gathering momentum, growing seven times faster than trade in manufactures and accounting for one-third of all global trade.

Competition within international trade is intensifying. Communications technology is a factor underlying this. Another is the rapid emergence of low-labour-cost economies capable of producing high-quality manufactured goods. Success in future can no longer be linked solely to price, but will depend on a deepening process of innovation, quality enhancement and responsiveness to customer needs: factors, in other words, that raise the value associated with the product.

The spatial pattern of international trade is also changing. New and emerging markets are set to capture an increasing share of world trade.

The transition of the Central and Eastern European economies and the former Soviet Union to market principles significantly extends the scope of the global market which plays by market rules. Despite the growing importance of new and emerging markets, the UK and the European Union should remain the main focus of attention of Irish exporters, even until 2010. The UK will continue to be the first step to exporting for many small to medium-sized firms. That market will be enhanced by the prospects of increased cross-border trade, if a permanent peace is established in Northern Ireland.

The importance of trade in international exchanges is changing. Trade is increasingly linked to foreign direct investment (FDI), but both are increasingly dwarfed by capital movements facilitated by the liberalisation of capital markets and the removal of exchange controls. The resulting volatility in foreign exchange markets is a potential threat to the stability of the open trading system.

The trend in FDI, itself, is a matter of considerable importance to Ireland. Overseas companies located in Ireland account for 55 per cent of the output of manufacturing industry, 44 per cent of employment and 70 per cent of industrial exports. This degree of dependence is much higher than in other countries. The major threat to continuing FDI growth in Ireland stems from increasing competition. Apart from traditional competitors like Scotland, Wales, Benelux, France, Spain and the Netherlands, there will be much stronger competition in the future from Eastern European countries and from countries in south-east Asia.

Finally, the regulation of international trade is changing. The successful conclusion of the Uruguay Round and the establishment of the World Trade Organisation to monitor and police the agreements which have been reached are hopeful signs that trade will be governed by stable and predictable rules. However, the rapid growth of government intervention and regulation, in response to the need to manage environmental concerns, protect consumer welfare and ensure social solidarity, is a potential source of tension in international trade in the future. The likely emergence of non-tariff barriers to trade as a result of this intervention will need to be vigorously fought against.

The size, structure and organisation of the workforce

The international evidence suggests that the nature of employment in the developed world will change substantially in the next fifteen years. The major trends expected include:

- more self-employment
- a reducing working week
- more part-time and other atypical forms of employment, e.g. temporary, contract, job sharing.

These developments are expected to be paralleled in Ireland. The increasing trend to employment in services, the continuing development of information and communications technologies and the replacement of the old hierarchical approach to the organisation of work by a new flexible entrepreneurial approach are likely to stimulate the growth in atypical forms of work. If present trends continue, self-employment could double by 2010 to around 24 per cent of the total at work, and there is expected to be a sharp increase in part-time and temporary employment which currently account for 7 per cent and 8 per cent respectively of the total number in employment.

A major issue is the likely size and composition of the Irish labour force in the future. This has major implications for achieving one of the primary goals of the strategy: halving the current rate of unemployment. The structure of Ireland's employed labour force differs substantially from that of other European countries in terms of its sector composition. Of the total number employed, 13 per cent are engaged in agriculture compared with 8 per cent in the EU as a whole, whereas both industry and services' share of employment, at 28 per cent and 59 per cent respectively, are below the EU average. The long-term fall in agricultural employment from its earlier higher level has contributed to Ireland's unemployment problem. While the pace of decline is expected to ease, agricultural employment is expected to continue declining. A fall to the EU average of 8 per cent would involve the loss of a further 50,000 people from agriculture.

Another structural feature of Ireland's demography is its age structure. The proportion of Ireland's population in the 0–14 year age category is well above the EU average (26 per cent against 18 per cent in 1992). Correspondingly the proportion in the 'working age group' of 15–64 years and the over 65 age group is well below the EU average (74 per cent against 82 per cent). This age structure has contributed to a historically high dependency ratio in Ireland and has restricted Ireland's ability to raise living standards to the EU average, another of the key goals of the strategy being put forward. Recent demographic trends in fertility mean that in the future Ireland's age profile will gradually move towards the European average. This will assist the aim of raising Ireland's living standards to the EU average.

However, there are other features of demography which will pose challenges in the future. While Ireland has experienced a rapid increase in educational participation in recent years, it still lags behind many of the more advanced EU countries. At 75 per cent, the participation rate amongst 15–19 year olds has the potential to be raised to 85–90 per cent. Participation amongst the 20–24 year age group, at 15 per cent, is low. If Ireland is to exploit the economic potential offered by technological developments, there will need to be a major drive to raise the educational attainment of the workforce and population.

The scale of the challenge to halve the present rate of unemployment is influenced to a significant degree by the likely growth in the labour force. However, there are numerous hazards involved in projecting future trends. For one, the Irish labour market is very open, especially *vis-à-vis* the UK. This means that large migration flows between these markets can have a significant impact on the total number in the labour force. For example, in the decade 1971–81, Ireland experienced net inward migration of 11,000 per annum. In the 1980s the trend was reversed; in the period 1986–91 net outward migration was 27,000 per annum. It is estimated that net outward migration had fallen to 5,000 by 1994. While Ireland's relative economic performance compared with that of other countries (and the UK in particular) may be a principal cause of these flows, there is not an accurate model available that would enable them to be predicted with any degree of reliability. In framing labour force projections to 2010, it has been assumed that emigration will continue, although at a progressively slower rate (see Table 2). The projections are sensitive to this assumption. For example, compared with the 'benchmark' shown in Table 2, a scenario of zero migration would involve an additional 134,000 in the labour force by 2010.

Another major source of uncertainty concerns the female participation ratio. In Ireland, this is low by comparison with other European countries. In 1988 the overall participation rate of females was 37.6 per cent in Ireland. This may be compared with an EU average of 52.2 per cent and rates of 63.5 per cent in the UK and 78.3 per cent in Denmark. Research indicates that, at present, there are significant inflows of women in the 40–50 year age group entering the labour force.[3] In the period to 2010 it is expected that female participation rates will increase significantly in Ireland and that they will converge to the already increasing trend in other European countries. Again the projections are sensitive to this assumption; as an illustration, if participation rates were to stay at their present level, the increase in the labour force to 2010 would be 153,000 fewer.

The 'benchmark' labour force projections used in the strategy are summarised in Table 2. They show that the labour force is likely to expand significantly over the period to 2010. The rate of increase, currently 22,500 per annum, is expected to taper off to under 12,000 per annum after 2000 and to 9,000 per annum after 2005.

Table 2: Population and labour force projections to 2010

	1995	2000	2005	2010
Population (000s)	3,575	3,585	3,574	3,594
Birth rate per 1,000	3.2	2.2	11.4	11.0
Death rate per 1,000	8.9	8.9	9.0	9.0
Emigration (000s)				
(annual five-year period averages)	*11.4*		*12.0*	*3.4*
Labour force (000s)	1,423	1,536	1,595	1,640
Growth in labour force (000s)				
(annual five-year period averages)	*22.6*		*11.8*	*9.0*

Source: *Shaping Our Future: A Strategy for Enterprise in Ireland in the 21st Century*, Dublin: Forfás, 1996

Key issues which must be addressed

A number of key conclusions emerge. These, along with the principal implications which they give rise to, are set out below. Future strategy will have to address these effectively if the overarching goals are to be attained.

Six basic conclusions are drawn about the nature of the enterprise sector in the future, namely:

- most employment growth will arise in services
- economic performance will be determined increasingly by the skills of people in being able to exploit the potential of a small number of pervasive technologies
- the structure of enterprises and work will adapt to a much more flexible and entrepreneurial form
- international trade will continue to expand rapidly but competition will increase, especially in manufactures, and international trade in services will expand most rapidly
- global competition will intensify: the nations that will thrive will be those whose people are most advanced in knowledge, skills, adaptability and organisation, and who share a coherent vision of their future
- competition for foreign direct investment will intensify and the character of FDI will change.

It is worthwhile elaborating on these conclusions in terms of: the necessary actions which arise; priorities that need to be established;

appropriate policy responses; and the implications and issues that are likely to follow.

Most employment growth will arise in services

In these circumstances a number of *necessary actions* are to:

- recognise that the services sector will be the key jobs provider, potentially creating 300,000 new jobs, which is 80 per cent of the expected total, by 2010.
- adapt policy to encourage dynamic growth in locally based services; lower income taxes so as to reduce costs and boost consumer spending as a way of encouraging employment growth; and progressively reduce the standard rate of corporation tax to a single low rate not exceeding 12 per cent, commencing with introducing a low rate of tax for small business enterprises. Tourism, leisure, entertainment and a range of services associated with an ageing population such as health and home help will be key growth sectors.
- aim for substantial growth in internationally traded services, of the order of a fourfold increase. This implies an increase in employment from 21,000 now to 80,000 by 2010. Key new growth areas will be telecommunications-based services and a whole range of business services where Ireland can offer an efficient multilingual service. Policy should also build on existing strengths in sectors like software, which is expected to be the world's largest industry by 2005.
- raise tourism revenue as a percentage of GNP to equal or exceed the EU average, i.e. from the present 7 per cent of GNP to 13 per cent or more. Aim to create over 80,000 jobs in tourism services.

Economic performance will be determined increasingly by the skills of people in being able to exploit the potential of a small number of pervasive technologies

Given this, a *main priority* has to be to:

- raise education and skill levels and focus them in the areas which will provide Ireland with an advantage to exploit the opportunities that are arising and will continue to emerge from technological developments.

The structure of enterprises and work will adapt to a much more flexible and entrepreneurial form

This will require *policy responses* in terms of:

- a proactive competition policy to reduce costs, eliminate restrictive practices and increase efficiency
- the development of a system of public administration which is more efficient and geared more towards supporting enterprise
- bringing about a market culture in which individuals and enterprises find it more rewarding to engage in commercial risk-taking
- reducing the burden of taxation and shifting more of the economy's resources into the market sector of the economy.

International trade will continue to expand but competition will increase, especially in manufactures, and international trade in services will expand most rapidly

In relation to Irish-owned manufacturing industry there are several *implications*, namely:

- There is a need to adopt the goal of reversing the downward jobs trend of the last twenty years and setting this sector on a path of steady jobs growth, from 128,000 now to 140,000 by 2010, with many more jobs supported elsewhere in the economy as performance improves.
- Much greater attention needs to be given to innovation, i.e. doing existing things in new ways and doing new things, not only in research and development but in all areas of operation including marketing, production, management and organisation.
- Companies need to reposition themselves into better business areas. This can be achieved through companies in traditional areas developing new higher value products or, instead of manufacturing, concentrating on specialising in sales, marketing, distribution or design, all of which are increasingly important areas. There is a need to focus on directing new start-ups to higher growth sectors.
- Developing the scale of Irish-owned firms needs to become a key concern so that they can compete more effectively on world markets.
- There is a need to focus on substantially improving the profitability of Irish-owned firms.
- There is a need to introduce policies to contribute to these objectives and to explore new approaches by which the state may work with these companies. To succeed, companies must invest in research and development, adopt modern manufacturing techniques, improve

employee training and develop access to new technologies and markets. This will require proactive company capability development initiatives, particularly developing management capability. The state should continue to promote growth sectors, directing entrepreneurs towards them and investing public funds in developing centres of excellence in research, technology and marketing.

More widely there is a need for much greater emphasis on:

- overcoming the disadvantage of peripherality in terms of higher transport and communication costs by investing in these infra-structures and improving the operating efficiencies of the agencies providing these services
- logistics, i.e. the management of goods and services across the economy and into export markets; the aim should be to become a world leader in this field
- increasing the language skills of those engaged in business and trade.

Competition for foreign direct investment will intensify

Ireland's policy to attract FDI in the future will have to respond to a number of *issues*, for example:

- maintaining a competitive total cost base and financial package
- shifting the balance of inward investment towards higher value-added and, increasingly, service sector projects
- developing higher skills, knowledge and a technological infrastructure
- ensuring that the transport infrastructure overcomes the disadvantage of peripherality
- continuously identifying emerging new sectors and gaining early market leadership positions.

Foreign direct investment will remain a key source of growth and the government should target an increase in employment in overseas-owned manufacturing industry from 107,000 now to 140,000 by 2010. As well as creating jobs, FDI will also help Ireland to develop a strong position in new-technology sectors. Overseas industry also provides an important market for Irish-owned companies.

The strategy

The strategy described below addresses the key issues for the future raised above and draws on the lessons from past experience. The critical elements revolve around:

- supporting the traded goods and services sector as the engine of economic growth
- encouraging an enterprise culture and a system which rewards entrepreneurs in order to ensure that the full growth potential of the traded sectors is realised
- setting new targets for reducing the national debt and the level of taxation so as to rebalance the economy's resources more towards the market sectors of the economy
- investing in a skilled labour force as a key source of competitive advantage
- developing the ability of business to innovate
- improving competitiveness and opening all sectors of the economy to competition and appropriate regulation
- leading the way in developing information industries by investing in telecommunications infrastructure and services
- putting a whole new emphasis on excellence in logistics.

These aims could be accomplished best by pursuing two broad strands:

- directly promoting the growth of the enterprise sectors
- implementing a consistent and co-ordinated set of key support policies.

Promoting the growth of the enterprise sectors

The focus of the strategy for promoting the growth of the enterprise sectors should be to:

- harness the immense potential of the services sector by rapidly developing the scale of the internationally traded sector and creating as many jobs as possible in locally based services
- reposition Irish-owned industry into new growth segments and transform its ability to innovate and compete
- maintain a strong flow of inward investment from overseas companies as a key source of new jobs and fresh technologies.

Services

The key success factors for developing services fall under six headings.

- *Achieving an early leadership position in telecommunications-based services.* Advances in telecommunications are revolutionising the services sector and will allow many more services to be traded internationally. Among the opportunity areas are banking, education, shopping, publishing, logistical services, back-office administration and tele-medical services. Irish-owned companies have the opportunity to be 'early movers', getting into these fields as they are growing rapidly. A key goal for state agencies will be targeting support at companies which are able to do this. A small number of dedicated state agency staff should work with companies to develop the sector. The development of demonstration projects on an advanced communications 'nursery' run on a cable system to homes and offices would help businesses to develop new applications. Changes in the personal and corporate tax environment will also be needed to encourage entrepreneurs. Over 40,000 new jobs can be created in this sector, provided the underlying telecommunications infrastructure develops as required.

- *Establishing Ireland as a multilingual European services hub.* As companies increasingly buy in services rather than conduct them in-house, Ireland will have a major opportunity. In the US many mid-western and southern states have gained as back-office service jobs migrated from the expensive east and west coasts. A multilingual Ireland can become a centralised administration, back-office and sales/services location for European-based companies, offering services in areas like accounting, purchasing, invoicing, treasury management and systems development. In order to win contracts from major corporations stand-alone companies will need to operate under an 'umbrella organisation' which will guarantee standards and offer recourse to the international corporation through a bonding-type system. A further 40,000 jobs could be created in this area.

- *Promoting Ireland as a location for headquarters for Irish-based service multinationals.* Many Irish companies already provide services internationally. Companies like Aer Rianta and Campbell Catering are operating successfully overseas and many more can follow.

- *Establishing a competitive local services market and fostering its development.* This general services sector will be the main source of new jobs. Higher disposable incomes and a reduction in the burden of taxation, together with demographic changes, will create a major boost to this sector and accelerate employment growth. Growth areas will include tourism, security, business services, child-minding, home-help, environmental services and education. The tax changes recommended will be critically important.

- *Continuing to grow the established internationally traded services sector.* The existing internationally traded services sector employs 21,000 people and has the potential for strong growth. Software, publishing, animation, financial services, health care services and other sectors all have the potential to increase employment.

- *Promoting tourism.* This can be done by developing scale, focusing on product positioning and market segmentation, and developing a positive image of Ireland as a tourist destination.

Meeting these challenges will require a number of developments in policy and the establishment and pursuit of priorities with respect to:

- *Improving competitiveness.* A proactive implementation of competition policy across all sectors and actions to maintain and enhance a competitive labour cost base and labour market flexibility will be essential.
- *Investing in telecommunications.* The information superhighway will increase competition for domestic industry but also open new markets to Irish service companies. If a 'do nothing' approach is adopted, Ireland could forfeit up to 40,000 extra jobs in this area. Telecommunications policy is one of the key levers left to governments to influence industry, and the Irish government must set the development of communications infrastructure and services as a priority.
- *Developing language skills.* Steps must be taken now to improve language skills by introducing an expanded programme of training for those in work and about to enter work. The introduction of modern continental languages at primary level must become universal and their teaching expanded at second and third level.
- *Changing the tax structure.* Most of the services sector is now taxed at a 38 per cent rate, almost four times the 10 per cent rate applied to manufacturing and some internationally traded services. A 20 per cent corporation tax rate should be introduced for small businesses as soon as possible, with the goal of a single low overall rate of corporation tax by 2010.
- *Developing appropriate state supports.* Major opportunities can be developed in the services sector through strategic alliances and technology transfers with overseas firms. This will require specialised promotional activities in this area by An Bord Tráchtála, Forbairt and IDA Ireland.

Irish-owned industry

A summary of expected future growth opportunity areas for Irish-owned industry is presented in Table 3.

Table 3: Overview of opportunity areas for indigenous industry

Pharmaceuticals

- Drug delivery device development and manufacture
- Contract manufacture (chemical synthesis)
- Biosynthetic manufacture
- Neutraceutical sector development – health promotion
- Specific treatments – gene therapy, diagnostic molecular biology, cell/tissue therapy
- Contract R&D
- Software services
- Tele-medicine
- Generic supplier

Medical/surgical

- Traditional products – hospital/clinic supply
- High-tech equipment manufacture – implantable devices, minimally invasive products
- Development of specific assays – configure as disposables, configure with interface for remote monitoring
- Screening – generic, major disease, discovery
- Software development – products, applications, services
- Distribution – tele-services

Electronics

- Product design – indigenous companies, multinational corporations
- Software development – multimedia, tele-services, security and encryption
- Manufacture – sub-assembly, final assembly
- System integration – localisation and customisation
- Sales, marketing and distribution – direct selling, technical support, non-physical software distribution

Publishing and print

- In-house origination, composition and printing
- Electronic publishing on telecommunications networks
- Multimedia
- Security printing
- Direct mail
- Telemarketing

In order to take advantage of the opportunities that will arise in these areas, a strategy which revolves around four headings is needed.

- *Innovation.* This is likely to be the key to profitable growth. Essentially, innovation involves firms doing new things in new ways which increase productivity, product development and profitability. It involves new ways of identifying the needs of new and existing clients, and new ways of making and marketing the products and services that satisfy them. The development and implementation of new, cost-effective technology is central but innovation also involves other areas such as general management, finance and administration. It applies to the services sector as much as to manufacturing.

- *Repositioning*. This will happen if firms become more innovative. There are a number of aspects to the repositioning challenge facing Irish business:
  - Companies in traditional sectors need to develop new, higher value products for existing and new markets. This requires new investment, the development or acquisition of new technology, the development of higher management capability, particularly in marketing, and more highly skilled employees.
  - Existing firms in traditional sectors must reposition themselves to other areas of the value chain. Where higher returns are available, manufacturing activity is accounting for less and less of the total value or production chain. Many firms which are not competitive in manufacturing can specialise in other areas such as sales, marketing, distribution or the provision of services such as product design.
  - Irish-owned industry must reposition from traditional to growth sectors. While most existing firms will choose to develop new products or reposition themselves in areas of the value chain where returns are higher, some will enter new growth sectors through diversification; where required the development agencies will have to provide proactive support.

The key to achieving a significant repositioning will be to ensure that the highest possible number of start-ups are in the new growth sectors. The development agencies will be required to work with firms in identifying these areas of high potential growth, developing incentives which support companies entering these new areas, promoting related education and training initiatives, and developing centres of excellence in research, technology and market assessment.

- *Developing the scale of Irish-owned firms*. Very few Irish-owned businesses have developed into true global players. The exceptions include Jefferson Smurfit, CRH, Glen Dimplex and the two main banks, AIB and Bank of Ireland. Most firms remain small, and lack of scale is a substantial barrier to growth in increasingly global markets. Achieving the scale needed to become significant players in global markets by a significant number of Irish-owned firms will require heavy investment. The required investment will materialise only if the potential profitability is high relative to alternative investment opportunities. It will also require strong partnership between firms and the development agencies in sourcing the investment required through internally and externally generated equity, grants, loans and other supports.

- *Profitability.* The above initiatives will contribute to improving profitability. In addition, the proactive company capability development programmes of the development agencies – Forbairt, An Bord Tráchtála, FÁS and Shannon Development – should be fundamentally reviewed and redeveloped as an integrated and co-ordinated set of supports. It is vital that companies are given the necessary support to address specific deficiencies in key functional areas such as general management and innovation, marketing, product development, operational efficiency, distribution, quality and general workforce skills.

Foreign direct investment

The central thrusts of strategy on foreign direct investment should be concerned with:

- *Developing the existing overseas base.* Many overseas firms located in Ireland are still based on manufacturing production and assembly. As such, these firms have weak links with the Irish economy and are thus vulnerable to competition from other countries for new rounds of investment. Policy must encourage existing overseas companies to locate more business functions in Ireland in areas like marketing, research and product design.
- *Focusing on higher value-added products.* Low-skill, low-wage jobs will increasingly flow to low-wage-cost countries. Ireland can compete for knowledge-intensive jobs in areas like electronics, pharmaceuticals and biotechnology. It must also achieve greater success in attracting other elements of the manufacturing process such as research, design, customer support and administration.
- *Early identification of growth sectors.* Ireland has done well in the past through identifying and exploiting FDI high-growth sectors at an early stage of their development, e.g. telemarketing, electronics. This strategy will continue to be important in attracting FDI.
- *Targeting new modes of investment.* As greenfield investments decline in relative importance, Ireland must focus to a greater extent than in the past on 'follow-on' investments and attracting joint ventures, alliances and acquisitions.
- *Attracting entrepreneurs.* New business start-ups will continue to be important and so attracting entrepreneurs from overseas to locate their businesses in Ireland will be essential.

In order to successfully implement this strategy in an increasingly competitive environment it will be necessary to achieve and maintain:

- *A competitive cost base.* This applies to all costs facing incoming industry including not only labour but also inputs, services, energy, telecommunications and others. Achieving high productivity levels will also help control cost per unit of output.
- *A sophisticated low-cost communications infrastructure.* This will be crucial, particularly if combined with improvements in communications.
- *An attractive incentive package.* This must include advisory services and grants as well as a competitive corporate tax regime. New ways of forging joint ventures and alliances between overseas and Irish-owned industry will be essential.

Key support policies

The Culliton Report argued that government policy in a whole range of areas had paid too little attention to job creation. It recommended changes in a number of areas including taxation policy, education and training, and competition policy.[4] To be most effective, changes in these areas must be set within a long-term vision of where the economy is heading. In this way, the actions of different sectors can be harmonised in a consistent way towards a common objective. The role of key supporting policies should be to assist in bringing about the required transformation of Ireland's enterprise economy. *Shaping Our Future* sets out the appropriate policies in a wide range of areas including:

- taxation and public finances
- education and training
- telecommunications
- logistics and transport
- labour market regulation
- science and technology
- energy policy
- the physical environment
- marketing and trade
- competition policy
- public administration
- regional policy.

It is beyond the scope of this essay to consider all of these. However, it would be inappropriate if consideration was not given to the first topic, in view of T. K. Whitaker's life service at the Department of Finance.

Taxation and public finances

A fundamental change is needed in the approach to planning the public finances. The central priorities must be reducing taxation and lowering public indebtedness, rather than deciding on public spending first and then deciding how it will be financed. Lower taxation – and reforms to its structure – will be essential to provide a greater incentive for enterprise and job creation. The future of the tax system can only be considered in the context of the evolution of the public finances. The goal must be to expand the market economy.

Provided economic growth continues at a steady rate, the overall size of the public sector can still expand. However in many respects policy now starts with accepting increased public expenditure programmes as given and then moves on to examining the tax and public finance aspects. A change of approach is needed.

- *Debt target.* A steady reduction in the debt burden – as measured by the ratio of national debt to GNP – is essential to free resources for cutting taxes or increasing public spending. The Maastricht Treaty already sets a debt to GDP target of 60 per cent. This provides a target to be achieved within five years, and an appropriate fifteen-year target (to 2010) would be a debt ratio of 40 per cent.
- *Overall level of taxation.* To achieve a significant shift of resources from the public to the private sector requires a steady reduction in the tax burden. Currently, taxation, including Pay-Related Social Insurance (PRSI), is 39 per cent of GNP and the target for 2010 should be to reduce this to 30 per cent.
- *Public spending.* With targets set for debt levels and taxation, the scope for public spending growth then depends on the level of economic growth. For example, if growth averaged 5 per cent in real terms over the period, there would be room for average annual expenditure growth of 2.5 per cent in real terms.

Tax policy must take into account the need to be competitive. A key problem for Irish enterprises, for example, is the lower cost of taxation and social insurance in the UK. A crucial factor is the tax wedge – the gap between what the employer pays out and what the employee takes home. For single workers in particular, the tax wedge in Ireland is above the international average and well above UK levels. A recent survey of eleven industrial countries found that the so-called marginal tax wedge on a single worker, i.e. the percentage of an extra pound earned taken in taxation, was second highest in Ireland. The rate of PRSI for both employers and employees is also higher in Ireland than in the UK. Particular competitive problems are faced by firms in labour-intensive sectors.

Further problems are caused by so-called unemployment and poverty traps. The unemployment trap is where somebody who is out of work can end up worse off in employment due to the combination of the loss of benefits and taxation of income. The poverty trap is where an increase in gross pay to an employee can lead to a fall in disposable income, resulting from higher taxation and the loss of family income supports.

The policies required to address these problems include:

- *Widening the tax base.* The tax base should be further widened to allow a lowering of the average burden. All remaining tax reliefs should be eliminated or reduced to the standard rate, remaining accelerated capital allowances should be removed, the VAT net should be expanded, and a broadly based property tax should be introduced.
- *Reducing corporation tax.* Tax on corporate profits is falling across the industrialised world. Ireland should aim to progressively reduce the standard corporate tax rate, now 38 per cent, to a single low rate not exceeding 12 per cent by 2010. Lowering the rate for small business to 20 per cent should be the first priority.
- *Personal income tax.* The aim should be that 80 per cent of all taxable personal income be liable at a standard 25 per cent rate, with the remaining income taxable at 40 per cent.
- *Indirect taxes.* Any opportunity should be taken to shift the burden from direct to indirect tax. There is a strong argument for having a single VAT rate chargeable on a wide range of goods and services.
- *Capital taxes.* Capital gains tax should be reduced to 25 per cent for entrepreneurs running a business. Capital acquisitions tax should be cut to 25 per cent for those inheriting a business.
- *Property taxes.* These should be increased to about 5 per cent of revenue through a broadening of the tax base. The yield from property taxes – including residential property tax, business rates, stamp duties and capital acquisitions tax – was 4.4 per cent of revenue in 1992.

NOTES

1. *Economic Development*, Dublin: Stationery Office, 1958, p. 1.
2. *Ibid.*
3. For example, see *Implications of Major Trends for the Size, Structure and Organisation of the Workforce to 2010*, Dublin: Economic and Social Research Institute, 1996.
4. *A Time for Change: Industrial Policy for the 1990s – Report of the Industrial Policy Review Group*, Dublin: Stationery Office, 1992.

13

The Role of Science and Innovation

T. P. HARDIMAN AND E. P. O'NEILL

Introduction

Discovery and application

As science is the systematic descriptive explanation of the physical world in which we live, it undergoes development and change as researchers explore the universe. Changes in our knowledge provide opportunities for innovation in things we make and in services we provide. Technology is the use of that new knowledge and innovation in meeting various physical needs. New technology provides a potential competitive advantage to both the supplier and the supplied, through improved and more economical processes or through superior products and product performance. This advantage may in turn earn improved revenues and induce further investment. This apparently simple process, extending from research to market activity, summarises many complex events which may occur over a long period of time. *Yet it lies at the heart of how many Irish people must earn their living in future.*

Private corporations and public bodies invest heavily in scientific research and technological development. Illustrative examples are provided in Appendix 1. This activity results in changes to the way we understand the physical world. Changes arising from new knowledge are welcomed when they provide a deeper understanding or a more accurate definition of the material universe. Changes in engineering result from applying scientific methods to the selection and use of materials, and also from creative design flowing from advances in understanding. Both lead to improved economic performance or to entirely new facilities that are judged worthy of exploitation.

The correctness of this new knowledge or understanding may be judged by the results of experiments. The experiments may be contrived situations where specific circumstances are isolated for inquiry as in laboratories or in pilot projects. Equally often, the universe itself will provide us with phenomena that can be observed and measured. These procedures are slow and expensive and require highly trained manpower. The investment in that manpower may be slow to generate a return, and is to be viewed as a social, educational or cultural investment; it is truly an important element of capital formation. The process of building up our scientific knowledge has been one of cumulative growth. Much of this growth is quite recent, reflecting society's increased capacity and willingness to invest in the creation of this knowledge.

The fundamental background of culture and infrastructure which allows the growth of technology can be arranged to facilitate the process: the details cannot be prescribed by the state. An extreme version of this view leads to the hypothesis that if markets are sufficiently rewarding, then the necessary investment will occur and the state need not interfere. But the evidence from countries that are technological leaders is that where the state takes a leadership role in promoting science and technology over several generations, the results are cumulatively rewarding. Yet, in conventional analysis, inadequate attention is given to the role of science and technology in driving economic development.

The intellectual arguments for the study of science and technology are cultural and basic to the understanding of the human condition. The level of investment we make in basic science reflects both society's attitude to science and society's expectations, rational or perceived, from such investments. Since science and technology are the bases for much economic development, changes in how science and technology are developing may cause huge changes in the economic conditions of society.

Knowledge in the economy

Knowledge is not of itself of any great commercial value in most economies but its application in a well-defined system can be a remarkable tool in the advancement of mankind. The uniqueness of new knowledge creates intellectual property, a concept that has developed into the patent and copyright systems that are in force today. Knowledge is therefore a valuable commodity when it is properly protected, and one from which significant commercial profit can be directly earned. Knowledge is advanced almost daily; what was accepted as fact by eminent scientists has often been later proved erroneous. That advancement is a process that moves before our eyes: what has changed for us, and hopefully for our descendants, is the very pace of change. Information on these changes is of vital importance, and the access to and use of up-to-date information is a major key to advancement. To avoid misunderstanding, we note that science and technology are not the only areas of human endeavour with legitimate claims to our attention because they enable rational behaviour and productive development; markets, financial and legal structures, and political stability are also crucial to the realisation of the benefits flowing from scientific and technological advance.

Technology can create new wealth and extend economic advantage in appropriately organised social systems. Technology itself also provides tools for further scientific measurements, so that the process of knowledge growth is non-linear. Representations of the growth of invention are usually exponential, more by convention than by strict analysis. The basic result of the advances made internationally, year upon year, is that what was impossible and could be excluded from rational decision-making becomes possible and challenges existing practices. In no area is this as immediately important as in business. The globalisation of markets and the ease with which information is disseminated force change on us.

Business in the future will be increasingly knowledge dominated. Much of the knowledge has yet to be uncovered. Innovation is the process of applying that knowledge, and we must master its techniques if we are to have a sustainable future as a country. Given the increasing level of investment in R&D internationally, it is reasonable to forecast that science and technology will continue to cause rapid changes in the type and nature of the production process worldwide with consequential impact on employment. Traditional fears about the short-term impact of technology on employment must be balanced by consideration of the new opportunities for productive work that can be seized by an appropriately trained workforce. Such changes and effects of change are likely to dominate whole economies, including that of Ireland, unless other darker political events overshadow them. Much effort has been invested in the developed countries in designing policies that will capture for local economies more of the expected future flow of benefits from technology. The identification of critical elements of successful policies will be of particular importance to efforts in achieving accelerated progress.

Despite the logic of using the results of science in the pursuit of economic development, the process can be haphazard, as has been the case in Ireland. The position of science and technology has been uneven in the political and administrative culture of the country. (We show in Appendix 2 the organisational structure of the state's efforts to organise its science policies and practices over the past thirty years.) Although we are not alone in our confusion on this issue, the reason why this should be is worth exploration.

Management and control of the environment in which the application of new knowledge flourishes is increasingly a function for good government. Scientific thought and knowledge must constitute fundamental building blocks in economic planning in the private and public sectors, rather than an optional addition to the political agenda. We must change the long-standing perception in Ireland of our role in the world around us as one where we must accept whatever technology outside forces choose to give us. Our future, in our view, lies in active participation and not in spectator status.

Science and technology – past and future

The importance of change

Many long-held scientific beliefs have been overthrown in recent decades. A simple example is the case of the so-called inert gases, believed for practical and theoretical reasons to be incapable of forming chemical compounds. Their very inertness lent credibility to the entire system of classification of chemical elements and formed a cornerstone of the justification for believing that the outer electrons of an element determine largely the chemical reactions of that element. These elements, however, do form compounds, a fact demonstrated by experiment in the early 1960s. Strangely, their reactivity can be explained without abandoning basic theories of chemical reactivity. Science changes its mind. Change can be as difficult for scientists as for those in other human endeavours. Kuhn (1957, p. 3) describes this as 'the transiency of treasured scientific beliefs'. Today's technology may blind us to the obvious openings which only the most creative minds can explore.

Technology perspectives in the nineteenth century

The technical abilities of the most developed countries at the start of the nineteenth century were radically different from those we enjoy today. People then relied on animals for transport, sailing ships for inter-country travel, letters for communications, cut stone and brick for civil buildings, and plants and animals for fabrics. Their food came from animals, plants and aquatic/marine life, and their social structure depended largely on dominant hierarchies of families and overriding property rights. Their artistic and cultural achievements were almost as highly developed as those of people today although the distribution of access was highly skewed. They lacked access to the means to distribute and utilise energy, mineral wealth, machinery, industrial production systems (in business and agriculture), universal education and a generally available money economy. They also lacked for the most part a scientific knowledge of the world. Research mathematicians were often unable to set their knowledge accurately in its future context of utility. A typical quotation of Jean-Baptiste Delambre (permanent secretary of the mathematics and physics section of the Institut de France) from his commentary of 1810 (quoted in Kline, 1972, p. 623) illustrates the limitations of contemporary thinkers:

> It would be difficult and rash to analyse the chances which the future offers to the advancement of mathematics; in almost all its branches one is blocked by insurmountable difficulties; perfection of detail seems to be the only thing which remains to be done. All these difficulties appear to announce that the power of our analysis is practically exhausted. . . .

But what actually happened in the next century was 'a vast expansion in the number of research journals'. Kline (1972, p. 624) attributes the increased number of mathematicians in the nineteenth century to 'the participation of universities in research, the writing of textbooks and the systematic training of scientists initiated by Napoleon'. Research, information dissemination and education became enablers of technical advances: while they did not guarantee it, they enabled it in countries where conditions were favourable in other respects.

A common analogy used in France to focus our attention on the recent rapid development of technology is to remind us that had Napoleon wished to send a message from Paris to Rome, he would have sent a messenger on horseback (and sailing ship), the method available to Julius Caesar while pursuing his Gallic wars more than eighteen hundred years previously.

Progress at the start of the twentieth century

One hundred years later, the engineering disciplines of civil, electrical and mechanical engineering (with resultant energy production systems) and the scientific knowledge of mathematicians, chemists, biologists and medical specialists were developing at remarkable speed. (Lorenzi and Bourles (1995) note that in one twelve-year period in late-nineteenth-century Germany, a large chemical manufacturer increased its number of employees from 7,000 to 77,000, a feat which would be noteworthy even in the larger markets of today.) Social change and economic organisation were developing in parallel in Western society. Steel bridges, railroads, apartment buildings, hospitals, schools, libraries, surgery, photography and animal breeding on scientific lines were contemporary manifestations of new knowledge. But there were still major differences from today: energy production and application were largely in the discovery stage and personal transport was still dominated by the horse. Correspondingly, scientific theory was (from our perspective) dogmatic. The theories of matter still held that atoms were indestructible. Biological systems were still a class apart from chemical phenomena.

Our perspective on the future of science

In considering today the future of science, the necessary tools of logic and measurement are already available to us. The volume of new work published by mathematicians during the past century outweighs in a literal sense the output of the previous two thousand years. There have been two important developments: the universal spread of software packages (facilitating the use of computers by professionals in many aspects of their work) and of powerful high-performance computers (enabling professionals to address and solve large complex problems); these ensure that new mathematics will be more accessible to the engineer than ever before. Science has tended to grow and its applications have been most effective where mathematics has been employed. The increasing use of sophisticated mathematics in molecular biology illustrates the trend.

The traditional economic fundamental input of natural resources – whether of land or minerals – has been complemented by the development potential of the educated mind. Added to the correct level of investment of capital and the appropriate management of the resource, the economic advantage created is substantial.

Any projection of discovery into the middle or end of the next century, based on progress over the past two centuries, suggests that the state of knowledge our grandchildren will inherit and enjoy will be one that is unthinkable for us. In the long run, the wisdom of our time will fail to understand the world's evolution. It is evident now that stating basic scientific principles for the future is dubious. For example, many eminent scientists believe that all human behaviour and physical characteristics will be exposed as the consequences of the same simple laws of chemistry and physics that ultimately derive from the atomic and subatomic constitution of matter and the basic forces that apply to such particles. This view is strongly dismissed by equally dedicated scientists:

Chemistry is never going to be collapsed into physics even though physical principles and knowledge profoundly illuminate chemistry. And still less are sociology and psychology going to be collapsed into biochemistry and genetics (Rose, 1995).

Even modest projections of progress in important technologies can still expose an exciting prospect for the near future, a prospect of providing citizens with the knowledge they need as they need it:

- teraflop computers (capable of one thousand billion floating point operations per second) as everyday commodities will arrive within decades, perhaps within the next decade
- medicines based on individual human gene structure will become commonplace
- microelectronic systems that monitor and control various physiological functions will become routine, leading to informed and inexpensive medical ailment diagnosis and treatment tailored to the individual and the individual's environment.

In this last case, the feedback of this information into and from very large computer databases will improve the expertise level available to the ordinary medical practitioner and serve to inform judgements on a scale that is quite impossible for any individual to match. Similar expansion of the expertise resources available to engineers and to other professions will improve the efficiency with which resources are extracted, consumed and recycled for most purposes.

An indication of the utility provided by new knowledge storage and dissemination techniques (libraries) is given by the simple observation that some fifty million documents can be scanned today from an inexpensive desktop computer and an ordered set of reference documents provided for inspection on screen within seconds (Appendix 3). Important features of these new systems of distributing knowledge are their low cost and the ease with which young people adopt such new procedures and technology into their working habits. This acceleration of the use of new knowledge on a global scale is an exciting prospect.

None of these developments requires new science on a fundamental level, although all require the investment of prodigious resources of time and brainpower. What are the processes by which these advances in science will be made? Who are the people who will make them, interpret them, harness them and use them for our benefit? Who will direct the national resources according to policies that will accelerate our country's ability to profit from such knowledge? How is this relevant to Ireland?

Management of science and technology

Although we know that investment in science and technology has produced great wealth, we cannot immediately specify where exactly the resources should be directed to repeat the process. From the vantage point of the firm (how does business use the investment in science and technology?) and from the perspective of the individual participants (what makes the inventors of new technologies successful?), and from the point of view of the economy itself (i.e. state policy and linkage between the institutions), this question of selective investment is important for the future.

The development of technology in firms

From the perspective of individual firms, development of technology is a risk-laden process. Cooper (1988) has made extensive studies of the process of introduction of new products by firms (particularly in highly organised economies), focusing on the market expectations of a new product and how management makes its judgements as it commits resources. What is important about these processes is that they are subsequent to the basic research phase. Economies with a local level of basic research that funds innovation on a lavish scale are not science and technology limited: they produce a surplus of potential new technologies. Founding research laboratories in 1902 and 1903 was probably the easiest decision Du Pont's leaders ever made regarding research and development (Hounshell and Smith, 1988, p. 7). The basic research phase is a given, and what is in question is whether or not a future market can be induced to accept the product. Once the product is to be made, the logistics of delivery to market and the availability of well-trained labour are important factors in locating new industry.

For a country like Ireland, where the new product stream arises overwhelmingly in other economies for delivery in yet a third marketplace, it has been supposed that the local scientific and engineering base is not of great importance other than as a training ground for cost-effective labour. Yet the companies that establish bases in Ireland are the technology-driven corporations of our age: IBM, Hewlett-Packard, Hitachi, Motorola, the pharmaceutical giants and the software leaders such as Microsoft. These companies are distinguished by the advanced nature of the products and services they provide. Many of the products now made by these firms did not exist at the beginning of this decade. Clearly their integration into the Irish economy with the consequent spin-off of multiple layers of jobs will require that the supporting environment be capable of responding effectively. So the key industrial investment in our infrastructure needs to be geared at the advanced products and services of these modern industrial sectors. The genesis of those future products lies partly in the research laboratories they operate and in the university laboratories that study the relevant technologies. Increasingly, major firms are contracting out research to university laboratories across the world. What is it that will throw up these new products? Takeda's opinions, discussed later, give us a corporate view.

The perspective of the scientist

Scientific discoveries become important in economic terms for a variety of reasons and through many channels, but useful generalisations are difficult to extract from experience. It is widely believed that the time elapsed from concept to application for new ideas is shortening: certainly many new products and ideas now come to market in some form within a short time period from their initial discovery. The products of science are impinging with increasing frequency on more and more aspects of our daily lives. The process of discovery and of application is highly variable and seldom predictably planned or managed. It is widely accepted that the process of innovation and the national system of innovation (to use the current terminology: Mjøset, 1992) are determining factors in the growth of most modern economies. How this process works in practice, particularly in a local context, is a crucial question for any assessment of the prospects for the future economic well-being of our country. The process can of course be summarised by saying that the development of a new idea awaits an understanding that its time has come to enter the economy or that a market evolves more or less naturally in response to needs and available resources. One group of French analysts (Lorenzi and Bourles, 1995) has remarked that technology is a process of providing people with products they never knew they wanted. In a review of Japanese culture, Sansom (1973) noted that 'invention in its widest sense is the child, not of necessity, but of leisure and riches'.

The study of the innovation process itself is therefore important for Ireland. An example of innovation in practice is the development of the widely used smoke detector which is found increasingly in houses and the merits of which are promoted by professional fire chiefs throughout Ireland. It has been manufactured in Ireland and exported successfully for twenty years. The economic consequences of the saving of lives and property achieved by this device are considerable. The product was developed for domestic use from research instrumentation in the late 1960s by a former student from a research group in the University College Dublin Physics Department: this group under Professor P. J. Nolan had acquired an international reputation in the field of atmospheric physics over the preceding fifty-year period.

Access to and dissemination of information have been the key to the use of science and technology, while telecommunications – the technology for the transmission of that information – has itself undergone a revolution. The revolution is far from completion. Managing the use of the new telecommunications technology and systems is one of the critical processes in the management of economic development. The generation and storage of new knowledge have also undergone a step change with the availability of vast computing power at modest cost to every desk-worker and to some in manual occupations. For example, a 'desktop computer' in 1975, e.g. Wang 2200, could store about twenty pages of text in its machine memory, while the 1997 PC successor can similarly store about two million pages of text. The exploitation of these new technologies has been successful in Ireland to date but to maintain the progress, new attitudes and a deeper understanding of the opportunities facing us will be required. The life sciences with applications in medicine and agriculture are no less subject to major change and discovery.

Agriculture

The roles of applied and basic research are often rigorously segregated for the purposes of analysis. This may be a useful political method of segregating the work to be done by various institutions with allocated resources (see Ireland, 1996) but it often makes no particular philosophical sense. We may refer to examples of practical research, drawing on an article by Daie and Wyse (1996). They list the singular discoveries made by departments of agricultural chemistry in the US:

- role of vitamins in nutrition
- role of trace minerals in nutrition
- discovery of streptomycin in soil organisms
- first blood coagulant (coumarin) extracted from mouldy hay
- immunological tolerance (the basis of organ transplant successes) first studied in fraternal calf twins
- embryo transfer in dairy cows.

To oppose the use of this knowledge would seem perverse; to oppose the process of developing the knowledge would seem incompetent; to abandon the possibility that the analogues of these discoveries could emerge in Ireland from modest institutions employing well-equipped scientists and engineers would indicate despair or ignorance. Yet in Ireland, we reduced support for the state institutions (An Foras Talúntais, Institute for Industrial Research and Standards, Eolas) that could have continued this path of discovery if they had been funded. The alternative or additional path of funding university research was also largely ignored until the late 1980s. As the work of Cunningham (1996) exemplifies, such research is of great importance to Ireland. Yet it has been underfunded due to the need to reduce public expenditure and the isolated position of technology development agencies which were remote from direct political and administrative influence.

The achievement of the individual

Perutz (1995), himself a Nobel laureate, explains that Pasteur gave mankind two discoveries of the highest importance of a practical nature, i.e. vaccination and pasteurisation. But prior to these discoveries, he had engaged for ten years on an exotic project, the study of the different optically active crystalline forms of tartaric acid (an investigation into the sediments of old wine).

In the course of this study Pasteur invented the modern science of biotechnology. It is conventional in our time to add after such descriptions of the intellectual capital we inherited from the past that Pasteur would have had no hope of sourcing funds for such a research project today. His project proposal would have failed in the selection process precisely because he could not predict the brilliant outcome of his experiments in a manner convincing to the savants of his time. Had he done so, he would have limited himself to what was already conventionally known and understood and he could not, even with all the conventional wisdom of his age, have predicted bacterially produced chemical products. Pasteur's work would probably have failed almost every test for investment efficiency adumbrated for scientific research in the Irish White Paper on science and technology (Ireland, 1996) and in its antecedent documents.

Examples of the linkage between applications and theory, or between basic and applied research, abound. The common lasers found in our CD players where music is reproduced without the mechanical devices of the old-fashioned record/stylus system arise from experiments in the early 1960s in physics laboratories in which coherent light was discovered. The coherence arises from the synchronous behaviour of assemblies of molecules pumped with focused energy. In plain language, the atoms emitting light are orchestrated to act in time and in tune with one another. The forerunner of the laser was the maser (where the light is microwave radiation). A decade after the maser's discovery in the laboratory a giant system of masers in outer space was identified by astrophysicists (Moran, 1976). What had been apparently created in the laboratory was in fact already a process used by nature for billions of years.

In Ireland, even allowing for the modest scale of scientific and technological research, efforts in these areas make consistent contributions as detailed elsewhere (*The Irish Scientist*, 1994, 1995, 1996, provides a readable account). The range, quality and impact of this work are likely to impress those unfamiliar with recent progress in Ireland. Most of the work comprises incremental improvements that fill in our knowledge in detail, following progress in some well-established disciplines. Recent analytical work investigating the true international stature of university science in Ireland is being published as this paper is being written (CIRCA Group Europe, 1996).

E. P. Cunningham (1996), in a personal account of his own career, has reviewed some aspects of the successful application of science to agriculture. His account makes particular reference to Ireland and to his own contributions to international efforts in science. In his work, he developed a discounted gene flow method to evaluate the consequences of breeding decisions. He himself initiated a programme on cattle genetics with a team of molecular biologists which has given improved under-standing of the archaeology and anthropology of cattle domestication from Asia and Africa through Europe since the dawn of time. Cunningham (p. 19) says: 'as so often happens in science, the results produced useful information on the questions we had posed, but the real significance lay in a totally different direction'. His description may be recommended as an excellent indicator of the value to the community of support for scientific research. But his depiction of a generation of scientific research work from 1960 to the present day raises many questions about science policy in Ireland. The institutional changes that have been effected and the continuing parsimony in supporting basic research that underpins his area of work (ranging from high-performance computing to genetic manipulation) strongly suggest that in many respects Ireland could be relatively less well served scientifically in the next century than it was in the past half century.

We may emphasise here the enormous personal effort demanded of individual researchers who work in an indifferent intellectual climate. Even in the best of circumstances, adventurous technologists must learn to live with failure. Support of their work and recognition of its intrinsic value are two of the main motivators for experts in their fields. At present, Irish practitioners of innovation through science and technology must largely look abroad for these supports. In future, a greater commitment of domestic resources will be essential.

Research-led business in Ireland

Such applications that arise from changes in our knowledge of science and technology will continue to have marked effects on the economies of countries large and small. The Iridium project for example (one of several proposals by various consortia) offers to provide telephone systems by satellites to countries with poor existing telecommunications, mainly those with no terrestrial telephone systems. The software to manage the intricate communications will come from a product developed by Iona Technologies in Ireland. Iona's genesis lay in a European Community research project in Trinity College and by 1996 the company employed some 240 people, mostly in Dublin. Their product was a research idea in the late 1980s. Their launch as a company coincided with the analysis by the National Software Directorate that little relevant research was carried out in Irish universities. Earlier notable spin-offs from university research (for example Drumm's battery train in the 1930s) lacked both the international market access necessary for survival and the indigenous investment sources to match the potential of the invention, but the future pattern for such development is now much clearer, with the development of university–industry technology transfer programmes.

Policies

National administrations struggle with the management of science

The marked effects of technology on economies and on politics have been recognised overseas and have led governments and institutions to study the generalised phenomenon of the growth of science, and how to plan its future activities for the benefit of individual countries. This process was greatly accelerated during and after the Second World War, particularly in the United States.

The questions regarding the themes of why science and technology are important are universal as can be seen from recent reviews of strategic R&D policies respectively entitled:

- *Endless Frontier, Limited Resources* (USA, 1995)
- *Inventing Tomorrow* (EU, 1996)
- *Science and Technology: Foundations of Development* (Brazil, 1994)
- *Science, Technology and Innovation* (Ireland, 1996)

- *Striving to Become a Front-runner in Research Activity* (Japan, 1995)
- *Technology Ventures: Commercialising Scotland's Science and Technology* (Scotland, 1996).

The Scottish document is to be recommended for the directness of its conclusions. The first of its main priorities is admirable:

> to create mechanisms or institutions with responsibility for placing science and technology originating from Scottish institutions into companies located in Scotland (Scotland, 1996, p. 21).

The analyses carried out by all the countries mentioned reflect some common themes of concern. For the larger groups the possibility of a gap between the principal competitors and the target country or federation is a major policy concern (Lafay and Herzog, 1989). The analysts usually urge proactive government investment. The education and training of engineers is becoming problematical for the most advanced countries, since market signals invariably indicate that personal wealth concentrates in other professions. One of our concerns must be to make the world of technology more inviting for young people. Linking education to immediate areas of economic growth is the tempting path to follow and it is likely to be followed exclusively to the detriment of those to be educated. A balanced and basic education pursued to a high standard in secondary schools will maintain our reputation for high competences that are broadly based.

The leaders

Few will argue convincingly with the observation that the United States has the world's leading technological community: almost half of all the research students in the world spend time in the US. The indifferent level of much of the US second-level education system hides the reality that in postgraduate education, resources invested in excellence are awesome. A historically high level of investment in public facilities, a science-oriented defence budget, a system of recognition of excellence in leading institutions, and a liquid market at all stages from venture investment to mature product marketplace have supported the human resources that enabled this outcome. In addition, individual states plan and support local initiatives.

The other major forces

Other countries have particular strengths: Japan has a system of basic education that has delivered a uniform degree of opportunity to its citizens that surpasses most countries' efforts. Japan has a system of industrial R&D linked to production and backed by a coherent and a hitherto largely isolated market that has attracted imitators, detractors and analysis from around the world. A particular area of attention has been the relatively diminished role played by government investment in R&D in Japan (Japan 18 per cent; OECD 45 per cent). This fact has often been used to suggest that government intervention is not necessary: in fact high corporate taxes of 50 per cent and full allowances for R&D are powerful inducements to Japanese industry to fund its own R&D. Recent Japanese policies have emphasised that Japan is, relative to the EU and USA, a laggard in basic research. New government programmes for stimulating basic research in 1996 in Japan are about twice the total government R&D spend per capita in Ireland. These advances in Japan's capability are based to a large, but not exclusive, extent on scientific inquiry in well-supported institutions. Europe still maintains a position in science and technology which is at the same time fragmented among the larger countries and significant in world terms. Its influence on Ireland has been dominant.

The European influence

Support and dependency

The European Community has sustained Irish science and technology over the past decade and a half. In recent years the Structural Funds programmes have funded most of the scientific research undertaken in Ireland. Without this support, over 80 per cent of the research training and development in Ireland at present would not occur. The obvious difficulty arises from the likely decrease in general EU Structural Fund support for Ireland after 2000. The importance of indigenous scientific activity to economic development is not yet adequately appreciated, raising questions about the funding from taxes of a thriving scientific effort in Ireland. Although an improved infrastructure will by then exist, its future is very uncertain and if the past experience of Irish scientific institutes (Institute for Industrial Research and Standards, An Foras Forbartha, An Foras Talúntais, National Board for Science and Technology) is a guide, then the facilities may not be funded on a scale to permit economically beneficial, internationally competitive work.

Quite apart from the funding aspect, EU support for the interchange of scientists and the training opportunities for young Irish researchers in major facilities abroad have raised the level of science in Ireland. The impact level of Irish research papers in 'condensed matter' (i.e. solid state physics and chemistry) rose considerably during the 1980s judged by the average citation rate (an index of the use made by the international community of new knowledge).

The European Commission's 1995 *Green Paper on Innovation* addresses a key question: how can Europe profit from its clear strengths in scientific research? The Green Paper is helpful, particularly to the smaller member states, in focusing political attention on the question of innovation. Each of the major industrialised nations consciously invests in science and technology in the search for competitive advantage. It is a common perception in Europe that the EU is losing its position relative to Asia and the Americas in several industrial sectors because of comparatively lower investment in advanced technology.

Achievement based on European support

Funding for research work in science and technology in Ireland improved when the European Community developed its Framework programmes for the conduct of research by transnational teams in the period from 1980 to date. Conceived as a method of supplementing national efforts and drawing researchers together from across Europe, the programmes have breathed life into the Irish scientific community. They have provided facilities, equipment, networks and connections for specialised scientists and engineers, and have made a modern career in science within Ireland practicable for our best scientists in many disciplines. A good example is the European consortium on permanent hard magnets led from Professor J. M. D. Coey's laboratory in Trinity College (Coey, 1991). Coey's work was recognised with the award to him of prizes at the Seville World Fair in 1994 and by the London-based Institute of Physics (The Cree Prize 1996), while he was also conferred with an honorary degree by the University of Grenoble, one of the major European centres for research in magnetism. Over 90 per cent of the funding of £1 million secured by Coey in the past decade arose from sources outside Ireland.

European Union funds are intended to supplement national programmes, but funding of these national programmes has not developed to any realistic level. Over 40 per cent of the research funding of Irish universities comes from the Framework programme and similar European initiatives.

The European Commission's 1996 paper on the future scientific research programmes of the Union, *Inventing Tomorrow*, identifies a much stronger connection between research and the lives and welfare of Europe's citizens than has been articulated in previous documents. The major problems to be addressed – growth and unemployment, health and the environment – are all to be solved by using science and technology. Ireland funds the bulk of its scientific infrastructure and running costs from European Commission sources. This must be a matter of real concern for Irish science policy. European funding will inevitably diminish as the improving Irish economic performance indicates a reduced need for Cohesion and Structural Funds support.

Objective analysis of the present use of European funds would question the preoccupation with physical communications facilities to the relative exclusion of new modes of computing or new materials research. The supposed emphasis on subsidiarity also raises questions: the European programme is not designed to replace national programmes but in Ireland's case, this is precisely what it does. An aspect of particular interest in Ireland is the stated objective of the European support funds of enabling small and medium-sized enterprises to benefit from the research programmes. Irish policy-makers have yet to devise suitable mechanisms to achieve this objective, even though the bulk of Irish industrial effort falls into this category of small and medium enterprise.

The Irish White Paper on science and technology

The Irish White Paper (Ireland, 1996) took into account the STIAC Report (1995) chaired by Daniel P. Tierney and the Response chaired by John Travers in setting out the priorities to be addressed in Ireland. (The Response was a document prepared for the government to inform its deliberations on the STIAC Report, and is not publicly available). Many of these needs reflect the urgency of catching up with the marketplace reality. These needs include the introduction of a planning process to ensure a coherent approach to science policy across government departments; expert and independent advice from a new permanent Science and Technology Council; improving public perception of science, technology and innovation; improved organisational structures for government research programmes; a higher profile for technology transfer; improvement in the capability of firms that have little or no technological competence; increased networking of firms; and addressing barriers to the availability of seed and venture capital for technology-based companies.

Specific actions required include a substantial increase in business expenditure on R&D and provision of extra funding for research in the third-level education sector as resources permit.

Regrettably, the White Paper is silent on the vital question of the timing of implementation, giving credence to the view that the economic significance of science and technology has yet to register effectively in the consciousness of policy-makers.

Parsimony

Because of the relative absence of scientific institutions in Ireland, the bulk of research expenditure is found in the third-level colleges. Measures of relative resources are extremely difficult to determine. McBrierty (personal communication, 1997) has compared state expenditure on Queen's University Belfast with that on Trinity College Dublin. Making allowances for the observable differences, he concluded that Queen's received 33 per cent more money annually to fund its activities and much of this funding is spent on science and technology. Similar if wider differences emerge from cursory examination of the figures for third-level institutions in Europe. Nonetheless, the White Paper assigns priority in this area to ensuring that the state gets value for money and that efficiency is ensured. In reality, the present state of Irish science and engineering might be described as undernourished but very much alive.

The White Paper is welcomed by those aware of and concerned with the vital economic importance of the issues, but, regrettably, like previous official publications dealing with science and technology, it does not have a substantial basis in analysis. The Culliton Report (1992) was hailed politically as a well-informed analysis of Irish industrial development backed up by a series of 'in-depth' reports on a variety of aspects of the Irish economy. None of these reports dealt specifically with science and technology. In the five years since the publication of this report, the industrial scene in Ireland has been marked by increasing employment in high-technology industry and by new technology based indigenous start-ups. Traditional sectors such as agriculture and heavy industry have been languishing, losing employment and following declining paths.

Planning and revival

The deficiency in public policy relating to science and technology is less evident in the area of the environment. Ireland has a well-delineated programme of research in this area and a scientific analysis of the state of the environment has been published as a statutory requirement by the Environment Protection Agency (1996), some twenty-five years after the United States first established such an agency. Once again, European programmes have been decisive in initiating action in Ireland. The STRIDE (Science and Technology for Regional Development) programme provided the funds for the initial research work and the projects themselves were selected by requesting suggestions from the scientific community. Of their nature, environmental programmes are long term and address many of the intractable difficulties that have arisen from the commercial exploitation of natural resources, including scientific farming. The ubiquity of such problems and the costs of addressing them have led to the widespread demand for financial accounting policies which respect the laws of nature rather than count the costs within the closed systems that the law allows. External effects, long held to be economically irrelevant, have cumulated to the point where they can no longer be ignored. In the next century, monitoring material inventories and effects of processes on the environment may be sufficiently detailed to enable such 'green accounting' to be realistic.

The activities of the transport, energy, manufacturing and agricultural sectors will also be open to creative innovation because of environmental concerns. A measured scientific policy in this area is of particular strategic importance (Wallace, 1995).

The White Paper identifies the need for co-ordination between departments of state, yet the ongoing work of several departments with a recognisable research policy based on science and technology – the Department of the Environment, the Department of Health and the forestry section of the Department of Agriculture – is largely omitted.

The central conclusion of the STIAC Report of lack of government support for science and the need for £25 million of expenditure for the correction of obvious defects is not really accepted in the White Paper. It is important to observe that, whatever the reason, public policy is other than implementation of the advice sought and received from those with knowledge and understanding of the issues mooted.

Science policy and technology foresight

In the OECD study on investment in education in the early sixties the significance of science and technology to economic development in Ireland was identified. The setting up of the National Science Council (NSC) was a result, as was the well-informed study and report on technological education which brought in its train the establishment of the network of regional technical colleges strategically located around the country.

The NSC, operating on an advisory basis, did remarkable work in difficult circumstances in developing an awareness of the benefits to be derived from the public funding of research in Ireland and in creating a basis for a systematic approach to priority setting. The statutory National Board for Science and Technology (NBST), which followed the NSC in 1978, expanded and elaborated the basis of university research funding and, in particular, the funding of university research co-operation with industry. The NBST produced an annual science budget, developed a national programme in science and technology, and opened up an active participation in European Community science and technology programmes which were then at an early stage of development.

Regrettably, the political perception of problems in the public finances in the mid-eighties overshadowed the emerging recognition of the real economic benefits to be derived from a planned and coherent approach to public investment in science and technology. Public expenditure concerns led to the closing down of some agencies and the merging of others. The development of science policy, in the sense of charting the economic consequences of public investment in science and technology, was not pursued and that lacuna still exists.

Foreign direct investment in Ireland has been beneficial to economic growth and employment. It brings with it technological skills and production know-how, but few foreign-owned companies have developed beyond the production functions to become integrated business entities, and linkages with the indigenous industrial sector have been largely limited to subsupply.

The STIAC Report (1995) included the proposal that a technology foresight programme should be examined in the Irish context. Technology foresight is a process that systematically attempts to look into the longer term future of science, technology, the economy and society with the aim of identifying the areas of strategic research and the emerging technologies likely to yield the greatest economic and social benefits. The iterative processes in the technology foresight arrangements ensure that the two-way exchanges between the planners and the key actors in technology application bring an improved shared understanding of possible future developments.

There are many possible futures and the destination reached depends on the decisions taken now. The aim of technology foresight is to explore these possible futures through a process of consultation with business and industry people, researchers, the public sector and the general public with the objective of identifying areas where the country can derive maximum economic benefit by bringing a more deterministic attitude to the future than is achieved by relying on simple extrapolative forecasting. Technology foresight is not about prediction – its primary purpose is to influence decision-taking in a coherent way.

The Japanese were first in the field of technology foresight back in 1970. The technique used then and much developed since was the Delphi survey where experts give an indication of the scientific and technological developments they foresee within a given time horizon.

The first assessment of the responses is fed back and a further expression of expert opinion is elicited, enabling a picture of likely future trends to be built up. This approach is possible because of the existence of parallel analyses of the technological capability of Japan and the strength in key areas relative to its competitors (e.g. Science and Technology Agency of the Japanese Government, 1996).

Other approaches to technology foresight include scenario writing, now used by the Dutch, which involves building logical sequences of events in the external environment in order to show how future technological trends might evolve from the present. Direct consultation, used in the UK, employs workshops to involve a wide circle of interested organisations and individuals. Technology foresight programmes have been pursued in Germany (using the approach developed in Japan), France, Finland, Australia and New Zealand. It is to be hoped that a technology foresight process in Ireland will be put in place in 1997.

Industrial policies since the late sixties have facilitated the attraction to Ireland of the multinational technology-driven corporations. Their presence has initially been driven by the moderate tax rate and access to the European market. The continuing public investment in the second and third-level education system since the sixties now brings the added attractions of an educated workforce. The predictable cost environment, the reasonable business climate and the competent telecommunications infrastructure have facilitated the significant increase in high-technology investment in recent years. The time-scales of investment programmes become ever shorter and it is vital that we deepen our capability of adding to the incoming advanced technology and incrementally provide the competitive advantage that anchors in Ireland entities with world market access.

Specific technologies that are vital for Ireland are those that enable access to markets and those that advance our ability to cope with new information. Telecommunications and computing are obvious examples. Our opportunity is not limited to the use of these tools – innovative and productive work in these technologies continues in Ireland in research, in development, in new product design and in manufacturing.

Telecommunications and the information society

Telecommunications is the key infrastructure of the communications future and is the critical resource in the emergence of the knowledge-based society. For long perceived as a natural monopoly suitable for provision by the state or by a closely regulated private sector monopoly, telecommunications entities are now being opened up to competition. As the sophistication and diversity of the computer have increased, so too have the demands on the telecommunications networks carrying the information and knowledge generated. The transmission paths must carry scientific data, extensive business data and everything from entertainment to plain voice telephony.

The European Commission initiated reform in European telecommunications with the publication of a Green Paper in 1987, several years after the ending of monopoly and the opening of competition in the US telecommunications sector. During 1997, ten years after the process began, European telecommunications will be largely deregulated and opened up to field competition with significant benefits to the emerging information society.

The wide-ranging implications of the knowledge-based information society have been considered at European level by the Bangemann Report released in May 1994, *Europe and the Global Information Society*. The Bangemann Report called for concerted action by the member states and the European Commission in the achievement of necessary institutional and regulatory reform to meet the challenge of competitive suppliers of networks and services from outside Europe who are increasingly active in the European single market.

The Irish telecommunications service, as in other member states, had been provided directly by a department of state operating as a monopoly. Business criticism of the serious inadequacies of the service in meeting burgeoning business needs following Ireland's accession to the European Community led to the setting up of a review group in the late seventies. The review group reported within twelve months, and its recommendations were accepted by government and rapidly implemented through the establishment of a state-sponsored entity and the launching of an accelerated development programme utilising advanced digital switching and transmission technology. Remarkable progress was achieved through the eighties in providing modern and reliable telecommunications services in Ireland.

Responding to Commission and Council directives, liberalisation and preparation for full competition have been progressively pursued in recent years. The opening up of competition in Ireland, initially in the cellular telephony area, will undoubtedly ensure that the existing performance of the telecommunications services, which is still below the better comparable European efficiency indices, will significantly improve. The opening of competition in cellular telephony brings with it the statutory setting up of the independent regulator of the telecommunications sector.

Mobile cellular telephony is the fastest growing area in the telecommunications sector worldwide, and it is beneficial in the Irish context that competition in this area has already started. The market is being driven by rapid advances in communications technology and by the commercial opportunities evident. Growth rates in certain member states have exceeded 40 per cent, the Scandinavian countries being particularly advanced with penetration exceeding 25 per cent. The growth rate in Ireland has been significant and a penetration of some 7 per cent was achieved at end 1996. The opening up of competition will accelerate the growth and increase the penetration rate.

It is apparent that society benefits with the progressive shift from wireline fixed-location connection to person-to-person radio connection. Mobile telephony is now a normal part of business life and is expected to make significant inroads into the mass consumer market. The market potential for personal communications services is clearly very big. The maximum density for fixed wireline telephones is not expected to be much more than 50 per cent of the population – with one connection per household plus business use – whereas radio personal communication has the potential to reach some 80 per cent of the population – i.e. one connection per adult.

Mobility has a particular significance in the broader context of the European Union. The basic objective of the Union for the free movement of goods, people, services and capital is facilitated by the near prospect of European-wide advanced mobile communications services. The pan-European digital mobile system, GSM, is a world-leading technology in this key area of the future global communications market.

High-performance computing

One of the principal conclusions of our age has been the realisation that the simplification of physical systems to extract simple physical laws has limited utility. Most real world systems we really want to investigate are subtle and complex. In certain conditions, systems are dominated by the results which are the same as those arising from great simplification. But apart from those conditions, nature is complex, and interactive, and does not conform to simple analysis.

High-performance computing (HPC) is a name given to the most powerful arrays of computers used to solve large-scale problems. Within high-performance computing, *parallel* computing is a growing trend in improving the scale of computing; it enables faster processing and allows modelling of larger problems within a reasonable time. Earlier high-performance computing (scalar and vector) will gradually be displaced for complex or large uses by parallel hardware and software.

In Europe, weather forecasting has been routinely serviced by HPC machinery, while research, defence and computer development have increasingly drawn on this technique. More advanced regular use of HPC has been evident in the USA and Japan with industrial applications ranging from car design to telecommunications and traffic management. The relative absence of European sites in the industrial application of this technology is noticeable but in the academic and research fields, European HPC sites are significant. It is to be expected that academic and research sites will be followed in the near future by the spread of industrial application; certain of the academic and research sites are now also industrially linked.

Industry and university perspectives

The future development of science-based industry in Ireland will depend on the external perception by potential investors of the Irish workforce as being qualified academically and on the systems developed to support indigenous innovation. These two factors are somewhat out of balance at the moment. Inward investment is dominant, particularly so in the perception of the establishment culture. The corresponding need in Irish industry for R&D management skills was identified by the colleges and noted in the White Paper (Ireland, 1996).

The views of industry technology managers on the question are relevant. The future prospect, on a world scale, has been described recently by a leading research manager, the executive vice-president of Hitachi, Yasutsugu Takeda (1996).

Takeda reflected on the impact that short-term business management goals have on the process of investment in science and technology – a matter of concern to society. He defined the problem as that of providing opportunities for intellectuals and stressed that companies that succeed in this endeavour can confidently expect beneficial returns. He saw R&D investments in four categories, the first three of which relate to whether profit can be expected in the near future, medium term or long term and the fourth being that which creates intellectual property. He termed this latter endeavour North Star research to distinguish company basic research from Blue Skies research. (Blue Skies research is so called to indicate that the research has no clear object in view other than to voyage into the unknown.) The absence of a sense of direction (sometimes implicit in the Blue Skies name) is considered unnecessary. A portfolio of research projects each at a different stage of development should be sustainable for a company. But as the most important resource for research is knowledge, global partnerships with the aid of computer networks can contribute to this form of technology management. Takeda has elsewhere emphasised the global networks required for first-class research – even the world's largest corporations must form partnerships and spread risk. This trend has been repeated in many fora, e.g. Nicholson (1996).

The origins of university-led innovation are widely held to have commenced with the production of Warfarin by the Wisconsin Alumni Research Foundation in the 1930s, although the University of Glasgow stakes a claim to the development of the effective steam engine from theories of latent heat in the eighteenth century. In progressive countries with effective public policies in science and technology such as Japan, Sweden, the Netherlands and the USA the growth of university-based science parks testifies to the beneficial collaboration between municipal, national and educational bodies to promote knowledge-based enterprise. Major corporations such as Hewlett-Packard sprang from campuses such as Stanford University in California.

In Ireland, early pioneers such as Drumm in the 1930s and Timoney in the late 1960s (both University College Dublin) have been succeeded by successful linkers of the campus to commerce in the late 1980s and 1990s. Relevant descriptions have been published by Hardiman (1994) and in the work cited here by Corish, Kinsella, McBrierty and O'Neill. In each of the modern techniques of campus companies, technology transfer arrangements, licensing of intellectual property, industrial laboratories on campus and marketing of research internationally, substantial progress has been made in Ireland. In a recent review of research management conducted for the Higher Education Authority, the CIRCA group of consultants, a campus entity based in University College Dublin but independent of the college, described the university–industry interaction function in the Irish colleges as state of the art in Europe (CIRCA Group Europe, 1996). As actors in this vigorous and developing activity, we may add that the further utilisation of university research in attracting and holding foreign investment in industry and services and in encouraging indigenous entrepreneurship in high added value activity has the potential for large-scale expansion. The returns from investment are highlighted by the successes of two spin-off companies – Silicon and Software Systems, and Iona Technologies – in employing about five hundred graduates. Similar companies are emerging from campuses across the country and their success has the possibility of being replicated often in the coming decades.

The middle ground between researcher and product developer will continue to be the springboard for applying new scientific knowledge. Irish universities can benefit from successful interaction with the network of clients supplied by the multinationals located in Ireland and a culture that has transformed its directions in the past two decades at the cutting edges of many technologies. It is important that a supportive environment in public policy facilitates the translation of this potential into entrepreneurial new companies on a scale that captures wealth in significant terms. Unless the administrative and political environment in Ireland changes to a considerable extent, much of the golden opportunity will be lost.

This paper has reiterated the view, from a variety of differing perspectives, that government policies on science and technology and on R&D can be of singular importance. In countries with successful modern industrial economies, an effective science infrastructure supports the future development of industry. In Ireland, we will have to invest in institutions that can support the earning industries by successful research and innovation effort and by supplying personnel with superior training to that of our competitors. Global partnerships with major scientific and technological development corporations across the globe are possible. The next decade will see the emergence of new trading patterns and the creation of new supply alliances that will dominate the first quarter of the next century.

Conclusions

Attempts to define the precise outcomes from science and technology in our future are unlikely to be successful. Knowledge of how we will use the unfolding information provided by science is not attainable, but some general observations are permissible regarding the opportunities ahead for Ireland and the means required to grasp those options that can support our society. As a corollary, a view that we should focus only on certain narrow areas of research in our science is a recipe for missing the next revolutions in knowledge that will affect our economy.

The basic elements for harnessing the present and future knowledge needed for new technologies are present in our educational systems. Support and strengthening of these systems can help the emergence of an indigenous entrepreneurial business culture. Investment in education is the enabling activity without which nothing can prosper and the investment required will increase into the next century. Human capital formation is our real natural resource and it is renewable, flexible and productive. Investment in that human capital should follow the logic of the marketplace and be directed at those who excel and who have the best chance of success in international arenas. Policies to meet their needs with focused support will pay handsome rewards to the country.

Management of new technology is a second imperative. The country is in a period of significant growth and major economic development with inadequate technological support systems of information and analysis. The increasing complexity of the economic environment as the process of further European integration gathers pace requires the mastering and effective management of the activities and opportunities created by technologists.

The level of confidence created in Ireland by effective public policy and by foreign direct investment requires a second stage of activity in which some level of transition from technology importation to technology development inevitably occurs. That transition is now under way in Ireland, however hesitantly. It is critically important that the process be seriously nourished and that knowledge-based enterprise be recognised as the way that Ireland can grow and prosper.

Good communications is possible between key interest groups in Ireland, and the internal co-ordination of resources and potential speed of response can be a major factor in enabling us to move to the leading edge as a supplier of new technologies. If the other factors are positively reinforced, then the inward investment will focus on our ideas and our implementation of them as well as on our adaptability to technology importation.

Ireland has a significant history in science over the past two centuries, but we are too often prisoners of a mentality that reduces the value of our own creations. The Shavian wit that produced the comment that science 'never solves a problem without creating ten more problems' (Patch, 1951, pp. 193–4) was distinctly Irish: the thought was more creatively expressed by Faraday who saw the diverging possibilities of future paths as the beauty of science.

Appendix 1: The scale of international investment in R&D (principally science and technology)

	Japan	USA	Germany	France	Ireland*
Per cent science and technology in national budget (1994)	3.23	4.5	3.5	5.6	6.4
Per cent of patents granted in USA by origin of applicants (1993)	22.7	54.1	7.0	3.0	–
Share of R&D financed by government (excluding defence) (per cent)	20.8	22.9	33.8	33.6	23.0
R&D expenditures (trillion yen)	13.7	17.9	6.3	3.4	0.03

*Derived from STIAC Report (1995). The widely inclusive nature of the Irish science and technology figures are not reflected in the actual investment in R&D. Figures published by Forfás in *The Irish Times*, 15 May 1997, show reduced science and technology expenditure.
Source: Science and Technology Agency of the Japanese Government (1996)

Appendix 2: Irish institutions – growth and decay

Era	Agency	Function	Growth pattern	Perceived output	Function then transferred to:
1946–87	Institute for Industrial Research and Standards	Industrial research and standards	Grew rapidly to 1980	Not a success	Eolas
1967	National Science Council	Advice to government on science and technology	Developed reporting mechanisms	Sound	NBST
1978	National Board for Science and Technology	Statutory mandate to advise and analyse	Grew very rapidly	• Technically sound • Supportive for researchers • Failed to acquire administration legitimacy	Eolas
1987	Eolas	National science and technology agency – adviser, analyser, performer	Initial decline followed by growth with Community Support Framework funds	• Managed many national efforts in science and technology • Perceived as falling between academia and industry – pleasing neither	Forbairt
1994	Forbairt	Indigenous industry	Decline anticipated	Less technology – more support to business and to small and medium-sized enterprises, but not clear	Shared with IDA
1994	Science, Technology and Innovation Advisory Council	Similar to National Science Council	Produced one report	Report leading to White Paper on science and technology	Non-executive council
1997	Science and Technology Advisory Council	Similar to National Science Council			

Appendix 3: Use of the Internet – A search engine examined the World-Wide Web (WWW) and produced the following list of documents, each of which could then be called up on screen for inspection

*Solar Cooking Archive – Documents. New. Country Reports. General. Technical. New. Teaching for a Better World: Making Solar Box Cookers. Country Reports. Tom Sponheim: Continuing.
—http://www2.accessone.com/~sbcn/docs.htm

*No Title – L'ONU LOUANGE LE PROJET DE CUISSON SOLAIRE CHEZ LES RÉFUGIÉS AU KENYA. En janvier 1995, Solar Cookers International inaugurait un programme...
—http://www.accessone.com/~sbcn/95sep15f.htm

bobzimb1 – UNESCO Funds Solar Cooking Project in Zimbabwe. An interview with Dr. Bob Metcalf of Solar Cookers International. Tom Sponheim: Tell us about your most ...
—http://www2.accessone.com/~sbcn/bobzimb1.htm

Solar cookers – Reduction of tropical deforestation by massive use of solar cookers. Ari Lampinen, Technology for Life, Finland, 18.10.1994. Deforestation problem. From ...
—http://kaapeli.fi/~tep/keitin4e.html

3.Thermodynamical review of solar box cookers – 3.1 Introduction. A typical solar box cooker consists of two boxes with insulation between them, a black ...
—http://kaapeli.fi/~tep/petri/petrithe.htm

6.5 Evaluating the teaching and solar cookers appropriateness – 6. Field study of the project in Namibia. The field study of the project was carried out between February 14th and May 2nd, 1995. The work included ...
—http://kaapeli.fi/~tep/petri/petrinam.htm

Solar cookers – Reduction of tropical deforestation by massive use of solar cookers. Ari Lampinen, Technology for Life, Finland, 8.10.1994. (This text will be soon ...
—http://www-com.grenet.fr/inesdev/ala.html

Solar Cookers – Next: SSIN Up:NEWS Previous: NEWS. Solar Cookers. If you have WWW access, check out the Solar Cooking Archive: http://www.accessone.com/~sbcn/index.htm ...
—http://aix 12.hrz.uni-oldenburg.de/~kblum/nl_0295_html/node6.html

Devel-L: Solar cookers at IUFRO congress – Solar cookers at IUFRO congress. Ari Lampinen (mailto:ala@KANTO.CC.JYU.FI) Mon, 24 Jul 1995 13:25:55 +0300. Messages sorted by: [date][thread][...
—http://library.wustl.edu/~listmgr/devel-1/Jul1995/0079.html

ACKNOWLEDGEMENTS

Although we are indebted to many people for discussions on relevant matters over the years, and also to those of our colleagues whose work is referenced in the paper, recent interactions with Dr James Sexton (Trinity College Dublin), Professor John Hegarty (Trinity College Dublin), Professor Carlos Alberto Schneider (Federal University of Santa Caterina) and Dr Pat Frain (University College Dublin) have helped us to formulate our own views. We thank the Irish Embassy in Tokyo for securing Japanese reports for us and Mrs Bridget Noone of Trinity College Dublin who managed various evolutionary stages of this manuscript.

REFERENCES

Bolton, William, Fabian Monds, Eoin O'Neill and Carlos A. Schneider (1995). *Policy for Innovation: A Discussion Paper on Incubator Management for Universities*, 2nd edn, Paris: CRE-UNESCO

CIRCA Group Europe (1996). *A Comparative Assessment of the Organisation, Management and Funding of University Research in Ireland and Europe*, Report presented to Higher Education Authority, Dublin, February (available December)

Coey, J. M. D. and I. V. Mitchell (1991). 'The Concerted European Action on Magnets', *International Journal of Technology Management*, Vol. 6, p. 547

Conselho Nacional de Desenvolvimento Cientifico e Tecnologico (1994). *Ciencia & Tecnologia Alicerces do Desenvolvimento*, Sao Paulo, Brazil: CNPq

Cooper, R. G. (1988). *Winning at New Products*, London: Kogan Page

Corish, John and E. P. O'Neill (1992). 'Industrial Development Policy and Implementation: The Role of the Colleges, Post Culliton, Higher Education and Industrial Development – A Response to the Culliton Report', Conference Paper, Dublin City University, April

Culliton, Jim (Chairman) (1992). *A Time for Change: Industrial Policy for the 1990s – Report of the Industrial Policy Review Group*, Dublin: Stationery Office

Cunningham, E. P. (1996). *History, Genetics and the Provisioning of Mankind*, Dublin: The Boyle Medal Lecture, Royal Irish Academy

Daie, Juleh and Roger Wyse (1996). 'All Roads lead to Rome', *Science*, Vol. 274, p. 701

Environmental Protection Agency (1996). *State of the Environment in Ireland*, ed. Larry Stapleton, Wexford: Environmental Protection Agency

European Commission (1995). *Green Paper on Innovation*, Brussels: European Commission, December

European Commission (1996). *Inventing Tomorrow: Europe's Research at the Service of its People*, Brussels: European Commission, July

Faulkner, Wendy and Jacqueline Senker (1995). *Knowledge Frontiers, Public Sector Research and Industrial Innovation in Biotechnology, Engineering Ceramics, and Parallel Computing*, Oxford: Clarendon Press

Fegan, Lorraine (1995). *Environmental Research: Discussion Document on a National Programme and Priorities*, Wexford: Environmental Protection Agency, April

Gibson, David V. and Everett M. Rogers (1994). *R&D Collaboration on Trial*, Cambridge, Mass.: Harvard Business School Press

Hardiman, T. P. (1994). 'Industry–Higher Education Interaction: The Challenge of the 1990s', *Industry and Higher Education*, March, pp. 29–35

Hounshell, David A. and John Kenly Smith Jr (1988). *Science and Corporate Strategy*, New York: Cambridge University Press

Ireland (1996). *Science, Technology and Innovation: The White Paper*, Dublin: Stationery Office

Kinsella, R. P. and V. J. McBrierty (1994). *Economic Rationale for an Enhanced National Science and Technology Capability*, Report commissioned by Forfás, Dublin

Kline, Morris (1972). *Mathematical Thought from Ancient to Modern Times*, New York: Oxford University Press

Kuhn, Thomas S. (1957). *The Copernican Revolution*, Cambridge, Mass.: Harvard University Press

Lafay, Gérard and Colette Herzog (1989). *La Fin des Avantages Acquis*, Paris: Economica

Lorenzi, Jean-Hervé and Jean Bourles (1995). *Le Choc du Progrès Technique*, Paris: Economica

McBrierty V. J. (1994). 'The University and Research: Aims, Conditions and Resources', in *The Role of the University in Society*, Proceedings of NUI conference held in Dublin Castle, Dublin: National University of Ireland

McBrierty V. J. and E. P. O'Neill (1991). 'The College Role in Innovation and Entrepreneurship: An Irish Experience', *International Journal of Technology Management*, Vol. 6, pp. 557–67

Mjøset, Lars (1992). *The Irish Economy in a Comparative Institutional Perspective*, Dublin: National Economic and Social Council

Moran, J. M. (1976). 'Radio Observations of Galactic Masers', in Eugene H. Avrett (ed.), *Frontiers of Astrophysics*, Cambridge, Mass.: Harvard University Press

Nicholson, Geoffrey C. (1996). 'Innovation Working for You', Presentation at the Third Annual Research Directors' Conference – New Strategies for Managing Corporate Technologies and the R&D Portfolio, MIT, Cambridge, Mass., 18–19 April

O'Neill E. P. and J. Corish (1996). 'Marketing Scientific Endeavour', in Christopher Moriarty (ed.), *Science, Technology and Realism*, Proceedings of conference held at the RDS in 1994, Dublin: RDS

O'Neill E. P. and V. J. McBrierty (1992). 'Technology Transfer in a Changing Environment', *Industry and Higher Education*, Vol. 6, p. 213

Patch, Blanche (1951). *Thirty Years with G.B.S.*, London: Victor Gollancz

Perutz, Max (1995). *The New York Review of Books*, Vol. XLII, No. 20 (September)

Rose, Stephen (1995). 'Minds, Brains and Rosetta Stones', in John Brockman and Katuka Matson (eds.), *How Things Are*, New York: William Morrow & Co.

Sansom, G. B. (1973). *Japan: A Short Cultural History*, Tokyo: Charles E. Tuttle Company

Science and Technology Agency of the Japanese Government (1996). *Fifty Years of Postwar Science and Technology in Japan*, White Paper on Science and Technology in Japan, Tokyo: Japan Information Center of Science and Technology

Scotland (1996). *Technology Ventures: Commercialising Scotland's Science and Technology*, ed. Tom Johnston and Cranford W. Beveridge, Glasgow and Edinburgh: Scottish Enterprise and the Royal Society of Edinburgh

STIAC (1995). *Making Knowledge Work for Us: A Strategic View of Science and Technology in Ireland*, Dublin: Stationery Office

Takeda, Yasutsugu (1996). 'Innovation Management for the Company of the Future', Sixth International Forum on Technology Management, Amsterdam, 16 October

Wallace, David (1995). *Environmental Policy and Industrial Innovation*, London: Royal Institute of International Affairs and Earthscan Publications

14

Towards Free Trade for Agriculture

S. J. SHEEHY

Introduction

THE agricultural industry today is vastly different from that analysed in *Economic Development* in 1958 (Whitaker, 1958). The volume of gross output has more than doubled in the intervening years, while at the same time the farm workforce has declined from 400,000 to 130,000. In 1958 output was allocated equally between on-farm consumption, the domestic market and the export market; by 1996 the domestic market still absorbed one-third of output but on-farm consumption had virtually disappeared, and the export market accounted for some 65 per cent of total output. The industry had therefore become much more productive and export orientated.

At processing level the biggest change relates to beef. In 1958 the only beef processing occurring related to the slaughter of TB reactor cows; all prime cattle were exported live to Britain. In 1996 some 90 per cent of cattle exported were in processed form and only 10 per cent were exported live. In dairying the main change relates to skim milk, which after EEC accession in 1973 was processed, whereas before that it was fed directly to calves. The doubling of the volume of farm output and the increased processing intensity of that output did not lead to any increase in employment – the number employed in food processing in 1996 was similar to the 1958 level.

Perhaps the greatest change over the forty years has been in the market environment. In 1958, and even more so in the 1960s, the market for Irish agricultural produce was confined to Britain, and that market became progressively more restrictive as Britain became increasingly more self-sufficient. In the years immediately preceding EEC accession the Irish exchequer was spending 3.4 per cent of the GDP on the kinds of price subsidies on which today 0.6 per cent of the EU GDP is spent under the Common Agricultural Policy (CAP).

The EEC/EU experience to date

Given this background it is easy to understand why EEC accession in 1973 was so enthusiastically welcomed. EEC membership offered the prospect of a substantial price increase, a doubling of real per capita incomes in agriculture and unlimited market access. These were of enormous consequence, not just for farmers, but for the economy generally in which agriculture represented at that time about 50 per cent of total net exports.

In the event, EEC membership proved to be much more turbulent than anticipated, as may be seen in Table 1. In 1972 and 1973 real farm incomes were boosted by international scarcities, but this was followed in 1974 by a sharp reversal attributable to inflation in input prices and chaos in the cattle industry (Review Body, 1976). However, incomes recovered strongly up to 1978, and at that time Irish farmers had realised the income increases that had been predicted from EEC membership. Associated with the recovery, farmers embarked on a wave of borrowing to fund investment and land purchase. Nobody – including the author – saw much wrong with this. People knew in 1977–78 that incomes had peaked, as the transition period to full EEC membership was completed and surpluses were mounting under the CAP. But expectations were for a continuation of the prevailing high incomes or possibly a gradual decline from the 1978 level.

Table 1: Real per family worker farm income of Irish farmers

1970	100	1980	108	1990	199
1971	106	1981	113	1991	198
1972	136	1982	125	1992	227
1973	168	1983	142	1993	244
1974	130	1984	172	1994	264
1975	167	1985	161	1995	277
1976	162	1986	145	1996	284
1977	202	1987	182		
1978	210	1988	217		
1979	152	1989	219		

These comforting expectations proved totally wrong. In the following two years, 1979 and 1980, average incomes were halved, falling back to pre-EEC levels, and farmers were plunged into the greatest credit crisis ever. It seemed that all the great promise of EEC membership – high prices, unlimited markets, high incomes – had evaporated. The causes were twofold: a doubling of interest rates from 9 per cent to 18 per cent and a fall in real prices of 23 per cent. The sharp price fall was confined to Ireland among the member states and was mainly attributable to the revaluation of sterling after Ireland joined the European Monetary System in 1979. That revaluation deprived Ireland of £ green increases which were needed to offset continuing high inflation.

While no obvious basis for a reversal of fortunes was in sight in 1980, the record in Table 1 shows a strong income recovery during the 1980s to reach once again the levels of 1977–78 in the late 1980s. Even the trauma of imposing milk quotas in 1984 did not prevent this. The income growth was greatly assisted by the gradual decline in inflation and interest rates and by the benefits of a series of IR£ devaluations and consequent £ green increases, especially an 8 per cent devaluation in 1986. Despite the rise in incomes, farmers and bankers remained cautious; there was no net increase in either investment or borrowing during the 1980s.

The main event of the 1990s to date was the reform of the CAP by Agriculture Commissioner Ray MacSharry which was implemented over the three-year period 1993–95. These reforms were an integral part of the Uruguay Round trade negotiations, as they were made to enable the EU to accept the disciplines in agricultural trade of the emerging trade agreement.

The MacSharry reforms consisted of three main components:

- reduced prices for beef and cereal/oilseed/protein crops offset by direct payments to farmers
- extension of supply control beyond sugar and milk, where it already applied, to beef, sheep and cereal/oilseed/protein crops, and
- a set of Accompanying Measures.

The support prices for beef and cereal/oilseed/protein crops were cut between 1993 and 1995 by 15 per cent in the case of beef and 29 per cent in the case of cereals. These price reductions were offset by compensation paid directly to farmers per head of livestock or per hectare.

Supply control was extended to cereal/oilseed/protein crops and to beef and sheep by capping the direct payments at the level of production prevailing before the reforms were put in place. Any production beyond these levels would be sold at the lower prices but without compensation. In addition, in the case of the crops, land set-aside at specified levels was required to qualify for receipt of the compensatory payments, and in the case of livestock extra premia were paid for low stocking rates.

The Accompanying Measures consisted of three schemes: one to promote afforestation; a second to encourage early retirement of farmers; and a third as payments for the 'public good' of improving the rural environment in the form of the Rural Environment Protection Scheme (REPS). Payments for such public goods are thus receiving increasing emphasis and are expected to be a growing source of income for farmers into the future.

When MacSharry revealed his proposals in 1991 he was bitterly attacked by EU farming organisations. But an objective assessment concluded that 'the comprehensive compensation involved is sufficient to prevent any reduction in aggregate nominal farm income in Ireland' (Sheehy, 1992, p. 49). While this analysis was considered by critics to be optimistic, at the end of 1995 it proved to be well short of the outcome. Real family income per worker rose by 22 per cent between 1992 and 1995, and the level of that income stood at an all-time high in 1995. In effect Irish farmers experienced a windfall gain, because market prices did not fall as expected while compensation payments still grew.

High income levels continued in 1996 despite the BSE crisis. In 1997 and beyond, incomes are destined to decline, with the outcome in the short term depending on the success of the measures being implemented to restore market balance in beef.

The evolution of the Accompanying Measures is also of interest in light of the expectations. The prospective value of these was impossible to quantify in any meaningful way because their detailed operation and their uptake were unknown. Nevertheless, the Department of Agriculture, Forestry and Food did go on record as saying that these programmes could amount to £55 million per year. The budget provision for them in 1997 was £236 million.

The Uruguay Round Agreement

After eight years of negotiation agreement was finally reached in the Uruguay Round, and the agreement came into operation in July 1995. It is proceeding on its six-year course to June 2001. The commitments made by all countries under the Uruguay Round Agreement (URA) relate to reduced domestic support, increased market access and reduced export subsidies. However, by tough bargaining the EU succeeded in keeping these commitments to a minimum.

The domestic support conditions will have no impact in the EU up to the end of the agreement period, since the price reductions already made – largely in the MacSharry Reforms – are more than sufficient to meet the required reductions, while the MacSharry price reductions are fully offset in all member states by direct payments to farmers.

Under market access all existing non-tariff forms of protection were converted to equivalent tariffs to make protection more transparent.

This tariffication process resulted in such high tariffs that, even after the required average 36 per cent reduction, they will still be high enough to exclude most products from EU markets. But there is also a minimum access requirement, and this will allow in some extra materials, especially dairy products, which are expected to enter up to the extent of about 2 per cent of total consumption by 2001.

The restriction on export subsidies is the commitment most likely to have an impact, the precise magnitude of which will depend on how EU production and consumption evolve up to 2001. The effect on dairy exports is likely to be a reduction of up to a further 2 per cent. The total impact on EU milk production could thus be a reduction of as much as 4 per cent in the absence of growth in consumption. In the case of beef the phasing down of subsidised exports will aggravate the already large beef surplus problem arising from BSE effects.

The next trade agreement

Thus, the URA will not have major short-term effects, but its real significance is that it has put in place a foundation which will be built upon in future trade agreements. The new trade round talks will not begin formally until 1999, but there will be an extended build-up to this event. Already the European Commission has outlined its train of thought in a Strategy Paper published in November 1995 (European Commission, 1995a). Basically the Commission has argued for further reform of the MacSharry type, and it has promised to publish its evolving views on future policy in the autumn of 1997. In addition, the EU is committed to opening negotiations for enlargement sometime in 1998, and clarification of its own position will be desirable before these talks begin. Further reform of the CAP must be such as to simultaneously accommodate the demands of the EU's trading partners and the accession of a number of the Central European countries (CECs) (European Commission, 1995b).

The debate that has already begun on the future of the CAP will therefore intensify over the next few years and will climax in 2001. Further reforms will build on the reforms to date. Thus, the commitments under the URA will have to be extended in the next trade agreement to meet the demands of the EU's trading competitors. This is quite significant because, while the URA effects will be very modest up to 2001, any extension of commitments beyond that date will intensify pressures on EU markets. That is the case under all three headings of the agreement.

Further reductions in domestic support will not be as conveniently cushioned in the next agreement as they were in the URA, where reduced prices were offset by increased direct payments linked to production. This link to production will come under severe attack from negotiators of other exporting countries, who will argue that the link continues to encourage subsidised production and exports even after prices have been reduced. The US has already severed this direct link in its 1996 Farm Bill in anticipation of other countries being forced to do the same. The outcome will probably be a greater degree of 'decoupling' than in the MacSharry Reforms whereby payments which are now made on a headage basis will be converted to area payments, leaving farmers free to produce as they wish without affecting their entitlements.

Increased market access is achieved in the URA by (i) reducing tariffs generally and (ii) affording a minimum level of market access under low tariffs. The pace of tariff reduction will be especially important in the next trade agreement. As stated above, because the initial tariff is so high, the early reductions are having no market impact during the current agreement. But as the process continues, the declining tariffs will begin to allow low world prices to undermine high EU prices. How quickly this will take effect will vary by commodity as explained later.

Relating to the third dimension of URA, namely, reduced export subsidies, again the EU will be under massive pressure not just to phase them down gently, as under the URA, but to abolish them altogether. Such an outcome would exclude the EU from world markets unless it reduced its internal prices to world levels to be able to export without subsidies. This might not be so drastic as it appears viewing low current world prices, as these prices should rise in the years ahead. This has already happened for cereals in 1995 and 1996 when world prices rose above EU levels. While world prices of Ireland's main commodities, milk and beef, are most unlikely to rise to current EU levels, some firming would at least narrow the gap to be bridged (MAFF, 1995).

The merits of milk quotas beyond 2000

The reforms of the CAP which are required to arrive at a new trade agreement are the same as those required for enlargement. They involve, as already outlined by the Commission, further price reductions compensated to some degree by increased direct payments, the details of which will be central to the debates ahead. In particular the future of milk quotas has to be decided as the present system extends only to March 2000. The author has argued elsewhere that, given the commitments already agreed in the URA and their likely extension in the next trade agreement, and given the political imperative of enlargement, the Commission will have cogent reasons to propose the early abolition of milk quotas after 2000 (Sheehy, 1996). Such a proposal would have to be accompanied by a sharp reduction in prices, probably of the order of 20 to 30 per cent, to prevent an upsurge in milk production as farmers dashed to exploit their surplus capacity. At the same time compensation would have to be paid, probably in the form of area payments.

Regardless of what the Commission will propose, it is necessary for Irish interests to re-examine the merits of continuing with milk quotas in a rapidly changing policy context. The arguments in favour of quotas in 1983 were simple and decisive: to curtail surplus production there was the stark choice between quotas and a sharp price reduction. Most dairy farmers quickly came round to accept that quotas were the lesser of the two evils. And the record since 1984 has verified that stance: if quotas had not been introduced, prices would have had to fall drastically to contain milk production within acceptable limits.

While many people still see quotas in the simplistic framework of 1983, the policy environment has changed utterly since then, so the analysis of that time is irrelevant to the decisions ahead. In particular, the introduction of comprehensive compensation in the MacSharry Reforms, and its proposed extension in future reforms as outlined in the Commission's Strategy Paper, is a critical change in the balance as between the quota and price approaches. No such compensation was even dreamed of in 1983 when the proposed milk quota was being debated. Now it is possible to envisage compensation generous enough to cancel totally the price merits of quotas. Of course, it is not possible to anticipate ahead of negotiations the degree and form of compensation that will be agreed, though for various reasons the generosity of the MacSharry formula is unlikely to be on offer.

The second change to be noted in the policy environment is the threat to the quota of continuing the URA commitments into the next trade agreement as outlined earlier. Even now the tariff on dairy products is falling at the equivalent of 5 pence per gallon per annum, but this will not begin to affect farm-gate prices until early in the next trade agreement. Unless tariffs are frozen in that agreement – a very unlikely prospect – further declines in the tariff will progressively erode producer prices. At the same time increased market access and falling export subsidies will shrink markets for EU produce. In that situation the power of the quota to sustain high prices will be undermined, and efforts to retain a quota policy will increasingly be seen as counterproductive: prices would be falling while at the same time production would be curtailed and market shares would diminish. EU farmers would then have the worst of both worlds, falling prices and falling production.

Likewise persistence with a quota policy through the next trade round would be a short-sighted approach to enlargement from both the EU and Irish points of view. If the EU retains the quota as the CECs join, then presumably the CECs would be obliged against their will to impose quotas while at the same time raising producer prices towards EU levels. Then in a short few years, as EU prices fall under the next trade agreement, the CECs would have to join the EU in cutting their prices again. Along the way they would have established the right to compensation from Community funds, thus reallocating funds away from other member states. The only pay-off from this would be the retention of higher prices for a limited period in the early years of the next trade round – a poor exchange for the damage done to the CECs and existing member states.

A further benefit from abandoning quotas, with associated price reduction and compensation, would be the positive impact on EU consumption. The steady decline in dairy markets over a number of years would be reversed, thus providing scope for expansion instead of the contraction which is inevitable under quotas. Since 1984 the milk quota has been cut cumulatively by 9 per cent and, as indicated earlier, a further 4 per cent reduction may be necessary by 2001. At the same time the capacity of farmers to produce grows with improved technology and better yielding cows. The result is a growing frustration among farmers, especially younger farmers, and an intensifying scramble for diminishing quotas.

This has been very evident in Ireland in recent years and will get worse. Already one in every seven gallons of milk is being produced with expensive leased quotas, which pushes the returns net of lease rent down to world prices. Persisting with such a policy of progressive strangulation is only warranted if the pay-off makes it worthwhile. That has been the case to date but is unlikely to be the case beyond 2000.

Related to this frustration is the state of competitiveness of the industry. In high-cost dairy regions of the EU, such as southern Europe and the mountain regions, limiting production by quotas is less restrictive than in low-cost regions across northern Europe – and Ireland in particular. Irish agriculturalists constantly proclaim their competitive status based on low-cost grass production. If they really believe this they should be seeking opportunities to displace high-cost producers. Sometimes mobility of quotas across national boundaries is advocated in this regard, but this is not going to happen. And even if it did, it would be a very inefficient approach, as most of the competitive advantage would be absorbed by lease rents, exactly in the same way as for efficient Irish farmers who have currently to lease quotas. To exploit efficiently our competitive advantage within the EU, the quota has to be abolished.

Competitiveness of Irish production in global trade is less certain than competitiveness within the EU. But the common practice of considering competitiveness only *vis-à-vis* the most efficient producer in the world, New Zealand, is blinkered. In global free trade there would be a hierarchy of competitive players, and for success it would not be necessary to be competitive with the most competitive; it would suffice to be just among the most competitive.

Given the changing policy environment – because of the availability of compensation, because of the URA and its successor and because of prospective enlargement – Irish and EU dairy industries have to reappraise the merits of persisting with quotas long beyond 2000. The Irish may choose to be reactive rather than proactive and to await the Commission's proposals, but sometime along the way they must clear their heads in relation to the national advantage.

The EU has decided to retain quotas until 2000, but phasing out quotas after 2000 and cutting prices across the EU to restrain expansion has a lot of attractions for the Irish dairy industry provided that reasonable compensation is available. Irish dairy farmers and processors would be released from the shackles of quotas. Some might quit production while others would expand. All would be free to exploit the competitive advantage of Irish grass-based production and to force out of production more costly producers in other member states. At the same time consumers would get cheaper dairy products and would consume more of them; enlargement could be achieved with minimum cost both to the CECs and to the EU; and a second world trade agreement would be facilitated.

Those in less competitive regions in the EU, including such regions in Ireland, will have a special concern about the threat to continuing production. Undoubtedly, when compensation is further decoupled from production in those regions the dairy industry could rapidly contract, causing serious social problems. To avoid this, much more resources will have to be channelled into such schemes as rural development, REPS and disadvantaged area payments. In addition, there is a strong case for a special EU Farm Adjustment Scheme in less competitive areas, which would consist of EU-supported intensive advice and generous investment grants targeted at smaller farmers with competitive potential. The Irish government should be willing to supplement the EU scheme with a tax holiday similar to that operating in designated urban areas. The policy challenge here is to find the appropriate balance between economic, social and regional concerns.

The alternative of attempting to slow down the tide of change by hanging on to a crumbling quota has little to recommend it. The debate is no longer about a quota approach versus a price approach. Ireland already opted for the eventual abolition of the quota when it agreed in the EU to sign the URA. The only issue now is the choice between an early abolition and a delayed abolition.

Other major commodities

The URA and the next trade agreement will impact more or less on all agricultural commodities. Sugar has much in common with milk under the CAP. Its production is controlled by farm-level quotas, and its price within the quota is raised well above international trading prices – in recent years at around double world prices. It is also unreformed in the MacSharry sense, as the Council of Ministers decided in 1995 simply to roll over the existing policy rather than to reform it. Furthermore, the sugar regime is affected by the URA in very similar ways to dairying. In particular, if tariffs continue to be reduced during the next trade round, farm-gate prices for sugar beet must fall. The merits of the quota approach would then be diminished as for milk.

The main difference between the milk and sugar regimes is the 'self-financing' of the latter through the imposition of levies on producers. This could be an important influence in decisions regarding the future of the policy in the next trade round, where it is anticipated that the budget limitations will be a serious constraint. Already in the URA sugar tariffs are being reduced by only 20 per cent as against the average reduction of 36 per cent. It could be decided in the next trade round to further slow down the rate of tariff reduction and to retain the quota system while thus limiting price reduction. Such an approach would minimise any new budget demands from the sugar sector and would continue the gradual pace of reform in that sector.

This caution would be bolstered by political circumstances. In particular, the ACP countries would wish to maintain the status quo under the Lomé Convention to protect their favourable access for 1.3 million tonnes of their produce. Along similar lines, US pressure for trade liberalisation is likely to be very much weaker for sugar than for milk. The future of sugar quotas, therefore, seems more secure than in the case of milk.

The situation for cereals and beef under the URA is quite different from milk and sugar. Tariff reduction does not appear to threaten the price levels of these commodities in the next trade agreement unless tariff reduction is greatly accelerated. What does threaten their prices are the mounting surpluses which have been predicted by the Commission in both cases (European Commission, 1997). The BSE scare is compounding the beef problem.

Faced with these growing surpluses, the EU will have to fall back on the two standard instruments to contain them, namely, further supply control or further price reduction. Intensifying supply control for either of these two commodities is not an easy option. In the case of cereals it would involve ever-growing areas of set-aside, at which society would be likely to recoil. In the case of beef it would involve, among other things, the slaughter of growing numbers of calves, which again would be anathema to EU citizens. Furthermore, the supply control approach would increase the gulf between EU and world markets at a time when trade liberalisation was being intensified.

For these reasons it appears that price reduction will be relied upon more than further supply control. In the case of cereals the surplus problem may well be resolved by strong international markets, where prices were so high in 1995 and 1996 that export taxes were used to keep EU prices uncharacteristically below world levels. But if world markets weaken again as most people expect, then further price reduction may be necessary. In that event a modest further reduction would bring EU cereal prices down to world levels, in which case market limitations would disappear as subsidies would no longer be required on exports. Of course, compensation would again be claimed as part of this package.

Beef prices would have to fall much more than cereal prices to reach world levels – by 25 to 30 per cent according to the UK Ministry of Agriculture, Food and Forestry (MAFF, 1995). Yet if they are not reduced by this amount, import tariffs and export subsidies will continue to shrink market shares both within the EU and in world markets.

Free trade in agriculture by 2005?

The foregoing analysis points to an acceleration in trade liberalisation after 2001 to the extent that global free trade would be approached sometime during the decade ending 2009. Since agricultural trade has always been heavily protected this would be a new experience for farmers everywhere. As a result they are increasingly enquiring as to the shape of a free trade world. This has been extensively modelled in recent years, though of course models can only produce guidelines and not answers. Model output is a consequence of model input and specification, so there is considerable variation in the literature (see MAFF, 1995).

However there are common strands. One is that free trade prices will be higher than they have been in the past when they are no longer depressed by systematic dumping. But they will still be much lower than current EU prices. A second is that free trade prices will fluctuate over time because of the price inelastic character of agricultural produce and the tendency for production to vary because of weather and disease. This could be cushioned in the EU if the compensatory payments were arranged to vary inversely with market price as is already the case for oilseeds.

In these circumstances the competitive position of Irish agriculture is a critical consideration. At farm level that position seems quite favourable based on grass, but rapid restructuring would be called for to achieve appropriate scale. Many see this as a threat to the family farm and therefore a reason to oppose liberalisation. In this regard it is useful to focus on three distinct categories of farmer, namely, (i) commercial farmers, (ii) part-time farmers and (iii) redundant farmers. These are to be found in all countries but in different mixes. Commercial farmers are those with the human, physical and financial capacity to increase their scale and efficiency over time. In these ways they offset the market pressures from falling margins and thereby continue in business. Part-time farmers achieve the same objective by diversifying their efforts into non-farm employment.

Many farmers are not able to make either of these responses, in which case they continue in farming until retirement or death but experience a declining income. They are in effect caught in a process of creeping redundancy. In the case of employees the redundancy experience is usually a sudden one at the time when employment ceases. But in the case of self-employed people such as farmers the process is prolonged, because as income is eroded the farmer continues farming, there being no better option available.

The movement towards free trade will intensify market pressures. But there will be four streams of income available to farmers to cushion the shock. These comprise two streams of market income in the forms of farming income and non-farming income, compensation payments and payments for 'public goods' relating to the rural environment and landscape. A favourable combination of these would modify the impact of free trade and could maintain rural viability.

Downstream

The food-processing industry will be challenged by trade liberalisation just as much as farming. In the dairy sector there is a great sense of comfort under the quota regime, with volumes static or declining and minimal pressures for modernisation and amalgamation. This will all be shattered when the quota is abolished. Volumes in Ireland will resume growth and seasonality will be accentuated, so substantial new investment will be called for unless milk is to be shipped out of Ireland for processing abroad. Hopefully the industry will not be lulled into a false security but rather will have the foresight to anticipate the responses that will be necessary.

In the beef sector the BSE crisis has reversed the slow but steady progress towards product and market development. That progress must resume as soon as possible and, paradoxically, will probably be accelerated by the necessity to guarantee quality and safety to worried consumers. The Irish food industry has made major advances over the past four decades. The scale and nature of many Irish food companies have also been transformed beyond all recognition. Through a combination of organic growth and acquisition, some of the larger players have carved out substantial niches in overseas markets. Who would have thought in 1958, for example, that a company from Kerry would be one of the leading manufacturers of food ingredients in the world, or that a company from Dungarvan would be the largest cheese manufacturer in the UK?

Despite this progress, the structure of the food industry in Ireland remains flawed. The two largest sectors, dairying and beef, remain sheltered from the rigours of a free market by a range of quotas and price support mechanisms.

In all sectors of food processing, as in farming, scale is part of free market requirements. This will be achieved by amalgamation and joint ventures within countries and between countries as the globalisation of markets will dictate. As intervention and export subsidies disappear dependence on commodity products will have to be replaced by own label and branded products, a process that will be facilitated by multi-national linkages.

Conclusion

The EU agricultural industry must recognise that the agricultural world is on the road to free trade – at a very slow pace initially under the URA, but at an accelerating pace in the next trade round. In addition, EU enlargement is a political imperative. The policy challenge then is to make a virtue out of necessity. As argued in this essay, these developments need not damage Irish national interests as most agriculturalists seem to fear. Given the right policy responses, free trade will provide

new and exciting opportunities for Irish agriculture. The alternative of
attempting to slow down the tide of change, in particular by hanging on
to a crumbling dairy quota system, has little to recommend it for
Ireland.

REFERENCES

European Commission (1995a). *Agricultural Strategy Paper,* CSE(95)607,
Brussels: European Commission
European Commission (1995b). *Preparation of the Associated Countries of
Central and Eastern Europe for Integration into the Internal Market of the
Union,* COM(95)163, Brussels: European Commission
European Commission – DGVI (1997). *Long-Term Prospects for Grains,
Milk and Meat Markets,* DOC/97/1, Brussels: European Commission
MAFF (Ministry of Agriculture, Food and Forestry) (1995). *European
Agriculture – The Case for Radical Reform, Working Papers,* London:
Ministry of Agriculture, Food and Forestry
Review Body (1976). *Report of the Review Body on Beef Intervention and
Cattle Slaughter Premium Systems,* Dublin: Stationery Office
Sheehy, S. J. (1992). 'Evaluation of CAP Reform Proposals', in National
Economic and Social Council, *The Impact of Reform of the Common
Agricultural Policy,* Report No. 92, Dublin: National Economic and Social
Council
Sheehy, S. J. (1996). 'Milk Quotas to be Abolished in 2001', paper
presented to the Irish Agricultural Economics Society, Dublin, May
Whitaker, T. K. (1958). *Economic Development,* Dublin: Stationery Office

15

The Tourism Dimension to Irish Economic Development

JAMES DEEGAN AND DONAL A. DINEEN

Introduction

THE relative neglect of the tourism sector in Ireland's economic development for most of the period since Whitaker's seminal work on *Economic Development* in 1958 was arrested only with the availability of EU Structural Funds in 1989. Ironically, it was the opportunity to access external sources of funding in the late 1940s/early 1950s from the US Marshall Aid plan for European reconstruction that provided the previous most significant impetus of development for the sector. It was clear from the First Programme for Economic Expansion, 1959–64, that tourism was very much the poor relation (to agriculture and manufacturing) of economic policy. The programme projected capital expenditure of £220.5 million; of this the relatively minuscule amount of £2.5 million was projected for tourism development. The actual amount expended on the total programme was a little over £297 million (35 per cent above target) yet the expenditure on tourism at £1.21 million was less than 50 per cent of target.[1] While the overall programme was undoubtedly a success as the performance of economic growth was almost double the target,[2] it does appear that the new-found emphasis on industrial development led to a relative neglect of the services sector in general and tourism in particular. This relative neglect was to continue for many years and the emphasis on tourism in the late 1980s only emerged when the relative failure of manufacturing industry became manifest.

The impressive macroeconomic performance in the Irish economy since the late 1980s has been accompanied by a phenomenal turnaround in the fortunes of Irish tourism compared with a rather poor record in the previous twenty years. Currently, average tourism industry revenue growth throughout Europe is running at around 3 per cent, yet Irish growth is closer to 12 per cent. Undoubtedly, the performance of the sector has contributed significantly to the economy-wide growth, and tourism contributed 35 per cent of the net job creation in the economy in the period 1987–94 though its share of total employment averaged only 7 per cent. To better understand the recent performance it is useful to examine the development of Irish tourism policy and this essay begins with an assessment of tourism policy and performance from 1970 to 1985. It then reviews the background to the emergence of a focus on tourism in the late 1980s before going on to evaluate policy and performance to 1995. The essay then focuses on policy issues relevant to the future development of Irish tourism and ends with some brief conclusions.

Tourism policy and performance, 1970–85

Tourism performance, like that of any other sector of the economy, is determined by the complex interaction of endogenous and exogenous factors. On the endogenous side the tourism policy of the government, access transport policy and more generally prudent domestic macroeconomic management can play a significant role in determining tourism outcomes. On the exogenous side the tastes of international tourists, the general levels of disposable incomes and the exchange rates prevailing in outbound markets contribute in no small way to the tourism outcomes in host countries.

Tourism setbacks and recovery in the 1970s

The Irish tourism industry went into decline during the first half of the 1970s through a combination of the conflict in Northern Ireland, high inflation rates and poor product development. The outbreak of the 'troubles' in Northern Ireland in the late 1960s reversed the sustained expansion in Irish tourism of the previous ten years. The 1970s and subsequent experience in Irish tourism confirmed the interdependency between both parts of the island (North and South) when it comes to the performance of their respective tourism sectors, with overseas tourist flows to each part closely correlated from 1960 to 1994.[3]

The tourism industry recovered from the mid-1970s at a steady if unspectacular pace. The increased prominence afforded to public sector bodies and government participation in the economy led to a more proactive policy stance in relation to tourism, even though this was not matched by appropriate resource commitments. A comprehensive report in 1980 concluded that the government grant support schemes, originally intended as a pump-priming exercise, had generally been successful though the report also concluded: 'with the passage of time, what was started as a means of stimulating an underdeveloped tourism sector has become accustomed practice and is considered at this stage by many within the industry to be an inviolate part of tourism development policy' (NESC, 1980, p. 103). This dependence on the state has continued to the present day and is now recognised as a constraint on the further development of the industry.

Tourist flows

Overseas and Northern Ireland tourists together represent the international dimension of Ireland's tourism industry.[4] The balance consists of domestic tourism. Given that tourist flows from Northern Ireland are quasi-domestic in terms of influencing factors on destination choice and ease of access, we focus here on overseas flows (Figure 1).

Figure 1: Tourism flows to Ireland from principal overseas origin zones, 1970–85 (000s)

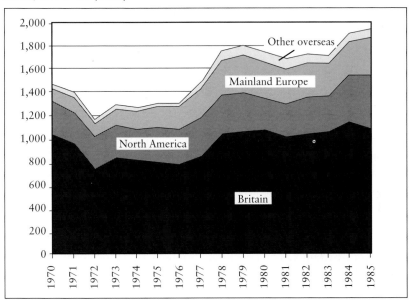

Source: Derived from Bord Fáilte, *Tourism Numbers and Revenue*, 1970–85

The impact of the 'troubles' is clearly seen in the early 1970s especially from the British market. The recovery in the latter part of the decade coincided with improved economic conditions in the principal origin markets. The 1970 level of overseas visitors was exceeded again in 1977, though it took a further two years for a similar outcome from the British market. The tourist flows to Ireland were static if not declining in the early part of the 1980s, with all markets affected, though signs of improvement were evident from 1984 onwards.

There has been a steady growth in visitor numbers from mainland Europe – 12 per cent per annum during the 1970s, with the numbers exceeding those from North America from 1977 through 1981. However, the North American market performed robustly in the first half of the 1980s, showing a 63 per cent increase to 1985 (helped particularly in that year by a strong dollar) while Europe was more sluggish with the same number of visitors in 1985 as in 1980 (336,000). The numbers of all overseas tourists to Ireland was 19 per cent higher in 1980 compared with 1970, and 34 per cent higher by 1985.

The trend growth rates of overseas tourists to Ireland from the principal origin markets are shown in Table 1.

Table 1: Annual average percentage change in numbers of overseas tourists to Ireland by principal origin zones, 1970–85

	Britain	North America	Mainland Europe	Other overseas	Total overseas
1970–75	–4.2	–0.2	11.3	–1.3	–2.2
1975–80	5.5	0.3	12.3	19.1	6.1
1980–85	1.0	10.2	0.0	0.6	2.4
1970–85	0.4	3.4	7.7	5.7	2.0

Source: Derived from Bord Fáilte, *Tourism Numbers and Revenue*, 1970–85

Ireland's share of the US market to European destinations fell throughout the 1970s, from 8 per cent (1970) to 6 per cent (1980). Overseas tourists to Ireland also increased much less rapidly than to other European countries during the 1970s with the result that Ireland's share of total international tourists to European country markets fell from 1.6 to 1.2 per cent and of total international tourists from 1.1 to 0.8 per cent between 1970 and 1980. In terms of the distribution of overseas tourists to Ireland, Britain's share declined from 73 to 58 per cent by 1985, North America's increased from 18 to 22 per cent while that of mainland Europe increased from 7.5 to over 17 per cent. These changes occurred at a time when overseas tourist numbers to Ireland showed an average annual increase of only 2 per cent from 1970 to 1985.

Thus, overall it was a period in which Ireland's expanding international tourism sector was halted in its tracks and went into reverse until 1974, recovered strongly to 1980 and less so to 1985. The Northern Ireland 'troubles' and the oil-induced recession of 1973–75 were important factors in explaining the slow-down which was observed.[5] In addition, the rapid expansion of keenly priced package tours for mass tourism to Europe's sun destinations of the Mediterranean militated against the relatively more expensive Irish destination in which price inflation – both in general and in tourist goods – was much higher than in other northern European countries (excluding Britain).[6] The improvement in economic growth rates throughout the OECD countries in the latter half of the 1970s assisted the resumption of growth in overseas tourists to Ireland, though the UK and general recession of the early 1980s dampened growth rates to 1984 while growth from the North American market was strongest at this time.

Expenditure patterns of overseas tourists

Tourism makes an important contribution to the Irish balance of payments through expenditure of incoming tourists, both on Irish carriers and on goods and services while on holiday.[7] While increasing the number of tourists has frequently been the policy target, the economic benefit of overseas tourism is much more sensitively reflected in the expenditure per tourist and the aggregate expenditure derived from all out-of-state visitors. The expenditure trends in real terms are presented in Figure 2.

Figure 2: Real expenditures* by tourists to Ireland by principal origin zones, 1970–85 (£m)

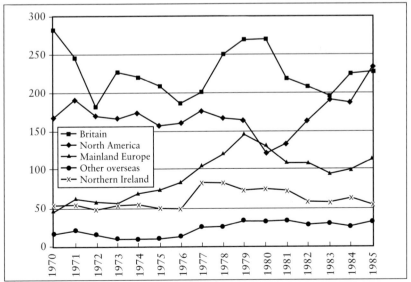

*1995 prices
Source: Derived from Bord Fáilte, *Tourism Numbers and Revenue*, 1970–85

With the exception of visitors from the European mainland all other zones registered annual average decreases in real expenditures in the first half of the 1970s of more than 1.5 per cent. There was some recovery in all markets in the 1975–80 period with the exception of North America where real expenditures declined even more dramatically (–4.3 per cent per annum). Ironically the North American market was most buoyant during the first half of the 1980s when the other principal short-haul markets exhibited limited or negative growth. Real tourism revenues in 1984 were below the 1980 level. Real expenditure growth by mainland European visitors averaged 11.2 per cent annually throughout the decade, 1970–80. These differential trends had a dramatic effect on some market shares. For example, mainland Europe's share of overseas tourism expenditure in Ireland doubled from 9 to 18 per cent between 1970 and 1985. The corresponding proportions for North American expenditures were 33 per cent (1970) and 39 per cent (1985). It was remarkable that in expenditure terms Ireland was more dependent on the North American market than on the British market in 1985 though the latter generated almost three times the volume of tourists.

If we compare Ireland's share of British spending on foreign holidays in 1968 with that of 1977 we find a dramatic reduction from 22.3 to 8.8 per cent. Ireland's share of US travel expenditures in Europe declined from 3.2 per cent in 1968 to a low of 1.9 per cent in 1972 but recovered subsequently to over 4 per cent by 1977 (NESC, 1980). The trends in international tourist receipts were much stronger in other OECD countries during the 1970s where they increased by an annual average of 6.5 per cent while Ireland's corresponding growth in real terms was only 1.2 per cent for overseas tourism expenditures. Thus Ireland clearly lost international market share of tourist receipts during the 1970s and declined further to 1984.

Contribution to the economy

This lower share combined with more rapid expansion of the goods-producing sectors reduced tourism's contribution to the Irish economy over the period 1970–85. Foreign tourism (including carrier) receipts more than halved from 13 per cent (1970) to less than 6 per cent (1985) of total exports, while tourism's share of invisible exports declined from 41 to 33 per cent. While not absolutely accurate it is reasonable to assume multiplier values close to unity for export tourism which suggests that the impact on the economy of the sector, having been as high as 5.3 per cent of GNP in 1970, averaged 4 per cent during the 1970s and declined to 3.9 per cent in 1985.[8] Domestic tourism augmented this impact by 1.0 to 1.5 per cent of GNP, ignoring any displacement effect of the latter.[9]

Government's interest in the tourism sector is critically related to the sector's contribution to employment generation. There was no clearly agreed estimate of the numbers employed in Irish tourism as variations in multiplier estimates clearly affected the outcomes.[10] Indeed some estimates for the late 1970s were as high as those for a decade later when the numbers of visitors were significantly higher. Using Deane and Henry's (1993) methodology, retrospective estimates were made of tourism-dependent employment to the early 1980s which showed that the sector (domestic and foreign) employed 52,300 people – equivalent to 4.8 per cent of total employment or 8.7 per cent of services sector employment – in 1985.[11]

Supply-side developments were constrained during the fifteen years from 1970 by the obvious demand-side problems and uncertainties of the period. The accommodation stock declined in the 1970s. Tourism did not receive much priority in government circles and the amounts for subventions for capital projects were generally small and thinly spread during this time. Ireland's attractive scenery and friendly people were the prime assets on which the industry was built and insufficient investment was undertaken to ensure the tourism 'product' itself was being enhanced. One other constraining factor was the cost of access transport, particularly air transport, a point which was highlighted in NESC (1980).

Summary of performance

Overseas tourism numbers and revenues dipped downwards towards the end of the 1960s in response to the onset of the 'troubles' in Northern Ireland, a feature that continued to depress tourist flows in the first half of the 1970s, particularly from the dominant market of the UK. During the 1970s and early 1980s, the core tourism product was not being developed, promotional policies were geared to the traditional ethnic and VFR (visiting friends and relatives) markets, and there was heavy reliance on the traditional characteristics of beautiful scenery, friendly people and a relaxed easy-going style of holiday. Policy design and delivery were largely left to Bord Fáilte and there was no clear strategic focus on how the industry should develop. The economic environment was not benign as two oil crises (and associated recessions) and rapid price inflation, combined with the successful packaging and marketing of alternative destinations, reduced Ireland's market share of international tourism. Trends improved somewhat in the latter part of the 1970s, though the mainland European market performed strongly throughout, averaging over 10 per cent annual growth. The North American market was the star performer in the first half of the 1980s (helped by the strong dollar) as the European short-haul markets performed sluggishly. Tourism product innovations, which featured strongly in the 1960s, were conspicuously absent in the following fifteen years.

Increasing focus on tourism

In 1980, the National Economic and Social Council produced a major report on Irish tourism policy (NESC, 1980). The report was rather critical of the manner in which tourism policy had developed in Ireland and stressed that major policy changes were required if the sector was to develop. While the report contained many excellent recommendations, the lack of emphasis on the sector hampered development in the early years of the 1980s and the lacklustre tourism performance continued. The poor performance of the tourism sector was however just one of the serious difficulties facing the government. At the time, government expenditure was spiralling out of control, the debt/GNP ratio was a phenomenal 118 per cent, agricultural employment was declining and manufacturing employment had remained at the 1977 level despite significant incentives and investment. In order to redress the poor and declining macroeconomic environment a policy of fiscal retrenchment was initiated in 1987 and since that time the fortunes of the economy have improved dramatically.

It was against this rather bleak performance and outlook for the economy in the mid-1980s that there was a renewal of government attention to tourism. This may have had more to do with the negative performance of other sectors of the economy than any abiding belief in the tourism sector. The first manifestation of this renewed interest was to be found in the government White Paper on tourism policy (Ireland, 1985). While the White Paper could be described as the first articulation of government policy for the sector since the 1939 Tourist Traffic Act, it significantly downplayed the role of public expenditure in financing promotion and capital development schemes. While this view was to change dramatically in subsequent years, a decision on aviation policy initiated in 1986 was to provide the first dramatic boost to tourism development. The decision to allow a new independent airline, Ryanair, on to the previously 'duopoly-controlled' (i.e. Aer Lingus and British Airways) Dublin–London route had an immediate and dramatic impact on traffic movement. Between 1986 and 1989 passenger numbers on the route increased by 1 million to 2.3 million (Barrett, 1991).

The development of tourism traffic occasioned by the relaxation of legislation on the Dublin–London route provided a catalyst for serious discussion on the underperformance of the tourism sector over the preceding years. A new government was elected in 1987, and its publication of a planning document entitled Programme for National Recovery (Ireland, 1987), which highlighted the potential for tourism to create employment, was concrete evidence of a shift in emphasis towards tourism. While the renewed focus on tourism was welcomed by many in the sector, finding the finance to pump-prime development remained the major obstacle. In this regard Ireland's membership of the European Union was to become critically important.

Ireland, like other members of the Union, had the option of grant aid for tourism under the terms of the European Regional Development Fund (ERDF) which had been established in 1975. Data available on ERDF funding show, however, that Ireland received its first tourism allocation only in 1985. A tiny fraction (0.9 per cent) of the 1,157 MECUs (million ECU) received under the ERDF between 1975 and 1988 was allocated to tourism.

A new system of funding the less developed regions and member states of the EU was introduced from 1989 as part of the preparation for the introduction of the single European market. These Structural Fund transfers were designed largely to enable the less developed parts of the EU to implement structural improvements to their economies and, in Ireland, were to have a significant impact on the tourism sector, one of the key sectors singled out for support. Under the new system, Community Support Frameworks (CSF) were drawn up by the EU for each member state, introducing the European Commission's structural action for that member under defined objectives. Each CSF defines the sectors, including tourism, to which the funds should be directed. Assistance under a CSF is then provided predominantly in the form of Operational Programmes. The movement to Operational Programmes replaced the previous approach of allocating funds on a project-by-project basis and also coincided with a period during which Structural Fund allocations across the Union were to double by 1993.[12]

The change to Structural Fund arrangements and the additional finance available provided the final link in the overall movement of tourism to the public policy mainstream in Ireland. Given this opportunity of available European finance for tourism investment the Irish government quickly moved to develop an Operational Programme for Tourism. In anticipation of the increased funding the government had already established ambitious targets for the sector in the Programme for National Recovery (Ireland, 1987). A target was then set to double both the number of overseas tourists and real revenue over the five-year period of the programme which took 1987 as the base year.[13] It was anticipated that achievement of this target would result in 25,000 additional jobs. Bord Fáilte responded to the targets by developing a strategy, within its existing resources, to achieve the stated targets. This strategy was set out in a document published by Bord Fáilte in December 1988 (Bord Fáilte, 1988). It consisted of four elements:

- product development in specialist activities, cultural heritage and genealogically related markets
- competitiveness improvement with an emphasis on both price and quality
- promotion of Ireland as an attractive holiday destination
- distribution of Irish holiday products through appropriate channels, appropriately packaged.

These components were designed to develop both the supply and demand sides of the tourism market and were reflected subsequently in the first Operational Programme for Tourism, 1989–93. The strategy of doubling numbers and revenues was adopted by Bord Fáilte on a prorata basis for each country market. This was rather surprising and took no account of the fact that major shifts were occurring in the origin markets for Irish tourism, for example the steady shift towards mainland European country markets (which subsequently accelerated) was not reflected in the marketing plans prepared at the time. As we shall see, the outcomes that occurred in subsequent years may have therefore had more to do with exogenous demand factors than with any strategic action of the planners. While the relationship between the tourism objectives and outcomes will be explored later in this essay, we focus now on the Operational Programmes that were implemented from 1989.

In the period 1989–93 it is estimated that some £450 million (about 557 MECUs) was invested in tourist facilities, training and marketing in Ireland. The bulk of this investment (£380 million or about 470 MECUs) was supported through the Operational Programme for Tourism. Table 2 shows that the initial investment targets for EU co-funded expenditure under the programme were exceeded.

Of the £380 million invested, approximately 53 per cent was funded by the EU, 30 per cent by the private sector and the remaining 17 per cent by the Irish exchequer. During this period all ERDF project grants to Ireland amounted to £1,387.3 million, of which tourism grants accounted for £157.6 million (11 per cent).[14] While comparison with the period prior to the new Structural Fund arrangements is difficult due

Table 2: Total co-funded investment achieved by the first Operational Programme for Tourism, 1989–93

	Programme targets (£m)	Programme out-turn (£m)	Out-turn/ target (%)
Product development	263.4	278.7	106
Marketing	23.0	48.3	210
Training	49.2	52.1	106
Technical assistance	0.3	0.7	233
Total	335.9	379.8	113

Source: Ireland (1994)

to the late investment of ERDF expenditure in tourism in 1985, Table 3 gives some indication of changing priorities in the period 1989–93. The most notable change is the sharp decline of investment in port facilities, from 22.3 per cent to a little under 1 per cent. The second major change is the investment of funds into sporting activities, a priority under the Operational Programme. Finally, the allocation of 37 per cent of funds to museums/historic centres and for restoration is indicative of the emphasis placed in the Operational Programme on one of the unexploited assets of Irish tourism.

Table 3: Distribution of ERDF assistance by type of tourism project, 1975–88 and 1989–93 (%)

Type of project	1975–88	1989–93*
Infrastructure	18.9	19.9
Accommodation	–	–
Leisure tourist complexes	–	9.4
Port facilities	22.3	0.9
Winter sports facilities	–	–
Other sports facilities	–	13.2
Thermal resorts	–	–
Museums/historic centres/restoration	24.0	37.0
Cultural and visitor centres	34.8	–
Conference centres	–	3.3
Other	–	16.3
Total	100.0	100.0

*The figure of £157.6 million to which this refers includes known tourism expenditure undertaken under the Operational Programme for Tourism, INTERREG, LEADER and the agri-tourism scheme of the Operational Programme for Rural Development. The figure does not include expenditure on training undertaken under the auspices of the European Social Fund, estimated at £30.5 million over the period.

Source: Derived from Pearce (1992) and Department of Tourism and Trade, Dublin

Government authorities were in no doubt that the first Operational Programme was a resounding success. The foreword to the second Operational Programme for Tourism stated: 'The Operational Programme for Tourism, 1989–1993 has been a major success. The ambitious strategic targets set for the development of Irish tourism at the outset of the Programme have been substantially met' (Ireland, 1994). After attributing the strong performance of the sector to the first programme, the second programme goes on to point out that there are still some major deficiencies to be tackled. The new programme stressed:

- the need to increase marketing spend to promote facilities developed under the first programme
- the urgent need to improve facilities at major national cultural institutions
- the requirement to preserve fish stocks and angling facilities to help ameliorate seasonality
- the need to develop a major conference centre, and
- the continuing need to upgrade training for the tourism sector.

The commitment to tourism is endorsed by a significant investment programme to run from 1994 to 1999. The financial plan is outlined in Table 4.

Table 4: Financial plan of the second Operational Programme for Tourism, 1994–99 (£m)*

	Total cost	EU	National/public	Private sector
Product development	287	139	19	129
Marketing	125	51	5	69
Natural/cultural tourism	125	94	31	–
Training	110	82	28	–
Technical assistance	5	3	1	1
All sub-programmes	652	369	84	199

*Based on 1 ECU = £0.80824
Source: Ireland (1994)

The financial plan shows that the EU contributions to the programme will be about 57 per cent (53 per cent in 1989-93), the private sector 30 per cent (same as in 1989–93), with the direct contributions from the national exchequer falling slightly to 13 per cent (17 per cent in 1989–93). Figures produced under the Community Support Framework for Ireland for the period 1994–99 estimate that Ireland will receive a total of 5,620 MECUs in Structural Fund support. Of this, the ERDF will account for a total of 2,562 MECUs, of which spending on tourism will account for 354 MECUs, or approximately 14 per cent, which shows an increase of 3 percentage points on the first programme. Figures of this magnitude confirm that tourism has finally received the attention and commitment of financial resources from government that for many years were not forthcoming.

Irish tourism performance, 1985–95

Tourist flows

The performance of Irish tourism since the latter part of the 1980s has been quite remarkable by comparison with the record of the previous twenty years. The total number of overseas visitors to Ireland increased by 117 per cent over the period 1985–95, from 1.951 million to 4.231 million, and a breakdown of this growth by the principal source markets is shown in Figure 3.

Figure 3: Overseas visitors to Ireland by principal origin zones, 1985–95 (000s)

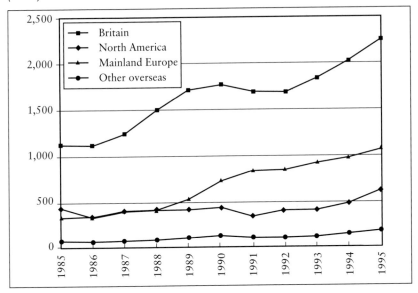

Source: Derived from Bord Fáilte, *Tourism Facts*, 1985–95

Dramatic growth of tourist numbers from Britain was experienced from 1987 to 1990; numbers dipped in 1991–92 and resumed a high rate of expansion from 1993 to reach 2.3 million in 1995. The strong growth in the latter part of the 1980s, especially from the mainland

European (+228 per cent) and other overseas (+196 per cent) markets, was renewed again from 1992 onwards. The acceleration in overall growth rates is noted in the latter years of the 1980s with the compound average annual 15 per cent growth rate target (equivalent to a doubling of numbers over five years) being practically achieved over the three-year interval, 1988–90. Mainland Europe (primarily Germany, France and Italy) displaced North America as the second largest source market for overseas visitors to Ireland. North American visitors exceeded those from mainland Europe in each year from 1982 to 1988, during which time they averaged 350,000 visitors annually; the dramatic upsurge in European visitors since then is illustrated by the 1995 data when 1.1 million visited Ireland. While various factors can explain the growth in tourism from mainland Europe – for example, cheaper access fares and more convenient charter air services, the turn away from sun destinations, environmentally attractive location and more information about Ireland – it seems also as if Ireland was suddenly 'discovered' by a sizeable number of Italian and Spanish tourists (almost quadrupled between 1986 and 1991) in addition to increased numbers of visitors from the more well-established German and French markets.[15] The paramilitary ceasefires in Northern Ireland in 1994 had a positive impact on all markets but particularly North America (up 52 per cent in 1993–95). Britain is still the principal market for overseas holidays in Ireland though its share declined from 58 to 54 per cent between 1985 and 1995; the North American share declined from 22 to 15 per cent while the mainland European share increased from 17 to 26 per cent.

Ethnic tourists account for a high proportion of overseas tourists (for example, 30 per cent of British visitors to Ireland were VFRs in 1995 compared with slightly less than one-sixth of North Americans). The strong ethnic dimension has helped the Irish tourism industry perform well, especially during years of adverse circumstances connected with the political situation on the island. The initial upturn in visitor numbers in the mid-1980s was due to an increase in VFRs from a buoyant British economy encouraged by cheaper air fares on cross-channel routes. By contrast, the expansion of tourists from mainland Europe was dominated by those in the 'pure' tourist category (50 per cent of the total) though stronger overall growth rates in business tourism were experienced in the 1990s (Table 5). The exceptional growth rates experienced during 1988–90 are shown separately in this table.

There was sustained growth in 'pure' tourist numbers during the period 1985–90, with particularly dramatic growth in the years 1988–90. This coincided with the strong growth in mainland European visitors to Ireland noted above. In terms of the relative importance of those coming to Ireland principally for holiday purposes, these increased from 39 per cent of overseas visitors in 1981 to 42 per cent in 1995, a small but important shift representing over 1.1 million additional visitors in 1995 compared with 1981.

Table 5: Average annual percentage changes in visitor numbers to Ireland by reason for journey, 1985–95

	1985–90	1988–90	1990–95
Business	11.8	7.6	8.6
'Pure' tourist	10.9	28.0	5.0
VFRs*	8.3	7.3	5.5
Other	8.4	–0.8	9.8
Total	9.9	14.4	6.4

*Visiting friends and relatives
Source: Derived from Central Statistics Office, *Tourism and Travel*, various years and Bord Fáilte survey data

Irish tourism expenditures

The revenue receipts from foreign visitors to Ireland showed a steady improvement in real terms from 1986 to 1991 (Table 6). The replacement of higher spending North Americans by lower spending mainland European visitors did not lead to overall revenue reductions because of the sustained growth in visitor numbers.

Table 6: Tourism revenue* from out-of-state visitors to Ireland, 1985–95

Year	£m†	Annual % change
1985	889.1	–
1986	812.3	–8.6
1987	883.3	+8.7
1988	1,005.8	+13.9
1989	1,147.6	+14.1
1990	1,278.4	+11.4
1991	1,320.1	+3.3
1992	1,297.3	–1.7
1993	1,426.7	+10.0
1994	1,527.1	+7.0
1995	1,669.0	+9.3

*Total expenditure (excluding international fares) plus passenger fare receipts of Irish carriers from visitors to Ireland.
†Constant 1995 prices.
Note: Includes expenditures by staying visitors from Northern Ireland.
Source: Ireland (1985); Central Statistics Office, *Tourism and Travel*, 1992; Bord Fáilte, *Tourism Facts*, 1995

From 1987 the real growth rate of more than 9 per cent was maintained until 1990. The setback in real revenue growth in 1991 and 1992 was reversed in 1993–95, during which time the Northern Ireland ceasefires reinforced the other favourable factors (short-break holidays, access costs, fashionable destination) contributing to the growth in tourism expenditures.[16]

The average real expenditure per tourist was relatively static during the years 1984–90; this may have been due in part to the quality of the tourism product which was available and the mix of tourists visiting Ireland. This outcome may also explain the preoccupation in policy circles with increasing numbers in order to boost revenue generation from overseas tourists.

The segmentation of the Irish international tourist market into the low-spending British and the relatively affluent non-British markets is also notable. As with other sectors (agriculture and manufacturing) of the Irish economy at earlier stages of development, the excessive dependence on the British market may operate to constrain the economic potential of the tourism sector. Britain accounted for 55 per cent of Irish overseas tourism revenue in 1970, a figure which had fallen to 48 per cent by 1980 and to 39 per cent by 1995; in the latter year 54 per cent of all overseas tourists were from Britain. Thus dependence on the British market has been falling, especially in revenue terms.

Should the trends towards higher volumes of low-spending tourists be sustained, ever-increasing numbers of tourists would be required to maintain a given real expenditure target. Apart from the environmental consequences, this highlights the need to develop marketing strategies which are targeted at higher spending segments of the market (such as those linked to particular sports, e.g. golf, angling, or special interest holidays, e.g. conferences), at segments which would generate longer stay holidays or at the second holiday market. The last two segments require continued investment in product development and improved/ cheaper access to the country.

Tourism's relative share of Irish GNP increased especially from 1987 onwards, with the contribution from foreign tourism rising from an estimated 3.6 to 4.8 per cent of total GNP. This is quite significant in the light of the rapid growth rates achieved in the economy overall in recent years. Domestic tourism contributed about 1.8 per cent in addition to this. Total employment dependent on tourism also expanded, rising from 52,300 in 1985 (4.8 per cent of total employment) to 95,100 in 1995 (7.7 per cent of the total). These estimates ignore the 30 per cent tax recycling which is included in the 'official' estimates for tourism employment dependent on foreign tourism revenues and carrier receipts. Export tourism accounted for between 5 and 6 per cent of total exports during the period 1985–95 (5.8 per cent in 1995) and slightly less than one-third of invisible exports over the ten years. However, as Deane and Henry (1996) point out, the net contribution to exports is much higher than the equivalent volume of manufactured exports because of the low import content of tourism exports.[17]

Summary of performance

The performance of Irish tourism since the mid-1980s has been impressive relative to the remarkably weak performance of the previous fifteen years.

The principal outcomes during the period 1985–95 were as follows:

- Irish tourism increased its overseas market share for the first sustained period in almost twenty years.
- Specific targets to double foreign tourist numbers over the five-year period 1987–92 were roughly on target for the first three years but fell short of the ultimate 1992 target by 26 per cent (i.e. over 1 million fewer overseas tourists than target).
- There was a significant shift to mainland European visitors towards the end of the 1980s while visitor numbers from North America remained relatively static, i.e. their numbers declined in relative terms; there was some recovery in North American visitor numbers in 1994 and 1995 (up 17 and 30 per cent respectively on the previous years).
- The 1995 revenue figure (foreign tourism revenue less carrier receipts) was over twice the level of ten years previously in real terms.
- Total tourism employment increased by 43,000 or 83 per cent over the period, which was 27 per cent of Ireland's net employment growth during that time.
- There was a significant improvement in the tourism product over the period, principally due to EU Structural Funds and the significant increase in investment in Irish tourism under the two Operational Programmes for Tourism, 1989–93 and 1994–99.

Explaining performance

The previous section of this essay has shown that by historical standards the recent performance of Irish tourism has been spectacular. What has received far less attention is the extent to which the outcomes can be clearly traced to government policy. This section explores those factors that have contributed to the success of Irish tourism and argues that it is vital that these factors be understood if the current boom in Irish tourism is to be sustained.

Empirical evidence for successful tourism destinations suggests that three characteristics are important: firstly, a competitive macroeconomic environment with low inflation and a stable exchange rate; secondly, frequent and adequately priced access transport; and thirdly, quality of the tourism product. The tourism product *inter alia* includes the quality of the environment, service quality and service delivery. By the early 1980s it was clear that the macroeconomic environment was poor, Ireland was perceived as a high-cost destination and generally the tourism product was rather jaded though the environment was perceived as being 'clean and unspoilt'. Most importantly, access transport was inadequate and extremely expensive. It was against this background that the sector began to develop in the mid-1980s.

Of immense importance to the development of the sector was the liberalisation of air access between Britain and Ireland that began in 1986. As previously noted, the entrance of an independent airline to the Dublin–London route broke the duopoly of Aer Lingus and British Airways and the increased competition led to a significant reduction in fares and a massive increase in traffic on the route. An additional benefit of the reduction of air fares was a reduction of sea access fares between Ireland and Britain. Another factor of note was the buoyancy of the British labour market in the late 1980s which attracted many young and well-educated Irish graduates. The fusion of cheap air fares and well-paid Irish emigrants provided the impetus to the significant growth in Irish–British traffic that initiated the remarkable and sustained Irish tourism growth. In relation to macroeconomic matters the policy of fiscal retrenchment that began in 1987 significantly improved the national finances and also helped tourism by reducing inflation. Thus, on two fundamental characteristics related to tourism performance it is correct to argue that government policies played a significant role in the turnaround that began in 1986.

On the third issue of product quality the evidence is far from clear. While it is accepted that the Operational Programmes with an investment of approximately £1 billion from 1989 to 1999 will undoubtedly improve the overall product it is not possible to demonstrate any strong link between the first programme and the performance to 1993. This arises for three reasons:

- Since the majority of the investment outcomes resulting from the first programme were not in place until the early 1990s, it is hard to see how these investments could have affected industry performance.

- An analysis of the tourism data shows that the tourism numbers from Britain and mainland Europe began to grow significantly before any investment had occurred.
- Our analysis has already shown that the improved outcomes from Europe could not be explained as a result of strategic marketing. It should be stressed that while expenditure growth during the period of the first programme was 102 per cent of target, the actual number of visitors was 1.17 million below target, which suggests very limited understanding of the key market variables (numbers and average spend). An understanding of these issues is a prerequisite to an effective strategic marketing initiative.

Thus on the fundamental issue of explaining the growth of tourism from Europe and other overseas markets the official explanation, at least to 1993, is incomplete. Growth in tourism since 1993 will no doubt have been helped by the IRA ceasefire (until its termination in February 1996), the product improvements in the first programme and the increased expenditures on overseas marketing; there is however insufficient evidence on direct causality.[18]

What is most likely lacking in the official explanation are exogenous factors that have been driving tourism growth. Tourism like any other sector of the economy is subject to change, as much from outside as from inside forces. An amalgam of factors that are difficult to quantify can have a significant impact on lifestyle preferences and holiday habits. The tourism market is increasingly comprised of niche tastes and requirements. In this regard the tourism industry has seen the rise and decline of many tourism destinations in recent years. Since the mid-1980s one driving force in the industry has been the environment with many tourists wishing to travel to destinations where environmental quality is deemed superior to that of their own country. Ireland, more by accident than design, possesses an excellent physical environment and the easy pace of life and the friendliness of the Irish people are prime tourism assets, much desired by international visitors but often overlooked by policy-makers. Ironically, Ireland's failure to industrialise may now be proving to be a major tourism asset. In addition to the environment, it is increasingly evident that the renaissance of Irish culture, music and literature, which have become prevalent in the international media in recent years, is playing a significant role in the tourism performance. While the Operational Programmes for Tourism can build on these assets by helping to provide better facilities and quality of service it should be recognised that the environment and the 'friendliness of people' are prime assets that can very quickly be destroyed.

Failure to fully understand all the factors that have driven tourism growth could lead to policies that destroy the assets that are so important for sustainable tourism development.

Issues for the future development of Irish tourism

Tourism is a dynamic industry. Policy-makers and planners alike must forever be cognisant of the changing international market trends and respond effectively to them. The future development of Irish tourism requires appropriate supply-side measures to ensure that tourists enjoy a good quality product and service, a clean and unspoilt environment, and reasonable access transport options both to the country and within it. It is critical also that a more balanced spread of tourists throughout the year and throughout the country be achieved. International marketing strategies should optimise the supply of tourists to the island; this requires genuine co-operation between the tourism authorities in Northern Ireland and the Republic. The public sector has had a dominant investment role in Irish tourism in recent years but it is not clear that appropriate investment appraisal methods have been used in many projects, thus leading to less than optimal use of the resources available; besides, this public sector dominance has served to continue the dependency role of the private sector in Irish tourism.

The current internationally competitive tourism market requires that Ireland continue to develop quality tourism facilities matched with appropriate service delivery. Significant investment has been expended in the past decade on developing the human resource capacities of those entering the industry though the emphasis on the quantity throughput of trainees has not always been matched by evaluations of the impact on overall service delivery. While the tourism sector of the future will increasingly require well-educated, linguistically capable personnel, the current pay and conditions in the industry in Ireland are not conducive to attracting this workforce. This is an issue which the industry itself must address collectively.

The environment is a crucial component of the Irish tourism product and is much lauded but often neglected by policy-makers. There is increasing evidence that certain parts of the country suffer environmental degradation associated with tourism, and the balance between tourism and non-tourism land uses can also be a delicate one. By the time an environment becomes a visible problem, it is probably too late to do anything effective about it – hence the need to take a long-term perspective on its conservation. A coherent strategy needs to be developed which would focus on management techniques, planning controls and market-based solutions if the current emergent problems are not to be exacerbated in the years ahead.

Appropriately priced, convenient and frequent access transport is a necessity for a peripheral island tourism destination. Air access and frequency from mainland Europe and the west coast of the United States continue to constrain the development of Irish tourism. Further moves towards greater liberalisation of air fares within the EU and the removal of remaining artificial barriers to access (as still pertain on US–Ireland routes) should enlarge the potential pool of tourists to Ireland. Continued investment in primary road networks within Ireland, especially to the less developed western regions, is required to facilitate a more even geographical spread of tourists when they visit.

The need to ensure a more even spread of tourists throughout the year has not stimulated any effective policy measures to ensure this desired outcome. With 30 per cent of arrivals in the peak July–August period, the negative effects of poor plant utilisation for many months of the year (and consequent poor return on investment) together with the deleterious effects of congestion in the peak months (environmental pressures and negative tourism experiences) is not a sustainable combination in the long term. The doubling of tourism numbers since 1987 means that peak season pressures are considerably worse than they were ten years ago. The required policy responses include targeted marketing for shoulder (April–May, September–October) and off-season (November–March) niche tourist groups, staggering of domestic school and work holidays, and an overall co-ordinated supply-side delivery of products.

Considerable public funds continue to be allocated to support the promotion of Ireland to overseas markets as an attractive tourism destination with an almost 'blind faith' in the effectiveness of these promotional efforts (e.g. the Overseas Tourism Marketing Initiative and the 'Ireland Brand' campaign). But Ireland is a small player internationally and the entire promotional budget must be examined realistically in the context of what can be achieved compared with the advertising spend of, for example, some individual airlines. As a service industry, tourism success is critically dependent on 'word of mouth' as a promotional vehicle and this relies on three factors – price competitiveness, quality of product and appropriately priced and adequate access transport. If these factors are in place the responsibility of the national tourism organisation, Bord Fáilte, is more appropriately viewed as a provider of good information for those who are considering a visit to Ireland. Furthermore, the failure to monitor the relationship between promotional campaigns and returns needs to be addressed as a matter of priority.

North–South co-operation is a critical component of overseas promotional measures and other initiatives to develop tourism on the island. Notwithstanding the successes with such measures as the INTERREG programme and the International Fund for Ireland, there still remains a 'co-operation deficit' (Teague, 1993) on economic matters. Much could be learned from the Italian model of 'co-operative competition' which could contribute significantly to progress on tourism on the island. In this model, co-operative initiatives are adopted to increase market share (of European and world tourism) and, once that is established, the parties compete vigorously. Significant benefits could be gained from pooling resources in such fields as tourism education and training, product development, and research and information services in addition to the more obvious market promotion measures.

Tourism has traditionally been seen as a sector which could assist the regional distribution of incomes and employment in Ireland. A clear east–west divide has opened up since 1981 with a less than proportionate share of expenditure growth accruing to western regions, already lagging behind in average income levels. The lack of product innovations to attract the changing visitor profiles and the attractiveness of Dublin as a European city destination explain some of this decline. It is ironic that many of the earlier innovations in Irish tourism were developed in western rural regions, notably the mid-west in the 1960s, with a strong public sector involvement. However, in recent years many tourism areas and enterprises have been characterised by an absence of an innovating approach. Given the greater dependency culture associated with less developed regions of the country, this deficiency may both explain the relatively poor performance of the western regions and, more importantly, augur poorly for the future development of tourism in these regions. Furthermore the regional tourism organisations have been undermined by the range of subregional bodies with a tourism remit (county enterprise boards, county tourism committees, LEADER groups) and this has not been very helpful to the development of a coherent regional strategy. Such a strategy should build on the outstanding natural advantages of rural regions, exploit the opportunity to develop tourism traffic through regional airports, and identify and design imaginative product innovations for the twenty-first century.

A final issue which is critical to the future development of Irish tourism is the respective future roles of the private and public sectors. Significant public sector subventions to the tourism sector from the 1950s created a dependency culture whereby the private sector seemed unwilling to undertake tourism investment in the absence of public sector support. The EU Structural Funds bonanza since 1989 has given rise to further unprecedented levels of support which are likely to be scaled down considerably post-1999. The dependence on public sector funding is exacerbated by an inherent supply-side approach to tourism investment with a concomitant lack of innovation in recent years. Mature tourism industries are characterised by a more dominant role for the private sector with the role for the public sector being confined to clear cases of market failure. The reorganisation and refocusing of Bord Fáilte in recent years was predicated on the assumption that the industry is (or should be) in this mature phase. The transition will be difficult as the current very effective energies directed towards various forms of rent-seeking behaviour, through political and institutional lobbying activities, will need to be directed instead towards building a more self-reliant, market-focused and innovative tourism sector.

Conclusion

This essay has shown that Irish tourism, relatively neglected by policy-makers for years, suddenly received considerable attention in the mid-1980s. The failure of other sectors of the economy and the availability of significant investment funds from the EU provided the catalyst for a focus on tourism. In tandem with government emphasis, there has been a sudden turnaround in the performance of the sector. The analysis in this essay has shown that government decisions on access transport and in relation to fiscal prudence have played no small part in the turnaround. It has also been shown that the significant investment of funds through the Operational Programmes for Tourism may lead to stronger performance in the future, though the current assumption by government that the first programme was the catalyst for much of the recent improvement in tourism performance seems at best to be premature. A number of favourable exogenous factors including the general renaissance of international interest in Irish culture and the existence of a relatively clean environment would appear to have been strong factors in the recent resurgence of tourism rather than any strategic action of the Operational Programme. Issues which are crucial to the long-term development of Irish tourism have been identified; these need to be addressed sooner rather than later. With more tourists visiting Ireland than the resident population (which means that questions of carrying capacity will soon emerge) and growth rates likely to slow down to more manageable levels, the time is ripe for proactive long-term strategic planning of the industry which will emphasise sustainability in the broadest sense.

NOTES

1. See Ireland (1958 and 1964).
2. The external economic environment was important to the out-turns achieved though the strong belief among policy-makers, supported by their political masters of the time, was the paramount importance of the programme in the achievement (and sometimes exceeding) of the stated targets.
3. These interdependencies are discussed in some detail in Deegan and Dineen (1997), and a recent report by the Northern Ireland Economic Council (1997) also recognised the similarities in the nature of and demand for the tourism product in both parts of Ireland.
4. In the sense that these tourists generate foreign currency earnings for the host destination. Perhaps with the advent of the new European currency, the euro, this criterion of internationalism may need revision within the European Union.
5. It has been argued that the slow-down in Irish tourism growth began in the late 1960s but had been masked for a number of years by the imposition of exchange controls on British tourists, which restricted the amount of British currency they could take outside the 'sterling area'. This had the effect of diverting more tourists from this source market to Ireland from 1967 to 1969 in line with the substitution effects within international tourism (Britons diverting from non-sterling to sterling area countries outside the UK) and between domestic and international tourism (Britons diverting to domestic holidays in the UK). For further discussion of the impact of these restrictions see O'Hagan (1972), Institut du Transport Aerien (1970) and Oliver (1971).
6. See NESC (1980, p. 45) for comparative data on this aspect of international tourism; the point in the text refers to the inflation rates in these countries and Ireland and not to the absolute levels of prices. Ireland was still regarded as a relatively cheap destination though this advantage was being eroded. In economic terms it had the hallmarks of an 'inferior' good where lower incomes induced by the recession encouraged British visitors to substitute the relatively cheaper holiday in Ireland (including access costs) for more expensive destinations elsewhere.
7. See Kennedy and Dowling (1975); excluding foreign passenger receipts of Irish sea and air carriers, the tourism and travel share of total exports of goods and services ranged from 11.5 per cent in 1970 to 5.9 per cent in 1976.
8. Though tourism may decline in relative importance as an economy grows (as Ireland's did during the 1970s) the declining relative importance of the tourism sector noted here was a combination of a poorly performing sector and a growing economy. Multiplier values relate the initial tourism expenditures to the total final incomes generated in the economy by these expenditures.
9. Expenditure on domestic tourism can be assumed to be diverted from other domestic leisure or recreation spending (thus displacing other forms of domestic expenditure); alternatively, it could be a diversion from holidays abroad or from expenditure on other imports – in such cases, this expenditure represents import substitution and is equivalent in impact to export tourism.

10. It was not until the early 1990s that some consensus emerged on the estimates, based on Henry's input–output analysis (Deane and Henry, 1993 and 1996; Henry, 1996). Tax recycling (whereby it is assumed that taxation raised from tourists is re-spent by government, thus generating additional income and employment) of 30 per cent of the taxes generated from overseas revenues is included in the 'agreed' estimates though there is no clearly defined economic rationale for this.
11. See Deegan and Dineen (1997), Table 4.10.
12. The ERDF, the European Social Fund (ESF) and the guidance section of the European Commission's Agricultural Fund (EAGGF) are the three primary Structural Funds.
13. Subsequent detail provided in government documents changed the base year to 1988 which provided a more favourable outcome.
14. We are indebted to Paul Appleby, Department of Tourism and Trade, for providing this figure and the estimates of expenditure based thereon.
15. The impact of special high-profile events may have an important though indeterminate influence on tourism destination decisions, e.g. European and World Cup finals in Germany (1988) and Italy (1990), and successive Eurovision song contest finals hosted in Ireland.
16. For a further discussion on these factors see ITIC (1996).
17. For a more detailed discussion of the economic impact of tourism in Ireland during this period, see Deegan and Dineen (1997), Chapter 4.
18. The general lack of research on the industry is reflected in limited allocations under the Operational Programmes for technical assistance, and the nature of the latter has more to do with the accountability requirements of the programmes and ensuring full draw-down of funds than a better understanding of the forces affecting the growth and development of the industry.

REFERENCES

Barrett, S. D. (1991). *Transport Policy in Ireland*, Dublin: Gill & Macmillan

Bord Fáilte (1988). *Strategy for Growth*, Dublin: Bord Fáilte

Deane, B. M. and E. W. Henry (1993). 'The Economic Impact of Tourism', *Irish Banking Review*, Winter, pp. 35–47

Deane, B. M. and E. W. Henry (1996). *The Economic Impact of Tourism*, Dublin: Bord Fáilte

Deegan, J. and D. A. Dineen (1997). *Tourism Policy and Performance: The Irish Experience*, London: International Thomson Publishing

Fitzpatrick, J. (1961). 'The Role of the ITA in Tourist Development', *Administration*, Vol. 9, No. 3, pp. 236–7

Henry, E. W. (1996). *Estimating Irish 1995 GNP and Employment Multipliers by Input–Output Modelling*, Dublin: Bord Fáilte

Institut du Transport Aerien (1970). 'The Effects of Currency Restrictions on British Travel Abroad', *Institut du Transport Aerien Magazine*, Vol. 15, pp. 261–6

Ireland (1958). *First Programme for Economic Expansion*, Dublin: Stationery Office

Ireland (1964). *Second Programme for Economic Expansion*, Dublin: Stationery Office

Ireland (1985). *White Paper on Tourism Policy*, Dublin: Stationery Office

Ireland (1987). *Programme for National Recovery*, Dublin: Stationery Office

Ireland (1994). *Operational Programme for Tourism, 1994–9*, Dublin: Stationery Office

ITIC (Irish Tourist Industry Confederation) (1996). *Regional Distribution of Tourism in Ireland: Responding to Changing Market Needs*, Report by Tourism and Leisure Partners, Dublin, April

Kennedy, K. A. and B. R. Dowling (1975). *Economic Growth in Ireland: The Experience since 1947*, Dublin: Gill & Macmillan in association with the Economic and Social Research Institute

Lynch, P. (1969). 'The Irish Economy since the War, 1946–51', in K. Nowlan and T. Williams (eds.), *Ireland in the War Years and After 1939–51*, Dublin: Gill & Macmillan

NESC (National Economic and Social Council) (1980). *Tourism Policy*, Report No. 52, Dublin: Stationery Office

Northern Ireland Economic Council (1997). *Rising to the Challenge: The Future of Tourism in Northern Ireland*, Report 121, Belfast: Northern Ireland Economic Council

O'Hagan, J. (1972). 'Export and Import Visitor Trends and Determinants in Ireland', *Journal of the Statistical and Social Inquiry Society of Ireland*, XXII (V), pp. 17–28

Oliver, F. R. (1971). 'The Effectiveness of the UK Travel Allowance', *Applied Economics*, Vol. 3, No. 3, pp. 219–26

Pearce, D. G. (1992). 'Tourism and the European Regional Development Fund: The First Fourteen Years', *Journal of Travel Research*, Vol. 30, No. 3 (Winter), pp. 44–51

Share, B. (1992). *Shannon Departures: A Study in Regional Initiatives*, Dublin: Gill & Macmillan

Teague, P. (ed.) (1993). *The Economy of Northern Ireland: Perspectives for Structural Change*, London: Lawrence and Wishart

Part IV

Other Policy Areas

=16=

The Irish Language

PROINSIAS MAC CANA

When a language dies, a possible world dies with it. There is here no survival of the fittest. Even where it is spoken by a handful, by the harried remnants of destroyed communities, a language contains within itself the boundless potential of discovery, of re-compositions of reality, of articulate dreams, which are known to us as myths, as poetry, as metaphysical conjecture and the discourse of the law. Inherent in After Babel *is the accelerating disappearance of languages across our earth, the detergent sovereignty of so-called major languages whose dynamic efficacy springs from the planetary spread of mass-marketing, technocracy, and the media.*

George Steiner, *After Babel*

ONE thing I have in common with Dr T. K. Whitaker is that we both learned Irish, more specifically the spoken Irish of the Gaeltacht, in the same neighbourhood, the little peninsula of Rinn na Feirste that lies tucked away between Dungloe and Gaoth Dobhair in the Rosses of west Donegal. When I began to frequent Rinn na Feirste a decade or more after Dr Whitaker it was still renowned elsewhere in Donegal and further afield for the quality and vigour of its Irish and for the remarkable gallery of gifted storytellers, *seanchaithe* and traditional singers who both sustained and reflected its extraordinary linguistic heritage. We were both fortunate enough to experience in generous measure the linguistic abundance, clarity and inherent sense of style of this oral tradition which had been touched but not yet grievously undermined by the impact of the neo-commercial age. For Ken Whitaker it was clearly an experience which became an essential part of his own cultural formation and one which left him with a lifelong regard and affection for the Irish language in all its various phases and mani-festations. It was not by accident that he came to preside for many years over the affairs of Comhairle Bhéaloideas Éireann (The Irish Folklore Council) with the same care and dedication as he has given to all his other manifold public service and voluntary commitments.

That he and so many others over the years should have visited and frequently revisited one or other of the Gaeltacht areas in search of the living language in all its fullness is in itself something of a phenomenon with few if any close parallels elsewhere in the world, and it is only explicable in the broader context of the progressive exploration and reassertion of cultural identity and autonomy which took place in Ireland in the course of the last two centuries and particularly in the last decades of the nineteenth century. So far as language and literature are concerned this process was influenced in its early stages by the eighteenth-century Romantic movement and also, and perhaps more profoundly, by the increasing interest in Irish antiquities among members of the ascendancy class, an interest clearly reflected for example in the proceedings of the Royal Irish Academy and in the rich treasury of artefacts and manuscripts which it accumulated by purchase or by presentation from the late eighteenth century onwards. This progress was marked by the establishment of several societies to promote the study and publication of Irish literature: the Gaelic Society in 1807, the Iberno-Celtic Society in 1818, the Irish Archaeological and Celtic Society in 1840 and the Ossianic Society in 1853 – all of them helping to prepare the ground for a new era of scientific enquiry into language, literature, history and institutions. In 1853 the publication of the German philologist Johann Kasper Zeuss's *Grammatica Celtica* provided an exciting and exacting model for future scholarly work on medieval Irish and at the same time established the importance of Irish within comparative studies in general and Indo-European studies in particular, thereby foreshadowing the immense international interest and participation in Irish and Celtic studies which have continued to this day. The second half of the century in the wake of the Great Famine saw a growing consciousness of the decline of Irish as a spoken vernacular and a correspondingly increased emphasis on the need for conservative action. Several organisations were formed towards that end, culminating in the establishment of the Gaelic League in 1893 and the launch of the long campaign to stabilise and restore the position of the language. But the primary motivation remained largely cultural and literary and essentially retrospective.

It is true that the great majority of the multitude of people who were drawn in one way or another within the ambit of the language movement would have had only a vaguely romantic notion of the Irish literary tradition, yet it is inconceivable that the movement would ever have come about without this cultural validation. In striving to restore and extend the use of the modern language enthusiasts believed that they were also reaffirming the lines of continuity extending back to the integral tradition of medieval and ancient Ireland. It was more than mere chance that the founding fathers of the Gaelic League included Douglas Hyde who was to publish some years later (in 1899) his *Literary History of Ireland from Earliest Times to the Present Day* and Eoin MacNeill, who was, some would hold, the most gifted of all scholarly interpreters of early Irish history and tradition and who, perhaps more than any other, provided the revival movement with its philosophical motivation. This exercise in cultural retrospection and self-knowledge was of course fully justifiable for its own sake, but in the uncertain final years of the nineteenth century it also had the considerable therapeutic effect of recalling an age when an independent Ireland with its own language and institutions cut a highly respectable figure among the nations of Europe.

Instead of the contemporary experience of a language which had been progressively degraded and marginalised over the preceding two or three centuries by its association with poverty, social inferiority and educational deprivation the Irish people were offered the image of an earlier period when Irish had flourished as a language of high social prestige and a vehicle for extraordinary artistic achievement. In the fifth and sixth centuries it had learned to coexist with the Christian Church and with the rich and diverse resources of the Latin language, and in the process, through the good offices of scholars in the newly founded monasteries, it also became a written language and an effective and flexible instrument for the redaction of native traditional learning as well as for the new cultural synthesis which was to develop within the monastic schools. Even before the coming of Christianity Ireland had been more or less unique among European nations in having a well-organised, self-perpetuating learned class who conserved and controlled the whole body of professional tradition – historical, juridical, mythical, ritual – on which social order and custom were founded, and who by virtue of the sacred origins of their office enjoyed an authority equivalent and complementary to that of the kings whose patronage ensured them a comfortable living. Now, as the result of a quite remarkable development, a flexible *modus vivendi* came about by the end of the sixth century between this learned sodality and the growing fraternity of monastic *literati*, facilitated no doubt by the fact that both would have drawn their membership largely from the same upper stratum of society, and probably in some instances from the same households. Their combination released a fresh creative energy that expressed itself in manifold ways – endless metrical innovation, lyrical invention, updating of myth and hero tale, and so on – and which sustained much of its original momentum throughout the eighth and ninth centuries and left as its legacy the earliest and richest corpus of written literature outside of Greek and Latin. For MacNeill this was Ireland's Golden Age, 'the crowning glory and the greatest pride of our nation', when the Irish, confident in their own culture, became in his by now somewhat time-worn phrase 'the schoolmasters of Europe'.[1]

During the next phase, from approximately the early tenth to the late twelfth century, there was no slackening in literary and learned activity nor any quenching of the creative imagination, but there is evidence of a growing emphasis on the compilation and recasting of extant materials, and it was during this period that most of the great narrative and didactic texts were redacted in the form in which we know them. It was also during this phase, in the eleventh and twelfth centuries, that two things occurred which in their different ways were to have fateful, and in the long term potentially fatal, consequences for the Irish language and its culture. These were of course the reform of the Irish Church and the Norman invasion and settlement. As a result of the restructuring of the Church and the introduction of continental orders the older monasteries which had cradled the fruitful symbiosis of pagan and Christian learning were now rendered obsolete and their learned functions and personnel obliged to find themselves a new *foyer*. The promotion and recording of vernacular learning passed into the charge of certain families who specialised in one or other of its several constituent disciplines – poetry, history, law – handing on their professional skills by hereditary succession. New prose and verse continued to be produced in considerable abundance and variety during these post-Norman centuries, but all the rest has tended to be overshadowed, rather unjustly it may be said, by the remarkable phenomenon that goes by the name of 'bardic poetry'. Between the beginning of the thirteenth century and the middle of the seventeenth a huge volume of highly sophisticated verse was composed by professional poets, or *filidh*, for the noble patrons who sustained them. The schooled poets who composed these poems of eulogy, elegy, counsel or complaint observed a highly detailed and prescriptive grammar of language and metrics, and so rigorously did they adhere to this code that, as has often been pointed out, it is virtually impossible to decide from style and language alone whether a poem was composed in the thirteenth or the sixteenth century or whether in Munster, Ulster or Gaelic Scotland. Whatever it may have lacked in artistic innovation, this was a poetry, and a language, of classical precision and consistency.

Meanwhile the historical process triggered by the Anglo-Norman settlement proceeded inexorably if unevenly. The fortunes of the Irish language ebbed and flowed with the fortunes of war and colonisation and even entered on one of their most prosperous phases in the fifteenth century, but the Elizabethan wars and plantations in the sixteenth century and the Cromwellian conquest in the seventeenth finally destroyed the social and political system which had sustained the complex professional culture articulated through the Irish language. Despite the heroic endeavours of talented groups and individuals such as the Franciscans of the Louvain school the intellectual and artistic dimension of vernacular culture was thrown upon its own slender resources and the remarkable linguistic unity which had characterised Irish literature since the beginning of its written history was now utterly fractured so that Irish poets and poetry, for example, were no longer viewed automatically in a national context but defined first and foremost in terms of their regional and dialectal affiliations. Yet paradoxically, however catastrophic the impact of this disintegration on the language as a whole, it had the fortuitous effect of ensuring that the spoken Irish to which MacNeill and Hyde and their colleagues dedicated their efforts towards the end of the nineteenth century was an exceptionally rich and nuanced medium of expression. Those elements of the literary tradition which survived the virtual eclipse of the native system of schools and patronage in the seventeenth century did so by being assimilated into the general body of popular culture and in doing so gave it a depth and sense of style which it might otherwise have lacked. According to Kenneth Jackson this was one of the principal factors why folk tradition in Irish and Scottish Gaelic was 'practically unique in the world' for its quality and its large literary content,[2] and since that tradition depended mainly on the spoken word and popular interest for its dissemination – through songs and poems and storytelling – its influence permeated the general spoken language and engendered in its speakers an inherent feeling for idiom and style and the resonance of a witty well-turned phrase (*deisbhéalaí*), those same qualities which at a later date were to make such a deep impression on scholars like Robin Flower and writers like J. M. Synge.

Once the traditional Irish-speaking ruling class had been displaced and dispersed it was perhaps inevitable that the future of the language would be one of gradual contraction and decay unless and until a new enlightened leadership should arise with the influence and the will to reverse the cultural decline while the language was still numerically strong in the land. In the event the leaders who did appear had other priorities which they perceived to be more pressing in the circumstances of the time. However they may have differed in the methods they chose to redress the social and political wrongs which weighed upon the country, they all assumed that this could only be done by adopting the language of the colonising power, particularly since their arguments and propaganda had to be directed increasingly towards Great Britain and the United States. Given the populist nature of their campaigning at home the effect of their choice was profound: as the late Maureen Wall observed, 'perhaps one of the greatest forces of all which hastened the displacement of Irish by English, and which prevented any genuine practical effort to preserve the language, was the involvement of the people as a whole in Irish politics from the end of the eighteenth century on'.[3] For equally sound and sensible reasons the Catholic Church opted for English in higher education when it became legal to establish Catholic colleges and thereby determined the linguistic and cultural orientation of both clergy and middle class: with the foundation of St Patrick's College, Maynooth in 1795, 'English became the dominant language in it and in effect was henceforth – apart from Latin – the official language of the catholic church in Ireland'.[4] The combined result of these changes was to associate the Irish language with poverty and illiteracy and to foster the belief that the best way to escape both conditions was to learn English. In such circumstances the drift from Irish was inevitable and the effect of the Great Famine when it came together with the rising flow of emigration was to render it virtually irreversible without a national change of purpose and governance of heroic proportions.

And indeed the sustained surge of enthusiasm which followed the founding of the Gaelic League was in its own way heroic with its countless thousands of people throughout the land giving freely of their time and energy to teaching and learning the language and seeking to recover their cultural origins. This enthusiasm acquired a sharper edge and clearer focus from its increasing association and identification with the political campaign for national independence. Something of it even survived the bitter disillusion of the Civil War and inspired the government of the Free State to adopt a programme of measures designed to restore the language. That it did not achieve its ambitious goal is self-evident (though the true measure of what it did achieve is often underestimated), and the question may be asked, and is often asked, why not?

Rather than attempt a comprehensive answer – considerations of space preclude it and some of the reasons are obvious in any case and most have been discussed from time to time by more closely informed commentators – I shall merely offer a few somewhat impressionistic observations based on a combination of personal experience and documentary evidence. One factor that has been noted by others is the expectation among language enthusiasts – heightened by the close conjunction between language and political nationalism – that with the advent of a native government they could rest on their oars, their cause assured. The inevitable result was a relaxation of voluntary effort and the beginnings of disillusionment as the Civil War took its toll and sectional

and local politics got to work on their own priorities; a dramatic index
of the change was the decline in the number of Gaelic League branches
from 819 in 1922 to 139 in 1924.[5] Even in less unpromising circumstances
than obtained in Ireland independence is not the cultural panacea it
sometimes appears in prospect: national aspirations become state
obligations and the transition is often difficult. In 1962 Saunders Lewis,
the most distinguished figure in the history of modern Welsh literature,
chose to end a remarkable BBC radio lecture, a lecture which effected a
profound shift in popular attitudes towards the Welsh language, with the
following passage:

> In my opinion, if any kind of self-government for Wales were obtained before
> the Welsh language was acknowledged and used as an official language in
> local authority and state administration in the Welsh-speaking parts of the
> country, then the language would never achieve official status at all, and its
> demise would be quicker than it will be under English rule.[6]

This declaration was all the more significant coming from one who was
first president of the Welsh Nationalist Party (subsequently Plaid Cymru)
and a firm believer in autonomy for Wales. The circumstances to which
he refers were of course different in some important respects from those
obtaining in Ireland, but his reasoning would have been relevant, *a
fortiori* one might say, to the Irish situation. It could hardly be claimed,
for example, that Irish county councils whose jurisdiction includes
Gaeltacht areas have distinguished themselves over the years by their
concern for the well-being of the Irish language.

The gravity of the task facing the Free State government can be
illustrated by continuing the comparison with Wales. According to the
census of 1891 only 3.5 per cent of the age group under ten years, that is
30,785 individuals, were returned as Irish speakers, from which we can
deduce fairly accurately the strength of the adult community of
traditional Irish speakers at the inception of the Irish Free State in 1922.[7]
By contrast if Wales had become self-governing about the same time
something between a third and a half of its population would have been
Welsh-speaking.[8] The implications of this are profound and far-reaching.
For one thing the linguistic base was already dangerously low, and native
speakers of Irish were extremely thin on the ground in the population at
large, among politicians, and among the various professional and
administrative classes whose function it was to formulate and execute
public policy on matters concerned with or having a bearing upon the
language (which in the modern environment of state intervention means
practically every aspect of life). This disparity is one reason, though not
the only one, why when I was living in Wales in the fifties, well before

Welsh was accorded the official status mentioned by Saunders Lewis, one could walk into a bank, police station, state agency or business house in large areas of the country with a reasonable expectation of transacting one's business through Welsh, whereas in Ireland, where the national language has long enjoyed nominal priority, officials representing central and local government generally tended to use English even in the Gaeltacht, where they have always been a very effective force for the marginalisation, spatial and functional, of the Irish language.

One consequence of the relative paucity of native or indeed fluent speakers of Irish among politicians and administrators was that they had little awareness of the practical realities of a functioning bilingualism and therefore no real comprehension of the scale and complexity of the undertaking to which they were committed. Popular sentiment towards the language had been transformed since the early nineteenth century and politicians constantly affirmed their support for it, but when the chips were down they were as a body unable or unwilling to deviate essentially from Daniel O'Connell's decision that English was to be the language of Irish politics. Unlike the situation in Wales where the sense of nationality was intimately linked to the national language and its associated culture, and hardly at all to the idea of political autonomy, in Ireland the growth of political nationalism had in fact undermined the position of the language; even the Gaelic League, which had begun as a cultural, non-political movement, was drained of much of its vigour and clarity of purpose by the very success of the political campaign which it had done so much to motivate. In his fine study of the literature of the Irish revival until 1921 Philip O'Leary documents how the confident expectation among members of the Gaelic League that the future of Irish would be made secure under a native government was confounded by the news of the signing of the Anglo-Irish Treaty and all that followed from it. The sentence with which he closes his long history says all: 'The four glorious decades of the Gaelic Revival were at an end.'[9]

Whether the new state could possibly have measured up to such high expectations is open to question. In the event there is little evidence of a coherent language policy with phased, co-ordinated objectives, and many of the government's initiatives would appear to have been dictated by well-intentioned expediency with little attempt to assess their actual as opposed to their assumed results. Nothing perhaps epitomises the government's predicament better than the contentious topic of 'compulsory Irish'. Since the education system had played a considerable role in anglicising the country, it was not unnaturally assumed that it could also be instrumental in undoing that process, and to that end certain language requirements were made obligatory in education as well as in the public service. Unfortunately little thought was given to reinforcing the work of the schools within the wider social context. Whereas the imposition of English through education had been backed by the combined pressures of politics, Church and the various instruments of the state, now it was left to the schools to save the language with little active support and often a good deal of hindrance from all three sources. While the teaching of other subjects through Irish was actively promoted the provision of suitable textbooks was woefully inadequate to the task. In Gaeltacht areas children were often obliged to attend English-language schools in mixed catchment areas. I recall that when free school transport was introduced in the late 1960s it was officially arranged that the children of one neighbourhood in the Donegal Gaeltacht would be carried by bus to the secondary school in a nearby English-speaking town. Fortunately this grave threat to the survival of the existing Gaeltacht school was averted at the eleventh hour by the prudent and resolute response of the local parents' representatives – and, be it said, by the willing co-operation of Department of Education officials when the case was firmly and effectively presented to them. What is, however, most significant about this instance is the reason for the original decision. When I pointed out to an official in the department that the neighbouring town was English-speaking his response was yes but that it was located within the Gaeltacht by the maps of Gaeltacht boundaries from which they worked. Just one of the innumerable instances of form prevailing over fact in the government's dealings with Irish. Not that form itself was always secure. When the late John Kelly, who was nothing if not logical, persistently inveighed against the sheer sloppiness that litters our signposts with barbarous misspellings of Gaelic placenames, he saw that it was indicative of a national malaise that went much deeper than forms on road signs or even than the Irish language. He also saw that authorities who would not ensure correct forms on road signs (as is done for example in Wales) were unlikely to accomplish the much more complex task of formulating and executing a comprehensive and effective language policy.

When in 1973–74 the government finally abolished the rule making the award of the Intermediate or Leaving Certificate conditional on the candidate obtaining a pass in Irish and also abandoned the obligatory qualification for entry to most public-sector appointments, this marked a decisive stage in the official retreat from earlier language policy. The emollient publicity that accompanied the change – it would release a wave of love and enthusiasm for the language which would ensure its increase – was a fair reflection of the temporising which coloured so much of state policy towards Irish. The truth is of course that no minority language can survive in direct competition with a major world language without some measure of what Americans might term 'affirmative action', if only partly to redress the stark imbalance of social pressures; and the irony is that 'compulsory Irish', for all the crudeness and inadequacies of its application, did create a widespread level of competence in the language and that that competence has contracted noticeably in the intervening twenty-odd years. Soundings of public opinion have consistently shown that a substantial majority of the Irish people are in favour of Irish, but this does not appear to have any material effect on the decline of the language. The uncomfortable reality is that goodwill does not normally translate into linguistic fluency except by dint of a measure of toil and determination that is beyond most ordinary individuals or else by virtue of constant environmental pressure and stimulus, and, for obvious but different reasons, neither has been an active factor in regard to Irish. Yet the curious fallacy that the ordinary individual could acquire mastery of a language by a sheer act of the will was shared equally by benevolent political leaders who continually exhorted the Irish people to speak their own language and by the inveterate opponents of Irish who insisted that the Irish people had already 'voted with their tongues' on this issue.

It could be said of these and other inadequacies of state policy and its implementation that they were crucial but not of themselves fatal. What was potentially fatal, however, was the continuing reduction of the area and population of the Gaeltacht. Beset as they were by numerous other emergencies succeeding governments lacked the experience and expertise and perhaps the resources to resolve a problem compounded of a variety of equally intractable elements, economic, geographical and cultural. Apart from several stopgap measures designed to slow the erosion of the spoken language within the resident Gaeltacht community the main concern was to reduce emigration by creating jobs through economic development at home. The scope of this enterprise increased very considerably during the 1970s and particularly since Údarás na Gaeltachta, a semi-elective body under the aegis of the Department of the Gaeltacht, assumed the mantle of its predecessor, Gaeltarra Éireann, in 1979. Their efforts have been instrumental in stemming the flow of emigration from the main Irish-speaking areas of Conamara and west Donegal; in the Gaoth Dobhair neighbourhood, the one I have been in a position to monitor most closely over the years, the flat rock-strewn waste of the Screabán was transformed in a few short years into a compact industrial estate which has reversed demographic decline and created an unprecedented level of material prosperity in the surrounding area.

There was however a price to be paid for this progress. In the first place, the official definition of Gaeltacht boundaries (in 1926 and 1956) generously overstated their real extent – for reasons which ranged from the optimistic hope of consolidating and expanding these areas to more pedestrian considerations of administrative convenience and political pragmatism – but the consequence was that a considerable proportion of the resources of Gaeltarra and the Údarás were directed towards locations which could not possibly be regarded as Irish-speaking. There may have been good socio-economic arguments for some of the enterprises in question, but they have little bearing, except occasionally a very negative one, on the conservation of the Irish language. Secondly, and perhaps more crucially, it is a matter of personal observation that state initiatives in the Gaeltacht have always, for fairly obvious reasons, tended to promote the use of English rather than fortify Irish, and this experience had to be taken into account when from the seventies onwards Gaeltarra and the Údarás adopted a more ambitious approach to economic development, introducing a range of modern, including high-technology, industries. In effect the choice was, and is, between allowing the language to die a lingering death through atrophy or risking killing it off with some *élan* in the effort to revitalise the communities who speak it. For example, in the 'rural town' that is the Bun Beag–Doirí Beaga area of Gaoth Dobhair the considerable success of the development project has attracted back emigrant workers some of whom in their time abroad had acquired families who were not Irish-speaking and consequently acted as a constant pull towards English in schools, shops and throughout local society; because of their lack of numerical strength and their virtually universal bilingualism Gaeltacht communities have no longer their old capacity to automatically assimilate English-speaking newcomers. Despite the precautions of Údarás na Gaeltachta it can hardly be doubted that economic development has strengthened the influence of English in the community at large. At the same time, however, it is creating the kind of vigorous and viable community without which Irish cannot possibly survive.

Prospects

Whether Irish will survive is another question. Logic and the realism born of experience suggest not, and one is tempted to echo Saunders Lewis's rhetorical comment on the prospects for the Welsh language in the early sixties: 'Is the position hopeless? It is, of course, if we are content to give up hope.'[10] But hope must be anchored in realism; otherwise it is little more than self-delusion. And yet, unless I am mistaken, there has long been a feeling abroad among the Irish people, including intellectuals, politicians and media people, that the Irish language is a constituent of national identity which is always at risk but by the same token will always be there – with institutions like Scoil Merriman as living and lively evidence of its cultural continuity. That way we are not haunted by a too stressful sense of urgency. The facts are less comfortable however. There is less Irish now in the schools than there was forty years ago and there are fewer teachers properly competent to teach it. There is less Irish in the public service and it is quite impossible for Irish-speaking families outside the Gaeltacht (or indeed within it) to transact their normal dealings with state agencies in their home language. Most crucial of all, the communities which constitute the Gaeltacht have been so grievously weakened through erosion on their boundaries and dilution within that, if this trend were to continue, one could foresee a time when they could no longer survive as viable socio-linguistic entities.

Fortunately, there are also positive indicators. The Irish revival, from what was virtually a cold start in terms of the printed text, generated an extensive and quite impressive literature embodying a cumulative reflex of the Irish mind and tradition that could never have been adequately replicated through English. On a quite different plane of relevance there is the remarkable fact that despite all the glaring defects of the language programme since the foundation of the state there should still exist such widespread goodwill towards Irish among the public, as confirmed by numerous polls and census returns. Census statistics for the speakers of minority languages are of course notoriously unreliable and often tell us more about attitudes than about the real extent of linguistic competence; when, for example, in the census of 1981 almost a third of the population of the Republic claimed to be able to speak Irish – 1,018,413 out of a total of 3,226,467 – this may tell us more about their disposition towards the language than their degree of fluency in it, though it is still significant coming as it did in a period when there remained few material inducements to make such a claim. During the sixties and seventies Irish went through a lean period in education: the state adopted a revisionist and reductive approach towards it, it was the butt of sustained criticism in the media, it experienced radical dilution in the teachers' training colleges, and the number of Irish-medium primary and secondary schools suffered a veritable collapse,[11] and still and withal in the last comprehensive survey of attitudes to Irish, in 1993, almost a third of the respondents said they would be willing to send their children to an all-Irish primary school and a quarter to an all-Irish secondary school, while about 70 per cent believed that the government should provide all-Irish schools where there was a public demand for them.[12]

Perhaps the most impressive corroboration of these indicators is the rapidly rising demand for *gaelscoileanna* or all-Irish schools which is at present testing the goodwill and cultural pluralism of a Department of Education facing the prospect of a declining school population. In numerical terms they are still far short of compensating for the earlier haemorrhage of all-Irish schools and in linguistic terms they still lack the reinforcement of a supportive social environment; what is remarkable however about these schools is that in almost every instance the initiative by which they come into being emanates not from the state but from groups of interested parents who must in many cases contend with official resistance in the initial stages and are obliged to maintain their makeshift establishments by voluntary co-operative effort until such time as they are accepted under the wing of the department. Moreover, in sharp contradiction to the conventional image of the Irish revival as a middle-class phenomenon, many of the groups most active in promoting such schools are found in 'working-class' areas. Whatever the eventual linguistic impact of this movement, and it is not easy to assess this in its present environment where linguistic competence is continually eroded by lack of social reinforcement, it is still a notable development at this time both because it arises from within the community and because it seems to reflect an interesting sense of cultural affinities – as opposed to more specifically political or nationalist loyalties – that is in itself a not insignificant phenomenon.

In the end, however, Irish must survive in the Gaeltacht if it is to survive elsewhere, and yet, as we have seen, the dice would appear to be heavily loaded against it there and there are those who have confidently predicted its imminent demise.[13] If one hesitates to assent to their admirable logic it is not so much that other similar predictions have already been disproved by the passing of the years as that there may be factors, untested or imponderable, which, coming together, have the potential to create a fresh momentum. There is for instance the seeming paradox that languages in serious decline can be curiously tenacious of life. Over the last fifty years and more I have observed in Gaeltacht areas the vernacular being overwhelmed by the sheer volume of English from tourism, television, state and semi-state bureaucracy, and burgeoning commerce and industry, so that year by year its disintegration seemed inexorably at hand, and yet year by year I have wondered at its sheer capacity to survive, bruised perhaps but still far from broken. One new factor that will test this resource is the advent of Telefís na Gaeilge. Perhaps its greatest importance is that virtually for the first time in its dealings with Irish the state has taken a rather bold and imaginative (and reasonably expensive) step that has no direct connection with the educational system. In terms of the medium (or in comparison with television in Welsh) its resources are quite limited, but as an expression of confidence in the language and the Gaeltacht it may well act as a stimulus to both. By itself Teleifís na Gaeilge cannot save Irish; without it Irish cannot be saved.

The question remains therefore: what, if anything, can save Irish? If pressed to name one central desideratum I would have little hesitation in opting for a measure of equal validity for Irish which would underscore the right of individual citizens to learn Irish and to use it in their day-to-day affairs rather than, as hitherto, stressing or assuming their personal obligation to do so. Only those parents throughout the country who have tried to raise Irish-speaking families can appreciate the endless frustration of striving to comply with a state policy which encourages them to use Irish in the public domain while struggling with a state system which – if only through sheer inertia – constantly inhibits them from doing so. This applies even to the Gaeltacht areas. In 1996 the Minister for Arts, Culture and the Gaeltacht acknowledged the findings of a survey carried out in the Galway region which confirmed systematically what has long been a commonplace of personal observation: that state organisations fail to provide anything approaching a satisfactory service through Irish for the people of the Gaeltacht.[14] To alter the present situation and give an assurance of equal validity would be less grandiose than the nominal priority accorded the Irish language in the constitution and in political manifestos but it would require a much more substantive commitment on the part of the state and a much more serious and effective co-ordination between the several departments of government and between their agencies. It would be an interesting exercise in creative bilingualism and in cultural pluralism. Whether Irish governments have the will to implement it remains to be seen.

NOTES

1. Eoin MacNeill, 'The teaching of history in Irish schools', *Claidheamh Soluis*, 5 October 1907, pp. 7–8. By a curious irony MacNeill's enthusiasm for Gaelic Ireland's teaching and civilising influence in the medieval period would appear subsequently to have fed into his own university's preoccupation with its concept of the heritage of John Henry Newman and with the notion that it was Ireland's destined role, as a Catholic English-speaking country, to send forth its teachers and professionals to reflect and uphold Christian standards throughout the English-speaking world.

2. Kenneth Jackson, 'The Folktale in Gaelic Scotland', *Proceedings of the Scottish Anthropological and Folklore Society*, Vol. 4, No. 3 (1952), pp. 133–4.
3. Maureen Wall, 'The Decline of the Irish Language', in Brian Ó Cuív (ed.), *A View of the Irish Language*, Dublin, 1969, pp. 81–90, at p. 88.
4. Brian Ó Cuív, 'Irish Language and Literature, 1691–1845', in T. W. Moody and W. E. Vaughan (eds.), *A New History of Ireland*, Vol. IV, Oxford, 1986, pp. 374–423, at p. 380.
5. Breandán S. Mac Aodha, 'Was this a Social Revolution?', in Seán Ó Tuama (ed.), *The Gaelic League Idea*, Cork, 1972, pp. 20–30, at p. 29.
6. 'The Fate of the Language', in Alun R. Jones and Gwyn Thomas (eds.), *Presenting Saunders Lewis*, Cardiff, 1973, pp. 127–41 at p. 141; translated from the original Welsh, *Tynged yr Iaith*, BBC Publications, 1962, by G. Aled Williams.
7. Cf. Máirtín Ó Murchú, 'The Irish Language', in Glanville Price (ed.), *The Celtic Connection*, Gerrards Cross, Bucks., 1992, pp. 30–64, at p. 43.
8. Glanville Price, 'The Welsh Language Today', in Price (ed.), *The Celtic Connection*, pp. 206–15, at p. 207. In the earlier part of the century the Welsh census figures are relatively unaffected by the distortions deriving from sentiments of language loyalty.
9. Philip O'Leary, *The Prose Literature of the Gaelic Revival, 1881–1921: Ideology and Innovation*, Pennsylvania, 1994, p. 496.
10. Jones and Thomas (eds.), *Presenting Saunders Lewis*, p. 139.
11. S. Ó Buachalla, 'Educational Policy and the Role of the Irish Language from 1831 to 1981', *European Journal of Education*, Vol. 19, No. 1 (1984), pp. 75–92, at p. 89; also Reg Hindley, *The Death of the Irish Language: A Qualified Obituary*, London and New York, 1990, pp. 139–40.
12. Pádraig Ó Riagáin and Mícheál Ó Gliasáin, *National Survey on Languages 1993: Preliminary Report*, Dublin, 1994, pp. 3–4.
13. The most notable and most recent is Reg Hindley whose *The Death of the Irish Language* is a remarkably comprehensive and detailed survey of the modern decline of the language. His array of statistical evidence is impressive and his comments on it often highly perceptive. However his analysis of the evidence and the inferences he draws from it seem to me to be coloured, and to some extent invalidated, by certain preconceived ideas on the subject of language in a colonial and post-colonial situation. This is reflected for example in his preponderantly utilitarian view of the societal role of Irish, in his dubious comments on class attitudes in the Gaeltacht, and in the attention he accords the less than objective, or representative, views of the British and Irish Communist Organisation.
14. Mícheál Ó Cinnéide agus Sorcha Ní Chonghaile, *An Ghaeilge san Earnáil Phoiblí i gCeantar na Gaillimhe*, Gaillimh, 1996.

17

The Constitution Review Committee of 1934

GERARD HOGAN

Introduction

AT first sight, an essay detailing the background to the replacement of the Constitution of the Irish Free State of 1922 by the Constitution of Ireland of 1937 might seem out of place in a Festschrift in 1997.[1] Yet, a moment's reflection will demonstrate why this is not so, since any proper evaluation of the challenges faced by the Constitution Review Group – which was chaired by Dr T. K. Whitaker – in its work between 1995 and 1996 requires an understanding of this important historical context. This essay seeks to illuminate the manner in which the transition from the Constitution of 1922 to the present Constitution came about. That this transition succeeded against the odds was largely thanks to the work of the Constitution Review Committee of 1934, whose work is the focus of this essay. The measure of the committee's success can be judged by the fact that, as we shall presently see, by the 1930s the 1922 document had ended 'in almost total failure',[2] but the committee by their recommendations managed to save the best features of that document while coming up with new innovations, thus paving the way for a new Constitution which has proved 'resilient and robust and is still thriving in its sixth decade'.[3]

Against this background, it is somewhat curious that outside of the confines of the legal community,[4] the Constitution of Ireland has not received a good press. Part of the reason for this, of course, is that key features of the Constitution were or are seen as being confessional and highly nationalistic in character.[5] Critics have also rightly drawn attention to the manner in which certain rights are subject to considerable qualifications and, indeed, to what appear to be internal contradictions within the Constitution itself. And yet, perhaps, it is only now with the passage of time and the dissipation of the passions of the politically charged 1930s that the virtues of the Constitution have been fully realised. At a political level, the Constitution had achieved stability:

> After nearly thirty years of incessant war, revolution and political change the twenty-six counties had at last achieved a kind of equilibrium so profound and so firmly based that even the final step towards the formal realisation of the republic, when it came in 1948–9, could be taken by the passing of a simple act of parliament and without the necessity of far-reaching constitutional amendment.[6]

At a legal level, the achievements of the Constitution are, perhaps, best summed up by the following observations of the Constitution Review Group:

> The provisions made for the protection of fundamental rights in the Constitution were more elaborate than heretofore and the drafters had clearly learnt from the experience of the 1922 Constitution ... Indeed, to an extent, the new Constitution reflected some sophisticated legal thinking (especially by the standards of the day) even if this was not widely appreciated at the time. This sophistication, coupled with skilful and elegant drafting, ensured that the Constitution was sufficiently flexible and had an in-built capacity for organic growth through judicial interpretation. Moreover, the fundamental rights provisions have, generally speaking, proved to be an effective method of safeguarding individual rights so that 'the overall impact of the courts on modern Irish life, in their handling of constitutional issues, has been beneficial, rational, progressive and fair'.[7]

The objects and background of the 1922 Constitution

How, then, did it come about that these twin virtues of stability and respect for individual rights were achieved by the new Constitution? As we shall presently see, the report of the 1934 Constitution Committee proved to be particularly influential in this regard, even though the work of this committee appears to have been hitherto largely overlooked by historians.[8] But before we can proceed to analyse the significance of the committee's work, it is necessary first to examine the state of constitutional law in 1934.

The Constitution of the Irish Free State 1922 had represented a new and potentially dramatic fresh start in Irish legal life. The Constitution not only sought

> to harmonise republican ideals with membership of the Commonwealth, it also attempted to combine the pragmatic British approach to the business of government with an attachment to those ringing declarations of human rights which were common to so many revolutionary constitutions in various parts of the world after 1918 ...[9]

Prior to 1922 there had been, of course, no Irish constitutional law to
speak of. The 'political and legal constitutional studies in this Country'
had in practice been 'limited to the British Constitution and the working
of the British Parliament',[10] of which the doctrine of parliamentary
sovereignty was – and is – the most striking feature. Accordingly, Articles
65 and 66 of the 1922 Constitution which vested the High Court (and,
on appeal, the Supreme Court) with express powers of judicial review of
legislation[11] represented a radical break with the previous British
tradition. Indeed, these provisions may be thought to represent the
coping-stone of the entire constitutional experiment – at least, so far as
the 'republican' element of that Constitution[12] was concerned – for
unless this power to adjudicate on issues of constitutionality was to be
exercised with at least some frequency, the fundamental rights
provisions would be thereby undermined.

The erosion and ultimate failure of the 1922 Constitution

In the event, the 1922 Constitution did not prove – in this respect, at
least – to be a success, chiefly because the legal culture was unreceptive to
the novel concept of judicial review of legislation based on fundamental
concepts of human rights and because Article 50 of that Constitution
contained the seeds of its own destruction. In the period between 1922
and 1937, there were only two occasions on which this power was
actually exercised[13] and a combination of circumstances conspired to
ensure that the power of judicial review never played the significant role
that the drafters of the Constitution had evidently intended.

This failure must first be ascribed to the hostility and unreceptiveness
of the legal culture. As Professor John Kelly perceptively noted:

> The judges [of this period] were used to the idea of the sovereignty of
> parliament, and notions of fundamental law were foreign to their training and
> tradition. The effect of these clauses in the 1922 Constitution was thus
> minimal.[14]

Secondly, the manner in which the language of Article 50 of the
Constitution was judicially interpreted effectively set at naught the
possibility of the evolution of any significant constitutional juris-
prudence. Article 50 originally provided in relevant part as follows:

> Amendments of this Constitution within the terms of the Scheduled Treaty
> may be made by the Oireachtas, but no such amendment, passed by both
> Houses of the Oireachtas, after the expiration of eight years from the date of
> the coming into operation of this Constitution, shall become law unless the

same [is submitted to and approved by a majority of the people at a referendum].

While the original intention of the drafters was that the eight-year period permitted by Article 50 was intended to facilitate minor drafting amendments of a kind not warranting a referendum,[15] in fact this clause proved to be the eventual undoing of the Constitution. The first drastic change was effected by the Constitution (Amendment No. 16) Act 1929 whereby the eight-year period within which the Constitution might be amended by ordinary legislation was extended to sixteen years. This ultimately proved to be the mechanism whereby the Crown, the oath of allegiance and the Senate were all removed from the Constitution in the years subsequent to Eamon de Valera's accession to power in 1932. Amendment No. 16 also facilitated the enactment of the Constitution (Amendment No. 17) Act 1931 which inserted Article 2A into the Constitution. Article 2A was in reality an elaborate anti-terrorism law which had been inserted into the Constitution by ordinary legislation. It provided for the establishment of the Constitution (Special Powers) Tribunal, consisting of five senior members of the Defence Forces. The breadth of its powers may be judged by section 7 of Article 2A, which provided that the tribunal might impose any punishment, up to and including the death penalty, greater than that provided by ordinary law for the offence 'if in the opinion of the Tribunal such greater punishment is necessary or desirable'. Moreover, for so long as Article 2A was in force, section 2 thereof provided that:

> Article 3 and every subsequent Article of this Constitution shall be read and construed subject to the provisions of this Article, and in the case of any inconsistency between this Article and the said Article 3 or any subsequent Article, this Article shall prevail.

Prior to 1931, however, amendments to the Constitution had also to be within the terms of the treaty which had been scheduled to that Constitution. In that year the Statute of Westminster 1931 was enacted by the British parliament following a Dominion Conference. This legislation enabled dominion parliaments (such as the Oireachtas of the Irish Free State) to legislate in a manner contrary to earlier British legislation. Since the requirement that any amendments had to conform to the treaty had been imposed (in the British view) by an Act of the Westminster parliament, the Oireachtas was now free to legislate to repeal these restrictions contained in the Constitution. This was done by the Constitution (Removal of Oath) Act 1933 which not only abolished the oath of allegiance (contained in both the Constitution and the treaty), but also amended Article 50 by deleting the words 'within the terms of the Scheduled Treaty'.

Finally, it should be noted that the validity of amendments to the Constitution and the treaty was upheld by the Judicial Committee of the Privy Council in May 1934 in *Moore v. Attorney General for the IFS*[16] applying the 'British view' of the effect of the Statute of Westminster. Some months later, however, the Supreme Court was to take a different view of these questions in *The State (Ryan) v. Lennon*.[17] While a majority of the court upheld the validity of Amendment No. 16 (extending the time for amendments from eight to sixteen years) and Amendment No. 17 (inserting Article 2A), all members of the court were agreed that the Oireachtas had no power to disregard the terms of the treaty, since the Dáil when sitting as a constituent assembly which had drafted the Constitution and created the Oireachtas had entrenched the treaty and had put it beyond the amending power of the Oireachtas.[18] On any view, therefore, the 1922 Constitution had by this stage been reduced to such tatters that the time for a new Constitution had come and de Valera was determined that such a new Constitution would acquire a legitimacy by reason of its popular enactment by the people in a referendum.

Establishment of the Constitution Review Committee

While it may be surmised that Eamon de Valera had toyed for some time with the idea that a new Constitution was necessary to replace the Constitution of the Free State, the initial impetus for the establishment of the Constitution Review Committee resulted from an opposition amendment which had been put down in respect of the Constitution (Amendment No. 24) Bill 1934. This bill proposed to abolish the existing Senate, but the opposition amendment sought to ensure in the wake of such abolition that certain provisions of the Constitution could no longer be amended by ordinary legislation unless a general election had intervened in the meantime.[19] While the proposed amendment was rejected by the government, de Valera availed of the opportunity to explain his attitude to fundamental rights:

> This [1922] Constitution was framed originally under exceptional circumstances. There were certain Articles in the Constitution which were forced upon the people of the country. There are certain Articles which represent democratic ideals, and which in so far as a thorough examination by people who have had experience of administration goes, are consistent with practical government. These Articles ought, with all possible speed, to be examined, and be made as lasting as it is possible for anything to be made

lasting, in a Constitutional way, without the danger of a cast-iron Constitution which, as I said, is always a temptation to revolution.[20]

De Valera returned to this subject a few days later on 25 May:

> If we agree in this House that a selected number of Articles guaranteeing fundamental rights are to be preserved, if we decide, for their preservation, that they cannot, for example, be changed by the Dáil except by a specified majority or on approval by the people by way of Referendum, I believe that an alteration of the Constitution embodying that will be effective ... To meet the views of those who fear that either this Dáil or a subsequent Dáil might ignore these fundamental rights in the Constitution, I propose at a later stage, when this examination shall have been completed, to indicate certain Articles and bring them forward in a simple measure with safeguards by which they cannot be changed by a simple majority.[21]

The Constitution Committee had, in fact, been established on the previous day by oral direction of de Valera; its task was to examine the Constitution

> with a view to ascertaining what Articles should be regarded as fundamental, on the ground that they safeguard democratic rights, and to make recommendations as to steps which should be taken to ensure that such Articles should not be capable of being altered by the ordinary processes of legislation.

The committee consisted of four senior civil servants: Stephen Roche, secretary, Department of Justice; Michael McDunphy, assistant secretary, Department of the President of the Executive Council;[22] John Hearne, legal adviser, Department of External Affairs; and Philip O'Donoghue, assistant to the Attorney General. The composition of the committee was in itself significant, as the latter three members were subsequently to play a pivotal role in the drafting of the new Constitution.[23]

The work of the committee: terms of reference and remit

The committee set about its work with impressive speed. It held ten meetings in all, commencing on 28 May, and submitted its final report to de Valera on 3 July 1934. At its second meeting on 29 May the committee decided that its report 'should take the form of an entirely new Constitution', although it was not proposed 'to present a finished draft, that being considered a matter for the Parliamentary Draftsman'.[24] The committee observed that it was at first intended to limit the new Constitution to matters 'relating to fundamental rights', but it was found that 'the insertion of others, e.g., those relating to Parliament etc. was essential if a complete Constitution were to result'. The committee's

minutes then set out briefly in a schedule the reasons 'for the proposed
inclusion or exclusion of the various Articles of the present Constitution,
with other relevant notes'.

At the third meeting, however, it became clear that this plan was too
ambitious and it was agreed that the committee should confine itself to
the original terms of reference, as 'it was now clear that what the
President wanted was not a new Constitution ...'[25] McDunphy had
confirmed this in a separate memorandum dated 31 May, which was
circulated between the second and third meetings:

> Subsequent to [second meeting of the committee] of 29th May it became clear
> as a result of pronouncements by the President and of conversations which
> individual members of the Committee had with him, that what he really
> wanted was not a new Constitution, but
>
> (a) a selection within the framework of the present Constitution of those
>   Articles which should be regarded as fundamental; and
> (b) a recommendation as to how these should be rendered immune from
>   alteration by ordinary legislation.
>
> The President himself had already created a precedent which should serve as a
> guide in regard to (b).
>
> In Constitution (Amendment No. 24) Bill, 1934 ... which provides for the
> abolition of the Seanad as a constituent House of the Oireachtas, he has
> provided in respect of Article 63 (The tenure of Office of the Comptroller
> and Auditor General) and Article 68 (the tenure of Offices of Judges) as
> follows:
>
>> 'Notwithstanding anything contained in any other Article of this
>> Constitution, a Bill for legislation to amend this Article in relation to the
>> passing of the said resolution shall not be introduced in Dáil Éireann unless
>> or until the amendment proposed by such Bill has been approved by a
>> resolution of Dáil Éireann for the passing of which not less than four-
>> sevenths (exclusive of the Chairman or presiding member) of the full
>> membership of Dáil Éireann shall have voted.'

This memorandum is clearly of great interest, since it indicates that
while de Valera had not yet finally determined to introduce a new
Constitution, the idea had plainly crossed his mind. As it happened, the
first formal instructions to draft the heads of a new Constitution were
only given to John Hearne almost a year later in April 1935,[26] but, as
will be seen, the 1934 committee's report proved to be enormously
influential when it came to the drafting of the new Constitution.

McDunphy's memorandum is also significant in that it indicates that
de Valera was still in two minds on the amendment process. In his
speech to the Dáil on 25 May 1934 he had mentioned the possibility

that the fundamental rights provisions of the Constitution might only be amended either by way of referendum or by means of a special Dáil majority, but this memorandum suggested a preference at this time for the latter safeguard.

Core issues in the 1934 constitutional debate

The committee's work was to focus on three issues: the role of judicial review of legislation, the concept of constitutional change being subject to a referendum and the evolution of special courts operating outside a statement of emergency, thereby replacing Article 2A.

In fact, the outline of the committee's conclusions were already visible by its third meeting on 1 June. The committee had at this stage abandoned the suggestion to sketch the outlines of a new Constitution, but instead agreed that it should now proceed along the lines indicated by de Valera. Having spent the first two meetings examining the text of the existing Constitution, the committee appears to have reached broad agreement on which of the articles should be regarded as fundamental. The lengthy minutes of the third meeting record in summary form the views of the committee on practically every provision of the Constitution. McDunphy then prepared a first draft on 9 June which closely follows these minuted views.

This draft was further discussed by the committee at its next three meetings.[27] In the meantime, Stephen Roche, secretary of the Department of Justice, had prepared a memorandum for circulation to other members of the committee.[28] While the memorandum chiefly dealt with the topic of Article 2A, Roche first took the opportunity to express his views on the issue of constitutional change:

> I believe that in a unitary State with full adult suffrage the idea of a written Constitution, not capable of alteration by a majority of the elected representatives of the people is unsound in theory and dangerous in practice. It is unsound in theory *because no Parliament (whether it calls itself a Dáil or a Constituent Assembly or any other name) and no generation* has any right to bind future Parliaments or future generations. ... That is the theoretical side. The practical side is that majorities will have their way, anyhow, and if they can't have it 'constitutionally', or only after great delay, then they will (and quite rightly) have it 'unconstitutionally'.

The italicised words were underlined by McDunphy, who commented in the margins: 'not rigidly – but a Constituent Assembly should have some authority of an exceptional kind'. While Roche did not expressly address the question of amendment by means of a referendum, it seems

a fair inference from the tenor of his remarks that he was generally
against it.[29]

Roche then continued thus in a manner which suggests that he was
strongly opposed to the idea of judicial review of legislation:

> I believe that what this country wants at present and probably will continue to
> want for many years is a strong Executive, not liable, so long as it has the
> support of the people, to be delayed, hampered and humiliated at every step
> by long arguments in the Courts, or by propaganda of a threatening and
> seditious type. A Government should not allow itself to be insulted.
>
> Further, I believe that the doctrines of 'judicial independence' and 'the
> separation of the functions' are being overdone and that the Courts have been
> given or have assumed a position in our civic life to which they are not
> entitled. There was a time in England when the Judges' job was to save the
> people from an irresponsible Executive; it may be necessary, in turn, for a
> responsible Executive to save the people from irresponsible Judges.[30]

McDunphy placed a question mark in the margin beside the reference to
'irresponsible Judges' and then commented:

> A 'strong' Executive could conceivably be a real danger instead of a blessing.
> Something more than 'strength' is essential.

Roche continued by making comments on a number of specific
articles of the Constitution. These remarks are of exceptional interest to
any constitutional historian, since they contain the genesis of a number
of innovatory provisions of the present Constitution.

> With particular reference to Article 2A, I agree that, *in form* that Article is
> grotesque as an Article of the Constitution. It must go.[31] On the other hand,
> so long as we keep to the idea of a 'normal' written Constitution, with all
> sorts of snags and pit-falls for the Executive, we must have something,
> somewhere, on the lines of Article 2A. What I have done in my draft is to
> split the task into two parts, viz.:
>
> (a) The declaration of an 'emergency period' and
> (b) The measures which may be taken by the Executive once an emergency
>   period has been declared.
>
> I have put part (a) in the Constitution and left part (b) to be dealt with by
> ordinary legislation with the proviso that such legislation shall not be subject
> to the ordinary constitutional limitations. I see no other way of making
> adequate provision without overloading the actual Constitution with details.

Roche then went on to sketch out a scheme whereby the bringing into
force of such legislation would be contingent on the consent of the
judiciary voting in secret ballot. He added that he had taken this

approach 'mainly because he gathered from the President [de Valera] that he was anxious, for obvious and weighty reasons, to get some form of judicial, or at least non-political sanction for such a declaration'. We see here for the first time the outlines of what subsequently emerged as Article 28.3.3 of the present Constitution, whereby during the currency of a state of emergency the Oireachtas is freed from the ordinary constitutional contraints. It is significant, however, that Article 28.3.3 follows the main features of Roche's model.[32] As we shall see presently, following further discussion, the committee ultimately agreed to a further related proposal, namely, that in addition to the emergency powers provisions, provision should be made for the establishment of special courts where the ordinary courts proved to be inadequate for this purpose.[33]

Following the circulation of the McDunphy main draft report and the Roche memorandum, the committee spent its next three meetings working on these documents.[34] The McDunphy draft was more or less complete by the eighth meeting, 'various textual amendments being agreed upon'. There is only one significant feature of this first draft which did not find its way into the final report, namely, the issue of the amendment process itself. On this vital question the McDunphy draft stated as follows:

> The Committee are in favour of requiring that there must be a popular vote in a referendum in favour of any change in any of these fundamental Articles before such change can become law, except where a dissolution has occurred subsequent to the submission of the proposal in favour of the Bill. In such case it should be competent for the Executive Council appointed by the new Dáil to secure by ordinary legislation the enactment of the proposed amendment in the form in which it was submitted to or, in the case of any alteration, agreed to, by the Dáil prior to the General Election.

These comments are significant because, in the events that happened, the committee never reported on Part II of its terms of reference (i.e. the manner of constitutional amendment). McDunphy noted in hand on the cover of the committee's file:

> No action was taken on Part II of the Committee's terms of reference. The matter gradually became one of Government Policy and was dealt with on that basis.

Whatever reservations Roche may have had about the referendum process, it seems nonetheless fair to infer from this (admittedly draft) passage that the other members of the committee were in favour of this method of amendment. Since these three members of the committee were later to form the nucleus of the group who drafted the 1937 Constitution, it is scarcely surprising that the referendum option was the one chosen. With the exception of a transitory three-year period[35] Article 46 provided that the Constitution could henceforth only be amended by way of referendum. While this rigidity has certain disadvantages, this choice was ultimately to prove to be an enlightened one which ensured durability and continuity, guarded against emphemeral change and reinforced popular sovereignty. Indeed, it may be said that if there was one single change which ensured the success of the present Constitution, it was this.

The eighth meeting also considered Roche's proposals in relation to Article 2A and the matter was ultimately referred to him to revise 'in the light of the discussion'. Roche's revised draft – prepared overnight – was then discussed at the ninth meeting on 29 June where it appears to have suffered heavy revisions.[36] However, the revised draft had contained a most important new suggestion:

> 5. In addition and apart from 'emergency' periods and 'emergency' legislation, the proposed Article (or else an addendum to one of the 'judicial power' Articles) should authorise the enactment of special legislation as part of our permanent judicial machinery for the trial by Special Courts of persons accused of crime, as regards whose trial the ordinary Judge or Justice certifies at any stage of the proceedings, that it is desirable in the interests of justice that the trial be removed to a Special Court.

> 6. As regards this last suggestion we desire to point out, as against the obvious objections to Special Courts, that the ordinary Courts have been unable, in the past, to deal effectively with certain forms of crime, and that there is perhaps no optimism to hope for any permanent improvement in that respect. The choice appears to lie therefore between the alternatives of

> (a) allowing such forms of crime to go unpunished,
> (b) declaring a 'state of emergency' for the purpose of setting up a Special Court every time such crimes occur,
> (c) making permanent provision for a Special Court on the lines indicated in para. (5) above.

> As between these alternatives we recommend the last mentioned, mainly because we feel that its adoption will provide a remedy for outbreaks of disorder which would otherwise necessitate the formal declaration of a 'state of emergency' with inevitable damage to the national credit.[37]

Here we see for the first time the clear outline of what ultimately was to become Article 38.3 of the Constitution, which permits of the establishment by law of special courts quite independently of any declaration of emergency under Article 28.3.3.[38]

The minutes of the ninth meeting record that Roche's revised scheme was further examined and that while the principle was agreed on, 'it was decided to set it out in a different form'. McDunphy was deputed to do this and 'prepare for final consideration the text of the whole of the Committee's terms of reference'. The final version of the draft report was circulated by McDunphy on the following Monday, 2 July, and the report 'on Part I of their terms of reference' was 'approved and signed by all four members of the Committee as an unanimous report' at the tenth and final meeting on 3 July. The final version of the report was then presented to President de Valera by Roche later that day.

The committee's conclusions on the fundamental articles

The report consisted of an introduction and eight appendices.[39] The introduction recited the terms of reference and indicated the subsequent layout of the report. Appendix A contained the text of the articles regarded as fundamental by the committee which should, 'to the extent and with such modifications as are recommended in this Report, be rendered immune from easy alteration'. In those cases where amendments to such constitutional provisions were proposed, the committee indicated that:

> we have confined ourselves to indicating the nature of the changes suggested and our reasons therefor. We have assumed that it is not our function to submit drafts of articles as so revised.

The full version of Appendix A is too long to permit of reproduction here. It is proposed instead to list the articles regarded as fundamental and to identify in the notes some of the comments by the committee thereon:

Article 6: The liberty of the person (including habeas corpus)
Article 7: Inviolability of the dwellings of citizens
Article 8: Freedom of conscience
Article 9: Right of free expression of opinion and peaceable assembly[40]
Article 18: Immunity of members of the Oireachtas
Article 19: Privilege of official reports etc. of the Oireachtas[41]
Article 24
    (a) Summoning and dissolving the Oireachtas in the name of the king
    (b) Holding of at least one session of the Oireachtas each year[42]

Article 28
   (a) Date of assembly of Dáil Éireann after a general election
   (b) Duration of parliament
Article 41: Presentation of bills for the king's assent[43]
Article 43: Non-declaration of Acts to be infringements of the law
   which were not so at the date of their commission
Article 46: The raising and maintenance of an armed force[44]
Article 49: Participation in war[45]
Article 50: Amendments of the Constitution[46]
Article 61
   (a) Central Fund etc.
   (b) Appropriation of public money only in accordance with law[47]
Articles 62 and 63: Comptroller and Auditor General – tenure of office
Articles 64, 65, 66, 68, 69: The judiciary[48]
Article 70
   (a) Provision for legal trials of civilians
   (b) Trial of military offenders by military tribunals
   (c) The extension of the authority of military tribunals to civilians
   in time of war and armed rebellion[49]

Some specific comments of the committee in relation to particular topics merit further consideration.

The courts

The committee's comments in relation to the courts were particularly interesting. It first concluded that Article 64 – which provided, *inter alia*, that the judicial power 'shall be exercised and justice administered in the public courts established by the Oireachtas by judges appointed in manner hereinafter provided' – was to be regarded as fundamental, subject to the following proviso:

> We suggest, however, that it should be carefully re-drafted so as to meet the present position in which judicial or quasi-judicial functions are necessarily performed by persons who are not judges within the strict terms of the Constitution, e.g., Revenue Commissioners, Land Commissioners, Court Registrars etc.[50]

Indeed, following a discussion of this very point at the committee's third meeting, Roche had put forward a sketch of a possible addendum to Article 64:

> Provided for the removal of doubts and for the more expeditious and economical administration of justice and transaction of public business, that

nothing in this Article shall be deemed to render invalid any enactment, or any role, order, or arrangement made under the authority of any enactment, whereby powers or duties (not being powers or duties of a judicial nature in connection with criminal trials) have been conferred or shall hereafter be conferred on an officer of any Court in relation to the business of the Court or any Board, Commission, or Tribunal (by whatever name known) or any member thereof.

This draft proved to be very influential, since it clearly anticipates the present Article 37 which permits the Oireachtas to vest non-judicial personages with limited judicial powers in matters 'other than criminal matters'. Indeed, during the Dáil debates on the 1937 Constitution, de Valera expressly acknowledged that such concerns had given rise to Article 37:

> There were questions about the Land Commission, as to whether functions were of a judicial character or not ... So as not to get tied in the knot that judicial powers or functions could only be exercised by the ordinary courts established here, you have to have a provision of this kind.[51]

In our times, these questions also troubled the Constitution Review Group who wrestled with the problems thrown up by Article 37, but felt that since it could not devise a more satisfactory wording, it could not come up with a recommendation for change:

> The Review Group recognises that Article 37 as it stands is not wholly satisfactory. A majority of the Review Group considers, however, that, since experience has shown that there is no completely satisfactory answer to the problem raised and since there are great difficulties in formulating a different set of words which would deal adequately with these complex issues, Articles 34.1 and 37 should be retained in their present form.[52]

The 1934 committee also agreed that the express powers of judicial review of legislation vested in the High Court by Article 65 were fundamental. No agreement could, however, be reached on two very interesting suggestions which had been discussed by the committee. The first was whether:

> the power of deciding the validity of laws, having regard to the provisions of the Constitution, should be vested
>
> (a) in the Supreme Court alone, or
> (b) in a special 'Constitution' Court appointed or designated for that purpose, e.g., a combination of the Supreme and High Courts, or
> (c) in the High Court with a right of appeal to the Supreme Court as at present.

Had the suggestion that a special Constitutional Court might be established become public at that time, it would almost certainly have been regarded with deep suspicion by the judicial and legal establishments of the day. Hostility from the bar and bench had already killed off far more modest proposals for reform of court costume and dress in the 1920s[53] and radical, avant-garde proposals of this kind would doubtless have met a similar fate.[54] What is particularly significant, however, is that irrespective of the merits of such a proposal in the context of a small, common law jurisdiction such as Ireland, the fact that it was seriously considered by the committee (and, clearly, supported by some of its members) demonstrates that the members of the committee must have had a very sophisticated understanding of the dynamics of constitutional law. It provides yet further evidence of the ability and remarkable open-mindedness of what one leading historian has described as the 'merito-cratic administrative elite' who served on the Constitution's drafting committee.[55] Incidentally, the suggestion that a special Constitutional Court might be established clearly impacted on de Valera, who later admitted in the Dáil debates on the Constitution that he was wary of giving the powers of judicial review to the ordinary courts:

> This matter of the Constitution is going to be interpreted, ultimately, by the Courts. I know that in other countries courts are set up known, roughly, as constitutional courts, which take a broader view – I do not wish to be hurtful – which take a broader view, or not so narrow a view, as the ordinary Courts, strictly interpreting the ordinary law from day to day, have to take. If I could get from anybody any suggestion of some court to deal with such matters other than the Supreme Court, I would be willing to consider it. I confess that I have not been able to get anything better than the Supreme Court to fulfil this function.[56]

The second suggestion was that the Constitution should contain a time limit within which the constitutionality of legislation might be challenged. This proposal had first been put forward by Roche in his memorandum. He had suggested that Article 65 (which vested the High Court and Supreme Court with express powers of judicial review of legislation) should be amended by the addition of the following proviso:

> ... but no question as to such validity shall be considered unless it is brought before the High Court for determination within three months after the enactment of such law.

He added:

> The idea is that we should get certainty as to what is the law and not be discussing in 1934 whether a law which has been in operation since 1925 is valid or not.

The committee was ultimately to be divided on the question of a fixed time limit, but, like the Constitutional Court proposal, 'thought it well ... to place on record' that these suggestions had been put forward. McDunphy was, however, clearly against the proposal, since he had commented on the margins of the Roche memorandum: 'I am afraid of this.' Roche's proposal did not find its way into the corresponding provision – Article 34.3.2 – of the present Constitution and, indeed, by any standards, it would have to be rejected as unsound. Experience has shown that the constitutionality of most legislation cannot be tested on an a priori, abstract basis, but has to be judged by reference to the special circumstances of a particular litigant. The circumstances in which such a litigant may require to challenge the constitutionality of legislation affecting him adversely may not arise for many years or even decades after it has been enacted. Moreover, legislation which was valid at the date it was enacted may become unconstitutional by reason of changing circumstances, such as inflation, population movements and mortality tables.[57] In addition, where a court upholds the validity of legislation in a case which depends on an appraisal of the prevailing scientific or other relevant expert evidence as to the effect of such legislation, it would seem unjust if this question could not be reopened if new evidence were later to materialise.[58] At the same time, most constitutional lawyers would recognise that a procedure which provides for a swift and certain determination of the constitutionality of a particular law – which was the gist of Roche's proposals – might prove to be of great value.[59] And thus it may be that this proposal contained the germ of an idea which ultimately led to the present Article 26 of the Constitution (which had no counterpart in the 1922 Constitution) whereby the constitutionality of a bill may be determined before it ever comes into law following a reference by the President to the Supreme Court.[60]

The proposals for the Special Criminal Court

Appendix B contained the committee's recommendations in relation to Article 2A which closely followed Roche's proposals for the establishment of special criminal courts (Scheme A) and declarations of emergency (Scheme B). The committee clearly envisaged that the Special Criminal Court would be the first step in curbing civil disorder and that the declaration of a state of emergency would be necessary in the final resort:

> What may be regarded as the first serious phase in the development of a grave state of disorder throughout the country is the failure of the ordinary Courts,

either through intimidation of jurors and/or witnesses, or lack of civic spirit
on the part of either or both, to secure the conviction of offenders,
particularly in the case of offences of a semi-political nature. The resultant
immunity of offenders from punishment leads inevitably to the spread of
offences of this character, resulting sometimes in a serious situation with
which the ordinary processes of law are unable to cope. We are of opinion
that the development of a situation of this nature could in most cases be
arrested by the application of suitable measures in the early stages, and we
think that, to this end, the Constitution should contain a permanent provision
to supplement the operation of the ordinary Courts.

In its introduction to the report the committee had anticipated its
recommendations in relation to Scheme B, the declaration of emergency
provisions:

> We are of opinion that Article 2A in its present form is not a proper one for
> retention in the Constitution. We suggest that it should be replaced by a single
> Article which would enable the Oireachtas, by ordinary legislation, to
> empower an Executive to take any measures necessary to deal effectively with
> a state of public emergency not amounting to armed rebellion or a state of
> war, including, when necessary, the temporary suspension of many Articles of
> the Constitution which under normal circumstances are rightly regarded as
> fundamental.

As we have noted, these recommendations clearly formed the basis for
the present Article 38.3.1 and Article 28.3.3.

Recommendations in relation to the Irish language, education and jury trial

The committee dealt with three heterogeneous provisions dealing
respectively with language (Article 4), education (Article 10) and the
right to jury trial (Article 72) in Appendix C. In the case of Article 4
(which, unlike the present Article 8, provided that while Irish was the
'national language', English was 'equally recognised as an official
language') the committee observed that:

> While ... this Article is not fundamental in the sense that it safeguards
> democratic rights, we recognise that from the National point of view, it is
> important because of the status which it gives to the Irish language. We
> realise, however, that in the course of time it may be found desirable to
> modify the recognition which it accords to English as an equally official
> language throughout the State, and for that reason we are of opinion that the
> Article should be left open to change by ordinary legislation.

In relation to the guarantee contained in Article 10 that all citizens 'have the right to free elementary education', the committee recommended against including this in the fundamental list, having first obtained the views of Seosamh Ó Néill, secretary of the Department of Education,[61] who adverted to possible difficulties to which this provision might give rise:

(1) whether a small number of children, say, two, three, or four, living on an island, or at a long distance from a National School, could successfully claim the right to be transported daily to a National School; or to have a School established for their own use;
(2) whether the Article could be construed to put an obligation on the State not only to pay the teachers but also to build, equip and maintain schools, and provide free books and requisites for the schoolchildren.

While Article 42.4 still protects the right to free primary education, Ó Néill's letter – and the committee's evident support for his views – produced an important change. Article 42.4 provides that the State's duty is now only to 'provide *for* free primary education' (as opposed to 'provide free primary education') – a change which has somewhat diluted the extent of the State's obligations in this area.[62]

Somewhat surprisingly, the committee also recommended against the inclusion of Article 72 – guaranteeing the right to jury trial – in the list of fundamental articles.[63] They noted that in England and America the jury system had been subjected 'in recent years to very considerable criticism' and that 'in our State it cannot even claim to be a spontaneous national growth'. The committee continued:

With an Executive dependent on, and responsible to, a parliament elected on a full adult suffrage, and with judges whose independence is guaranteed by the Constitution which also forbids the setting up of extraordinary courts, the right to trial by jury has lost its original importance.

The committee concluded that if they had included the article in the list of fundamental articles, they would have recommended amendments designed to make it clear:

(a) that the Article does not bind us to the present English system of requiring a jury of twelve and an unanimous verdict, and
(b) that when the Oireachtas has designated any particular offence as a 'minor offence', fit to be tried summarily, it shall not be open to a defendant to raise the point that the offence is so serious that it cannot reasonably be called a 'minor' offence and that the law declaring it to be triable summarily is therefore ultra vires Article 72 and invalid.

While these recommendations were ultimately not acted on – and, if anything, the new Constitution strengthened and reinforced the right to jury trial, the provisions of Article 38.3.1 and the Special Criminal Court notwithstanding – they again demonstrate the far-sighted character of the committee's report. It is true that the constitutionality of section 25 of the Criminal Justice Act 1984 – which provides for majority jury verdicts in criminal cases – has been upheld by the Supreme Court in *O'Callaghan v. Attorney General*,[64] but one leading commentator has found the reasoning in that case to be profoundly unconvincing and disappointing.[65] However, whatever the merits of the second recommendation,[66] the committee correctly anticipated that this provision was likely to lead to the invalidation of legislation which incorrectly classified certain offences as 'minor' and therefore capable of being tried summarily.[67]

Conclusions

What does this examination of the report of the 1934 Constitution Committee tell us about the drafting of the 1937 Constitution? The drafting of the Constitution has been hitherto ascribed more or less exclusively to Eamon de Valera.[68] Of course, de Valera's pre-eminence as the political architect of the Constitution is beyond question, but it may be argued that historians have somewhat overstated the extent to which he was personally involved in the drafting[69] and more importantly have, perhaps, underestimated the extent to which he was influenced by his own drafting committee in which he had reposed so much trust.[70] Constitutional lawyers have been traditionally wary of attributing such a complete and exclusive influence to de Valera, mainly because the sophistication, style and general layout of the Constitution strongly suggested that its legal content and drafting must have been the work of very skilled lawyers and draftsmen. The 1934 report tends to corroborate this view, inasmuch as we can see in this report the origins of some of the innovatory features of the subsequent Constitution, among them the declaration of emergency, the refinement of the Dáil's power to declare war, Article 37, the Special Criminal Court, the proviso to Article 40.6.1.ii and the recasting of the language of what was to become Article 42.4.

Secondly, the entire tenor of the report was to emphasise the desirability of maintaining continuity where possible with the existing 1922 Constitution. It is true that de Valera had always maintained that the 1922 Constitution contained fine features, but the report clearly took the view that the better features of that Constitution should be retained, while at the same time paving the way for innovatory improvements, and the entire structure of the new Constitution follows these recommendations.

Thirdly, it is self-evident from the report that its drafters were people who were anxious to reinforce constitutional rights and (Roche perhaps excepted) who welcomed the prospect of vigorous judicial review of legislation to the point of suggesting the establishment of a special Constitutional Court. It has been often stated that de Valera did not anticipate that the new Constitution would lead to the development of extensive judicial review. As Professor Kelly has observed:

> Even Mr de Valera, though he entrenched this elaborate bill of rights in his Constitution, intended it to be primarily a set of 'headlines to the legislature' rather than a hurdle on which that legislature would frequently stumble and fall; his contributions to the Dáil debate on the draft Constitution seem to me to show that he did not see himself as calling into existence a sort of legal shredding-machine, which a later generation of lawyers and judges would use with devastating effect on the Acts of the sovereign Irish people's own parliament.[71]

While de Valera's comments in the Dáil debates on the draft Constitution clearly support this view,[72] his drafters probably privately hoped for – and expected – more from the elaborate bill of rights which they had constructed. After all, if some of their number had been pressing for a special Constitutional Court, this would have seemed like a futile exercise unless they had anticipated that such a specially established court would have had a significant amount of litigious business to discharge.

Finally, the 1937 Constitution succeeded against the odds in establishing a system where judicial review could flourish, even though this prospect excited considerable scepticism at the time.[73] Moreover, compared with the constitutions of the other emerging nations of Europe, the Irish Constitution succeeded where many other attempts failed.[74] It may thus be stated that the success of the 1937 Constitution is due in no small measure to the foresight and legal acumen of the members of the 1934 Constitution Committee whose report paved the way for its enactment.

NOTES

1. My thanks are due to John Conlon, assistant secretary, Constitution Review Group and Catriona Crowe of the National Archives for their assistance in securing a copy of the Constitution Committee 1934 SPO file, SPO 2979. All unreferenced quotations in this essay are taken from this file.
2. R. Humphreys (1994) 16 *Dublin University Law Journal* 222, 223.
3. *Ibid.*

4.   Thus M. Forde, *Constitutional Law of Ireland* (Cork: Mercier Press, 1987,
     p. 13) describes the Constitution as a 'model of superb drafting'.
     Humphreys, *loc. cit.*, p. 222 observes that:
     > And yet the Constitution has its strengths. It is one of the oldest in Europe, and
     > has developed organically to reflect and accommodate a changing society since
     > 1937. It has proved to be flexible enough to allow for contemporary public
     > administration and contemporary conceptions of human rights.

     See also the comments contained in the *Report of the Constitution Review
     Group*, Dublin: Stationery Office, 1996, below.
5.   Critics point to the terms of the Preamble, Articles 2 and 3, the 'special
     position' of the Catholic Church contained in Article 44.1.2 (deleted by
     the Fifth Amendment of the Constitution Act 1972), the divorce
     prohibition (deleted by the Fifteenth Amendment of the Constitution Act
     1995), and the general contents of Articles 41 and 42 dealing with the
     family and education. For a representative analysis of these provisions by
     eminent historians, see J. H. Whyte, *Church and State in Modern Ireland,
     1923–1979*, Dublin: Gill & Macmillan, 1979, pp. 50–56; F. S. L. Lyons,
     Ireland since the Famine, London: Fontana, 1973, pp. 536–50; J. J. Lee,
     Ireland 1912–1985: Politics and Society, Cambridge: Cambridge
     University Press, 1989, pp. 201–11.
6.   Lyons, *op. cit.*, pp. 549–50.
7.   *Op. cit.*, pp. 213–14. The quotation is from J. Kelly, *The Irish
     Constitution*, Dublin: Butterworths, 1994, p. xci.
8.   See the comments of Lee, *op. cit.*, p. 202:
     > Much remains to be uncovered about the planning and the drafting of the
     > constitution, including not least the roles of John Hearne, the legal adviser to
     > External Affairs, and of Maurice Moynihan. ... Any verdict on the genesis,
     > content, or consequences of the constitution must be even more provisional and
     > subjective than normal historical judgements.

     The work of the 1934 Constitution Committee was clearly appreciated by
     J. Faughnan in his seminal article, 'The Jesuits and the Drafting of the Irish
     Constitution', *Irish Historical Studies*, Vol. 26 (1988), p. 79, although, as
     its title suggests, this essay has a different focus. The work of the
     committee is briefly alluded to by A. J. Ward, *The Irish Constitutional
     Tradition: Responsible Government and Modern Ireland 1782–1992*,
     Dublin: Irish Academic Press, 1994, p. 239.
9.   Lyons, *op. cit.*, p. 472.
10. Foreword by Chief Justice Kennedy to L. Kohn, *The Constitution of the
     Irish Free State*, London: Allen and Unwin, 1932, p. xii.
11. I.e., the power to invalidate a statute on the ground that it contravened a
     provision of the Constitution. This was completely unknown in the British
     system.
12. I.e., in contrast to those features which either were inspired by previous
     British constitutional practice (e.g. the rules as to parliamentary privilege
     in Article 15) or established the institutions of the State in a manner which
     roughly paralleled the Westminster model (e.g. a government based on the
     principle of collective responsibility contained in Article 28).
13. *R. (O'Brien) v. Governor of the North Dublin Military Barracks* [1924] 1
     IR 32; *ITGWU v. TGWU* [1936] IR 471.
14. *Fundamental Rights in the Irish Law and Constitution*, Dublin: Hodges
     Figgis, 1967, pp. 16–17.
15. This is made clear by Chief Justice Kennedy (who, as law officer to the
     Provisional Government, had been one of the principal drafters of the

1922 Constitution) in his preface to Kohn's book, *op. cit.*, p. xiii:

> It was originally intended, as appears from the draft, that amendment of the Constitution should not be possible without the consideration due to so important a matter affecting the fundamental law and framework of the State, and the draft provided that the process of amendment should be such as to require full and general consideration. At the last moment, however, it was agreed that a provision be added to Article 50, allowing amendment by way of ordinary legislation during a limited period so that drafting or verbal amendments, not altogether unlikely to appear necessary in a much debated text, might be made without the more elaborate process proper for the purpose of more important amendments. This clause was, however, afterwards used for effecting alterations of a radical and far-reaching character, some of them far removed in principle from the ideas and ideals of the first authors of the instrument.

16. [1935] IR 472. This case concerned the validity of the Constitution (Amendment No. 22) Act 1933 which had abolished the right of appeal from the Supreme Court to the Judicial Committee of the Privy Council, a right which was not only provided for in the Constitution, but which was also contained in the treaty.

17. [1935] IR 170.

18. For a discussion of these issues, see I. Jennings, 'The Statute of Westminster and Appeals' (1936) 52 *Law Quarterly Review* 173, J. Philips, 'Ryan's Case' (1936) 52 *Law Quarterly Review* 241 and N. Lenihan, 'Royal Prerogatives and the Constitution' (1989) 24 *Irish Jurist* 1.

19. The amendment, which was in the name of W. T. Cosgrave, J. A. Costello and Patrick McGilligan, sought to amend Article 50 of the 1922 Constitution by providing that no ordinary law amending the Constitution passed by the Oireachtas in respect of:

> Articles 6, 7, 8, 9, 18, 19, 24, 28, 43, 46, 49, 50, 61, 62, 63, 64, 65, 66, 68, 69, 70 shall become law until after a General Election shall have been held and a Resolution approving of such amendment shall have been passed by Dáil Éireann on the recommendation of the Executive Council first elected after such General Election.

The background to this proposed amendment is discussed in D. O'Sullivan, *The Irish Free State and its Senate*, London: Routledge, 1940, pp. 363–5. The author comments (p. 364) that the opposition was concerned that de Valera's real object 'was to establish himself as a dictator behind the facade of single-chamber parliamentary government'.

20. *Dáil Debates*, Vol. 52, col. 1249 (17 May 1934).

21. *Dáil Debates*, Vol. 52, cols 1877–8 (25 May 1934).

22. I.e., corresponding to the present Department of the Taoiseach.

23. The drafting committee for the Constitution itself consisted of McDunphy, Hearne and O'Donoghue, together with de Valera's private secretary Maurice Moynihan who took Roche's place on that committee: see R. Fanning, 'Mr de Valera writes a Constitution', in B. Farrell (ed.), *De Valera's Constitution and Ours*, Dublin: Gill & Macmillan, 1988, p. 39. See also D. Keogh, 'Church, State and Society', in Farrell (ed.), *op. cit.*, p. 106. The detailed drafting of the new Constitution does not appear to have commenced until the late summer 'when the 1934 Committee was reconstituted, albeit on a more informal basis. One major change had been made. Roche's place had been taken by Maurice Moyhihan ...' see Faughnan, *loc. cit.*, p. 80. For an account of Hearne's role in the drafting process, see B. Kennedy, 'John Hearne and the Irish Constitution', *Éire-Ireland*, Vol. 25 (1989), p. 121.

24. Minutes of second meeting, 29 May 1934.
25. Minutes of third meeting, 1 June 1934.
26. D. Keogh, 'The Irish Constitutional Revolution: An Analysis of the Making of the Constitution', in F. Litton (ed.), *The Constitution of Ireland 1937–1987*, Dublin: Institute of Public Administration, 1988, p. 8; Ward, *op. cit.*, p. 240.
27. 18, 19 and 20 June 1934.
28. The memorandum was dated 14 June 1934 and was immediately circulated to other members of the committee.
29. His proposed addendum to Article 65 of the 1922 Constitution which would have required any constitutional challenge to be brought within three months of the date of the enactment of the law in question is discussed below.
30. If only Roche could have foreseen the vigorous judicial activism and the key role of the courts in constitutional matters which was to lie in the future, one wonders what his comments would have been!
31. McDunphy noted in the margins of his copy: 'I agree.'
32. Save that the emergency is declared only following the passage of resolutions by both Houses of the Oireachtas.
33. Roche then proceeded to make a number of comments about other specifc articles. His views on Articles 64 and 65 are discussed below.
34. Held respectively on 27, 28 and 29 June 1934.
35. Article 51 had provided that any provision of the Constitution (other than Article 46 and Article 51) might be amended by means of ordinary legislation for a period of three years from the date on which the first President took office. The First Amendment of the Constitution Act 1939 and the Second Amendment of the Constitution Act 1939 were enacted by means of ordinary legislation during this transitional period which expired on 25 June 1941. But even during this transitional period the President had a discretion to require that any such proposal be submitted to a referendum before it was enacted into law: see generally, Kelly, *The Irish Constitution*, pp. 1167–70.
36. The revised draft contained in the National Archives is very heavily annotated and lines have been drawn through several paragraphs.
37. A line has, however, been drawn in manuscript through these paragraphs and they do not feature in the final report.
38. Article 38.3.1 provides that:

> Special courts may be established by law for the trial of offences in cases where it may be determined in accordance with such law that the ordinary courts are inadequate to secure the effective administration of justice, and the preservation of public peace and order.

39. The contents of Appendices B and C are dealt with below. Appendix D contained extracts from foreign constitutions dealing with freedom of assembly, Appendix E contained extracts from foreign constitutions dealing with the annual assembly of parliament, Appendix F contained extracts from foreign constitutions dealing with the declaration of war, Appendix G contained an excerpt of a letter from the secretary of the Department of Education dealing with free primary education and Appendix H contained the text of Article 36 of the Constitution.
40. The committee recommended that Article 9 be amended so as to make it clear that:

> laws may be passed, and police action taken, to prevent or control open-air meetings which might interfere with normal traffic or otherwise become a

nuisance or danger to the general public. We understand that legislation on these lines has been delayed by reason of doubts as to whether such legislation could be validly enacted in view of the present wording of the Article.

The committee included in Appendix D copies of the relevant articles dealing with freedom of assembly which were contained in the constitutions of Belgium (1921), Czechoslovakia (1920), Denmark (1915), Estonia (1920), Germany (Weimar Constitution, 1919), Yugoslavia (1921) and Spain (1931).

The committee's recommendation was acted on, as Article 40.6.1.ii of the Constitution now provides by way of qualification of the right of the citizens to assemble peaceably and without arms that:

> Provision may be made by law to prevent or control meetings which are determined in accordance with law to be calculated to cause a breach of the peace or to be a danger or nuisance to the general public and to prevent or control meetings in the vicinity of either House of the Oireachtas.

41. The minutes of the third meeting record that the committee observed that Article 19 might be modified so as to secure that 'objectionable pronoucements in Parliament may not be utilised outside for the purpose of inciting to violence or other breaches of the law'. These comments – which, significantly, did not feature in the final report nor were they acted upon in respect of the corresponding provisions (Article 15.12) – were probably made in the light of the deteriorating security situation at the time, with clashes between the IRA and the Blueshirts: see generally, O'Sullivan, *op. cit.*, pp. 342–4, 359–62.

42. The committee recommended that the requirements that there be at least one session of the Oireachtas each year (now contained in Article 15.7) and that the Dáil should fix the date of reassembly of the Dáil following a general election should be regarded as fundamental. The committee examined the constitutions of Czechoslovakia (1920), Denmark (1915), Germany (Weimar Constitution, 1919), Yuogslavia (1921), Estonia (1920), Mexico (1917) and Poland (1921)(which were set out in Appendix E to the main report) by way of comparative analysis of these questions and concluded:

> In other Constitutions (see Appendix E) the desired result is secured by providing:
> (i) that Parliament shall meet on a specified date in each year, if not previously convoked, and/or
> (ii) that if a certain proportion of the total members so require, Parliament must be convened within a specified time.
> We recommend that an effective provision on the lines of (i) be substituted for the first sentence of Article 24. We also suggest for favourable consideration the insertion of an additional provision on the lines of (ii).

Article 15.7 incorporates a modified version of (i), but no action was taken in respect of (ii).

43. The committee observed that the principle that 'an Executive should have no power to delay the last formal stage of enactment of Bills which have been duly passed by Parliament through all legislative stages is fundamental'. As 'the trend of policy' was that it was not desirable 'to make permanent the present machinery of assent', the committee thought it desirable, if possible, to separate these two features of this article into separate articles, so that 'that relating to machinery of assent or promulgation [could be] left open to amendment by ordinary legislation'.

Article 25.1 of the Constitution now provides that, save for the special

case of a bill to amend the Constitution, a bill passed by both Houses of
the Oireachtas shall be presented by the Taoiseach to the President for
signature.

44.   The committee commented that '(a) the reference to the Treaty and (b) the
      limitation to the territory of the Irish Free State should be eliminated'. The
      committee added that the suggested amendment 'in regard to (b) is a
      corollary to recent constitutional developments whereby the right of
      Saorstát Éireann to raise and maintain armed forces outside of its territory
      has been recognised'.

45.   Article 49 provided that:

      Save in the case of actual invasion, the Irish Free State (Saorstát Éireann) shall
      not be committed to active participation in any war without the assent of the
      Oireachtas.

      The committee commented that:

      The restriction imposed by the word 'active' in reference to participation of the
      Saorstát in war should be further examined. This word was not in the draft of
      the Treaty before being submitted to the British Government in 1922. It is
      understood that it was inserted at the request of the British Government in
      conformity with the theory that once the King had declared war even though
      the actual declaration concerned Great Britain, it automatically involved the
      Dominions in the state of war created.

      In view of these comments, it is not surprising that the reference to 'active
      participation' has been omitted in the present Constitution. Article 29.3.1
      now provides that:

      War shall not be declared and the State shall not participate in any war save
      with the assent of Dáil Éireann.

46.   The committee originally commented that:

      The subject matter of this Article, which has a direct bearing on Part II of our
      terms of reference, will be dealt with in a separate Report.

      As we have already noted, the committee ultimately never reported on
      Part II of its terms of reference.

47.   At its third meeting the committee noted that the Department of Finance
      was to be consulted 'as to whether this Article is fundamental'. Roche
      wrote to J. J. McElligott, secretary of the Department of Finance on 2
      June 1934 requesting the urgent views of the department as to whether
      Article 61 'or any other Article should be so regarded'. The Department of
      Finance does not appear to have responded formally to this request, but in
      the final report, the committee observed that it understood 'from informal
      conversations that the Department of Finance regard this Article as
      fundamental'.

48.   The committee's comments are dealt with below.

49.   The committee noted that if its proposals in relation to the revision of
      Article 2A were to be adopted this might necessitate a revision of the text
      of Article 70, but 'this question would naturally receive attention in
      connection with the drafting of the new provisions'.

50.   The committee had already noted at its third meeting that the provisions
      of Article 64 might need to be re-examined as far as their effect 'on the
      exercise of quasi-judicial functions such as those exercised by the Land
      Commission, the Master of the High Court, etc. should be further
      considered'. It may be noted that, a few years earlier, the constitutionality
      of the Land Commission's activities had survived challenge only following
      very elaborate judgments from the Supreme Court which attempted to
      essay a definition of what constituted a judicial power: see *Lynham v.*

Butler (No.2) [1933] IR 74. In 1929 it had been held – but not, it is submitted, very convincingly – that an assessment of damages by the Master of the High Court did not represent the exercise of judicial power: see *Matheson v. Wilson* [1929] IR 134.

51. *Dáil Debates*, Vol. 65, cols 1511–12.
52. *Op. cit.*, p. 155.
53. See generally, R. Keane, 'The Voice of the Gael: Chief Justice Kennedy and the Emergence of the New Irish Court System, 1921–1936' (1996) 31 *Irish Jurist* 205, 221–3; T. Garvin, *1922 – The Birth of Irish Democracy*, Dublin: Gill & Macmillan, 1996, pp. 171–3; O'Sullivan, *op. cit.*, pp. 533–4.
54. The Constitution Review Group considered a similar proposal, but rejected it: see note 66, *infra*.
55. Keogh, 'Church, State and Society', in Farrell (ed.), *op. cit.*, p. 108. Keogh also observes (p. 107) that the drafters:

> were all people of wide culture. They were wholly free of the stridency associated with certain vociferous elements in the Irish Catholic Church in the 1930s. All ... had broad intellectual horizons. None were the victims of then fashionable ideological phobias.

56. *Dáil Debates*, Vol. 67, cols 53–4 (11 May 1937). Indeed, the draft Constitution had originally proposed that the Supreme Court alone should have original jurisdiction in constitutional matters. However, in response to opposition suggestions, de Valera agreed to an amendment at committee stage whereby the power was transferred to the High Court with a right of appeal to the Supreme Court: *Dáil Debates*, Vol. 68, cols 1492–5 (2 June 1937).
57. See Kelly, *The Irish Constitution*, p. 482. In *McMenamin v. Ireland*, Supreme Court, 19 December 1996 the court identified a breach of the State's constitutional obligations in circumstances where the failure to revise the pension arrangements of District Judges provided for by the Courts (Superannuation Provisions) Act 1961 having regard to the fact that revised mortality tables and increasing judicial longevity in the subsequent 35-year period had rendered the 1961 superannuation calculations objectively unfair.
58. This point was made by the Supreme Court in *Ryan v. Attorney General* [1965] IR 294 in dismissing a challenge to the constitutionality of the Health (Flouridation of Water Supplies) Act 1960. In this case the available evidence strongly suggested that the flouridation of water did not have the deleterious consequences apprehended by the plaintiff, but Ó Dálaigh CJ was careful to stress that 'if in the future the scientific evidence available should be such as to warrant a different conclusion on the facts, the question of the validity of the Act could be re-opened'.
59. See Kelly, *The Irish Constitution*, p. 219.
60. See generally *ibid.*, pp. 212–19. Of course, if the Supreme Court adjudges that the bill or any portion thereof is unconstitutional, then the bill falls in its entirety and the President must decline to sign it into law: Article 26.3.1.
61. Ó Néill's letter of 2 July 1934 to the committee was set out in Appendix G. Roche had written on 15 June 1934 requesting Ó Néill's views.
62. This point was confirmed by the Supreme Court in *Crowley v. Ireland* [1980] IR 102.
63. Although the committee noted with evident satisfaction that this article had not been included by the leaders of the opposition in the list of fundamental articles referred to in their Dáil motion.

64. [1993] 2 IR 17.
65. J. Casey, 'Interpretation of Constitutional Guarantees: An Antipodean History Lesson?' (1996) 31 *Irish Jurist* 102. As Casey so perceptively notes, the High Court of Australia's contrary conclusion in respect of an exactly parallel question in *Cheatle v. The Queen* (1993) 177 CLR 541 is more persuasive.
66. As it happens, the *Report of the Constitution Review Group* recommended (pp. 143–4) against the establishment of a Constitutional Court on the grounds that it would lead to a complication of appellate structures and that it was undesirable that there should be a 'proliferation of court structures in a small state where there should be maximum use of the existing courts'.
67. At least six major items of legislation have been found to be unconstitutional on this ground: see *The State (Sheerin) v. Kennedy* [1966] IR 379; *Re Haughey* [1971] IR 217; *Cullen v. Attorney General* [1979] IR 394; *Kostan v. Ireland* [1978] ILRM 12; *Desmond v. Glackin (No. 2)* [1993] 3 IR 67 and *Mallon v. Minister for Agriculture and Food* [1996] 1 IR 517.
68. See, e.g., the comments of B. Chubb, *The Government and Politics of Ireland*, 3rd edn, London: Longman, 1992, p. 42:
    > Bunreacht na hÉireann was almost literally de Valera's constitution. He drafted it or supervised its drafting, clearing its principles with his government and taking advice from officials and others, including a number of the Catholic clergy.

    See also Fanning, 'Mr de Valera writes a Constitution', in Farrell (ed.), *op. cit.*, pp. 32–45 for an expression of similar views.
69. It is also beyond question that de Valera was personally involved in the drafting of some of the key clauses. Keogh notes, for example, in 'Irish Constitutional Revolution', p. 29, that drafts of some of the amendments to Article 44 have been found in de Valera's own hand.
70. However, Keogh rightly acknowledges the central work of Hearne, Maurice Moynihan (then secretary to the government and chairman of the drafting committee for the Constitution) and the other members of the drafting committee in his seminal essay, 'Irish Constitutional Revolution', pp. 4, 65–6. It is, of course, clear from this essay that de Valera took a very keen interest in the draft and remained the ultimate arbiter of disputed points. The fact remains, however, that much of the sophisticated legal thinking evident in the Constitution must have come from de Valera's legal team and the 1934 report provides corroborative evidence for this argument. Ward, *op. cit.*, also comments (pp. 239–40) that:
    > de Valera himself took little part in the technical work of preparation but gave instructions to Hearne and responded to the numerous drafts that Hearne and his civil service associates presented.
71. 'Fundamental Rights and the Constitution', in Farrell (ed.), *op. cit.*, p. 163.
72. Thus, de Valera said in respect of the fundamental rights provisions (*Dáil Debates*, Vol. 68, cols 216–17):
    > Unfortunately … we cannot provide by any Constitution against the possible abuse of its powers by the legislature in future. It is vain to attempt to do it. All we can do is set headlines for the legislature, as we are doing here – headlines with regard to the things the legislature should aim at.
73. *The Irish Times*, 1 July 1937, described the declarations of fundamental rights in the Constitution as 'bunkum'. O'Sullivan, an admittedly fierce if eloquent critic of de Valera, writing in 1940 commented (*op. cit.*, p. 495) that:

> Large sections of the new Constitution consist of declarations of a homiletic character concerning personal rights, the family, education, private property, religion and directive principles of social policy. Many of these are so vague that they could not possibly be impleaded in the courts.

74.   Thus, the Finnish Constitution of 1919 also contained a brief catalogue of fundamental rights, but, as one noted Finnish human rights lawyer has observed:

> In everyday court practice, constitutional rights have never played a significant part and even today cases where constitutional provisions have been invoked by Finnish courts remain few in number.

M. Sheinin, 'Incorporation and Implementation of Human Rights in Finland', in M. Sheinin (ed.), *International Human Rights Norms in the Nordic and Baltic Countries*, The Hague: Martinus Nijhoff, 1996, p. 261.

18

Volunteer Service in the Elimination of Poverty

BILL JACKSON

As long as there is plenty, poverty is evil.

Robert F. Kennedy

Development is people: all else is technique.

Erskine Childers and Bradford Morse

WITH the possible exception of disarmament, the elimination of poverty – or at the very least its marked alleviation – remains the single greatest priority of humankind. It has been the key objective of the Agenda for Development and the related Agenda for Peace initiated by former United Nations Secretary-General Boutros Boutros Ghali as well as of the Irish government's Official Development Assistance (ODA) programme.

Perspectives on poverty

It is as well to remind ourselves what we mean by 'poverty', whether we are talking of nations or of individuals, or whether the poverty be on O'Connell Bridge or the Orinoco. The statistics presented in Table 1 underline that poverty is both objective and relative. The middle column is a sample of developing nations: all are in fact classified as 'least developed countries'. They are the seven which Ireland has singled out for priority help from the ODA programme: Ethiopia, Lesotho, Mozambique, Sudan, Tanzania, Uganda and Zambia.[1] The poorest in the ranges are objectively poor by any reckoning – one might say absolutely poor. The fact that all of them are also poor, *relatively* speaking, is

Table 1: Indicators of relative poverty and prosperity

Criterion	Irish ODA priority countries (range)	Ireland
Under 5 years mortality, 1993 (000)[a]	156 to 282	9
Life expectancy, 1993 (years)[b]	44.7 to 60.8	76.1
Population per doctor, 1993 [a]	9,210 to 85,690	980
Food production per capita, 1979–93 (average annual growth rate %)[a]	–2.2 to +0.3	+1.9
Adult literacy, 1993 (%)[a]	37.9 to 76.2	99
First, second and third-level education enrolment, 1993 (%)[b]	16 to 55	84
Real GDP per capita, 1993 ($)[b]	420 to 1,350	15,120

Source:
(a) World Bank, *World Development Report, 1995*, New York: Oxford University Press for the World Bank, 1995, pp. 168–9, 214–15
(b) United Nations Development Programme, *Human Development Report, 1996*, New York: Oxford University Press for the United Nations Development Programme, 1996, pp. 135–7

starkly brought home if we compare the sample with our own Irish situation (which is broadly speaking prosperous even when compared with some other so-called 'industrialised' nations).

However, stated in such macro terms, these statistics still cloak the obscenity of how poverty *affects human beings* and how in any society they can fall victim to it. Few authors have captured more graphically the inexorability of 'Third World' poverty than Dominique Lapierre in his magnificent novel set in Calcutta, *The City of Joy.*

> Yet further terrible trials lay in store for Prodip Pal and his family. Just like ten or twelve million other Bengali peasants during this second half of the twentieth century, they were to become the victims of that endemic phenomenon known to economists as the cycle of poverty – that unavoidable process of descending the social ladder by which the farmer becomes a sharecropper, then a peasant without land, then an agricultural labourer, then, eventually, is forced into exile.[2]

But that is only the *process*, and in one country. It still doesn't describe the end result, the general *state* of poverty, the degree of deprivation. Theorising about developing countries from the comfort of our armchairs, we'd probably instance the lack of sufficient food (seen in Ethiopia some years back, or most recently in Niger as the result of drought), lack of basic health provisions, of shelter, of opportunity for education and training. We might or might not remember to add the lack of transport and access, and perforce by extension the lack – or for all practical purposes, the remoteness and felt irrelevance – of the human rights of freedom of association, expression and the vote. In sum, poverty is lack of choice.

Which is pretty well how a local women's group in a disadvantaged neighbourhood of Dublin saw it, quoted by Hugh Frazer of the Combat Poverty Agency:

> Poverty means constantly scraping and never making ends meet.
> Poverty is the feeling of inadequacy.
> Poverty means never being able to get a bank loan.
> Poverty means social isolation.
> Being poor means constantly hiding your poverty.
> Poverty means denying your ambitions.
> Poverty means 'policing' the kitchen at night so the kids don't snack.
> Poverty is left over pie.
> Being poor is being tired of managing.
> Being poor means taking tranquilliser to be able to cope.
> Being poor means 'protecting' your kids.
> Being poor means not being able to host family and friends.
> Being poor means paying more for your goods and more for borrowing – the poor pay more.
> Being poor means being constantly in debt.
> Being poor means having no choice.[3]

As we approach the end of the second millennium, there are two fallacies about poverty at home and abroad which should give us cause for sober reflection. First is the temptation to think that the problem has gone or is going away as a result of the end of the Cold War. Not true: poverty is alive and well and living virtually everywhere. Second, that the solution to it is more readily to hand in free market forces than under the discredited central planning. On that the jury is still out. Robert I. Kuttner of the Washington-based Economic Policy Institute noted recently that as globalisation and liberalisation take root, the international community is reverting to a laissez-faire system that has been historically proven to be 'unstable, unreliable and unbearable in human terms'.[4] Apologising for ranting, novelist John le Carré puts it more baldly:

> The mere fact that communism didn't work doesn't mean that capitalism does. In many parts of the globe it's a wrecking, terrible force, displacing people, ruining lifestyles, traditions, ecologies and stable systems with the same ruthlessness as communism.[5]

Were Mr Hegel still alive, he would surely remind us that capitalism was thesis, communism the antithesis, and not the other way around.

Kuttner would have delighted Mr Hegel because he went on to say that, since an unfettered market economy is not beneficial either for a growing economy or for balanced human development, the task today is to reinvent a mixed economy, noting that

> Many of the things that markets price wrong – education, public infrastructure, health, research, the quality of public governance – are themselves necessary inputs to economic development.

Poverty and instability

But, since 'the poor always ye have with you', perhaps there is no need to worry that 20–30 per cent of relatively rich Ireland's people are living in poverty, or that a seventh are unemployed? Imprudent at the least, because poverty is the great destabiliser of the individual and the family, the community, the nation: and thus of the world. One doesn't have to be a card-carrying Marxist to know in one's heart that there will be no lasting peace without development, without policies which seek systematically to reduce poverty to a much greater extent than at present – and succeed in doing so. No peace in Summerhill, any more than in Somalia; no peace in Andersonstown, any more than in Angola.

In the USA, where 12 per cent of the population is black and 25 per cent of them are below the poverty line (only 7 per cent of whites are below it), blacks constitute 59 per cent of those serving prison sentences. There are of course well-off criminals in Ireland and elsewhere, whose anti-social behaviour requires a different explanation. But it has been interesting to have clear historical evidence of the broad linkage between poverty and violence against property and persons in Ireland in Brendan Ó Cathoir's 'Famine Diary' in 1996–97 issues of *The Irish Times;* this entry could as easily have come from Mexico's Chiapas Province in recent days:

> *September 12th, 1846.* In Clonoulty, Co. Tipperary, a curate tears down an 'inflammatory notice' posted on the chapel gate. It urged the people to assemble on the fairgreen to devise some means to keep themselves from starvation. Father Thomas O'Carroll speaks 'on the necessity of something being done immediately to mitigate the distress and inspire confidence, as the people are in a great ferment about food. It is much to be feared that outrages will take place' ... Some disorderly fellows, taking advantage of the alarm, are going about the country inciting the poor to seize the cattle of the gentry.

> *September 14th.* In pursuance of the notice about 200 persons tumultuously assembled today ... It is really provoking to witness the efforts which the youth of this parish are making to possess firearms ... It is quite a usual thing

for servant men and paupers employed on the public works to club a portion of their earnings in order to purchase a gun.[6]

While we may like to think that we now live in calmer times, we are blinkered if we deny that much of the violence still done to people and property which characterises the Ireland of the 1990s is either directly linked to, or substantially affected indirectly by, the poverty which persists in our society. The problem of development, and its implications for peace and social stability, is by no means confined to the countries of the Third World.

The 1995 White Paper on Ireland's foreign policy recognised and encapsulated the linkage well, in stating that there is a demonstrable interconnection between the economic and social well-being of all the nations of the world and the maintenance of international peace and security. 'Irish Aid and Development Co-operation', it said, 'are practical expressions of Ireland's foreign policy commitment to peace and justice in the world.'[7]

Irish Official Development Assistance and poverty

The White Paper enunciates the government's objectives in participating in development co-operation. They are commendably simple, modest for a small donor country, and people-oriented:

- to reduce poverty and promote sustainable development in some of the poorest countries of the world;
- to assist in establishing and maintaining peace in developing countries by fostering democracy, respect for human rights, gender and social equality and protection of the environment;
- to respond promptly to emergencies and humanitarian disasters, both natural and man-made, as they occur, and to support preventive measures so that such emergencies may, so far as possible, be avoided;
- to contribute to building civil society and social solidarity.[8]

Had that White Paper been written thirty years earlier, it would have reflected the aspiration, internationally widespread at the time, to 'balanced economic and social development'. The White Paper has an admirably social foundation and in that respect runs to some extent counter to currently prevailing donor thinking, which has swung emphatically to the economic component. It has been in reaction to that latter trend that, since first it was published in 1990, the Human Development Report issued annually by the United Nations Development Programme (UNDP) has been dedicated to ending the mismeasure of human progress by economic growth alone. The foreword to the 1996 report states:

> The paradigm shift in favour of sustainable human development is still in the making. But more and more policy-makers in many countries are reaching the unavoidable conclusion that, to be valuable and legitimate, development progress – both nationally and internationally – must be people-centred, equitably distributed and environmentally and socially sustainable.[9]

Gaps continue to widen

As long ago as 1979, Dr Garret FitzGerald wrote:

> That the average citizen of the United States consumes over thirty times the material resources used by the average citizen of countries such as Bangladesh and Bhutan in Asia, and Rwanda, Upper Volta and Mali in Africa, is a staggering statistic, which owes nothing to exchange rate distortion but is as near as it is humanly possible at present to arrive at a true measurement of relative material welfare.[10]

Nearly twenty years on, the position has significantly worsened. UNDP goes on in that Human Development Report to warn that

> In the past 15 years the world has become more economically polarized – both between countries and within countries. If present trends continue, present disparities between the developing and industrial nations will move from inequitable to inhuman.[11]

And it provides abundant evidence to justify the warning:

> The world has become more polarized and the gulf between the rich and the poor of the world has widened even further. Of the $23 trillion global GDP in 1993, $18 trillion is in the industrial countries – only $5 trillion in the developing countries, even though they have nearly 80 per cent of the world's people.

- The poorest 20 per cent of the world's people saw their share of global income decline from 2.3 per cent to 1.4 per cent in the past 30 years. Meanwhile, the share of the richest 20 per cent rose from 70 per cent to 85 per cent. That doubled the ratio of the shares of the richest and the poorest – from 30:1 to 61:1.
- The gap in per capita income between the industrialised and developing worlds tripled, from $5,700 in 1960 to $15,400 in 1993.[12]

In the very recent past Ireland was reflecting that trend, showing an increase in the number of people in poverty from 18.4 per cent in 1980 to 19.5 per cent in 1985. But the most recent research by the Economic and Social Research Institute suggests that the trend is beginning to be reversed: the *number* of people falling below the 60 per cent and 50 per cent of average income lines had increased by 1994 and the number below the 40 per cent relative line was falling or stable.[13] For example, about 20 per cent of Irish people were below half average income in 1987; by 1994 only about 8 per cent were below that line (uprated by the increase in prices over the period). Moreover, when alternative aggregate poverty measures are used, taking into account the *depth* of poverty shortfalls as well as numbers, a consistent fall is evident in aggregate poverty between 1987 and 1994. Nevertheless, writing in *Poverty Today*, Hugh Frazer can state that

> Overall, the unequal distribution of resources in Ireland, which underlies the high levels of poverty, has not changed sufficiently to lift many people out of poverty. Indeed, some groups, notably the elderly, single-adult households, female-headed households and households headed by someone working full-time in the home ... have an increased risk of being below key relative income lines.[14]

Having in its opening sentence articulated the fundamental principle that 'Human development is the end – economic growth a means', the 1996 Human Development Report (1996 being the International Year of Poverty Eradication) continued:

> Eliminating poverty requires a holistic approach to human development. Not hand-outs but empowerment. Not Band-Aids but the preconditions for self-help.[15]

The White Paper speaks in similar terms of

> a greater understanding of the need for the process to be a real partnership, with the beneficiary countries and communities being fully involved, instead of having models of development imposed upon them.[16]

That understanding has dawned at home too: the government has committed itself to set out an across-the-board national strategy to address all aspects of poverty and inequality. And at local level throughout the country there now exists a range of broadly defined partnership structures for development, including county enterprise boards, Leader companies and the area based partnerships and other informal partnership arrangements.

Agency for Personal Service Overseas

In 1973, twenty-three years before the White Paper, Dr Garret FitzGerald had responded as Minister for Foreign Affairs to the urgings of a concerned group of individuals and organisations and announced plans to set up the Agency for Personal Service Overseas (APSO). A non-commercial state-sponsored body, it was destined to be the first piece of machinery for implementation of part of the new ODA programme. Its founding chairman was to be the man whom that concerned group, at the suggestion of Professor George Dawson of Trinity College, had asked to chair the preliminary consultations: Dr Kenneth Whitaker.

The new body was to promote volunteer service in developing countries by persons from Ireland, and to that end to disburse its annual grant-in-aid (part of the International Co-operation Vote administered by the Department of Foreign Affairs) in funding and co-financing assignments, providing appropriate orientation and training, and seeking the removal of disincentives to such service.

APSO was of course far from being the first Irish organisation in this field. The missionary work of various denominations had welcomed the contribution of lay personnel for years through endeavours such as Viatores Christi, and in a more secular vein both Concern and Gorta were already active. APSO represented a new channel by which the government could support such work both for its intrinsic value and as an approach towards fulfilling Ireland's share of a duty to poorer nations, recognised as an obligation in the expanding European Communities and the wider international community of 1973.

United Nations Volunteers programme

Three years earlier again, in 1970, the General Assembly of the United Nations had resolved that the work of the UN for the development of countries recently enfranchised could benefit from the input of volunteers. In like manner to APSO on the Irish scene, the United Nations Volunteers programme (UNV) was not itself the pioneer of such service internationally. It was created in the wake of Service Civile Internationale (1920) and the more recently established Voluntary Service Overseas in the United Kingdom (1957), the Peace Corps of the United States (1961), the Deutscher Entwicklungsdienst (1963) and several other such national programmes. These were partly or, for the most part indeed, wholly funded as an element of their countries' bilateral aid efforts. While they were welcomed, they were nonetheless seen by the Third World as inevitably influenced to some degree in policy and practice by the foreign policy objectives of the sponsoring nations. The case was made and accepted for such volunteers, recruited on a universal basis from developing and industrialised nations alike, to be enabled to serve in neutral and disinterested fashion through the UN family of agencies.

From technical assistance to facilitation

Within both UN and national administrations such programmes were perceived in the 1960s largely as technical assistance: designed operationally to fill manpower gaps in ministries and directorates of newly independent administrations, and by giving training and education to transfer skills to those needing them. The fields of activity for UNV and bilateral volunteers alike were the classical and discrete sectors of development – agriculture, health, education, infrastructure, etc.

Only a decade later, in the 1970s, prevailing orthodoxies about tackling poverty in 'the South' were under challenge. Maggie Black, chronicling Oxfam's first fifty years, puts it well:

> Economic expansion brought about by the march of Western science, technology and industrial knowhow into developing societies, had been expected to sweep more and more people into its embrace as it spawned jobs and services, upgrading the quality of life for all ... No such thing had occurred.[17]

It has taken most of the subsequent two decades for the international community really to address Robert McNamara's landmark suggestion to the World Bank in 1972, that the developing countries should reorient their policies to attack directly the poverty of the poorest 40 per cent of their citizens, and that their donor friends should help them do it. It has largely been voluntary agencies and volunteers, rather than governments and international agencies, which have brought about the change. Maggie Black again:

> to ensure 'that the money really gets there', the philanthropists distributed their resources as close to the poor as they could reach. The projects they supported focused on the specific needs of a specific group of people ... The sensitivity of most voluntary agency projects to the human condition – what people thought, how they behaved, whether they were motivated, what they themselves could contribute – was beyond that of large impersonal government programmes.[18]

Today's volunteers, Irish or international, do not affect to be experts: but neither are they 'wet behind the ears'. They are mid-career professional men and women, averaging 35–40 years of age, with degrees and postgraduate diplomas and, on average, five to ten years of working experience under their belts. They have a motivation to be of service – as UNVs, some 3,500 of them every year from 125 nationalities (including Irish, by courtesy of APSO); and 1,500 directly through APSO. The overriding common feature is their willingness to – indeed, their conviction that for effectiveness they must – work with their hosts, the 'beneficiaries', on a peer basis.

Things have evolved considerably for both APSO and UNV. APSO's Strategic Plan 1994–1997 describes its ethos of service in the following terms:

> ... We operate at an individual, organisational and community level and we seek to identify with those with whom we work in developing countries as closely as possible. We believe this enables us to work at a level and pace which is appropriate to the circumstances. It enables a greater understanding of both the problems and the potential solutions. In this way, we emphasise the role of Irish development workers as supporters and advisors in the development process. The individual will provide a particular skill and experience but can only be one element in a much larger and longer-term process.[19]

So it is with UNV, too. The emphasis has been for some years on the community, on facilitating and helping empower local people at the grassroots to take and pursue the initiatives which they themselves prioritise in seeking to improve their lot. Asked by a Filipina UNV fieldworker in Sri Lanka what their priority was, the women of a village replied that it was a crèche. Not a dispensary, not a feeder road? No, a crèche. Why? 'Because we're told that our best prospects lie in growing more food; there's plenty of untilled land round the village and we do the planting here, but we can't possibly open up new plots if our babies are milling around our feet the whole time: we need a crèche.'

So why didn't they go right ahead and build one? They were ready, they said, to bring stones for the foundations and poles, wood and palm leaves for the walls and roof: but cement was the one thing they couldn't afford. The UNV informed them of their *right* as a duly constituted village development group to an allowance of cement from the District Commissioner. They wouldn't approach him, they said, they had never dared do that: 'We are only poor village women.' The UNV convinced them to make the request and accompanied them on the bus. They got their cement. They built their crèche. Facilitation. Empowerment.

Development as a trickle-up process

As in that example, the local community is where it happens. No prescription or magic formula from a capital city ever brought about development, whether in Ireland or anywhere else. GNP is the sum total of many *local* efforts, guided and influenced by the centre perhaps, but local in their origin. Thus if a nation such as Zambia wants its AIDS prevention programme to be effective country-wide, it must not only work up a strategy at national level: the programme is doomed unless it also *reaches down* to individual homes. Accordingly UNVs have worked as AIDS advisers at *national* level in Lusaka, have formed the core of *district* groups working with those infected or affected, have trained *community* educators, have guided *home-based* care teams and have identified *local* personnel to extend the outreach. Other UNVs, in Honduras, have taken the socio-economic data researched by the Population Teaching and Research Unit of the National Autonomous University and helped local authorities apply them to economic, social, health and environmental issues in outlying suburbs.

But one can – and should – also *build upwards* from the innovative achievements of communities. We completely underestimate the richness and endurance of local knowledge systems and coping mechanisms. And, thanks to our media, we ignore what developing country peoples do for themselves routinely every day, as well as in the face of particular adversity. (We have forgotten that Lester Pearson could point out in the 1960s that, even then, 86 per cent of the development effort of those countries came from them and 14 per cent from the rest of us.) Not only, as we have seen, can volunteers help communities access resources outside the locality, but, just as importantly, they can encourage them to compare their experiences, share their techniques and network their knowledge, so that they can hone their own skills and help their fellows avoid reinventing the wheel. Artisans in leather, weaving and bamboo in the four countries of Bhutan, India, Nepal and Sri Lanka were enabled by UNVs to compare within their own and in each other's countries their experience in obtaining and processing raw material and designing their products. They exchanged designs and ergonomic techniques and they went on to discuss common approaches in dealing with suppliers, middlemen and authorities. A Canadian UNV 'eco-volunteer' was enabled to attend a networking meeting in Costa Rica on analog forestry (systems planned to reflect the naturally occurring forest ecosystems, in their form and function). There she learnt and brought back to New Brunswick a model pioneered in Sri Lanka. National

UNVs working with the Pagayan waste-pickers who live off the gargantuan rubbish dumps on the edge of Manila were brought to Cairo to see how the Zabbaleen there had built up businesses from the city's garbage.

Worth adding, too, is that a holistic approach is vital, in contrast to the help of yesteryear for discrete sectors. Farmers cannot be effective if they are undernourished or sick and haven't the physical strength to work the fields or husband their livestock. Nor if they cannot read the instructions on the fertiliser bag, or have no access to microcredit to buy the fertiliser anyway, or no means of irrigating the crops. 'Development' is a complex process requiring the integration of many interlocking inputs – nutrition, health, literacy, technology, training, loans, water, environmental management, etc. There can be a degree of emphasis in a given initiative on one or another of these, say by assigning a volunteer specialist in microcredit in Zanzibar, in low-cost housing in Namibia, in income generation in Ecuador, or in small business management in Papua New Guinea: but all are indispensable.

In these various contexts, volunteers have been a key conduit to an approach, an idea, an appropriate technology, a resource which lay just beyond the reach of the local community and which could transform an aspiration into reality, could generate some small income to widen the area of choice. Inexpensively, too: take, for example, the UNV who has reduced pollution and disease in villages of southern India by substituting for the dirty bucket at the well a pump they use in his native Sri Lanka. It's made of plastic rope and wood, PVC piping and a bicycle tyre, and costs $10. Or the Congolese UNV teacher in Chad who fashioned all his classroom aids from locally available materials, including a perfectly satisfactory globe mounted on its axis – made from a gourd and with the continents painted on. Or the UNV from Togo who has helped locals bring on their small bakery in a Namibian village: it produces eighty loaves a day and has a monthly turnover of about $750. By the way, it bakes some smaller loaves 'so that even people with very little money can afford to buy some': has any Irish firm made this kind of gesture for the poor within living memory?

The 'value-added' of volunteer activity

There are of course parallels in the Irish context to the great innovations in the developing countries, like Bangladesh's Grameen Banks: the Ralahine co-operative in its time, Fr James McDyer's Glencolumbkille, Fr Harry Bohan's housing schemes, Brendan O'Regan's Shannon New Town and its pioneering industrial free zone. The parallels at home with

the approaches of APSO and UN volunteers abroad are striking; Hugh
Frazer of the Combat Poverty Agency summed them up well when he
said:

> Looking at the experience of voluntary groups in Ireland I can identify seven
> ways they can contribute to working for change in national policies to combat
> poverty:
>
> - winning the intellectual debate
> - winning the moral argument
> - empowering those affected by poverty
> - building alliances and coalitions
> - creating a climate for change
> - influencing policy makers
> - demonstrating alternatives.[20]

Thinking for the future and preparing itself for the World Summit for
Social Development in Copenhagen in March 1995, UNV recognised
that as government services crumble and more and more territory of the
so-called social sectors is left to the market, there is inevitably an
expansion of the numbers and categories of the marginalised and
excluded. It recognised, too, that many of the forces that shape society
today are much less visible, structured or identifiable as institutional
entities than before; that powers of decision-forming and decision-
making are more diffuse; and that many of the most important power-
holders do not participate in UN-organised conferences.

In UNV's belief, a very significant element of the response to this
situation can – indeed, must – come from volunteer action and service
which is already found abundantly in virtually every culture and in all
layers of human society. That is to say, volunteer effort as a form of
social behaviour which all of us practise as human beings and not just
volunteers as an occupational species: a form of social activism, non-
profit, non-wage and non-career action for the well-being of the
community, of society at large. Yet, there are extremes to be avoided:
volunteers have no wish to be exploited as a cop-out for societies which
cannot or will not accept that certain basic responsibilities are
incumbent on the state. Nor do they see voluntary service as an
alternative to the proper creation of remunerative employment.

With such pitfalls skirted, volunteer activity – usually involving
joining together for collective action – has enormous potential for
creating new alliances and partnerships, from the local to the global: it
crosses barriers of power and wealth, of nationality and geography, of
ethnic and cultural identities, of gender and age, of specialisation, even
of the gulf between government and civil society.

The missionaries were recognised for generations as the best expression in Africa and Asia of a caring and sharing Ireland. Effectively they were the source of Ireland's awareness, such as it has been, of the needs and hopes of those parts of the world. Albeit fewer in number, Irish volunteers convey as much to their overseas hosts of the Ireland of today. And the association for the volunteers who have returned, Comhlámh, has done an outstanding job of interpreting back home the aspirations of today's developing countries, and of seeking to influence the directions and content of Ireland's assistance, both official and non-governmental. The UNV programme is an APSO writ large, a global initiative with essentially the same purposes and the same very satisfactory track record. International volunteers represent an effective, inexpensive, humane (and largely incorruptible) means of helping our own societies in these ways, in the process of helping others. They were a cause for satisfaction as UNV celebrated twenty-five years of activity, and APSO and Comhlámh twenty-one. Far from having seen their day, the day of volunteers is still to come in Ireland and abroad, as civil society is called upon to bear a greater share of the load.

An International Year of Volunteers in 2001?

Which is why, together with a number of major international non-governmental organisations, UNV is advocating that 2001 be designated the International Year of Volunteers (IYV). Such a concentrated effort could bring volunteers' achievements more to the attention of governments and people, providing an opportunity to depict and talk and write about them, to stage demonstrations of examples, to give people a chance to experience their uniqueness, to campaign for them. Each society could define what encourages or inhibits volunteer behaviour among its people. What factors, what situations, which traditions, what messages come through from families, educators, religious authorities, media, the political leadership and élite? What are considered the best examples of volunteer-led activity? Which are the most representative profiles of exceptional volunteers, from the perspective of the given society? Country-wide studies could identify the broad impact of volunteer contributions – a recent official study in Australia indicated that the size of the volunteer 'workforce' was half as large as the country's entire labour force. And the case could be made for removal of disincentives to volunteer service: the grant of special leave of absence, for example, for voluntary work domestically or abroad, or the granting of tax-deductibility for donations in furtherance of such work.

It is earnestly to be hoped that the Irish government, encouraged by the fine record of its citizens as willing donors to voluntary activity and by the achievements of Irish volunteers within the ODA programme, will see fit to have Europe endorse the IYV proposal and ensure its resolution by the UN General Assembly. That would so well reflect what President Robinson has described as the spirit of *meitheal*:

> that sense of the interdependence of people, a sense fostered by the small village, the remote community, the conversation that goes on late in lonely parts, the treasured gift of sharing which maximises the resource loneliness and remoteness would otherwise erode. A sense which is reflected in all our countries, but which needs to be encouraged and harnessed in a more deliberate way.[21]

Reducing poverty is feasible

Meantime, let us note that deliberate reduction of poverty is feasible. The key to success, says a handbook resulting from a Ford Foundation-funded research project, is an effective partnership between the public and private sectors – the 'private sector' here defined as both for-profit private enterprise and non-profit institutions such as civic groups, community associations and other non-governmental organisations (led or supported by volunteers).[22]

- Since Chile returned to democracy it has maintained a commitment to an already open economy driven primarily by market forces with government expenditures in the social sector focused on the poor. In the five years to 1992, the percentage of homes classified as impoverished fell 10 per cent to a low of 27.7 per cent, four-fifths of the decrease being attributed to overall national growth but one-fifth to a gentle, evolutionary redistribution of income.
- Ten years after the Korean War, 40 per cent of the population of South Korea were regarded as destitute: today, barely 5 per cent are poverty-stricken. Prudent macroeconomic policies designed to secure stable demand and keep inflation low were key. But so also were enormous emphasis on education, one of the greatest of all equalising forces, and gradual extension of national health insurance.
- Malaysia boosted its income more than 7 per cent per annum over the past decades. But it also took steps to achieve equity, reduce poverty and ethnic tensions. It reduced its incidence of poverty from 49 per cent to 14 per cent between 1970 and 1993.

As they say in Mozambique, 'a luta continua': the struggle goes on. But the evidence is clear that, in Ireland and in developing countries, the task is not impossible. It is as much a matter of personal and political will as of know-how. In that sense and that context, volunteers and voluntary agencies can make a significant difference – because volunteering is, above all, an act of will to help other people help themselves.

NOTES

1. Department of Foreign Affairs, *Challenges and Opportunities Abroad: White Paper on Foreign Policy*, Dublin: Stationery Office, 1996, p. 232.
2. Dominique Lapierre, *The City of Joy*, London: Arrow Books, 1986, p. 8.
3. Hugh Frazer, 'Voluntary Action and Poverty Programmes', paper delivered in Madrid, 26 March 1992.
4. Robert I. Kuttner in the Paul G. Hoffmann Lecture for the UN Development Programme at the UN, November 1996.
5. Davis Streetfield, 'John le Carré: Lies, Damn Lies and the Spy Game', *International Herald Tribune*, 7 November 1996, p. 24.
6. *The Irish Times*, 14 September 1996, p. 4.
7. Department of Foreign Affairs, *op. cit.*, p. 230.
8. *Ibid.*, p. 229.
9. United Nations Development Programme, *Human Development Report, 1996*, New York: Oxford University Press for the United Nations Development Programme, 1996, p. iii.
10. Garret FitzGerald, *Unequal Partners*, New York: United Nations, 1979, p. 3.
11. United Nations Development Programme, *op. cit.*, p. iii.
12. *Ibid.*, p. 2.
13. T. Collins, B. Nolan, B. J. Whelan, C. T. Whelan and J. Williams, *Poverty in the 1990s: Evidence from the 1994 Living in Ireland Survey*, Dublin: Oak Tree Press, 1996.
14. Hugh Frazer, 'Viewpoint', *Poverty Today*, December 1996/January 1997, p. 3.
15. United Nations Development Programme, *op. cit.*, p. iv.
16. Department of Foreign Affairs, *op. cit.*, p. 233.
17. Maggie Black, *A Cause for Our Time: Oxfam, the first 50 Years*, Oxford: Oxfam and Oxford University Press, 1992, p. 177.
18. *Ibid.*, p. 179.
19. Agency for Personal Service Overseas, *Strategic Plan 1994–1997*, Dublin: Agency for Personal Service Overseas, p. 5.
20. Hugh Frazer, 'Voluntary Action and Poverty Programmes', p. 8.
21. President Mary Robinson, Address when accepting the Liberal International Prize for Freedom, Budapest, 27 November 1993, p. 4.
22. *Policies and Programs for Social and Human Development: A Handbook*, International Center for Economic Growth and International Center for Self-Governance, 1995.

$$===== \textbf{19} =====$$

Salmon and Sea Trout

KEN WHELAN

Introduction

FOR its size Ireland's freshwater resources are truly immense. Into a land area of 84,000 km² nature has packed some 26,000 km of river and stream and some 200,000 ha (500,000 acres) of lakes, all of these well populated with salmonids: salmon, sea trout, brown trout and in many places arctic charr.

The migratory salmonids, salmon and sea trout, are found in almost every accessible stream entering the sea but over one hundred are recognised as salmon or sea trout fisheries. There is probably no other country in the world which can boast such a concentration of sea running salmonids in such a confined geographical area. In this essay I will review the history of these valuable fisheries and the current national management and conservation objectives.

Ownership of salmon fisheries

Over the centuries the ownership and exploitation of this valuable self-renewing resource have taxed the minds and ingenuity of countless generations, not least those of religious communities. By the Middle Ages most religious establishments in Ireland were located on or near a river or lake. For example, Cong Abbey, an Augustinian settlement of monks in the far west of Ireland, at one time housed three thousand scholars. Not alone did the monks retain a so-called 'fishing-house' or trap on the neighbouring River Cong but they also had the tithes of the fishing on the River Moy, which is over 70 km distant! Indeed most of the numerous fishing weirs in Ireland belonged to religious orders at one time or another before their dissolution by King Henry VIII, after which the weirs fell mainly into private hands.

As may be imagined, quarrels often broke out regarding ownership or fishing rights, particularly on the more urban fisheries such as the River Liffey in Dublin. Here, in 1261, the Hospitallers of Kilmainham destroyed the fixed salmon net at Dublin bridge owned by the city, and the citizens in retaliation wrecked the Hospital's mill. When word reached King Henry III he ordered the city to pay a fine of ten pounds but stipulated that 'the Mayor and commonalty have to have free fishing in the Avenlif [River Liffey] ... and the passage of salmon great and small is not to be obstructed by nets, standards, weirs, other engines or impediments'. Eventually the city leased the fishery to private citizens but it took steps on every possible occasion to protect its interests.

The value put on their fisheries by the city's inhabitants is reflected in the anti-pollution legislation passed by Dublin Corporation in 1466! It stipulated that: 'no tanner, glover nor any person use limed ware or leather work in the River Liffey on account of the destruction of the salmon. Penalty 3s/4^d for each offence, one half to be paid to the detector and half to the court.' In 1585 Dublin Corporation reasserted its determination to keep the river clean by ordering the impoundment of pigs found on the strand and forbidding anyone 'to put any flax into the ditches near his ground'. Flax water is a destroyer of fish life and special precautions must be taken to keep it out of rivers. Dublin Corporation retained its fishery down to very recent times.

Fisheries legislation

Further legislation concerning the conservation and protection of salmon was enacted during the following three hundred years. Then in 1842 the Fisheries Act sought to consolidate and update earlier outmoded legislation. This Act was a landmark in salmon conservation but, unfortunately, because of ambiguities or other defects, not all its provisions could be readily implemented. However, provisions were made for the following:

- appointment of commissioners with extensive powers for the government, regulation and management of the fisheries
- annual close seasons and weekly close times
- a free gap (Queen's share) to be maintained in salmon weirs with conditions defined for the construction of these weirs
- fish passes over artificial and natural obstructions
- protection for fry and smolts, kelts and unseasonable fish
- prohibition of a number of poaching methods, for example strokehauls, lights
- protection against pollution or the use of fish poisons.

Penalties for conviction for infringements were specified and owners of fisheries could appoint water bailiffs to enforce the law with wide powers of entry and seizure.

Additional legislation introduced in 1848 and 1863 provided for the division of the country into twenty-three fishery districts and strict limitations on the location and number of fixed nets to be used in the sea and tideways. Each district was to be under the local control of a board of conservators consisting, in approximately equal numbers, of *ex officio* representatives from the owners of the larger rated fisheries and elected members. The elected members represented the licence holders firstly in tidal waters, i.e. commercial fisheries, and secondly in fresh waters made up of both commercial and angling interests. The entire catchment of each major salmon river was designated as being a district, with the catchments of less important rivers either being attached to the larger districts or, in some cases, being joined together as districts in their own right.

In 1922, with the formation of Northern Ireland and the Irish Free State, the fishery districts were reorganised to take account of these political changes. In 1966 the boards of conservators in Northern Ireland were dissolved and replaced by the Fisheries Conservancy Board for Northern Ireland.

In Ireland, following the recommendations of the Inland Fisheries Commission in 1975, the then seventeen boards were dissolved and reconstituted in 1980 into seven regional fisheries boards and the Central Fisheries Board which has a co-ordinating and management role. The regional boards consist of elected members and nominated members. The chairmen of each regional board form the membership of the Central Fisheries Board, together with a chairman and five members nominated by the minister responsible. In addition to the formation of the fisheries boards structure, the 1959 and 1980 Fisheries Acts updated and refined much of the inland fisheries legislation in Ireland.

Methods of capture

Traditionally commercial salmon fisheries in Ireland can be divided into two main types: fixed gear (or 'fixed engines' as they are known in Irish legislation) in the river or at sea, and moveable devices such as nets, spears, gaffs, snares, and rod and line. By far the oldest methods of catching salmon on a large scale were weirs built on the seashore and in rivers.

Riverine weirs were designed to wholly or partially blockade a river or stream channel. This method became so effective and popular that the rivers of Ireland were studded with such structures until the Fisheries Act of 1863 severely curtailed their use and re-enforced the concept of a free gap or Queen's share, originally introduced in the Fisheries Act of 1842.

Seine nets or draft nets (known as net and cobble in Scotland) have been in use in Ireland since at least the twelfth century. This type of net originally accounted for well over half of the total salmon catch. Stake nets and bag nets, similar to those in use in Scotland, have been in use in Ireland since the beginning of the nineteenth century. Another device, known as a snap net and consisting of a light net suspended between two light flat-bottomed boats or 'cots', was at one time popular in the larger southern rivers such as the Rivers Blackwater and Nore.

Drift netting for salmon was first attempted in the north-west of Ireland (Donegal) in the mid-1800s. The fishing was carried out from small open boats, using nets of a natural fibre, not exceeding a few hundred metres. The success of the method depended on locating massing shoals of salmon returning to the Irish coast, prior to their migration towards individual river systems. During the period between the two world wars drift netting on a relatively small scale spread to a number of locations along the coast.

However, in the 1960s a concerted effort was made to increase the Irish inshore fleet along the west coast. This was primarily achieved by the provision of grants and loans for the purchase of new larger vessels and more modern fishing gear. As a direct by-product of this general expansion in the fishing industry the numbers of drift net licences rose sharply from 363 in 1962 to 1,048 in 1974.

This expansion in the number of drift nets led to profound changes in the pattern of salmon exploitation. Up to 1961 catches by drift nets, draft nets, fixed engines and rods moved more or less in step, largely reflecting fluctuations in the size of runs and to some extent the number of active licences in a given year. From the early 1960s the proportion of the catch taken by drift nets rose steadily until by the mid-1980s it accounted for well in excess of 80 per cent of the total recorded catch. In recent years, due to pressures on salmon prices from the aquaculture industry and poor overall catch, both the number of drift net licences issued and their exploitation rate have declined somewhat. For example in 1993, 670 drift net licences were issued and these accounted for some 65–70 per cent of the total salmon catch. Much improved protection at sea by both the Irish Naval Service and the regional fisheries boards has also significantly reduced illegal fishing.

The sectors hardest hit by the expansion of the drift net fishery were the traditional inshore draft nets and the angling sector. The draft net component of the catch dropped from 53 per cent in 1960 to 20 per cent in the mid-1990s. Angling accounted for 15 per cent of the catch in 1960 and this had declined to 5 per cent in 1994. However, in recent years angling catches have improved somewhat, in line with a reduction in the proportion of the catch falling to the drift nets.

Salmon management

During the past fifty years the management of salmon stocks in Ireland has centred on major commissions or reviews. The principal recommendations of these groups are summarised in Appendixes 1 and 2.

Regarding the management of inland fisheries for salmon, all of these commissions agree on the potential value of the recreational fishery but they differ on how best to regulate the offshore fishery so as to achieve the maximum benefit from the freshwater fisheries. Two of these reports recommended the abolition of the offshore fishery, while three permitted its retention but with far stricter controls.

The Salmon Management Task Force (1996) was commissioned at a time when statistics for the North Atlantic as a whole were showing an absolute decline in catch for all methods of capture. The report of the task force recommends a radical approach to the management of salmon stocks which includes a shorter season, a shorter fishing week, the introduction of carcass tagging and the imposition of quotas on the commercial salmon catch (Appendix 2). Implicit in the report's findings is an assumption that there is a future for the tradition of salmon drift netting, provided that the number of licences is controlled and stocks are enhanced through strict conservation measures. The report also accepts that inevitably

> the balance of advantage on conservation, environmental and economic grounds should lie increasingly with redirecting salmon stocks from interceptory commercial exploitation towards recreational fishing.

To underpin these imaginative proposals additional technical research is required, particularly in relation to the targeting of the recreational salmon fishery as a principal source of future game angling revenue. Amongst the areas which need urgent attention are:

- stock recruitment relationships, in particular quantifying the effect of additional escapement on smolt production and spawning stock levels
- the value of catch and release as a salmon conservation and management tool

- relative effectiveness of angling under varying levels of stock abundance
- the role of ranching in boosting the value of minor fisheries
- survival of stocks under varying levels of total allowable catch
- development of catchment management technology
- selective enhancement of multi-sea-winter stocks.

The recently announced integration of the Salmon Research Agency with the Marine Institute should help to rationalise the overall national approach to salmon and sea trout research and lead to a speedy and effective response to the national research priorities outlined above.

Although these changes in the management regime are to be welcomed, some observers would not fully agree with the Salmon Management Task Force's analysis of the current commercial fishery, particularly as to its current economic value, nor would they see any prospect of a full recovery of salmon stocks without, at least in the medium term, a severe curtailment in exploitation. They would further argue that the task force did not give enough prominence in its report to the sustained long-term decline in the economic value of the commercial salmon fishery in the North Atlantic.

The task force was provided with a detailed economic analysis of the commercial fishery (Ó Muircheartaigh, 1996), which concluded that it was currently worth about £2 million, a drop of almost £10 million since the period 1970–74. The submission of the Wild Salmon Support Group (1996), of which T. K. Whitaker was a member, showed that spawning stocks were low, particularly in the smaller systems and required urgent and sustained enhancement. The group questioned the validity of introducing tagging and quotas for a fishery which would, according to their analysis, continue to decline in value due to the overpowering influence on salmon prices of fish farming. They felt it was misleading to claim that there was a future for the drift net sector when its economic value was in serious and terminal decline and when all observers agreed that, in maximising net income to the state on a long-term basis, the recreational fishery had far greater overall potential.

Following publication of the task force report the Wild Salmon Support Group argued for the contemporaneous introduction of all of its recommendations rather than the initial introduction of partial measures. They were particularly concerned that the use of longer, monofilament nets should not be permitted until a tagging and quota system was in place and that the extension of the season into August should be considered only when this system was seen to be working effectively.

Following consideration of the task force report by the Minister for the Marine, the Department of the Marine and the Dáil Committee on Economic Strategy and Enterprise, it was decided to implement its principal conservation measures for the 1997 season as a first and necessary step if salmon stocks are to be conserved. These include:

Drift net fishery
- reduction in prescribed maximum number of licences which may be issued by the regional fisheries boards from 847 to 773
- reduction in sea area in which salmon fishing is allowed from twelve to six nautical miles from the baselines
- deferral of opening date of fishery to 1 June
- weekend close period extended to three days – Friday to Sunday inclusive
- introduction of day-only fishing between the hours 4 a.m. and 9 p.m.
- use of monofilament netting legalised
- increase in maximum depth of mesh permitted from 30 meshes to 45 meshes.

Draft and other net fisheries
- revision of prescribed maximum number of licences which may be issued from 604 to 518 for draft nets and from 164 to 152 for other engines
- opening date of fishery deferred to 15 May
- weekend close period extended to three days – Saturday to Monday inclusive.

Institutional/organisational changes
- establishment of catchment management committees
- formation of consultative group to review quota regime for the 1998 season.

Sea trout fisheries

In comparison with the complexity of salmon management and salmon politics, the life of the sea trout and sea trout fishing seemed, until relatively recently, benign and simple. It was primarily a recreational fishery and of little real value to the commercial sector.

Indeed the discovery of the sea trout as a sport fish owes much to the great west of Ireland sporting lodges such as the Erriff, Delphi and Lagduff, which were originally the properties of the great Anglo-Irish families and flourished from the mid-1800s until the Second World War.

It is through the writings of T. C. Kingsmill-Moore, William Hamilton Maxwell, Francis Francis, A. A. Luce and A. W. Peard that we get an insight into the lifestyle and sporting passions of those who frequented these great houses – grouse, port, cigars, sea trout and salmon (although not necessarily in that order) appear to have been the main ingredients for a really successful lodge.

Reading between the lines of these accounts we see that the number of rods, particularly skilled rods, fishing these loughs and rivers was relatively small and it is not surprising that consistently large bags of good sea trout were regularly taken by competent anglers. Labour costs were also exceptionally low, indeed tenant labour was often available free to the landlord, and as a consequence the upkeep, maintenance and protection of these wild fisheries were easily supported by the rich landlords of the time.

As the era of the landed gentry gave way to private ownership, clubs and syndicates of passionate skilled anglers, it is not surprising that the catch per rod declined, though, overall, the fishing remained surprisingly productive and healthy.

Stock collapse, 1989

However, in the late 1980s concerns were expressed that the abundance of sea trout in specific areas of the west coast was in serious decline. The history of these tragic events culminating in a calamitous stock collapse in 1989 has previously been published (Whelan, 1991; Whelan and Poole, 1996). Not alone did the catch of sea trout decline dramatically on the Burrishoole Fishery (for example, from 614 to 24 in the years 1986 to 1992) but also the stock of spawning trout collapsed, from 3,200 in 1975–76 to 155 in 1990. This pattern of population decimation was repeated throughout the west of Ireland. By-laws were introduced in the early 1990s banning the killing of all sea trout in particular fisheries and areas of the coast and severely curtailing the level of commercial exploitation even when sea trout were taken as a by-catch.

The sea trout problem was obviously located in geographically distinct regions which were adjacent to salmon farms. As evidence grew that the problem was closely associated with the presence of exceptionally high levels of juvenile sea lice on the returning juvenile sea trout, controversy raged between the private fishery owners, who wanted lice levels on farms eliminated even if this meant the removal of the farms, and the fish farmers, who steadfastly claimed that the problem was based in freshwater and most likely associated with forestry-mediated acidification.

In July 1993 the Minister for the Marine established the Sea Trout Task Force to 'save the sea trout' and in particular to:

- consider the programme entitled 'Sea lice on salmon farms: programme of minimum action' recommended by the Western Gamefishing Association and report conclusions directly to the minister
- agree measures or actions which could be introduced or intensified to mitigate or halt the sea trout stocks decline
- make recommendations for improving communication and dialogue between the Department of the Marine, statutory bodies, fishery operators and fish farm operators.

The task force, chaired by T. K. Whitaker, represented all interested parties including the fisheries boards, the Department of the Marine, fishery owners, fish farmers and Bord Iascaigh Mhara (Irish Sea Fisheries Board).

In its comprehensive and unanimous report, issued in spring 1994, the Sea Trout Task Force concluded:

> [The] infestation of sea trout in the vicinity of sea farms [is] the factor most closely associated with the marked incidence of adverse pressure on sea trout in recent years.

The task force further concluded:

> If the sea trout is to be saved, the virtual elimination of lice on and in the vicinity of sea farms must be a constant priority of management and regulatory practice. . . .
>
> It is, at the same time, necessary to keep in mind that, besides lice infestation, other adverse influences have been, and probably still are, at work in certain fisheries. . . . The immediate need, however, is to ensure the effectiveness of measures for the control of sea lice. . . .
>
> For pressing economic and social reasons, the national objective must be to combine the commercial development of sea farming with the preservation of the sea trout as an important contributor to local [tourist] income and employment. It is important to ensure the compatible progress of both sea trout angling and sea farming as sources of jobs and income in disadvantaged areas.

The report listed recommendations regarding the establishment of a Sea Trout Monitoring and Advisory Group, the management of lice on farms and the steps which were required to rehabilitate sea trout stocks. The task force laid particular emphasis on the establishment of a scientific control area to differentiate between natural fluctuations in sea trout stock abundance and those attributable to other man-made factors; to differentiate between natural population increases and those resulting from stock enhancement programmes; and to guarantee future access to wild sea trout populations, as a source of broodstock, for additional stock enhancement programmes.

Slow recovery

In the intervening three years some success has been achieved in attaining the objectives outlined in the Sea Trout Task Force report: the levels of lice on fish farm salmon have been significantly reduced; a large broodstock of sea trout has been established by the Salmon Research Agency and over 1.5 million ova per annum are being used to replenish stocks in affected sea trout systems; strategies have also been developed by the agency to generate significant numbers of sea trout smolts.

Where fin-fish farms have been obliged to cut lice levels they have achieved reductions to less than one ovigerous female louse per salmon, levels which were widely considered unachievable some four to five years ago. Despite this impressive drop in the mean densities of lice there are still areas where sea trout smolts are encountering very significant numbers of juvenile lice in spring. However, recent experimental trials of novel chemical treatments for lice have proved highly effective and hopes are currently high amongst fish farmers that lice levels can be maintained at exceptionally low levels throughout the year.

The survival of sea trout at sea has also marginally improved over the past three years but the total spawning stock in some fisheries can be measured in hundreds, as against thousands in the past. The life cycle, longevity and slow growth rates of the sea trout are such that it will take at least eight to ten years for stocks to recover fully, assuming that pre-collapse marine survival rates can be achieved. This is not the situation which pertains at present. Sea survival rates have risen from 1 per cent to 8 per cent for finnock over the past seven years in the Burrishoole Fishery but are still well below the pre-collapse range of 11–32 per cent for first return as finnock and 19–66 per cent for one-sea-winter maidens. It would seem that even at sea lice levels of one ovigerous female lice per fish the gross number of salmon in cages (more than 7 million in 1996) may still cause problems for sea trout smolts and inhibit the full recovery of the stock. The challenge of achieving the twin national objectives of maximising income from the salmon farming sector and protecting one of Ireland's unique natural treasures is still formidable.

Ireland's anadromous stocks are a unique, self-renewing, living treasure which needs to be constantly nurtured and cared for in order to survive the rigours of the twenty-first century. Past experience has taught us that the biology of these stocks is subtle and complex and that it is difficult, if not impossible, to reverse fully the adverse effects of environmental change or overexploitation. However, with care and commitment the economic and aesthetic returns on good stewardship could prove immense.

Appendix 1: Principal recommendations of Commission on Inland Fisheries (1935), Inland Fisheries Commission (1975), Central Fisheries Board (1986) and Salmon Review Group (1987)

Commission on Inland Fisheries (1935)
1. Estuarine and weir fisheries to be vested in a Central Fisheries Board
2. Abolish sea and freshwater netting
3. Compensate displaced owners and fishermen
4. Central Fisheries Board to operate weirs or net fisheries in river mouths/ estuaries
5. State-owned or non-valued fisheries to be vested in Central Fisheries Board
6. Develop and promote salmon angling

Inland Fisheries Commission (1975)
1. Strict control on drift netting
2. Promote salmon angling
3. Enhance salmon (multi-sea-winter) runs
4. Ban monofilament net
5. Better salmon statistics
6. Devolve making of by-laws to fisheries boards

Central Fisheries Board (1986)
1. Phase out offshore drift netting
2. Comprehensive inshore fisheries policy
3. Promote salmon angling
4. Enhance salmon and grilse runs
5. Ban monofilament net
6. Better salmon statistics
7. Devolve making of by-laws to fisheries boards

Salmon Review Group (1987)
1. *Policy objectives*
   - Exploit potential for sustainable employment
   - Maximise net income on a long-term basis
   - Optimise income distribution
   - Optimise amenity and recreational value
   - Conserve and develop individual unit stocks

2. *Offshore fishery*
   - Permit monofilament net of less than 2,000 m x 45 meshes deep
   - Control effort and extent of fishery
   - Introduce quotas, dead salmon tagging and log books
   - Bring fishery closer inshore

3. *Estuarine fisheries*
   - Regulate with tags and quotas
   - Increase rates in line with increasing stock
   - Shorten season

4. *Freshwater fisheries*
   - Local involvement in management and ownership
   - Anglers to operate on a quota basis
   - Promotion of fisheries

5. *Ownership*
   - Clarify ownership of all fisheries claimed by the state
   - Help prepare management plans with private owners
   - Commence with the acquisition and development of pilot areas

6. *Research*
   - Integrate all salmon research
   - Agreed national plan of research

7. *Environment*
   - Monitor pollution – fisheries boards to be independent
   - Identify high-risk sources and deal with them
   - Full-time emergency service
   - Education and awareness programmes

Appendix 2: Principal recommendations of Salmon Management Task Force (1996)

1. **Mission statement**
   - To secure and augment national salmon stocks as a sustainable resource to be managed on a catchment basis for the social and economic benefit of the community within an overall national framework.

2. **Spring fish policy**
   - Drift net season to be delayed until 1 June
   - Draft net fisheries should not commence until the middle of May
   - Evaluation of a catch and release policy for rod anglers in spring
   - Spring fish enhancement in selected fisheries using modern techniques of genetics and husbandry
   - Special environmental protection to be afforded to the habitat of spring salmon, particularly spawning areas

3. **Grilse and summer salmon fishery**
   - Monofilament net to be legalised
   - Depth of net to be increased to 45 meshes
   - Cap number of drift net licences at 1995 levels
   - Confine nets to within six miles of the shore
   - Netting on a four-day week only
   - Fishing times to be restricted to 4 a.m. to 9 p.m.
   - Season to run from 1 June to 31 August
   - Draft nets to be restricted to defined areas
   - No further extensions to commercial or rod fisheries
   - Ban on the sale of rod-caught salmon

5. **Institutional/organisational changes**
   - Establishment of a National Salmon Management Commission to monitor strategic implementation of the Salmon Management Plan
   - Establishment of salmon catchment committees
   - Recasting of the regional fisheries boards to make them more representative of the community as a whole

6. **Control and management**
   - Introduction of a national total allowable catch (TAC) and a carcass tagging programme; TAC to be set at 900 tonnes in the initial year of implementation, to take account of the assumed level of undeclared catch

REFERENCES

Central Fisheries Board (1986). *Inland Fisheries: Strategies for Management and Development*, Dublin: Central Fisheries Board

Commission on Inland Fisheries (1935). *Report of the Commission on Inland Fisheries*, Dublin: Stationery Office

Francis, F. (1887). *Angling Reminiscences*

Inland Fisheries Commission (1975). *Report of the Inland Fisheries Commission*, Dublin: Stationery Office

Kingsmill-Moore, T. C. (1960). *A Man May Fish*, London: Herbert Jenkins

Luce, A. A. (1959). *Fishing and Thinking*

Maxwell, W. H. (1880). *Wild Sports of the West*

Netboy, Anthony (1968). *The Atlantic Salmon: A Vanishing Species*, London: Faber and Faber

Ó Muircheartaigh, F. S. (1996). *Economic Assessment of the Earnings of Commercial Salmon Fisheries in Ireland since 1960, and Estimates of their Residual Value*, Dublin: Economic and Social Research Institute Seminar Series, February

Peard, A. W. (1867). *Year of Liberty*

Salmon Management Task Force (1996). *Salmon Management Task Force – Report to the Minister*, chaired by Professor Noel Wilkins, Dublin: Department of the Marine

Salmon Review Group (1987). *Report of the Salmon Review Group*, chaired by F. S. Ó Muircheartaigh, Dublin: Department of the Marine

Sea Trout Task Force (1994). *Report of the Sea Trout Task Force*, chaired by T. K. Whitaker, Dublin: Department of the Marine

Vickers, Ken (1988). *A Review of Irish Salmon and Salmon Fisheries*, Moulin, Pitlochry, Scotland: Atlantic Salmon Trust

Went, A. E. J. (1964). 'The Pursuit of Salmon in Ireland', *Proceedings of the Royal Irish Academy*, Vol. 63 (C), No. 6, pp. 192–224

Whelan, Ken (1989a). *The Angler in Ireland: Game, Coarse and Sea*, Dublin: Country House

Whelan, K. F. (1989b). 'Priorities for Irish Salmon Research', *Proceedings of the Institute of Fisheries Management 20th Annual Study Course*, 12–14 September 1989, Galway: Regional Technical College, pp. 116–28

Whelan, Ken (1991). 'Disappearing Sea Trout: Decline or Collapse?, *The Salmon Net*, No. 23, pp. 24–31

Whelan, K. F. (1992). 'Management of Salmon and Sea Trout Stocks', in *Environment and Development in Ireland*, Proceedings of conference held in December 1991, Dublin: Environmental Institute, University College Dublin, pp. 457–66

Whelan, K. F. and R. Poole (1996). 'The Sea Trout Stock Collapse, 1989-1992' in J. Reynolds (ed.), *The Conservation of Aquatic Systems*, Proceedings of a seminar held on 18–19 February 1993, Dublin: Royal Irish Academy, pp. 101–10

Wild Salmon Support Group (1996). Submission to Working Group on Management and Conservation Strategies for Salmon

Appendix

Writings by T. K. Whitaker on Economic and Social Topics

Books

1. *Financing by Credit Creation*, Dublin: Clonmore and Reynolds, 1947; a pioneering study of wartime deficit financing in the USA and UK
2. *Economic Development* (with collaborators*), Dublin: Stationery Office, 1958
3. *Interests*, Dublin: Institute of Public Administration, 1983; a collection of essays including nos. 6, 14, 16 and 17 below but also 'Financial Turning-Points' (a survey of budgetary policy 1922 to 1982), 'The Central Bank, 1969–1976 – A Retrospect', 'Credit Creation for Government', and other essays

Research papers and essays

4. 'Ireland's External Assets', paper read to Statistical and Social Inquiry Society of Ireland (SSISI), 1949
5. 'The Dollar Problem Reviewed', *Studies* (Summer 1954)
6. 'Capital Formation, Saving and Economic Progress', paper read to SSISI, 1956 and published in *Administration*, Vol. 4, No. 2 (Summer 1956), pp. 13–40
7. 'Merits and Problems of Planning', *Administration*, Vol. 12, No. 4 (Winter 1964), pp. 262–8
8. 'Productivity and Full Employment', *Administration*, Vol. 17, No. 1 (Spring 1969), pp. 11–22
9. 'Monetary Policy'; 'Banking and Credit in Ireland Today'; 'The Role of the Central Bank', *Central Bank of Ireland Quarterly Bulletin*, 1969–70
10. 'World Poverty', *Administration*, Vol. 19, No. 1 (Spring 1971), pp. 12–21
11. 'The Changing Face of Irish Banking', paper read to the Manchester Statistical Society and published in *Central Bank of Ireland Quarterly Bulletin*, Spring 1972

*These are named in the first chapter. Whitaker's part in the study was (a) to initiate, direct and edit it, (b) to contribute key chapters (Chapters 1, 2, 3, 4, 12 and 24) and (c) to be responsible for the advice and recommendations.

12. 'The Future Roles of Gold and SDRs in a Reformed International Monetary System', *Central Bank of Ireland Quarterly Bulletin*, Spring 1973
13. 'Monetary Integration: Reflection on Irish Experience', in *Moorgate and Wall Street: A Review*, Dublin: Hill Samuel & Co, 1973
14. 'From Protection to Free Trade – The Irish Experience', First Lemass Memorial Lecture, published in *Administration*, Vol. 21, No. 4 (Winter 1973), pp. 405–23
15. 'Planning Irish Development', *Administration*, Vol. 25, No. 3 (Autumn 1977), pp. 288–96
16. 'Industrial Relations – Is There A Better Way?', *Administration*, Vol. 27, No. 3 (Autumn 1979), pp. 282–93
17. 'Ireland's External Reserves', *Journal of the Institute of Bankers*, January 1980
18. 'The Bank of Ireland – Origins and Consolidation, 1783–1826', in F. S. L. Lyons (ed.), *Bicentenary Essays: Bank of Ireland, 1783–1983*, Dublin: Gill & Macmillan, 1983
19. 'Ireland: Land of Change', presidential address to Royal Irish Academy, 1986
20. Foreword to Maurice Manning and Moore McDowell, *History of ESB*, Dublin: Gill & Macmillan, 1985

Some other publications

21. *Staid na Tíre* (Léacht an Oireachtais, 1960)
22. 'The New Ireland, Its Progress, Problems and Aspirations', Extrait du No. 2 da Vol. XIX, de la *Chronique de Politique Étrangère*, Institut Royal des Relations Internationales, Bruxelles, May 1966
23. 'An tÓr', *Central Bank of Ireland Quarterly Bulletin*, Autumn 1969
24. 'Productivity and Incomes', *Central Bank of Ireland Quarterly Bulletin*, Spring 1971
25. 'Ireland and Foreign Money', *Central Bank of Ireland Annual Report*, 1971–72
26. 'Ireland's Development Policy', Reykjavik lecture, *Central Bank of Ireland Quarterly Bulletin*, Autumn 1972
27. 'Currency Realignments and European Monetary Integration', *Central Bank of Ireland Quarterly Bulletin*, Winter 1975
28. 'Monetary Policy', *Central Bank of Ireland Quarterly Bulletin*, Winter 1975
29. 'An Ceangal le Sterling – Ar Cheart É Bhriseadh?', *Central Bank of Ireland Annual Report*, 1976